LAND TO THE TILLER

Land to the Tiller

The Political Economy of Agrarian Reform in South Asia

Ronald J. Herring

Yale University Press
New Haven and London

Published with assistance from
the Mary Cady Tew Memorial Fund.

Designed by James J. Johnson
and set in Trump Medieval type.
Printed in the United States of America by
Halliday Lithograph, West Hanover, Mass.

Library of Congress Cataloging in Publication Data

Herring, Ronald J., 1947–
   Land to the tiller.

   Bibliography: p.
   Includes index.
   1. Land reform—South Asia.   I. Title.
HD1333.A784H47   1983   333.3'1'54   82–48903
ISBN 0–300–02725–7

10 9 8 7 6 5 4 3 2 1

Sr, 30.00/15.00/8/5/83

Contents

List of Tables and Maps   vii

Acknowledgments   ix

1   Introduction: Policy Logic and Policy Models of Land Reform   1

2   The Venerable Tenure-Reform Model: Intervention and Regulation   17

3   Peasant Democracy, Tenure Reform, and the Liberal State: Ceylon's Paddy Lands Act   50

4   Land Ceilings in Pakistan: An Agrarian Bourgeois Revolution?   85

5   Transformational Logic and Ordinary Politics: Land Ceilings in India and Sri Lanka   125

6   The Logic of Land to the Tiller: The First Communist Ministry in Kerala   153

7   The Politics of Land to the Tiller: The United Front's Reforms in Kerala   180

8   The Politics of Land Reform: Class Interests and Regime Interests   217

9   The Economic Logic of Land Reform   239

10   The Argument for Land to the Tiller   268

References   289

Index   309

List of Tables and Maps

Tables   *Page*

3.1   Distribution of Landowning Families by Occupation
      (Ceylon, 1950–51)   57
3.2   Comparative Economic Condition of Agrarian Classes in
      Ceylon Prior to the Paddy Lands Act   84
4.1   Indicators of Technical and Social Organization of
      Production by Size of Holding (Pakistan, 1972)   110
4.2   Progress Officially Claimed in Implementation of Ceiling
      Reforms during the Bhutto Period   113
6.1   Agrarian Structures: Kerala and India, 1951   160
6.2   Agrarian Structure of Kerala, 1957–1958   161
6.3   Agrarian Livelihoods in Kerala, 1957–1958   161
7.1   Kerala's Agrarian Structure at the Time of the United
      Front Government   182
9.1   Yields by Size of Holding in Pakistan, 1972   247
9.2   Input-Output Ratios in Kerala Agriculture   248
9.3   Land and Rental Values by Size of Holding in Kerala   249
9.4   Paddy Production and Costs by Size of Holding in Kerala   250
9.5   Paddy Yields by Tenurial Status in Hambantota and Kandy
      Districts (Ceylon), 1971–1972   255
9.6   Yields of Major Crops in Pakistan by Tenurial Status   256
9.7   Investment on the Land by Tenurial Classes in Pakistan,
      1972   260

Maps   *following page 152*

South Asia
Sri Lanka
Pakistan
Kerala State

Acknowledgments

An intellectual debt is too complex an entity to acknowledge in a brief space. I can express here gratitude only for immediate and direct assistance in the production of this book. The research on which it is based was supported at various times by the University of Wisconsin Graduate School and Land Tenure Center, the Henry Vilas Fellowship Foundation, the American Institute of Indian Studies, the Ford Foundation, the Social Science Research Council, the Pakistan Institute of Development Economics, and the National Science Foundation and Government of India's University Grants Commission through the Indo-U.S. Subcommission on Education and Culture. Manuscript preparation was aided by the University Research Committee of Northwestern University. The manuscript drafts were prepared with consummate skill and good humor by Ann Larson, who thereby became one of the few citizens of the Chicago area able to spell *kudikidappukaran*. The maps were drafted by Marguerite Ney.

The individuals and institutions in South Asia who aided me are too numerous to mention, but some deserve special acknowledgment. Pradeep Mehendiratta and the staff of the American Institute of Indian Studies in New Delhi provided crucial and effective assistance. In Sri Lanka, the staff, faculty, and students of the University of Peradeniya, and particularly the collegial scholars of the Ceylon Studies Seminar, made important contributions. The Agrarian Research and Training Institute, particularly Hiran Dias and A. S. Ranatunge, and officials of the Department of Agrarian Services rendered invaluable assistance. Special thanks are due Nimal Sanderatne, Nimal Fernando, and Michael Roberts. In Pakistan, the Institute of Development Economics provided a research base, and a number of staff members, particularly Ghaffar Chaudhry, Sarfraz Qureshi, and Steve Guisinger, aided my research efforts. The Pakistan materials benefited from discussions with Hamid Kizilbash, Shahnaz Rouse, Abdul Qayyum, and Hamza Alavi.

For institutional support in Kerala, I am thankful to the Department of Economics, Calicut University, and the Centre for Development Studies, Trivandrum. I am deeply endebted to Professor M. A. Oommen for all manner of contributions, both intellectual and practical; the same applies to Mathew Kurien and Jacob Eapen and the Indian School of Social Sciences, Trivandrum. Special assistance was provided by A. O. Kuruvila and K. Ramadas. Colleagues and friends throughout South Asia made diffuse, important contributions that can be acknowledged in only a general way. It is particularly appropriate to mention John and Barbara Harriss, Janice Jiggins, Kumar David, Wayne Nilsestuen, Ijaz Nabi, V. C. Koshy, Bob Hardgrave, Tom Nossiter, Michael Tharakan, Chandra Mohan, and A. V. Jose, though there have been many others. Two men who dedicated their professional lives to the issues discussed in this book provided important encouragement and assistance: Wolf Ladejinsky and Daniel Thorner.

I am also obviously indebted to the many officials, farmers, politicians, bankers, clerks, and ordinary people throughout South Asia who patiently answered my questions; my gratitude to all of them is great. Institutional support in the United States was provided by the Land Tenure Center at the University of Wisconsin under directors Bill Thiesenhusen and Don Kanel and the Center for Asian Studies at the University of Texas, Austin, headed by Tom Jannuzi. Colleagues and staff at the Land Tenure Center too numerous to name helped me in the many cooperative ways characteristic of the Center. Discussions and comments on various pieces of the manuscript involved many people, but special thanks are due Vernon Ruttan, Carl Gotsch, Shahid Javed Burki, Barry and Aruna Michie, Bob Frykenberg, Sam Popkin, Meghnad Desai, Joseph Elder, Rex Edwards, Lloyd and Susanne Rudolph, Terry Byres, Charles Kennedy, and anonymous reviewers of Yale University Press. The original seeds of interest were planted and nourished by Walter Neale, Tom Jannuzi, Jim Roach, and—oddly enough—Khushwant Singh.

It is difficult to produce anything without moral support. I cannot adequately express my appreciation to my teachers and friends Henry Hart and Jim Scott, for both constructive criticisms of my work and, more importantly, for having faith in me. Finally, Valerie Bunce has suffered through the final stages of putting together this book in ways that exceed any conceivable notion of legitimate spousely expectations; my gratitude is simply too deep to express.

Land to the Tiller is dedicated to those who work to feed the rest of us.

Among the ancients we discover no single enquiry as to which form of landed property, etc., is the most productive, which creates maximum wealth. The enquiry is always about what kind of property creates the best citizens.
                                                                Karl Marx (1858)

The land reforms I am introducing are basic. . . . They will bring dignity and salvation to our rural masses who from today will be able to lift their heads from the dust and regain their pride and manhood, their self-respect and honour.
                        Zulfikar Ali Bhutto, President of Pakistan (1972)

There cannot be any lasting improvement in agricultural production and efficiency without comprehensive reforms in the country's land system.
Agrarian Reforms Committee of the Indian National Congress (1949)

We will not be able to answer anybody if he is hungry.
                C. Subramaniam, Indian Finance Minister (1975)

1 Introduction: Policy Logic and Policy Models of Land Reform

> All the ancient law-givers, and above all Moses, founded
> the success of their arrangements for virtue, justice and
> good morals upon landed property, or at least on secure
> hereditary possession of land, for the greatest possible
> number of citizens.
> —B. G. Niebuhr

"Land to the tiller" has long been a rallying cry of radical agrarian movements. The slogan evokes the image of crude red flags in the hands of peasants confronting landlords and police in the classic conflict over distribution of the land and its product. That image is one aspect of the reality in South Asia; but the issue of agrarian reform is simultaneously less dramatic and more profound than its popular image. At stake is the transformation of the basic structure, the political economy, of agrarian society. Marx noted that the "innermost secrets" of a society are revealed in its production relations; in the relations of men and women to the land are embedded relations of power, security, wealth, opportunity, and standing in rural South Asia.

The arguments for and meanings of "land to the tiller" as both political demand and public policy have emerged from various, often conflicting, intellectual and political currents. It is, on one level, a simple expression of peasant folk justice: those who work the land should enjoy the fruits of their labor; every family should have enough land to provide a decent living. At this level, the demand expresses what Erich Jacoby (1971: 88) has termed the transcultural "agrarian creed" of peasant societies—the normative position that the surface of the earth can belong to no one unconditionally and exclusively but should produce for those who clear and till it. For Mahatma Gandhi, the desirable form of socialism was embodied in the traditional Indic teaching that "all land belongs to Gopal" (literally, "shepherd") or "God" or "in modern language . . . the State, i.e., the people."[1]

1. "Sabhi bhoomi Gopalki. . . ." Chapter 6 briefly treats the traditional roots of redistributive agrarian impulses as communicated by Gandhi and others. There are ambiguities in the empirical validity of such conceptualizations, as well as tension between the normative ideal of land belonging to "the people," as Gandhi expressed it, and the political

At another level, land to the tiller is a demand for social justice and economic rationality emanating from intellectual critiques of existing property and production relations. Such critiques have emerged from the Marxian left, but also from what Lenin termed the "radical bourgeoisie." And, finally, somewhat ironically, land to the tiller has appeared as a policy model in planning documents as a pragmatic response to observed failures in implementing less fundamental agrarian reform, such as regulation of rents and security of tenure. Thus the Indian Planning Commission recently supported a land-to-the-tiller policy as representing "the logic of development in land reforms," citing evidence that halfway measures had not only failed to achieve the dual goals of agrarian reform—social justice and increased productivity—but had resulted in a net deterioration in the position of countless sharecroppers and tenants-at-will (India, 1973; 1974: 43).

The dyad of social justice and productivity is central to the policy logic of agrarian reform and runs as a central theme throughout this book. The interrelationships between these announced goals—trade-offs or complementarities—are complex, theoretically and empirically. Is it justifiable, or necessary, to sacrifice productivity for justice in the poorest sector of very poor societies? Or is the "equity–growth trade-off" a product of ideology and inappropriate theory? The social justice–productivity dyad is linked concretely in policy logic to a third legitimation of agrarian reform: the threat of rural violence. Citing evidence of "widening disparities between classes of rural population" and "a general accentuation of poverty in the rural areas," the Indian National Commission on Agriculture (1976: II, 28, 31, 35) approvingly cited Robert McNamara: rapid economic growth alone would not alleviate the poverty or inequality that would, in the absence of redistributive policy, "inevitably undermine the democratic foundations of the economy." Concern for rural "tensions," "harmony," and "stability" has dominated much of the policy logic, and even more the seriousness of policy response, in the subcontinent. That policy logic increasingly resonates with the findings of social scientists: an exploited peasantry may constitute an inherently destablizing social configuration.

But if there is growing agreement on the urgency of agrarian reform, the question of means remains critical and unresolved: what institutional mechanisms are capable of transforming agrarian systems that have persisted for ages? Agrarian reform thus poses a classic question of reformist public policy in bold relief: how can fundamental structural change be effected through the very institutions that service and reproduce the existing society and reflect the existing distribution of power and privilege? John Kenneth Galbraith wryly noted in 1951, in tones that need reemphasis today:

implications of overturning the existing system of land ownership—implications which Gandhi himself rejected.

> Unfortunately some of our current discussion of land reform in the under-developed countries proceeds as though this reform were something that a government proclaims on any fine morning—that it gives land to the tenants as it might give pensions to old soldiers. . . . In fact a land reform is a revolutionary step; it passes power, property, and status from one group in the community to another. [in Dorner, 1972: 29]

Although land reforms are universally argued for in terms of social justice and economic efficiency, the political reality in South Asian societies is that such reforms are promulgated by ruling elites largely composed of, or structurally or electorally dependent on, agrarian elites. Land reform, like all public policy, is in part a shadow play involving the manipulation of symbols; the actual policy demonstrably reflects considerations more pressing and mundane than abstract ideals of social justice and economic rationality. The empirical investigations in the following chapters underline the ambiguities in conceptualizations of and commitment to the announced goals of reform. The theory is important: in the mobilization of political and administrative forces behind reform, the claims of justice, productivity, and stability figure prominently. But the "ordinary politics" of policy formulation and implementation ultimately determine the net impact of reform.

Land reform is frequently the first legislative act of a new regime in an agrarian society; few issues arouse a comparable level of political controversy, manipulation of symbols, and administrative energies. A variety of regimes in South Asia have termed land reforms critical for the survival of the political system. In justifying her assumption of emergency powers in 1975, Indira Gandhi cited the inability of ordinary political, judicial, and administrative mechanisms to carry out land reform. Though it would be naive to believe that the Emergency was actually imposed to facilitate redistributive policies, there is good evidence that the compromises of ordinary politics and the character of ordinary judicial and administrative procedures have vitiated attempts at purposive agrarian transformation in South Asia.

The implications extend beyond the boundaries of the subcontinent. As the majority of the world's desperately poor are rural people, agrarian reform must figure centrally in any developmental strategy that seeks to benefit the least advantaged in society. Concern for the lowest 40 percent of the income pyramid is currently in vogue, supported by an emerging international paradigm of "equity with growth" and redefinitions of development itself to include reduction of poverty and inequality (e.g., Seers, 1969; World Bank, 1975). Indeed, both Sri Lanka and the South Indian State of Kerala are discussed internationally for having achieved marked success in development measured by "human needs" and "physical quality of life" despite aggregate low income and relatively slow growth (e.g., Mencher, 1980; Isenmen, 1980). Yet proposals for redistribution, both national and international, ring false, reflecting a certain naiveté about the political reality of agrarian transformation and the institutional dilemmas posed by so profound a change.

To explore these questions, I have studied a variety of reforms in South Asia representing the full range of redistributive policies in the independent period. Each of the case studies attempts to heed Doreen Warriner's injunction (1962: 3) that we should first ask about land reform: what did they do? and then: what did they think they were doing? What they thought they were doing is in part contained in the policy logic of the reform. In each case, I compare the policy logic to the actual reform. Gaps between the two add to our understanding of the political pressures, social mythologies, and ideologies that modify policy logic, and the possibilities excluded. Each measure of agrarian reform represents the outcome of a complex interaction involving the deep political-economic structure (the strength and level of mobilization of various classes) as distal causative conditions, proximate conjunctural political imperatives (regime interests, electoral tactics, rural violence, and so on) and the perceptual model of elites of the rural world: the prevailing understanding of what is wrong, what is possible, what will work. Implementation is another question; the answer is heavily dependent on the adequacy of the policy logic (a necessary but far from sufficient condition) and the relative strength and vector sum of forces of resistance and support, including the executive, legislative, judicial, and administrative organs of the state. In this analysis, I have found it useful to employ the concepts of policy models and policy logic.

Policy Models, Policy Logic, and Ideology

A policy model is an integrated set of propositions derived from distinct normative and empirical (causal-conceptual) paradigms. The use of the overworked concept "paradigm" self-consciously follows Thomas Kuhn's notion of a "strong network of commitments" that incorporates beliefs about what it is important to know and how we should evaluate knowledge (1962: 42 and passim). The policy model contains a view of the way the world is, the way it should be, and the possible means of moving from one state to another or maintaining the existing state. Though the normative and empirical elements are analytically separable, there is predictable confluence, as certain values are consonant with particular views of how the world works. These paradigms function together to screen and differentially weight perceptions of the social world and to limit policy options, explicating what is practicable, acceptable, and right. The policy model is, then, an elaboration of an ideology in the narrow sphere of some particular policy question—in this case land reform.

The policy model contains a normative paradigm that specifies values, defining, for example, what kinds and degrees of inequality are acceptable, what rights and duties vest in particular classes and for what reasons, and how power, privilege, security, and opportunity should be distributed. The paradigm also contains (or implies) the rules for moral reasoning, for justifying and ordering values, and specifies the kinds of questions that are the proper subject of normative inquiry. For example, consider the differences in three normative paradigms that would decide the proper share of tenants in the social product: "just price" theories (implying, in legislation, a "fair rent"), neoclassical economics, and Marxian value theory. These three paradigms differ not only in normative outcome (substantive values), but in methodology and irreducible assumptions as well.

Obviously the most crucial function of the normative paradigm is to define what constitutes a "problem" and how serious the problem is. It is immediately apparent that a great deal of policy thinking revolves around issues that many people (and regimes) do not consider problems. Likewise, issues emerge as "critical" and needful of "dramatic policy response" that were previously thought to be no problem at all and may in time fall into collective benign neglect, as in Anthony Downs's notion of an "issue-attention cycle" in policy (1972). The existence of poverty is considered intolerable in some normative systems, unfortunate in others, and inevitable, even functional, in others. Policy logic thus begins from a specific normative positions—the existence of a "problem"; the parallel to "normal science" is striking. As Kuhn notes, the object of normal science, like policy logic, "is to solve a puzzle for whose very existence the validity of the paradigm must be assumed" (1962: 80). That the normative bases of agrarian reform are not widely shared in important places is demonstrably one source of policy failure.

The normative paradigm not only posits basic values, but orders values, thus setting priorities. In Sartre's words, society chooses its expendables. The normative paradigm in actual policy logic performs, crass though it sounds, a type of normative cost-benefit analysis. Such analysis implicitly or explicitly weighs the costs implied by the policy against the value of a solution or partial solution to the original "problem," while simultaneously determining optimal, acceptable, and unacceptable policy mechanisms. It is in these subtle weightings that profound policy differences emerge. Conservative paradigms, for example, heavily weight the costs of uncertainty and risk of change relative to the benefits of a stable, though imperfect, existing situation. Radical paradigms weight potentiality positively and heavily and emphasize the costs, risks, uncertainty, and injustice of maintaining existing structures.

Analysis of underlying normative paradigms is critical for understanding the policy logic; the perception and definition of the problem shape the entire policy process, from conception through implementation. An analysis of normative paradigms in policy logic across a spectrum of important policies (or nonpolicies) provides an understanding of the *operative* values of specific regimes as opposed to those embodied in public pronouncements. Analysis of the connections (gaps, contradictions) in policy logic between problem definition and policy provides insight into operative distribution of political power and the operative political theory of elites. Particularly important are the leaps of faith that elites are willing or unwilling to make in concrete circumstances when the "facts" and empirical theory are characterized by demonstrable uncertainties and contradictions.

The empirical component of a policy model contains a description of the way things are. Descriptions are not simply mirrors of the social world, of course, but reflect selectively what constitutes a fact, what facts are significant, and how the bare facts are to be interpreted. The description may itself constitute a serious problem according to the normative paradigm (the severe poverty and increasing numbers of the landless) or may require processing through a chain of policy logic before entering the agenda as a problem (if landlessness breeds violence, a problem exists; if peasants are docile, fatalistic beasts of the field, little need be done).

More importantly, the empirical paradigm functions to explain how the world works—socially, economically, politically; it contains (often implicitly) an interrelated set of causal theories ranging from the relatively specific and testable (peasants allocate resources so as to maximize returns to the scarce factor of production) to the most basic and nontestable (it is immutable human nature for people to require individual material incentives to perform efficiently). Barrington Moore, Jr., has rightly emphasized: "In all ages and countries, reactionaries, liberals, and radicals have painted their own portraits of small rural folk to suit their own theories" (1968: 117). The notion of paradigm employed here is broader—it includes the portraits of rural social structure and social relations—and less purposive. As Kuhn notes of scientific paradigms, because we hold our theories as though they represented reality, the distinction between fact and theory is very difficult to sustain. Or, as Joan Robinson more bluntly expressed it: "No one, of course, is conscious of his own ideology, any more than he can smell his own breath" (1964: 41).

It is important that the empirical paradigm is not simply a structure of hypotheses but represents a "strong network of commitments." Though such theories claim empirical validity, in fact they are profoundly antiempirical in both mode of acquisition and retention, imposing severe limits on the kind of evidence that would serve as disconfirmation. Whereas more specific, limited theories may prove more amenable to change than deeper basic assumptions about the fundamental nature of human beings and social process, changes at the periphery are constrained by commitment to the deeper core.

The notion that policies presuppose a causal-conceptual model of the social world is widely accepted. Pressman and Wildavsky (1973: xv) note that: "Policies imply theories. Whether stated explicitly or not, policies point to a chain of causation between initial conditions and future consequences. If X, then Y." The type of theory suggested here is essentially Aristotle's "efficient cause," a theory about what conditions are necessary and sufficient to produce a particular change, the necessary institutional mechanisms for effecting change. Such theories impose constraints on the model by delineating what is possible, what will work.

The empirical-theoretic paradigm also contains specific theories of what caused or causes the problem in question, and what kind of change, or how much change, is necessary to alleviate the original problem. For example, if one theory locates the cause of some local insurrection in dissatisfaction with insecurity of tenures and food shortages, a second connecting theory relates complex measures of tenure reform to specific economic and social changes. But a third theory enters, a theory of practical politics. The third theory may hold, for example, that to appease the dissidents it is not necessary to overhaul the entire tenurial structure (an enterprise with significant costs); a few symbolic gestures will suffice, assuming perhaps that discontent has peaked and will dissipate, and that the complexity of the reform law will prevent most rural people from seeing through the ruse.

Different perceptions of rural social structure and relations necessarily produce different perceptions of the need for and urgency of land reforms. For example, official Indian concern about rural violence, especially the "land grab" movement in the late 1960s, was reflected in the Home Ministry's report on *The Causes and Nature of Current Agrarian Tensions*.[2] In a conclusion widely shared in high policy and planning networks, the report attributed increasing agrarian unrest directly to persistent social and economic inequalities and the failure of policy to narrow these inequalities. Prime Minister Indira Gandhi subsequently called for commitment to new policies to reduce rural inequalities. When she presented this analysis to the State Chief Ministers, they replied that the "land grab" was merely the work of "professional agitators" and therefore should not influence government policy.[3]

Mrs. Gandhi was explicit: political parties had not created the tensions but were exploiting existing tensions, which were caused by widening inequalities and government policy failures (including ineffectual land reforms). The alternative perception was that no tensions existed independent of the machinations of political agitators and that the urgency of land reforms argued by Mrs. Gandhi was consequently spurious.

2. India (1969), officially unpublished but circulated mimeograph. It is not clear whether the reported increased tension and violence reflected reality or simply a change in awareness and a fear of rural unrest consonant with the tenor of the "green revolution turns red" genre of literature and the tactical concerns of Indira Gandhi's faction of the ruling party.

3. *Economic and Political Weekly* (October 3, 1970: 1629). The prime minister's concerns are cogently expressed in her letters to the chief ministers dated February 20, 1970, and June 1, 1970, reprinted as appendices 2 and 3 in India (1970).

Policy logic is congruent with the major strains of ideology but represents a specification of ideology in terms of concrete situations, in a sense,
the tactical aspect of ideology. A number of competing policy models
may thus emerge from the same ideological base; for example, there may
be staunch conservatives who resist reform and conservative reformers
who see reform as necessary to preserve the basic structure of society. It
is then important to distinguish symbolic and reformist models from
transformational policy models that imply significant alteration of existing property and production relations. Transformational reforms reflect
fundamentally different understandings of the rural world in normative,
political, and economic terms.

Policy logic is thus separate from, but not irrelevant to, analysis of
the politics of agrarian reform. The gaps between expressed policy logic
and reality on the ground tell us a great deal about elite views of the rural
world, politics, and economics and about the operative political power
structure. The policy logic is also important in analyzing how those who
have power justify their actions to those who matter, thus providing insights into the legitimation functions of the state and a regime's perceptions of the normative structure on which its claim to authority rests.

My study of land reforms in South Asia suggests that the range of
policy experience can be analyzed in terms of three basic policy models
and their variants and combinations: (1) *Tenure reform* (the intervention-
regulatory model): the terms on which nonowning cultivators hold the
land are readjusted without fundamental alteration of the social organization of production. Typically, rents are lowered and regulated, and continuity of rights to use the land ("security of tenure") is mandated. Continuous supervision of and intervention in tenurial relations by the
administrative apparatus of the state is posited as the means to these
ends. Thus, some of the "bundle of rights" we often call ownership[4] are
transferred from owner to tenant; it is left to the tenant to exercise these
rights and challenge infractions on the part of the landlord. (2) *The ceiling-
redistributive model*: an upper limit, or ceiling, is placed on agricultural
holdings; land in excess of the ceiling is appropriated by the state, with
or without compensation, and redistributed among landless or poor cultivators, either gratis or at some cost, individually or collectively. (3) *Land
to the tiller*: the landlord–tenant organization of production, and hence
the institution of rent, is abolished and prohibited by law: cultivators
became the owners of the land they till, and in theory all cultivators
must be owners, all owners must be cultivators. A very low ceiling is
implicit, because no family is felt to deserve any more land than it can
till nor any land it does not till. The normative ideal is a classical peasant
society and economy.

4. For a learned explication of the notion of land as a "bundle of rights" in the
Indian context, see B. H. Baden-Powell, *The Land Systems of British India* (1892: vol. 1,
chap. 4, sec. 6 and passim).

Historically, tenure reform came first and persists tenaciously. It has been characteristic of conservative regimes desiring minimal change in rural society but fearful of agrarian discontent and economic stagnation. The policy logic, explicated in chapter 2, assumes that manifestations of structural defects (rack-renting, tenant evictions, and so on) can be remedied without alteration of the property distribution and the social organization of production. Instead, the administrative apparatus of the state is to intervene in and regulate the relations between landlords and tenants to correct the perceived abuses. The irony is that so limited and logical a reform has largely failed to achieve even its limited aims and has arguably led to the net deterioration of those most in need of its limited provisions.

Planners and political elites have recognized the failure of tenure reform to secure new rights and guarantee traditional rights for tenants. A common conclusion has been that local mobilization of cultivators is a necessary condition for even limited reform. Chapter 3 presents the policy logic of a modification of the tenure reform model designed to substitute administrative mechanisms and village-level bodies for the absence of peasant organization and consciousness. The Paddy Lands Act of Ceylon (Sri Lanka) is something of a paradox in tenure reform; it was drafted by a Marxist minister of agriculture who rejected the radical land-to-the-tiller model partly on the grounds that such reforms produce a politically conservative and economically stagnant peasant sector. This critique of land to the tiller from the left raises the critical issue of *embourgeoisement* to which the analysis returns in later chapters.

Chapters 2 and 3 demonstrate that though the policy logic of tenure reform is interventionist and regulatory, in practice the burden falls preponderantly on the tenant. A major cause of failure then becomes the demonstrably questionable rationality,[5] from the tenant's point of view, of demanding the legislated rights. Analysis of tenant rationality turns on the embedded character of production relations, the structural features of the liberal state,[6] and the tenant's experientially based percep-

5. By "rational," I mean simply that means and ends are connected in a way demonstrably congruent with experience and knowledge according to cognitive processes that are reproducible and understandable to an outside observer. Rational decisions take prior account of the consequences of different courses of action and involve choice among behaviors with concern for linking preferred ends with available means. For some insightful, though excessive, elaborations of the rationality of peasant action across a range of behaviors, see Popkin (1979).

6. By liberal state, I mean a state of the general ideational and structural form of the states that evolved in Western Europe and North America in accordance with liberal critiques of monarchism and feudalism, as transmitted to South Asia under colonial hegemony. Among the most important features for my analysis are the centrality of a separation of powers, implying an autonomous judiciary; adversary court proceedings between (presumed) legal equals as a mode of resolving conflict; an elaborate case law supporting private ownership of the means of production; procedural and evidentiary requirements derived from Western legal development; electoral succession between meaningfully opposed polit-

tions of the state's rural organs—the "embedded bureaucracy." The conclusion raises doubts about incrementalism and minimal compromise reforms as a strategy for agrarian transformation and provides insights into the obstacles to other types of regulation that nominally benefit the rural poor but neither restructure the rural world in which the poor live nor protect individuals from the negative consequences of demanding new rights. Ceylon's experiment with rural democracy as a means of implementing redistribution also raises serious unresolved questions about the consequences of local participatory democracy and decentralization, which are increasingly popular as models in development literature, in the absence of simultaneous restructuring of local power structures.

Chapters 4 and 5 analyze the politics and impact of land ceilings in Pakistan, India, and Sri Lanka. Ceiling-redistributive reforms have in policy logic appeared both as a means of "eradicating feudalism" by attacking the structural base of a "feudal" landed elite while fostering economic dynamism in agriculture—and thus as an acknowledged strategic lever in the bourgeois revolution—and as means of leveling rural inequalities while rehabilitating the landless. The Sri Lanka reforms, drafted in the shadow of a rural insurrection, produced the genuine transformational potential expressed in policy logic but denied in practice in India: a great deal of land was appropriated, and to a significant extent the core of the national economy was nationalized. The distribution of that land reflected a continuing tension in policy logic between political and economic imperatives—a tension between alienation in small plots, various collective forms of institutional experimentation, and state management.

The classic land-to-the-tiller model as explicated by theoreticians of the national Congress Party of India and of the Communist Party in Kerala is presented in chapters 6 and 7. The politics of translating the policy logic into legislation during the first Communist ministry in Kerala (1957–59) presented profound strategic and tactical dilemmas. Though closely following Congress Party and governmental prescriptions on agrarian reform, the legislation was central in the political conflicts that resulted in Nehru's dismissal of the Communist government in 1959 and in the subsequent intensified class polarization of rural Kerala. Land reforms languished until the victory of a Communist-led United Front ministry (1967–69). The dissolution of that ministry and competition between two communist parties (one heading the government, the other the largest opposition party) further politicized and energized implemen-

ical groupings as an ideal, if not a reality. At least in regard to tenure reform, liberal states of the region have tended to resort to the original premises of liberalism—a laissez-faire stance which places the primary burden of rectifying grievances on the individual, who is in a critical sense *free* from government intervention in his or her affairs. That, in practice, liberal states frequently belie their legitimating ideology, more so in some spheres than others, is undeniable.

tation of new reforms in an atmosphere of extreme partisan conflict and rural violence from 1970 to the present. The Kerala reforms emerged from the organized demands and decades of agitation of the peasantry, articulated through electoral victories of the Communist Party (later parties) in the State. The reforms illustrate the potential, and some ironic constraints, of a highly politicized agrarian system in which militant mobilization has played a major role in correcting both defects in the initial reform measures and the lapses in implementation imposed by ordinary administration.

Land reforms in Kerala illustrate several classic and poignant strategic and tactical dilemmas for the left. One section of the Communist Party which legislated the reforms feared that effective implementation would result only in the *embourgeoisement* of landless peasants and would thus close the system to progress toward the collective forms that were held to be necessary economically and politically in Kerala's severe agrarian crisis, an analysis similar to that of a contemporary Marxist minister of agriculture in Ceylon (chap. 3). An effective "radical" reform, in this analysis, replaces a radical political force with a conservative one (Lenin's "petit-bourgeois agrarians"); the irony is that without the radical peasant movement there would have been no possibility of the communists' political victories and thus no potential for a radical reform. A second classic dilemma for the left in Kerala is the tension between the partisan tactical demands of electoral competition within a parliamentary system and the strategic requirements of social revolution: how far can pressure for rehabilitating the poorest classes go without alienating politically important middle strata, inside and outside the left movement? How long will temporizing tactical compromises be tolerated by the poor?

These tactical and strategic dilemmas extend beyond Kerala. The current government of West Bengal, under the leadership of the Communist Party of India (Marxist) has opted for a kind of tenure reform— "Operation Barga"—instead of land to the tiller (see Bhattacharyya, 1979). Whether the Kerala reforms will indeed produce "embourgeoisement" or the West Bengal reforms will founder on the obstacles identified in chapters 2 and 3 are questions of great historical and theoretical consequence.

Chapter 8 turns to systematic consideration of the politics of land reform. Agrarian reforms worthy of the name transform rural society through alterations in the property structure and production relations, redistributing power and privilege. The policy logic of agrarian reforms in the region has often been transformational, though it is no secret that in practice the reforms have more often not been. That the policy logic— the internal logical structure of a reform model—correlates only imperfectly, if at all, with the political objectives of ruling elites must be stressed. The structure of power in agrarian societies reflects the distribution of the primary means of production—the land. Yet land reforms continue to be promulgated, to arouse powerful social forces and conflicts, to absorb enormous quantities of administrative resources. It thus becomes critical to analyze the contradictory imperatives facing governing elites and the nonredistributive functions of nominally redistributive policy within the context of the relative autonomy of the state.

The Kerala experience challenges a proposition of conventional wisdom that land reforms and parliaments are "incompatible," that power must be "concentrated" to effect change (Huntington, 1968; Tai, 1974). Genuine land reforms are indeed revolutionary and typically result from extraordinary, often cataclysmic, historical conditions, which are relatively rare. The Kerala chapters pose the question of the limits and possibilities of land reform within a nonrevolutionary situation, in the face of an acute agro-economic crisis. This issue is complicated by the federal power structure of India in which the Center (Delhi) has imposed serious constraints (termed "constitutional niceties" by a section of the left) on radical reform. Nevertheless, the Kerala Assembly (and, to a lesser extent, that of the Republic of Sri Lanka) has shown a capability for land reform unmatched by the concentrated power of the martial-law regimes of Pakistan. The comparison suggests that it is not concentration and parliaments that are the issue but rather the ensemble of forces represented by the parliament and executive, the configuration of regime and class interests and world-views of ruling groups, and the state of consciousness and mobilization of agrarian underclasses.[7]

Chapters 9 and 10 return to examine the universally announced goals of agrarian reform—economic rationality and social justice. The normative arguments for and against an existing social organization of production depend heavily on economic consequences. Chapter 9 presents the dominant paradigmatic economic case for land reform and compares the economic logic to reality. The economic logic, like all policy logic, is critically influenced by normative and conceptual-theoretic paradigms of the rural world. The economic case is far more ambiguous than its presentation in the policy logic of land reforms, emphasizing the importance of political explanations of land reform and simultaneously raising a serious question: if the economic case is empirically weaker than it logically seems, and large sections of the agrarian underclass have demonstrably suffered from the halfhearted reforms typical of the past, should land reforms be attempted at all in South Asia? The concluding chapter turns reluctantly to that question, centering on an analysis of the imperatives of social justice. The conclusion argues that land reforms have typically failed not because too much was attempted, but too little, producing strong incentives for all relevant actors to err on the side of conservatism rather than reformism, as the rural world was unlikely to be transformed by existing legislation.

---

7. For a treatment of the political development hypotheses concerning land reform, see Hart and Herring (1977) and the analysis of chapter 8.

The title of this book is meant to underline the ambiguity in the meanings of both "land" and "tiller." Once land is conceptualized as a "bundle of rights," rather than a simple commodity or patch of soil, "land to the tiller" takes on a spectrum of meanings, from redistribution of a minimal package of rights (transferability, hereditary security, specified share of product) to transfer of the full bundle of proprietary rights we usually term *ownership*. Reforms along the spectrum vary in their implications for economic consequences, as well as in the level and intensity of "political will" and administrative energies necessary for implementation. What the Indian Planning Commission termed the "logic of development in land reforms" is also the logic of exposition of the following chapters, from policy models of minimal redistribution of rights in land to the abolition of landlordism and rents as institutions.

The meaning of land to the tiller is relatively clear in the archetypal peasant society of landlords and tenants, but what does it mean in increasingly stratified and capitalist agrarian systems? Most work on Kerala's farms was done by hired labor—often for tenants; who are the tillers? If rents are illegitimate, are profits? Though the Kerala reforms were effective in abolishing landlordism and are widely hailed officially as a model in India, these issues are unresolved and raise new class conflicts in the meaning of land to the tiller. The land-to-the-tiller claim of agricultural laborers is structurally akin to the historic demands of tenants—a large enough share of the agricultural product to provide a decent living, security of access to production opportunities on the land, and freedom from arbitary control by those who formally "own" the land. Moreover, as non-land capital becomes increasingly important in production, agrarian reform can have meaning only by addressing the full range of inequalities in access to the means of production, distribution, and exchange. "Land" reform has always meant a reorganization of rights, privileges, and obligations in a system of production and distribution relations, not necessarily a rearrangement of physical plots; agrarian reform involves an explicit recognition of that fact and a corresponding acknowledgment that land is only one factor of production in agriculture.

Sources and Data: Appearance and Reality

Data on land ownership concentration and tenancy are presented throughout but present a dilemma for the serious analyst, particularly for the contemporary period. Although it is universally recognized that such data are misleading, scholars continue to make comparative statements based on manipulation of the numbers. Ironically, the data that would shed light on land reform questions are unreliable precisely because there is a question of land reform. The universal response of landowners to reform legislation or even intimations of reform has been to conceal the actual situation by altering records. It is axiomatic that holdings are far more concentrated than the data suggest and that there is a great deal more tenancy than is recorded. The case studies in this book contain sufficient evidence of such alteration to argue against accepting any existing aggregate data at face value. The specious precision of manipulation of systematically inaccurate data is the opposite of rigorous empirical inquiry.

Landholding data are more ambiguous than is frequently realized for specifiable reasons. It is in the interest of tenants-at-will to be recorded as permanent tenants, for tenants to be recorded as owners, and for rentiers to be recorded as cultivators. The juridical form of *individual* ownership reflected in most data obscures the real concentration of ownership by families. Moreover, data on land ownership (as opposed to operated area) frequently are not available; ownership units are typically far more concentrated than operational units. Indeed, one reason for not collecting ownership data in the 1960 Pakistan Census of Agriculture was the belief that the land reforms made it impossible to elicit honest responses to questions about ownership. Moreover, survey definitions and field methodologies change over time, often in quite haphazard ways; apparent agrarian structural transformations are frequently artifacts of such changes,[8] though this is infrequently appreciated. Definitions in official sources typically define tenancy in formal-legal, rather than structural-functional, terms, with the result that many categories of sharecroppers are not recorded as tenants; by sleight of hand definitionally, the Government of Bangladesh was able to declare its rack-rented agrarian system virtually free of the scourge of tenancy (cf. Jannuzi and Peach, 1980). And finally, it must be emphasized that officially published data are subject to political considerations before seeing the light of day. Regimes often try to present their reform accomplishments in the most favorable light; moreover, each level of the bureaucracy produces figures under pressure to "show progress" in implementation. Because of these constraints, intensive contextual investigation and analysis are important for understanding the actual situation.

The point about the unreliability of the numbers is so important that it justifies several examples. First, consider the simple question of the extent of tenancy in India. Even though Indian tenancy-reform legislation extends to volumes, and the state has made extensive efforts to collect data for planning purposes, there is no reliable answer to the question of the extent of tenancy. Household surveys (the National Sample Survey) show more than double the extent of tenancy shown in the Agricultural Census; independent village or district studies show even more

8. For example, Daniel and Alice Thorner, "Agrarian Revolution by Census Redefinition," in *Land and Labour in India* (1962).

tenancy than the NSS data. Laxminarayan and Tyagi concluded from an analysis of the available sources that "the longer the period of stay in the villages, the higher is the tenancy recorded" (1977: 880). This is to be expected because the terms of tenancy, even its legality, are controlled throughout India, leading to widespread concealment (cf. Sanyal, 1972). In a sense, the problem is analogous to trying to find the number of pick-pockets or black marketeers in a city by asking everyone a question about occupation. Both survey data and land records at the village level have been systematically distorted by decades of land reforms.

For some flavor of the problems encountered, consider the Government of Gujarat's Evaluation Study of Implementation of Land Reforms (1976: sec. 3.9). After noting puzzling discrepancies in the reported area leased in and leased out, the report concluded:

> It is not always possible to reconcile the figures of leased-in and leased-out areas as reported to the field staff. In the circumstances, the area of leased-out land and leased-in land as reported by the respondent families was taken as correct. In the course of the discussion, however, it was reported by the village knowledgeable persons and Talatis [record-keepers] that the extent and magnitude of concealed tenancy is much higher than what was reported. It was further revealed during the discussions with the village knowledgeable persons that persons cultivating the leased-in land are not willing to disclose the correct position. Such transactions of land take place as a result of mutual trust, need and convenience of the landlord and the lessee and they are not recorded in the Records. The agreement between the landlord and the lessee is considered as a gentlemen's word and it has a moral backing. It was also gathered that the lessees were generally in the know of the provisions of the Tenancy Act.[9]

It is crucial to consider data as social products and to recognize that the conditions of their production determine the relationship between the numbers and reality. Though this understanding produces messy analytical and methodological problems, it is central to any conceptualization of social science as social or as scientific.

The citations in the following chapters reflect another inevitable consequence of the social nature of social science. Wherever possible, I have cited accessible reports, studies, parliamentary debates, and so on, to indicate my evidentiary base; however, interviews with officers and politicians, peasants, landlords, rural bankers, and others over three years of field research were critical in the process of making sense of, evaluating, and interpolating among the written sources. Interviews with officers and politicians are sometimes cited explicitly, sometimes indirectly,

9. The same point appears continually in anthropological accounts, particularly in relation to the local power of local record-keepers (see chap. 2); cf. Lewis (1965: 104), Neale (1962: 245).

simply because the persons involved often requested that they not be identified by name or position. Given the political sensitivity of land reforms, and the common malpractices in their implementation, such requests are both expected and reasonable.

2 The Venerable Tenure-Reform Model: Intervention and Regulation

The rights of a tenant depend more on the size of his holding and his status in the village than on his status in law.
—Daniel and Alice Thorner

Tenure reform is logically and historically the place to begin. The policy model recognizes certain "defects" in agrarian systems and posits remedial measures addressed to exactly those defects. The degree of alteration of the agrarian system is thus minimal even in theory. Because the reform has limited objectives, the policy logic goes, success can be attained through limited measures. The tenurial defects which require attention in the model are moral, economic, and political: rack-rented tenants who can be evicted at the whim of the landlord suffer exploitation; such tenants are also less than optimally efficient producers and potentially threaten rural unrest. In response, rents are lowered by law and security of land-use rights for the tenant is incorporated into statutes; it is then left to specified organs of the state to intervene and regulate tenurial conditions.

The tenure-reform model is attractive to ruling elites because of the minimal disruption and cost implied by its modest aims; no physical land area changes hands and the social organization of production remains the same. But issues of rent and security of tenure are of enormous importance to landlords and tenants alike, evoking strong feelings and bitter conflict. Genuine tenure reform transfers significant prerogatives from owners to tenants, increasing the tenant's share in the "bundle of rights" we call ownership and simultaneously decreasing the landlord's share in the same bundle. In an effectively enforced tenure reform, the tenant may gain sufficient proprietary rights to retire from physical cultivation to become a petty rentier, subletting the field to a subtenant; this has historically been one source of "sub-infeudation."

The remarkable aspect of the reform model is its persistence in the face of widely recognized failures. Indeed, those familiar with the history of land reforms in South Asia may wonder if this chapter is not beating a dead horse, so well documented is the failure of tenure reform in the region. Yet the policy model survives, in South Asia and elsewhere, often in the programs recommended by development economists, foreign experts, and planning commissions to regimes which lack the "political will" to attempt more fundamental reforms (Mellor, 1976: 105–06; Myrdal, 1968: 1377–84; Ladejinsky, 1976: 103–10). It is a model typically utilized by governments seeking to defuse rural unrest and rationalize agricultural production but unwilling or unable to mount a full-scale confrontation with the landlord class. The conservative appeal of tenure reform is strong; although in theory the model is necessarily interventionist and regulatory and attacks important prerogatives of property, in practice it is fundamentally laissez-faire and allows rural dynamics to operate largely in accordance with existing power configurations.

Tenure reform often figures as a part of more comprehensive agrarian reforms, and in its main features is represented in the land-reform corpus of every nation in South Asia. But the model frequently stands alone; and even when combined with other reforms, the perceptions of defects and remedies are characteristic of the policy model. The central defects are the existence of exploitative ground rents and insecurity of tenure.

What Is a Fair Rent?

The perception of problems, the "defects in the agrarian system," focuses on rack-renting and insecurity of tenure. These phenomena are considered bad in and of themselves, but it is in their interaction with the causal theories of the model that the defects become so serious as to require reform. The normative position is that the institution of rent is justifiable and that sharecropping is an acceptable social organization of production, but that there is in some sense a just rent. The very notion of "rack-renting" presupposes such a just rent; the crop shares which are considered "exploitative" are thus reduced by legislation. Likewise, it is considered unfair that farmers who have worked a given field for many years, often stretching back generations, should be subject to arbitrary eviction by landlords. Thus the model includes explicit recognition of proprietary-like rights of tenants to continue tilling and to a given share of the product. Secure land-use rights are legislated along with rental controls, and eviction is allowed only under specified conditions.

The West Pakistan Land Commission, in its report to the World Land Reforms Conference in Rome (Pakistan, 1966: 6), summed up, somewhat defensively, the normative core assumption of the model: "There is nothing inherently wrong with the institution of tenancy." Six years later, Zulfikar Ali Bhutto claimed that his tenure reforms "lay down the foundations of a relationship of honour and mutual benefit between the landlord and the tenant" (Pakistan, 1972a: 2).

But if the institution of share tenancy is normatively acceptable, the distinction between "fair rent" and "exploitation" is difficult to understand. By what principle is the distinction justified? The absence of any generally accepted criteria is evident in the actual differentiations made in legislation. For example, the United National Party Government of Ceylon in 1951 proclaimed that tenurial conditions in the Hambantota and Batticaloa districts were "hardly tolerable," whereas in the rest of the country there was "a great deal of fair play and justice in the share the cultivator gets." The response was the 1953 Paddy Lands Act, a classic tenure reform, which lowered rents in the two districts. Yet the actual differences in the shares received by cultivators across district boundaries were small; evidently half the crop as rent was considered "fair play and justice" and anything more was "hardly tolerable" (Herring, 1972/74: 103). It is difficult to conceive of supportable normative criteria, other than tradition, which would sustain such a distinction. This is particularly evident when we understand that a half-crop share on five acres of poor land leaves the cultivator wretchedly poor whereas half the produce on five (or ten) good acres may allow a respectable standard of living in the terms of peasant society.

The one-half crop share is firmly rooted in the agrarian tradition of a number of diverse societies. Indeed, in Sri Lanka, as elsewhere, the word for sharecropping—*ande*—means "one-half" in Sinhala. But three years after the 1953 Paddy Lands Act, the one-half crop share rent was no longer considered "fair play and justice"; a Paddy Lands Bill was drawn up to reduce rents to one-fourth or less. In the new bill, the traditional half-crop share was considered exploitative, but one-fourth was held to be legitimate. Throughout the subcontinent we find this curious patchwork of rental limits. The early tenancy acts in Pakistan statutorily reduced share rents from 50 percent to 40 percent. The range in India in the post-independence acts of the various States ranged from very low shares for privileged-status tenants (one-eighth or less) to very high rates for tenants-at-will in Bengal and Madras (two-thirds of the crop was specified as the maximum rent under the West Bengal Bargadars Act, 1950).[1] Although the sharecropping rentals could logically vary with the share of working capital provided, it is difficult to conceive of consistent, defensible normative criteria which would define a one-half share of the crop as exploitation and 40 percent as just.

When tenure reform seeks to halt or reverse the deterioration of terms of exchange for tenants in a changing agrarian system, the normative appeal is indeed to tradition. If Marx and Malthus were right, the traditional division of the crop in conjunction with field size and soil fertility should allow bare subsistence to the sharecroppers in normal

---

1. India, *Agricultural Legislation in India* (1955), vol. 6, appendix 1, p. liii. For a review of Pakistan's early tenancy legislation, M. A. Cheema, deputy secretary, Ministry of Food and Agriculture (1954). Tenancy reform in Sri Lanka is covered in detail in chapter 3; see also Gold (1977), Sanderatne (1972b), Peiris (1976). For a summary of tenancy laws in Bangladesh, Jannuzi and Peach (1980: chap. 1). Sections of this chapter follow Herring (1981).

years. But with population growth, the intrusion of the market, or some-times simply the arrival of the external power of the colonial state to enforce property prerogatives, the rental share (or size of field) changes, often pushing large numbers of sharecroppers below the normal subsis-tence level. In these circumstances, tenurial reform is not conservative but restorative, seeking to reestablish the security and distributive prin-ciples of a passing age. Tenure reform employed under these conditions (as during the colonial period especially) becomes a liberal response to the intrusions of a liberal market economy into precapitalist agrarian for-mations. As Karl Polanyi (1944) suggests, the political response to such intrusions is frequently just such an effort to protect groups or sectors newly affected by the market by reestablishing traditional securities.

But in most contemporary tenurial reforms, the traditional share is seen not as just but as unfair, established through unequal bargaining power and "feudal" institutions. The modern reformist stance is simply that tenants pay too much, given that sharecroppers are a disadvantaged group in society, worthy of being benefited by redistributive public policy. Thus the Indian Planning Commission has consistently urged the States to reduce rents by law to between one-fourth and one-fifth of the gross produce (or monetary equivalent), though the individual States have typi-cally balked at accepting the recommendation.[2]

Whatever the circumstances in which the tenure reform model ap-pears, the normative core is that a secure tenant paying a "fair rent" escapes exploitation. The rack-renting and evictions which appear as evi-dence of exploitation, and thus of a defective tenurial system, are the same as those in the land-to-the-tiller model. The difference, of course, is that the latter rejects the justifiability of rent and landlordism alto-gether and abolishes both, whereas the former seeks to abolish the "abuses" but not the system.

Exploitation is a purely normative defect in the agrarian system; the only thing intrinsically problematic about an exploitative system is its unfairness. However, it is typically not the unfairness of rack-renting and eviction which counts heavily in the policy logic, but rather the pre-sumed political and economic consequences of these evils: agrarian un-rest and stagnant agriculture.

Land Tenure and Agrarian Unrest

If injustice is insufficient stimulus for tenurial reform, the consequences of tenurial "defects" must be something more than unjust. The paradigm

2. The proclaimed goal of rent reduction for sharecroppers in official publications originates in political tracts of the Congress Party before Independence. The *First Five Year Plan*, and subsequent planning documents, have reiterated the policy. See All-India Con-gress Committee (1949); India (1955, 1956, 1961, 1963, 1966b, 1969, 1973, 1978a); Koshy (1974).

holds that insecurity of tenure and high rents produce rural unrest and economic irrationality; thus, there are specific theories of collective political behavior and microeconomics embedded in the policy model. It is because of this perception that we so frequently observe tenure reforms in the wake of a food crisis or rural agitation.

As to agrarian unrest, the British *Report of the Commission on Malabar Land Tenures* stated the case precisely in 1884, with somewhat more colour (and honesty) than subsequent regimes:

> The political necessity for interference with the *janmies'* (landlords') rights we believe to exist in the grave discontent prevailing among the agricultural classes regarding the growing insecurity of their tenures; in the fact that, among one class in the community, agrarian discontent fanned by fanaticism, is ready to develop at any moment into agrarian outrage. . . . [Varghese, 1970: 60].

British colonial rule in northern Kerala, as elsewhere, rested on the support of traditional landed elites. Lord Cornwallis put the matter bluntly: "It is a matter of last importance, considering the means by which we keep possession of this country, that the proprietors of the lands should be attached to us from motives of self-interest." Cornwallis went on to note that insecurity of tenure, excessive rents, and high taxes potentially undermine support for the government in rural areas (Sen, 1955: 55).

In response to the Malabar Commission Report, some reforms came to Malabar, but these measures were limited to tenure reform, and only those tenurial defects which threatened serious social consequences were noticed or addressed (Hardgrave, 1977; Pannikar, 1979; Hart and Herring, 1977). The commission's report on Malabar was hotly debated in policy circles, but even the "radical" view sought only to provide security of tenure to all tenants; the dominant view, in rejecting full security of tenure legislation, officially argued "the best solution of agrarian questions to be that which involves least interference" (Varghese, 1970: 62).

The example from colonial Malabar represents one of the reasons why conservative regimes legislate land reforms—fear of agrarian unrest—when no agrarian transformation is intended. Elias Tuma (1965) has illustrated this phenomenon in a broad range of cultural and historical settings, dating to classical antiquity (cf. Anderson, 1978: 32–33, 56–57). As conservative reformers remind their more conservative opponents, there are times when the system must be changed marginally in order to preserve its fundamental character. Ironically, limited conservative attempts to improve tenurial relations in Malabar arguably contributed to the mobilization of tenants on agrarian reform issues by communists and other radical political groups.[3]

3. For a view of the situation by two venerable peasant organizers, see A. K. Gopalan (1959: 86 ff.) and E. M. S. Namboodiripad (1968: 110 ff.). For academic summaries, Paulini (1978), Koshy (1976), Pannikar (1977).

Ruling elites, like social scientists, hold different views on the nature and dynamics of rural society. A central dimension in differentiating the perceptual and conceptual bases of these paradigms is that of consensual-harmonious social structure and relations versus that of coercive-conflictual social structure and relations.[4] For example, in viewing the agrarian structure of Ceylon in the early 1950s, two successive ministers of agriculture came to diametrically opposed conclusions and produced correspondingly differing land reforms (Herring, 1972/74). In one view, the quiescence of landless tenants was confirmation that the agrarian social structure was essentially sound, that the landlord-tenant nexus was a contractual relationship mutually beneficial to the parties involved. Land reforms were necessary not to change the structure of land relations, but to *adjust* individual (aberrant) abuses by restoring the contract to its normal (traditional) form. The second perception viewed the same quiescence as evidence of the unequal and coercive nature of the relationship. The landlord-tenant nexus was conceptualized as a class relationship, hence characterized by latent conflict. The agrarian structure, in this view, was unsound and required thorough transformation. A land reform would, in effecting this change, require special attention to the conflictual nature of the relationship and the power imbalance between tenants and owners. The resultant policy prescriptions of the two ministers varied dramatically, as reflected in the 1953 and 1958 Paddy Lands acts to be discussed in the following chapter.

The Economic Evils of Share Tenancy

The economic paradigm of the evils of share tenancy goes back to Adam Smith and later neoclassical analysis. Basically, the argument is that high share rents depress the level of investment in operating capital by tenants because the tenant's marginal return is only one-half that of a comparable proprietor (assuming a rental share of one-half). Likewise, returns to tenant labor are reduced, because any increment to output must be shared with the landlord; thus less labor is applied to the field, lowering productivity. The tenant who bears the full cost of inputs, including the (opportunity) cost of labor, but receives only half of the increment to output, in theory will produce at a lower point on the production possibilities curve than would a comparable operator who did not pay rent.[5]

4. For an argument that this dichotomy is central to more general models of the social world, see Dahrendorf, *Class and Class Conflict in Industrial Societies* (1959), chapter 5 in particular.

5. There is a strong statement of the paradigm under South Asian conditions in Myrdal (1968), 2: 1064–69. A less neoclassical statement is Thorner (1956), especially chap. 1, which discusses the "depressor" introduced by the agrarian institutions of India. For a strikingly uncritical acceptance of the conventional view by the World Bank, see *Land Reform* (1974: 16, 27, and passim). Acceptance of the paradigm in official policy logic will be cited extensively in later chapters; the Task Force on Agrarian Relations (India, 1973: 7)

Essentially the same arguments apply to investment in fixed capital; by reducing returns to investment, share tenancy is held to discourage productivity-enhancing investment. Insecurity of tenure aggravates the problem; tenants would be irrational to improve the land if they may be evicted and receive little or no return on investment, or, ironically, see the rent raised as the land becomes more productive. The theoretical result is a less dynamic agricultural sector. Increasing agricultural productivity is a chronic policy problem; the price and availability of food are central political issues, affecting regime stability and national economic planning.

Though the economic issue will be treated in more detail later, it is useful here to give some of the flavor of the paradigm as incorporated into policy logic. Consider the position of the Bombay Government's Famine Enquiry Commission (1944):

> The tenant who cultivated land on lease . . . is not sure how long the lands would remain in his possession as the landlord has the power to resume the lands at the end of the year. . . . The tenant has thus no permanent interest in lands. . . . If the tenant sows improved seeds or puts in good manure or extra labor to improve the land, half of the increased produce so obtained at his cost goes to the landlord, and the tenant does not get a proper return on his labor and enterprise.[6]

These propositions are more than mere deductions from Marshallian economics; the inefficiency of share tenancy as a mode of organizing agricultural production seems congruent with common sense and has been bolstered by at least some field investigations of cultural practices. The Land Revenue Commission of the Punjab, for example, reported in 1938:

> The owner-cultivator feels the magic of property and puts more manure and effort into his cultivation than a tenant-at-will or a hired laborer. The tenant-at-will tends to exploit rather than develop the land . . . 'No tenant cultivated his fields as carefully as the owner,' said the headman of a village, 'he is apt to give the land a scanty amount of labor and get whatever he can, and is never a true husbandman.' Another cultivator of the same village, when asked if he cultivated his own land more carefully than what he took on rent, said, 'What else could you expect. When we cultivate our own land the produce is ours. When we cultivate land on rent we only get a share.' [Punjab, 1938: 36]

Thus, the policy logic goes, share tenants are often too poor to improve the land or supply proper inputs, and lack the incentive to do so,

---

termed exploitative tenancy relations "insurmountable hurdles in the path of the spread of modern technology and improved agricultural practices." The economic arguments are treated in more detail in chapter 9.

6. Quoted in Bhowani Sen (1955: 60). Investigations of tenure conditions figure prominently in famine inquiries, as in investigations of peasant unrest; cf. Sunil Sen (1972: 47–48).

as a consequence of onerous rental exactions by landlords. But what of the landlords? The tenure reform model specifies obstacles to optimal economic behavior by landlords as well. The Famine Enquiry Commission argued: "The absentee landlord cares only for his annual rent and takes no interest in the improvement of his land or the introduction of improved methods of cultivation" (Sen 1955: 60). The tenure reform model basically addresses the problem from below, by altering the microeconomic situation of the tenant. Other policy models, as we shall see, attempt to solve the problem of the "bad landlord," the geographically or functionally absentee rentier, from above.

The model of the social world in the policy logic thus contains a long and complex chain of causal reasoning. Tenurial institutions affect the microeconomic decisions of peasant producers, depressing both current yields and future investment and technological change, affecting national economic prospects and regime support. Remarkably, considering the impeccable logic of the model, there is very little evidence to support its behavioral suppositions. Not only is there limited decisive empirical evidence (and what evidence there is suggests more ambiguity than support for the paradigm), but the evidence available to policymakers who have recommended or legislated tenurial reform has been even *more* conspicuously absent, ambiguous, or contradictory. For example, the only study of productivity differences available when the Government of Ceylon legislated the Paddy Lands Act in 1958 showed yields on tenant farms *higher*, not lower, than those on owner-cultivated farms of similar size (Herring, 1972/74; Peiris, 1976; Sanderatne, 1974b: 344–46).

As suggested in the introductory chapter, cognitive paradigms are likely to be quite impervious to dissonant empirical information. This is true partly because paradigmatic thinking screens out, dismisses, or provides alternative explanations for seemingly disconfirming information, and partly because the roots of the paradigms are ideological; that is, the network of commitments is related to political realities.

To illustrate this point, we need only note that the mootness of the empirical case does not seem to affect the positions taken on the issue. This is true of politicians, policymakers, and most scholars of land reform. The politicians are very consistent; when land reform is debated in parliaments, conservative (typically landlord-dominated) forces argue it will be detrimental to production, liberal reformists argue it will improve production, the radicals argue that, if fundamental enough, land reform will "unleash the productive forces of society." Yet all three positions depend on similar evidence—typically very little at all. As scholar-scientists, we tend to dismiss the stances taken by politicians as ideological. Yet scholar-scientists of land reform tend to line up in similar positions, with better but clearly inconclusive and ambiguous evidence (as do policymakers, whose evidence is frequently that of the scholar-scientists in predigested form).

These points are illustrated by the origins, and demise, of the 1953 Paddy Lands Act in Ceylon, the only tenure reform legislated in eight years of rule by the conservative United National Party in the early independence period. In presenting the bill to Parliament, government ministers argued that their "sole intention" was to increase food production (Ceylon, *PD*, vol. 11 [1951: cols. 49, 296]). The plantation sector, which was the mainstay of the economy and thoroughly permeated by modern capitalist relations, was not considered in need of reform. The reform was to apply to only two districts—Hambantota and Batticaloa— where tenurial conditions were considered an impediment to rice production. Yet, curiously, there is no evidence that productivity was lower in those two districts than in other districts.[7]

Motives of regimes in land reform are, of course, extremely difficult to discern, given the symbolic posturing for political effect, but the regime's claim that the reform was a response to a food crisis was important considering the historical situation in which it appeared. The two districts where the reform was applied had traditionally been two of the leading exporters of paddy—the productive potential was great. Ceylon had a chronic rice deficit, and because of the Korean War prices of imported rice were rising; the cost of food-import subsidies was a heavy drain on the nation's foreign exchange reserves. On the recommendation of the Central Bank, the rice subsidy to consumers was cut, resulting in the "Great Hartal" (general strike) of 1953 and the resignation of the prime minister (Wriggins, 1960: 67, 289–90).

The claim that land reform was needed to increase food production was important even if the reform served other symbolic purposes as well— for example, to reassure the public that the government was concerned about the general welfare and willing to move against propertied elites in pursuit of the public interest, to steal a march on Marxist politicians, to blunt (limited) peasant unrest, and to emulate other Asian societies involved in modernizing land reforms (India, Japan, Taiwan, China).[8] The production imperative justification itself shows that the government considered the food crisis to be a plausible reason for instituting a land reform, a justification to be passed on to its supporters, both landed elites and urban nonagriculturalists. Such justifications are important for a re-

7. For analysis of available empirical evidence, see Herring (1972/74: 103–11). The only "evidence" linking tenure problems to low productivity available to the government was evidently an unsubstantiated report by the government agent in one of the districts.

8. Nimal Sanderatne (1974b: 345) correctly notes that a desire to emulate other Asian nations (Japan, Taiwan) by modernizing through land reform may have been important. But, significantly, the 1952 World Bank *Report on the Economic Development of Ceylon* did not recommend redistributive land reforms. Peiris (1976: 29–30) makes a similar point, using India and China as possible models, and stresses the desire of the ruling party to counter limited Marxist initiatives in rural Ceylon. Overt peasant unrest prior to the reform was evidently an extremely limited phenomenon, but has been given by one scholar as a contributing factor (M. S. Perera, 1970: 17).

gime which depends on the support of propertied classes and yet wishes to introduce a policy which nominally curtails the prerogatives of property. The justification also illustrates the pervasive paradigm of possible tenurial roots of low paddy productivity—the disincentives of rack-renting (more than three-fourths of the crop in Batticaloa) and extreme insecurity of tenure. The argument from the government was not only that these tenurial defects were unjust but, more importantly, that abuses sapped incentives for agricultural production.

The content of the resulting reform was quite limited even for the tenure reform model—security of tenure for share tenants for five-year periods and marginally reduced rents. Indeed, the provisions of the act were almost entirely voluntaristic and provided little more than a model contract for those landlords who wished to offer such a contract. However, the reform evoked fierce opposition, even violence, and obstruction from landowners, and was not seriously implemented. It was quietly abandoned as unenforceable several years after enactment.[9] As this has been the fate of similar reforms in a wide variety of settings in South Asia, it is necessary to consider systematically the dynamics of the failure of tenure reform in the subcontinent.

The Failure of Tenancy Reform

The evidence from South Asia is immense, ranging from anthropological accounts of single villages through scholarly studies of the workings of specific legislation to official evaluations by special task forces and commissions. For the most part, the evidence confirms the accuracy of Michael Lipton's broader summary:

> In general, tenancy reform in the 'soft states' of the Third World breaks upon the rock of landlord power, and the effects of evasion can include insecurity that worsens both rural income distribution and the standards of capital and land acquisition and maintenance on tenant farms.[10]

As Lipton suggests, the failure of tenancy reform is a phenomenon which is not limited to South Asia. An exploration of the dynamics of tenure reform in the subcontinent suggests explanations for the failure

9. The reform was administered by the district government agents; their reports illustrate its total failure; e.g., Ceylon, *Ceylon Administration Reports, Report of the Assistant Government Agent, Hambantota*, 1953, A 103; 1955, A 116; *Report of the Government Agent, Batticaloa*, 1955, A 190; *Parliamentary Debates, House of Representatives*, vol. 30 (1957: col. 2121). cf. Gold (1977: chap. 2).

10. In Lehmann, ed. (1974: 277). The United Nations, UNFAO, and ILO report, *Progress in Land Reform (Fifth Report)* (1970) reported a general failure of tenure reform in precisely those agrarian situations worldwide in which it was needed; little progress was noted in the official report of the World Conference on Agrarian Reform and Rural Development (UNFAO, 1979).

of the model in settings with different tenurial and cultural institutions but similar structural forces and political and social dynamics.

Failure or success in land reform is relative; of course, public policies seldom accomplish their stated objectives, even when the objectives are realistic and attempts at implementation are sincere. By success in tenure reform, I mean simply that in those situations in which cultivating tenants are in serious *need* of the protection offered by the reform, they have been able to secure the legislated benefits *in the face of landlord counterpreferences*. In this sense, the failure of tenure reform in general is clear. But it must be emphasized that rural South Asia is not neatly divided into homogeneous classes of tenants and landlords. Rather, the agrarian structure resembles a pyramid with gradations of propertylike rights in land. "Tenants" vary from insecure low-caste tenants-at-will to high-caste or peasant-caste tenants with large holdings and secure standing in the rural social structure. That tenure reform has institutionalized the rights of many of the relatively secure, relatively privileged tenants is indisputable. Where the reform has failed is in its efforts to alleviate the tenurial defects identified in the policy model for those cultivators who suffer from the defects.

The policy logic of the tenure reform model seems compelling: the "tenurial defects" are quite specifically delimited and are addressed through specific measures to correct exactly what is wrong in the relationship between owner and tiller. Indeed, the very limited nature of the reform recommends it to practical persons who recognize the extraordinary difficulty of more fundamental, sweeping reforms; limited reforms require minimal resources, produce minimal disruption, and yet seemingly address exactly what is defective in the tenure system, avoiding the burn-down-the-barn-to-roast-the-pig thrust of radical prescriptions. Yet it seems that, empirically, tenure reform has in the South Asian context proved unable to accomplish even its limited goals and has indeed often harmed rather than helped the tenants it claims to protect.

The institutional arrangements for achieving the ends of the policy model are constrained by the normative assessment that the landlord's proprietary rights in land should be preserved. The structural gap between ownership and production is held to be acceptable. If this is to be the case, the state must intervene to regulate the terms of contracts between innumerable landlords and tenants or assume that the legislated changes will be adopted voluntarily. Institutional innovation to effect the reform has typically been negligible; enforcement has been left to the civil courts, the revenue courts, or existing administrative mechanisms. The model assumes that tenants whose landlords refuse to comply with the law will take the landlord to court or apply to the administration for redress. The policy logic further assumes that the rural administration will be willing and able to determine the relevant facts in the case (how much rent is paid, and so on) and act to enforce the law. The critical assumption, then, is that tenants will come forward, pursue the cases, and that the administration will respond to correct irregularities.

A review of the evidence confirms reflective common sense: security of tenure and rent regulation are critically interdependent. If the tenant can be threatened with, or is afraid of, eviction from his farm (and often house site as well), other redistributive measures in the reform model—reduction of rent in particular—will not be demanded. Reciprocally, effective regulation of rent is a necessary complement to meaningful security of tenure; if the landlord can raise rents to ruinous levels, security of tenure is of little use to the tenant.[11] Since the policy model accepts maintenance of the landlord-tenant nexus, it must find effective mechanisms for guaranteeing security of tenure and a regulated rent.

Though the policy model posits the need for state intervention in and regulation of tenurial relations, in practice the burden of enforcement falls squarely on tenant initiative; aggrieved tenants must apply for redress. The policy logic thus depends in a fundamental way on the collective trust of rural have-nots in the organs of the state. Tenants must believe that the enforcers will act impartially and honestly to enforce the law, that the local courts and officials are *capable* of protecting tenant rights in the face of landlord opposition. Tenants will otherwise acquiesce in illegal tenurial relations, fearing a net deterioration in their position through landlord retaliation.

A strong case can be made, and will be made empirically in the next chapter, that the rational tenant-cultivator throughout much of the subcontinent would acquiesce rather than demand legislated rights. The central reason is that security of tenure has been virtually impossible to enforce for those tenants who are in need of protection. As Wolf Ladejinsky aptly remarked, security of tenure legislation in India became little more than a "pious hope."[12]

Tenure reforms in India were legislated primarily in the years 1948–54, varying from State to State, region to region, and subject to continual legislative tinkering. One of the first, most important, and most studied tenure reforms was the Bombay Tenancy Act of 1948. The most comprehensive investigation of the act concluded with surprise: "For all practical purposes the Act did not exist." More rents had been raised than low-

---

11. A. M. Khusro's study in Hyderabad (1958: 47) documents this obvious point, which extends to other factors of production; the tenant must be guaranteed access to ancillary inputs controlled by the landlord (water, for example) at less than ruinous prices, if security of *land* tenure, narrowly defined, is to be meaningful. The use of threat of eviction to nullify rent reduction is well documented. For a representative range of Indian sources see India (1955: xlix); India (1968: 18); India (1978a: 107–08); India (1972c); India (1976: vol. 15, chap. 66); Wolf Ladejinsky, for the Planning Commission (1965); Raj Krishna (1961: 221 ff.); All-India Kisan Sabha (Peasant Association) (1970: 16 ff.); A. M. Khusro (1973: 11). A perceptive overview of existing studies is P. C. Joshi (1975).

12. Ladejinsky's acerbic and accurate observations on land reform in India have been collected in one volume (1977); see, especially, sec. 44, 48, 50, 51, 60, 62.

ered and a large number of sharecroppers had been evicted.[13] These results are typical of the tenure reforms for which we have systematic evidence. In the *Report* of the Planning Commission's Committee on Tenancy Reform, we find a confirmation of the negligible impact of the reforms nationwide:

> We noticed along our tours that in spite of a new legislation on the statute book in the field the old practice still obtains. Tenancies continue to be governed by custom or agreement. Old rents still continue to be paid and accepted though law has scaled them down in many areas and the receipt of a higher rent is illegal. [India, 1959: 37]

The inertial resistance of village life to reformist state enactments is not surprising, of course. But tenancy reforms went beyond simply having no impact; that "waves of evictions" of tenants followed tenure reform legislation is a recurring theme of case studies and official investigations. Kotovsky's (1964: 139) conclusion from his survey of the early tenancy reforms of India was that "tenants have lost more land than they have acquired." Gunnar Myrdal came to the same general conclusion.[14] Daniel Thorner noted the darker side of tenant evictions in his study of Rajasthan: "A number of leases were shortened by the termination of the lives of the tenants."[15]

Though force and violence have been utilized to evict newly protected tenants (cf. Melchior, 1979), the more common mechanisms have been less dramatic—and less observable. Tenancy laws themselves, in accordance with recommendations of the *First Five Year Plan*, have typically sanctioned large-scale eviction of tenants by permitting landlords to "resume" land for "personal cultivation." Personal cultivation was virtually always defined so as to allow the owner to abstain from participation in or direction of cultivation. For example, personal cultivation legally could include arranging for cultivation by servants or hired labor or by "partners" in cultivation whose structural position was in no important way different from that of sharecroppers.[16] Moreover, "voluntary sur-

13. V. M. Dandekar, G. J. Khudanpur (1957: 187). Similar findings are reported by M. B. Desai (1958); Government of Maharashtra (1974: 281 and passim); Wunderlich (1964).

14. Myrdal (1968) 2: 1323–34. For supporting quantitative evidence, see A. M. Khusro (1958: 169). For evidence of intrastate variation in this pattern, see Maharashtra (1974); Desai (1971: 119–23).

15. Thorner (1973:32). The example could be multiplied many fold. For more recent archetypal accounts of the murder of tenants who demand legislated rights, R. Narayan (1977), Arun Sinha (1977).

16. The definitions of "personal cultivation" adopted in the various states are printed as Annexure 6 of India (1959). The "partners" in the Uttar Pradesh legislation—*sajhidars*—are not considered sharecroppers, but rather partners in cultivation, who supply the labor for a share of the crop given by another "partner," the landowner, who supplies the land. Precisely the same tenurial configuration, known as *koottu ande*, appears in Sri Lanka, depriving the sharecropper of legislated rent protection (ARTI, 1979: 57). Though the *Sec-*

renders" of land rights by tenants to landlords were typically allowed and a great deal of land was, predictably, "voluntarily surrendered." Both the Second and Third Five Year Plans noted, however, in classically understated official prose, that "most voluntary surrenders of tenancy are open to doubt as bonafide transactions" (India, 1961: 224). Likewise, most States enacted tenure reform laws which specified causes for legal eviction of tenants; such causes were often vaguely defined and open to arbitrary interpretation and abuse (for example, "failure to cultivate properly") (India, 1976: XV, 66–67).

The line between legal and illegal evictions thus blurred, but it seems clear that for every tenant who attained some improvement in tenurial rights, other cultivators lost ground. In part, this result could be expected merely from the conceptualization of the tenancy laws. There have always been strata of tenants in Indian law and practice, a hierarchy only partly the result of British legislation distinguishing between "occupancy tenants" and various kinds of tenants-at-will. Such distinctions have held in village usage as well, often as direct correlates of the caste standing of cultivator groups. Tenancy legislation typically accepted the continuation of this hierarchy and bestowed privileged status on the highest strata of tenants while denying any proprietary claim whatsoever to the lower orders of nonowning cultivators—the tenants-at-will and tillers whose structural status hovers between that of sharecropper and attached laborer: the *bargadars, sajhidars, bataidars, waramdars,* and so on.

Because the definition of tenant in virtually all of the Indian legislation was formal and legal rather than structural and functional—that is, not defined by the concrete place of the "tenant" in the structure of production relations—a great many actual tillers of the soil were denied benefits and deprived of what little security they had previously enjoyed. On the other hand, for the same reasons, a good many "tenants" who did not directly cultivate their land were given enhanced proprietary status. Yet is was this latter group which was least in need of protection, as such tenants tend to be of higher caste and status, to have better official and political connections, and to be better placed economically.

Thus the conceptualization of tenancy in the tenure reforms in India was partially responsible for the adverse effects of a seemingly mild and ameliorative land reform on the least secure and most marginal till-

---

ond Five Year Plan recommended that "personal cultivation" should require personal labor as a necessary condition, the recommendation suffered the fate of many other central initiatives in land reforms: it was not accepted by the States (India, 1961: 224–25). Personal cultivation may include cultivation of land with a "servant" as well, inducing landlords to have tenants sign a chit, known as *nauker nama* in Hindi-speaking areas (*majur kabuliyat* in Bengal), stating that the sharecropper is a servant and thus not entitled to protection as a tenant. A definition of "self-cultivated" that mandated significant contribution of personal labor would be quite radical in the Indian context, attacking both "feudal" and capitalist landlords and presenting a normative model of a purely peasant agrarian sector.

ers. As tenancy reforms were enacted, the giving of a lease, or allowing the continuation of a lease, threatened the property prerogatives of owners and resulted in countermeasures against the landless—refusal to lease land, denial of rent receipts or documentation of status, shifting of tenants from plot to plot to prevent continuous occupancy, shortening of leases, eviction, and so on. As A. M. Khusro (1958: 45) insightfully concluded from his study of Hyderabad:

> The antagonism of the landlord is not so much against the tenant as such but against his protected status. So long as he succeeds in depriving the tenant of this status he does not mind whether the land comes back to him (the owner) or goes to another tenant or indeed remains with the original tenant now shorn of protection.

Tenure reform in many situations thus had the ironic result of disrupting the traditional avenues to security of landless cultivators—striking an informal long-term tenancy agreement with noncultivating owners—or prompted evictions by pressuring landlords to "resume" the land for "personal cultivation" or accept diminished control of their land. These particular negative consequences are directly related to the provisions for landlord "resumption" and curious definitions of "tenant" and "self-cultivation" in the laws. But even those tenants who were unambiguously included in the legislation as worthy of protection often received no net benefits from the reforms. In order to understand the failures in implementation, as opposed to failures in conceptualization, it is necessary to analyze the particular social relations of production which the laws were to change, the mechanism through which the change was to be effected, and the relations between the two—state and society—at the village level.

Relations of Production:
Antagonistic Classes or Patrons and Clients?

Paradigms of rural South Asia frequently present two conflicting views, each with a different terminology, conceptual framework, and understanding of dynamics. One pictures landlords and tenants as patrons and clients involved in a diffuse, complex network of mutually beneficial exchanges predicated on close personal relations which sometimes take a fictive-kin form. A second model posits a class relationship based on profoundly unequal access to the primary means of production—a relationship which is structurally (if not experientially) coercive and potentially (if not overtly) conflictual. These two paradigms correspond to broader views of the social world—the latter paralleling what Dahrendorf terms the "coercion theory of society," with roots in Marxian theory, the former corresponding to Dahrendorf's "integration theory of society," with roots in gemeinschaft sociology and a Durkheimian emphasis on shared values and organic solidarity.[17]

Which view is correct? In explaining the failure of tenure reform, we seem to have evidence for both. The class conflict model is buttressed by the phenomena of forcible evictions, violence, and Thorner's macabre observation that "a number of leases were shortened by the termination of the lives of the tenants." On the other hand, we have the seemingly remarkable phenomena of well-documented "voluntary surrenders" of tenancies that were indeed voluntary (though many others were coerced) and of tenants acquiescing in an impoverished situation and foregoing any attempt to demand the reduced rent provided by law. Other tenants have accepted illegal evictions as the unquestioned prerogative of land-owners, suggesting a shared ideology of property rights and differential class privileges.[18]

The class conflict and coercion model of society posits class inequalities and disabilities across several important dimensions. The structure of economic, political, and social power (leaving aside authority for the moment) in the village typically makes for an unequal contest between landlords and tenants on a number of levels. Compared to the tenant, the landlord, through wider contacts and education, is more likely to understand the fine points of the law and its loopholes. He is more likely to be able to produce documents and to process them in accordance with technical requirements.[19] The landlord's power within the village is likely to extend to the local record keeper, allowing manipulation of the primary evidentiary source—the village record of rights. Tenancy contracts are frequently oral, whereas ownership rights are elaborately documented. In short, the tenant who choses confrontation may lose the battle before it appears openly in the judicial or administrative arena, partly because of the diverse consequences of inferior class standing.

Within the formal-legal confrontation system, the class privileges

17. Dahrendorf (1959), esp. chap. 5. I am ignoring here the neoclassical economic paradigm of landlords and tenants as equivalent economic actors drawn together in factor markets, differing only in the factors each contributes to the production process. For an (implicit) explication of these models in agrarian systems, Scott (1974). A useful collection of articles on the overlays and tensions between caste-*jajmani* explanations and class explanations of rural social relations is the special issue of *Economic and Political Weekly* (Bombay), "Caste and Class in India," vol. 14, nos. 7–8 (1979).

18. There are poignant examples of such attitudes with regard to land reform in the conversations recorded by Kusum Nair (1962: 29, 31, 66–68, and passim).

19. It is striking to read repeatedly field investigations which find that tenants do not even know the provisions of tenure reform laws; e.g., India (1959: 37–38); Mirich (1977: 11–12); M. B. Desai (1958: 94). Most accounts agree that the tortuous language and complexity of legal provisions prevent tenants, and even lower government officials, from understanding the laws, though ignorance of the reforms is also a reflection of the low priority given them by the government and the isolation and illiteracy of sharecroppers. The fact that the original legislation may be in English and only later (sometimes much later) translated into local languages compounds this problem.

of the landlord are likely to count heavily: superior knowledge of the arena, access to resources for lawyers and bribes, leisure time to pursue endless litigation, contacts in high places, and so on.[20] Outside the formal-legal arena, where most issues are settled, the landlord is more likely to be able to mobilize power in the various ways that power can be manifest in the village. A larger following, related to control of economic resources and derivative social status, is more likely to be available to the landlord. Compared to the tenant, a person of means in the village can get things done for people—or make life miserable for them. The mobilization of supporters is important whatever form the confrontation takes, whether physical in the back lanes of the village or political through the *panchayat* or social through a mobilization of diffuse pressures on a trouble-making tenant.[21] More basically, whatever the tenancy laws may say, the landlord still *owns the land* in a system in which the organs of the state are committed to protect the rights of private property. In concrete terms, this has meant that time after time landlords have been able to evict tenants in disputed cases by simply calling out the police. Court cases may drag on for years, but the local police can usually be counted on to enforce the prerogatives of ownership.

The fundamental weakness of the tenant is, however, the structural disability imposed by his or her own class position under typical economic and demographic conditions. Owning little or no capital, the tenant has only labor power to sell in a glutted market and can make a living as a farmer only if granted access to land and other means of production owned by others. A full-scale confrontation with a landlord threatens not only loss of the tenant's farm but also continued unemployment, as other landlords avoid taking on a tenant with a reputation as a trouble-maker or "bad tenant" (Albrecht, 1974: 88–89; Niaz, 1965: 29–30; ARTI, 1979: 56; Gold, 1977: 145). Moreover, a hostile landlord can urge caste and class fellows to deny a tenant other forms of employment. But the decisive vulnerability of the tenant—quite independent of the many and diffuse power handles of landlords—is the structural weakness of lacking independent access to the means of production.

The conditions described above are by no means universal, and some important qualifications deserve emphasis. Absentee landlords and very small landlords are less likely to have so many sources of power within the village. Vertical factional disputes may provide tenants more room for maneuver. Political parties with grass-roots cadres and vertical connections can change the balance, as can strong caste or religious organi-

20. The typical disabilities of the tenant-illiteracy, ignorance of the law, prejudice of officials, even language, etc.—will be discussed below; cf. India (1959), esp. p. 38. On the issue of corruption, a colonial adage ran: "Even the clearest print cannot be read through a gold sovereign." For relevant examples, Punjab (1938).

21. For a superb discussion of the social relations and dynamics of dependence in the context of class inequalities, Alavi (1971: 111–28).

zations. Peasant organizations in a few parts of India have likewise altered the balance. Moreover, the organs of the state have proved less responsive to landlord interests when regimes of the left are elected; in both Kerala and West Bengal, United Front State governments have pursued a police policy which proscribed interference on the side of property against labor: numbers then count, though the multiplex character of landlord power prevents any automatic or absolute reversal of the dynamics posited above.

The more important qualification is that the structural imbalance between capital and labor is neither static nor uniform across geographical and technical variations. Where there are seasonal or local labor shortages, or danger of losing a valuable crop to job actions, landlords may find it prudent to tie loyal retainers to the land, thereby improving the bargaining position of individual tenants. But these situations are atypical, and in explaining the failure of tenancy reform we have to analyze the exchange relations between land and labor that have normally obtained in rural South Asia.

The exposition of the class-structural model of rural production relations has already suggested one avenue of reconciliation with the integration model: if confrontation is virtually certain to lead to disaster, or has little chance of success, the rational tenant may acquiesce in an admittedly bad situation until conditions change. A great deal of acquiescent behavior must be explained by the irrationality of confrontation; coercion thus operates as a distal and unobservable, rather than proximate and overt, cause of acquiescence. Tenants understand the local structure of power. When Kusum Nair (1962: 64) interviewed villagers in Andhra Pradesh to ascertain the effects of land reform, one typical response was:

> Not a single man in this village has or will benefit by the land reforms. The tenants were so convinced that even if they went to court or to the tribunal the case would be decided in favor of the landowners that they thought it wiser to negotiate and come to terms with the landowner. So they got as much cash as they could out of him and surrendered their tenancies.

My own fieldwork in Sri Lanka discovered similar examples of voluntary surrenders of tenancy rights for cash which, while irrational in strict economic terms, made good sense in terms of the likely alternatives, given the local structure of power (Herring, 1977: 139–40; cf. Gold, 1977: 151).

The patron-client model of agrarian social structure builds upon the understanding that production and exchange relations are frequently embedded in broader, diffuse, and complex social, ritual, and political relations which have strong personalistic components. Even the terminology employed in landlord–tenant relations is often more indicative of fictive-kinship ties than of contractual economic relations. Indeed, connections of blood or marriage often overlap tenurial contracts. The fundamental point is that in much of rural South Asia a land tenure relation has traditionally meant much more than a mere economic contract.

The actual moral economy of patron-client relations is difficult to determine, however. Because the terms of exchange are profoundly unequal, observed deference and legitimating ideologies may obscure deeply felt bitterness and hatred.[22] Social scientists should expect, at least since Gramsci, a certain degree of incorporation of the dominant ideology in the world-views of subordinate classes; there is little doubt that a kind of legitimacy, or at least acceptance, is extended by large numbers of the agrarian underclass to privileges of landed patrons.[23] Though affective ties may prove quite ephemeral when subjected to pressure, it would be pure ideology to deny their reality and importance in the everyday consciousness of at least some clients. Moreover, the existing legitimacy, and legitimating ideology, clearly have a material base and provide important insights into the failure of agrarian reforms in the region.

Kusum Nair, in interviewing villagers to determine the prospects for agrarian change in India, found that many tenants opposed land reforms on moral grounds, believing it to be wrong to take property from others. There is no doubt that this attitude exists, and is an obstacle to tenant organization for land reforms, but it is important to note that such attitudes are in part conditioned by a belief that any attack on the privileges of the landed will only boomerang to make things even worse for the landless. One of Nair's respondents who opposed land reforms explained: "If they come, even the little some of us are still able to get on oral tenancy will be taken away" (1962: 66).[24] Empirical studies of tenure reform have confirmed the accuracy of this fear. Integration theorists frequently overlook, or underemphasize, as I believe Nair does, the roots of deference and acceptance of legitimating ideologies in structural inequality.

The material base of patron–client tenure relations is the ability of the landed patron to provide clients with goods and services which are

22. To relieve the geographical and cultural monotony of my discussion, consider the response of an American sharecropper: "There was plenty of things I was asked to do and plenty of things that was said to me. But at that time there wasn't no way to right every wrong. Sometimes the smartest dodge was just to take what the whites throwed at you and go on" (Maguire, 1975: 7).

23. This theme is developed nicely by James Scott (1974, 1977). In the South Asian context, the works of Harriss (1979) and Bremen (1974) introduce important conceptual refinements. On the extreme cases of acceptance of dominant ideologies legitimating exploitation, see Moore (1978).

24. Ameer Raza (1970: 9) argues that tenants in Sri Lanka shared the belief that land ownership confers the prior right in determining terms of tenure contracts. A recent official study in Gujarat State (1976: 57–58, passim) found that, though rural people generally supported land reforms, some landless agriculturalists complained that tenancy reforms had made their lives harder, particularly by drying up the market for leased land by dissuading owners from leasing except illicitly and without official records.

less available to patronless members of the same class. This relativity is crucial, for the client typically compares himself neither to landlords nor to some mythical or metaphysical potentiality that requires imagining a reordered society, but to class fellows who fare less well in the absence of goods and services (and, often, security) provided by patrons. The range of services provided has been elaborated effectively by James Scott and others; it may include consumption loans, production inputs and credit, brokerage functions vis-à-vis the external world, mediation with police, employment opportunities, leverage to obtain children's education or a daughter's marriage, and so on. A less tangible service is what Scott terms "subsistence insurance," a guarantee that the tenant's family will not be allowed to starve regardless of the severity of production disasters, so long as the patron's granary is full.[25]

To the outsider these services may resemble the "services" of a protection racket, since the need for the services is in part a function of the poverty of the sharecropper, which in turn is a direct result of the appropriation of half the produce by the landlord (allowing the latter sufficient wealth and power to provide the services). But in a context of general scarcity and insecurity, the tenant with a reliable patron may indeed count himself fortunate (compared not to landlords but to the unemployed and insecure).

The existence of patron–client overlays on tenurial relations potentially modifies tenant behavior in agrarian reform in two ways. At the normative level, some tenants may find demanding a lower rent or other rights from the owner morally unjustifiable; laws from an alien legislature lack the legitimacy of long-sanctioned local mores. To demand a better deal from the landlord would be unseemly, showing disrespect and

25. The elaborate statement is Scott (1976). On patron–client relations and their decay in the South Asian context, Breman (1974). It should not be assumed that patron–client relations are the dominant form of landlord–tenant relations. In many areas, the reciprocal exchanges were not dominant, and virtually everywhere market relations and the legal apparatus of capitalist society have hastened the decline of such institutions. Nor should we infer from terminology and overt deference the existence of actual reciprocity or legitimacy. Landlords seem to propound the legitimating myths long after tenants have discarded them. An investigation commissioned by the Government of Pakistan (Niaz, 1965: 29) to determine the credit needs of tenants following land reforms included interviews with twenty tenants: nineteen "reported that facilities like provision of credit, assistance in marketing their produce, patronage in personal affairs, etc., were never extended to them by landlords." A recent World Bank report on Bangladesh noted that fewer than 1 percent of the landlords provided agricultural inputs to tenants (1979: 38). The important work being done in India on "interlinkage of markets" (e.g., Bardhan and Rudra, 1978) indicates marked variation across villages. The explanation for persistence of clientelist attitudes in the face of declining or insignificant material contributions by patrons may partly be in Scott's insistence on risk-minimizing strategies of the underclass (it is safer not to jeopardize *potential* patronage functions, even if unreliable or typically inconsequential, in the face of potential disaster), and partly in the negative sanctions that village elites can enforce (deference and quiescence reduce the possibility of being denied employment or access to land, etc.).

ingratitude. But more importantly, at the material level, such demands may sacrifice more than is gained. A lowered rent is poor compensation if the concomitant sacrifice is off-season employment, interest-free loans, subsistence insurance against bad years, or the distant possibility of having a son appointed to a low-level salaried post. Thus, whatever the existing moral economy, very real and significant material costs may be incurred in violating the norms of a patron–client relationship. In sum, demanding the benefits of a tenure reform often proves economically irrational, particularly when the government is unwilling or unable to provide the goods and services previously supplied by the landlord, or to protect the landless from reprisals. This phenomenon is illustrated by the response of a Kerala landlord to an investigator's question about enforcement of the minimum-wage law:

> "My labourers are still working for me as before, on the same terms. They did ask for more. So I gave them the minimum wage but withdrew the other facilities—clothes, loans, and gifts on births, deaths, and festivals. Then they came back to me of their own accord and told me and the local revenue official that they wanted to continue the old system." This is, it seems, a fairly common occurrence. [Nair, 1962: 42]

The embedding of production relations in personalistic and customary social relations of a broader sort thus often alters the experiential quality of the class relationship, encasing it in an elaborate ideology of mutuality, quasi-familial intimacy, and norms of reciprocal diffuse obligation. But the patron–client relationship between owners and tenants is still structurally a class relation. Indeed, the inequality engendered by its class character *permits* and shapes the elaboration of connections other than those between producer and owner. For example, the very need for and possibility of "subsistence guarantees," and thus one strand of the ideology of legitimation in relations between landed patrons and landless tenants, are predicated on the existence of landed and landless classes, the wealth of one and the consequent relative poverty of the other, in interaction with the level of technique in agriculture and the particular natural ecology within which production takes place.

Although legitimating ideologies and personal attachments may obscure the structural conflict inherent in such production relations from both producers and outside observers, and may vitiate tenurial reform laws which presuppose tenant activism vis-à-vis owners, the class character of the relationship is crucial to understanding the dynamics of agrarian reform; indeed, that character is made manifest and accentuated in the reform process. Tenure reforms delineate beneficiaries and losers along class lines: tenants are to benefit at the expense of landlords. In the face of this threat to class privilege, latent structural conflicts emerge and coercion which had previously operated only as a conditioning potentiality becomes overt. Beatings, evictions, burnings of houses and crops, and murders accompany serious land reforms. And even when the conflict does not reach this stage, the reform process contributes to the transformation of harmonious patron-client production relations into more naked class relations. The reforms redefine the rural world, substituting the black and white of precise class categories—owner, tenant, laborer—for the richly textured categories of masters and dependents, patrons and clients. Thomas Metcalf provided an appropriate example from the mid-nineteenth century; the Chief Commissioner of Oudh noted:

> The majority of our *talooqdars* share the feelings of English landlords. Their demands are fair, and observed with good faith, and innumerable little kindnesses, so dear to the Natives of this country, are shown, which cease when our laws, creating rights on the part of the peasantry, set the two classes in antagonism. I firmly believe that half the bickering and bad blood that prevails between landlord and tenant have been caused by our ill-judged interference. [Merillat, 1970: 28]

Ordinary Administration and Tenure Reform

Most treatments of failures in tenure reform in South Asia focus on the twin villains of "lack of political will" and "failures in implementation" (or bureaucratic inertia, lethargy, and collusion). That emphasis is quite justified, but the issue is more complex. The contributions to the failure of tenure reform attributable to the implementation process can be analyzed under two interconnected headings:

    1. Relations between state and society locally—the embedded bureaucracy.

    2. Characteristics of the bureaucracy itself—ordinary administration.

The Embedded Bureaucracy

Though the administrative apparatus may be conceptualized as separable and distinct from society by both theorists and planners, a neutral mechanism for executing legislated directives, in fact the bureaucracy grows from and is linked to society in concrete ways. These connections condition administrative behavior at every level. The upper echelons of the bureaucracy constitute a distinct elite, and its members share some or all of the elite ideology of the parent society; high officials are drawn from classes which have access to a range of social perquisites, most importantly, superior education and "connections." Because control of land accords special privilege and status, security and opportunity, officials as a class, whatever their social origins, are likely to be interested in gaining or retaining control of land for themselves and their relatives. The class privileges of land ownership—that is, the objects of land reform—constitute an important normative component of the world-view of the administrative elite.

At lower levels, because tenurial reform legislation often has no extensive local support (either political or ideological) or even understanding, evasion of the letter or spirit of the law at the village level evokes few sanctions. The individual official has no real reason not to auction implementation prerogatives to the highest bidder. Pathetically inadequate pay scales reinforce the temptation. Corruption in the land revenue administration has historically been so rampant in Pakistan that a traditional folk saying runs: "Above, the Creator; below, the Patwari," meaning that the *patwari*, the village record-keeper and lowest echelon of the land revenue administration, has total power on earth as God does above, and no one in between makes much difference. Precisely the same phrase occurs in rural Kerala.[26] This power derives from the ability of record-keepers to falsify land records to the advantage of some and the disadvantage of others. Because the *patwari* is intricately involved in village society, the sanctions which the landlord can bring to bear in village society, the power imbalances discussed above, facilitate evasion of the law.[27]

The assumption that the bureaucracy constitutes a neutral instrument to be used by the state to act on and change society implies that values can be transmitted directly through the bureaucracy from the legislators. But in fact officials, both high and low, may not share the values in the policy model at all. Even if the values are shared, the concrete interests and social milieu within which the bureaucrat operates may prevent the consolidation of strong, enduring commitment to the reform's goals.

The lack of commitment on the part of the ordinary administrative apparatus is certainly understandable. The impetus for tenure reform has typically been narrow and shallow compared to the opposition; the reform itself is often a concoction of the intellectual center imposed on the rural periphery, where it is poorly understood. The economic arguments for land reform are either unknown or not widely believed; indeed, the opposite belief—that the large farmers are more progressive and that redistributive interference will be detrimental to progress in agriculture— seems to be more prevalent. The operative social mythologies run very deep; the image of the landless tenant as hapless, backward, dependent, perhaps dishonest, persists. There is little belief in or formulation of the potentiality of new structural relations on the land among important sectors of society, of which the bureaucracy is but one (cf. India, 1973: 9). In explaining why the attitude of revenue officers is frequently against the

26. "Upar Kartar, niche Patwar" (Punjab, 1938: 111). The phrase in Malayalam is (roughly) "mukalil daivom, chotil adhikari."

27. For typical accounts, see Thorner (1956: 47), India (1972c: 17), Neale (1962: 245).

tenant, the Planning Commission's Committee on Tenancy Reform insightfully noted:

> After all, ideas about the evolution of tenant's rights as against the landlord have been of a comparatively recent growth. The conception of land as property and the rights and privileges of the owner of the property is deeply rooted. The rights and privileges of the actual cultivator of land are not yet fully comprehended. We find their acceptance somewhat difficult even among politicians who should ordinarily have more liberal views than a revenue officer. The unconscious resistance of revenue officers to liberal ideas can, therefore, be easily understood. In the case of conflicting evidence, there is a greater tendency to believe the landlord than the tenant, the presumption being that a poor man is less likely to speak the truth. . . .[28]

Administrators quite naturally have difficulty separating perceptions of the tenant in social context—typically low status, illiterate, subordinate—from the tenant as legal equal to a person of power, influence, and standing, *even if* the official accepts the moral economy presupposed by tenure reform. The committee was right to point to the unconscious character of these psychological dynamics, though that insight should not deflect attention from conscious discrimination in favor of class, kin, and caste allies or locally powerful people that disables the tenant in the administrative arena. Likewise, the ambiguity of the political commitment that is passed down to the bureaucracy is properly stressed; as the committee noted, the passing of a reformist law may represent a contradictory and contentious ensemble of political forces and implies little about the effective political will for reform.

Just as the economic case for tenure reform is not well understood or widely shared, the normative case has shallow roots. The legitimacy of rent can hardly be questioned by officials whose ideal of retirement is to become landed gentry; the feeling that an owner's land is his to do with as he pleases is widespread. Traditional rental arrangements are widely accepted as right, and the argument for changing them is poorly received except in cases of extreme exploitation.

These attitudes are difficult to verify rigorously in the absence of systematic studies; moreover, the very act of formalizing the inquiry would affect the response behavior of officials—administrators are aware of what they should say. But the lack of commitment to, or even belief in, redistributive policies was frequently evident to me in the field. The following case is not meant to be representative, but does illustrate the phenomenon of the interpenetration of society and bureaucracy, structurally and normatively.

The Paddy Lands Board of Review was established as the final forum

---

28. India (1959: 38). P. C. Joshi (1978: A78–A83) elaborates this point nicely and comments on the interaction between "political will" and bureaucratic incapacity in land reforms.

of appeal in enforcing the 1958 Paddy Lands Act in Ceylon. A member of that board stated that the provision for reducing rent from the traditional one-half share to one-fourth or less was impracticable; tenants recognized this and thus brought no cases of excessive rent to the board, though it was universally recognized that rent on paddy lands was normally one-half or more of the gross produce. The official owned six acres of paddy, which he leased out *ande*. I asked whether this meant that he received one-half the crop as rent since *ande*, the traditional term for sharecropping, means "one-half" in Sinhala.

"Correct," he answered.

"But the Act specifies one-fourth or less."

"But the villagers always bring one-half. One-fourth is only the law; one-half is the custom."

The official went on to explain that tenants valued the security of tenure provisions far more than the rental provisions and did not demand a lower rent because they desired good relations with their landlords (interview, July 1973). When such attitudes characterize the enforcers, it is clear that tenants are acting rationally by hesitating to initiate cases to enforce their legal rights and that vigorous compensatory administrative action to balance the disabilities of tenants vis-à-vis owners is unlikely.

Ordinary Administration

For a variety of reasons too complex to explore here (cf. Bell, 1974: 67–69), the bureaucracies to which tenurial reforms have been entrusted are characterized by inefficiency. Even traditional tasks, such as collection of land revenue, are not performed at all adequately (India, 1972b). The "soft states" of Myrdal's analysis tend to be characterized by (selectively) soft bureaucracies.[29] Archaic procedures and rigid formalism engender vitiating delays. Lower officials are frequently underpaid and undertrained for their tasks. Frequent transfers from universally disliked isolated rural areas ("hardship posts") prevent officials from gaining a rich understanding of the local tenure structure and power configurations. Political interference and factional disputes delay action, punish initiative, and induce a security-oriented attitude toward role performance. Both tenants and landlords understand the bureaucracy—its permeability, corruption, inefficiency, lethargy—and this knowledge affects the willingness of both groups to obey the law, in each case undermining the redistributive impact of tenure reform.

Delays are not neutral, as the tenants lose their source of income for the entire period of eviction, even if eventually restored. The landlord

29. Myrdal makes this characterization in *Asian Drama* (1968). The "softness" of the bureaucracy varies with the task, as well as with the status of the subjects. The Emergency in India illustrated viciously the other face of the "soft" bureaucracy, a face long familiar to nonelite Indians.

typically loses nothing at all, as the evicted tenant is replaced. Conservatism—both attitudinal and behavioral (concern for job security by officials)—is not epiphenomenal; landlords are often powerful men, and it is risky to alienate them. This is particularly true when officials understand that reformist politicians and regimes frequently do not last; if they believe that the party of privilege will soon return to power after a reformist interlude, it would be risky to stand up for the "little people" in the villages. Moreover, savvy bureaucrats know that some legislation is meant purely for symbolic effect, not for serious implementation; it is safer to err on the side of conservatism than on the side of reformism. The composite of characteristics of the bureaucracy and its processes discussed here—conservatism, corruption, permeability, incapacity—may collectively be termed "ordinary administration" in the South Asian context. Such characteristics undermine the capacity of the bureaucracy to serve as an effective means of intervention and regulation in redistributing stoutly defended class privileges.

Conceptual Incongruities in the Reform Model

The tenure reform model in the liberal state assumes an activist position on the part of tenants. The bureaucracy will intervene and regulate, but initiative must come from aggrieved tenants. The quiescence of tenants for whatever reasons—fear, loyalty, rational calculation—saps the reform of energy and leaves it moribund, a familiar dead letter. Moreover, the punitive sanctions put in the hands of the bureaucracy, and the likelihood of success in wielding them, are typically incommensurate with the stake of landowners in evading the law and their ability to do so. It is striking to read reports that rental laws are almost universally ignored and simultaneously to find that no one has been prosecuted. I found landlords throughout the region quite willing to discuss openly and casually their evasion of the law.[30]

The absence or gross inaccuracy of land records is another slippage between conceptualization and reality. Particularly where tenancies are oral, it is naive to believe that even the best bureaucracy can intervene effectively to untangle the maze of customary usages and conflicting claims. The sheer magnitude of the task—intervention in the affairs of multitudes of tenants and owners, continuously—is sufficient reason to predict that failure and disillusionment will result. Particularly when the tasks of policing landlord–tenant relations are added to the existing responsibilities of the department, and no new administrative capability is engendered, there is a marked discontinuity between what the model

30. This has been the experience of other researchers as well; Dandekar and Khudanpur (1957: 187) state: "The surprising element of the situation is that even the landlords reported to us the true rents they received and that they found no reasons to conceal the facts."

posits as necessary and the possibilities on the ground. In most land reforms in the region, the commitment of personnel and resources has been pitifully inadequate relative both to the magnitude of the task and in comparison with Asian regimes which have carried out effective land reform.[31]

Purely technical problems in the reforms have likewise hamstrung the bureaucracy; poor drafting of legislation—ambiguous definitions, provisions contrary to existing law, inadequate specifications, and so on—provides the courts ample opportunity to strike down or cripple reform laws. The courts have done so with regularity, often with marked enthusiasm (India, 1973: 9–10). More fundamentally, in an unreconstructed liberal state the legal apparatus supports private property, and thus owners. Landlords have been able to call upon the police to evict tenants, quite simply on the ground that the owner owns the land: tenants can be prosecuted as trespassers. This access to coercive power in a liberal state does not typically rest with the tenant.[32] Indeed, it often proves more difficult for the tenant to obtain enforcement of a favorable decision than to obtain the favorable decision: where is the sharecropper to find the standing and resources to have himself physically reinstated on a plot and protected from future eviction or intimidation?

As the previous sections emphasize, a central conceptual problem concerns the capacity of the bureaucracy to intervene in tenurial relations. This problem, in turn, rests in part on a mistaken conceptualization of the bureaucracy as a neutral instrument for changing society rather than as an organism with strong and multiple connections to society, independent internal dynamics, and partial autonomy. Moreover, the model *assumes* the rationality and actuality of tenant initiative in enforcement, screening out or misinterpreting perceptions of the concrete power imbalances and multiplex relationships between tenants and owners that call into question the rationality and likelihood of tenant-initiated confrontation.

The failure to conceptualize the power imbalance is crucial. That imbalance conditions not only the likelihood of voluntary tenant initiative but also action throughout the reform process. Adversary court relations, for example, are profoundly affected by the resources and power of the participants. Staying power counts heavily when the reform pro-

31. Samuel Huntingon (1968: 395) noted the yawning gap between commitment of resources in Indian land reforms and reforms in Japan and Taiwan, as does Gold (1977: 85) for Sri Lanka. For an understanding of the extraordinary societal effort necessary for genuine land reform in backward regions, compare the accounts of land reform in China by Hinton (1966), especially parts 3, 6, 7, and Belden (1970), esp. part 7.

32. Again, for illustrating structural conditions, generalization is necessary. For brief periods during United Front rule in Kerala and West Bengal, the role of the police was reversed, but the exception illustrates the rule. Indeed, the first communist ministry of Kerala was dismissed by Delhi partly because of its police policy, specifically the refusal of police to interfere in agrarian struggles on the side of owners (see chap. 6).

cess is open-ended over time. Whatever political or administrative support greeted the reform legislation is likely to wane as the costs and difficulties of reform become apparent and opponents mobilize their formidable resources; but the model requires *continuous* supervision and regulation. Unless the basic structural imbalance is changed, the superior power of the landed and well connected will be reasserted over time.

Though the policy logic critically depends on tenant willingness to charge landlords with violations and seek redress, we have seen that for a number of reasons aggrieved tenants may rationally choose to acquiesce in illegal relations on the land. That decision is influenced by the possibility that the reformist regime will fall, replace an activist minister, or succumb to political pressure from landlords and rescind its commitment to the landless. Indeed, it would require an extraordinary leap of faith on the part of tenants to believe that regimes typical of South Asian societies have so fundamentally changed their character as to become dedicated champions of the dispossessed against the propertied classes. It would be an even greater leap of faith to believe such a regime could last. In such circumstances, the rational tenant may decide to refrain from alienating his landlord-patron-creditor, assuming that the reformers, despite their rhetoric, are not likely to reshape the rural world in which he lives, nor to last long if they try. The reasonable response to these reasonable perceptions would be to avoid irrevocably alienating powerful people, whether official or unofficial.

The emergence of a regime genuinely committed to tenant rights is likely to evoke counter-responses from privileged classes which shorten the life of the regime, particularly in an open and closely competitive system. Case studies from Sri Lanka and Kerala, discussed later in detail, concretely illustrate the ambiguous contributions of competitive political systems to land reform in introducing the likelihood of reversal of policy as a normal expectation. Tenure reform requires a continuous political commitment to redistribution, and yet, ironically, the liberal systems in which such reforms typically emerge posit in their legitimating ideology institutionalized changes in regime between meaningfully opposed political formations. If the political model works, the party of privilege will return and redistributive initiatives will fade.

A second major incongruity is the stark contrast between a view of society which is the liberal normative ideal and the reality of agrarian relations. If tenants and landlords entered into production contracts voluntarily, as legal equals, each needing the other equally, the liberal model of tenure reform might prove workable. The liberal view of society fails to appreciate the profound and fundamental dependence of nonowners on owners of the means of production when alternative means of livelihood are scarce.

Even the conceptualization of "tenant" in tenure reform is problematic. British law imposed a procrustean fit of tenants and owners upon a complex hierarchy of land rights[33] (and in the process made that hierarchy still more complex through subinfeudation); tenure reform legislation has typically not ventured into the mire of redefining tenurial classes according to structural and functional criteria. But so long as the definition of tenant is traditional and formal-legal, and not structural-functional, the new tenurial rights often do not accrue even in law to actual cultivators, but to lesser intermediaries (the *kanamdars* of Kerala, for example). Daniel Thorner (1956: 82) argued that any separation of proprietary rights from cultivation responsibilities leads inexorably to all the defects posited in the tenure reform policy model. So long as any individual can be assured a return from the land without laboring on the land, there will be the temptation to sublet, resulting in subinfeudation and tenurial discontinuities. This powerful logic is illustrated by the simple question of a Bihari landowner: "Why should I plough when I can get another man to plough for me?"[34] In an economy of impoverished men and women with nothing to sell for their livelihood but labor power in a buyer's market, it will always be possible to arrange subtenancies to accomplish exactly that.

Curiously enough, even the limited objects of tenurial reform are themselves poorly conceptualized. Rent is the center of the model's redistributive thrust, but rent is only one mode of surplus extraction; both tenants and owners recognize that if ground rent is reduced, other exactions can be proportionately increased. Landlords in Pakistan have frequently increased rental shares from one-half to two-thirds or three-fourths of the gross produce after adding expensive working capital, such as tubewell water and tractor plowing; since the charges can be termed returns to working capital, not rent, the relevant tenancy laws, limiting (ground) rent to 40 percent of the crop, cannot be invoked.[35]

A tenant may understand, as the laws do not, that what is gained through reduced rent may be lost through increased charges for working capital, tractor hire, marketing services, consumption loans, and so on. The model's view of landlord–tenant relations as concerned only with terms of access to the land factor ignores the multiplex character of the economic relationship (or "interlinkage of markets"), as well as the extraeconomic aspect of the patron–client relationship. The paradigm is land-

33. The most learned discussion is still the classic by B. H. Baden-Powell (1892), esp. vol. I, book I. For a flavor of colonial intellectual debates on the Indian land system, Ambirajan (1978), chap. 5. The points in the text were given great emphasis by Myrdal (1968), vol. 2, sec. 13, esp. pp. 1305–11.

34. Nair (1962: 62). For an informed discussion of this tendency based on extensive fieldwork, see Mencher (1975: 241–54); (1978: 349–66).

35. Author's field investigations, Pakistan, 1975. There is also evidence of rents at the high end of the spectrum in anthropological accounts and the latest Census of Agriculture (see chap. 4). The Planning Commission of India noted the same phenomenon (India, 1961: 222). The Pakistani laws' provisions are irrelevant in any event, as they have never been seriously enforced.

centered, but the structural economic position of the tenant is also determined by the "tenurial" relation to irrigation water, working capital, and marketing arrangements. Given these conceptual defects, not even energetic, committed, and honest officials could effectively police the complex production relationships which exist on the land. The rent regulation model thus fails in particular to appreciate the modernization of agriculture, during which non-land capital dramatically increases in importance.

The fundamental conceptual failure in the policy logic, however, is the failure to perceive "agrarian defects" as manifestations of deeper economic forces and structures. It is not simply the abuses of some landlords which create the problems of rack-renting, usury, and eviction, but rather a constellation of economic and demographic factors within a configuration of property institutions and production relations which defy piecemeal and partial tinkering. The very *existence* of rack-rented tenants fearful of and subject to eviction is but a manifestation of these structural forces and not, as the policy logic goes, constitutive of "the problem." The underlying causes of the "defects" addressed by the model are of course the concentration of the means of production in the hands of a minority of the agrarian population coupled with the existence of a class of rural people lacking independent access to the agricultural means of production or alternative employment opportunities.

Political Will, Implementation and Incrementalism

Reasons for the failure of tenure reform have been treated at a fairly abstract level in this chapter; the following case studies will flesh out these dynamics. Moreover, the explanations sketched at a high level of generality and abstraction here—structural imbalances, the miscarriages of ordinary administration, the embeddedness of production relations in a complex social matrix, the weak or contradictory political impetus behind the reform, and so on—are central to the subsequent analysis of other types of land reform.

Perhaps the most important issue in tenure reform is the serious question of whether it should be done at all. An impressive array of economists and planners, ranging from Gunnar Myrdal to Wolf Ladejinsky to John Mellor, with hosts in between, have recommended a limited tenure reform on the grounds of presumed political impracticability of fundamental structural change in land relations given the present constellation of political forces: the "political will" for radical reform is lacking. Mellor's comments are typical and paradigmatic:

> The new, high yield crop varieties greatly increase the value of land ... and the landowner's incentive to displace tenants.... Such circumstances demand more innovative legislation for institutionalizing tenancy.

Such legislation should encourage landowners to share in the risk and the capital needs of an expanding agriculture. Registration of tenants would guarantee their security, assist them in obtaining loans, and increase the certainty that they would benefit from increased production. . . . In this context it is of much greater practical benefit to the poor to protect existing rights of tenants than to attempt redistribution of land.[36]

Such views have long been pronounced gravely by practical analysts; land redistribution does indeed appear impractical. However, the analysis of tenure reform in this chapter, to be extended in later chapters, demonstrates concretely the quixotic impracticality of "registration of tenants" to "guarantee their security" when owners prefer otherwise. Mellor sees the dynamics—the pressure from technical change and the transformation to capitalist agriculture—and the threats posed for tenants, yet argues for more legislation to deny and mitigate those dynamics.

The alternative view was articulated by the late Daniel Thorner (1973: 75), one of the keenest students of India's agrarian situation: "If India's recent agrarian history demonstrates anything, it is that doing and saying nothing is preferable to taking small steps slowly and timidly."

Thorner's analysis is grounded in the indisputable evidence of net deterioration in the life prospects of countless landless cultivators in the wake of ineffectual land reforms. Partly because the limited tenurial reforms were encased in political rhetoric excoriating parasitic landlordism, signaling a general attack on agrarian elites by the state, and partly because even the weakest reform laws represented some threat to the political, social, and economic prerogatives of land control, landlords throughout the subcontinent fought back. Tenants were evicted, records distorted, patron-client bonds dissolved. Such changes are likely to be irreversible. Thus the incremental *logic*—do what is possible now to build the base for more fundamental improvement later—is confounded by the process.

To the extent that tenurial reforms have been beneficial to those at the bottom of the agrarian-class configuration, the effect has been more normative and ideological than economic. Tenure reforms delegitimize arbitrary landlord power and establish in law the partial proprietary claims of tenants to the land[37]—claims long recognized in village traditions, but

36. Mellor (1976: 105–06). Myrdal's position is carefully argued in *Asian Drama* (1968), vol. 2, chap. 26, pp. 1377–84. Wolf Ladejinsky's position was expressed in many of his articles, see, for example (1976: 103–10).

37. Breman, in *Patronage and Exploitation* (1974: 223), argues that government action has been effective in this "passive sense" of removing the aura of legitimacy of exploitation. Myrdal (1968: 1335) notes that the United Nation's *Progress in Land Reforms: Fourth Report* argues for the "exhortatory moral influence" of unenforced land reforms, the provision of a banner around which to organize, an impetus to courage, etc., but dismisses these positive effects in the context of the subcontinent. Myrdal's critique has merit and would still hold for some parts of the region, but there has been a qualitative change in the aware-

denied by the pure, or absolute, notion of land as property under market capitalism. Moreover, the denial of those rights in practice is not without long-term consequences. Tenants have learned what to expect from courts, bureaucracy, and politicians. Tenure reforms define traditional production relations in the terminology of economic class and the differential rights of property and labor in production and distribution. Land reforms have thus been an additional agent in defining and politicizing the agrarian underclass, even if effective mobilization is difficult for a number of well-known reasons. In those few situations in which tenants are mobilized and organized, dynamics quite different from those analyzed in this chapter operate.

The conclusion is that evaluation of tenure reform is fundamentally conditioned by the time horizon and focus of one's ethical stance. For a great number of insecure tenants—there is no way to count them; even the total number of tenants in South Asia is not precisely known—tenure reform has had negative consequences. Tenants have been evicted, sometimes beaten, their lives have been disrupted, sometimes ended, and they have watched the opportunities for sharecropping dry up and security guarantees from landlords disappear in the train of tenancy reform. Yet, these structural changes, part of Polanyi's "great transformation," proceed independently of tenure reform, though perhaps at a slower pace. Tenure reform, for all of its undeniably negative short-term impact on the life chances of landless agriculturalists, at least establishes normatively, in law, the traditional claims of labor on access to the means of production and a defined share of the social product. The establishment of these normative claims, when widely publicized and recognized, is of demonstrable importance in creating tenant organizations to demand these and other rights; later chapters devoted to the Kerala experience underline this point.

Tenure reform legislation is thus not without important consequences, but typically not those posited by the model. That tenure reforms are frequently legislated for purely symbolic purposes by regimes which have no intention of enforcing them is undeniable; the frequent complaint in the literature of lack of "political will" is well grounded. But political will alone is not a sufficient condition for land reform; even with an ensemble, or vector sum, of political forces which clearly supports reform—a strong political will—the policy model must be adequate. Flawed policy logic is sufficient cause for the failure of reform, though certainly not a necessary cause; absence of political will alone is sufficient to scuttle even the best-designed reform. This chapter has analyzed the obstacles to the implementation of tenure reform which would, and do, persist even in the face of concerted political commitment to

---

ness and political consciousness of depressed groups since *Asian Drama* was written, though effective organization and coordinated political action are still difficult and markedly rare.

reform, particularly in the liberal state. The obstacles are rooted in the isolation of tenure reform from a broader strategy of structural change and the attendant problems of a reformist policy in an unreformed society. These points are elaborated and etched deeply in the following chapter; the tenure reform efforts of a Marxist minister of agriculture in Sri Lanka recognized the dynamics and structural forces analyzed in this chapter, and proposed innovative responses to them. Yet the obstacles identified here—lack of tenant confidence in the state and its organs, embedded social relations of production, fluctuating commitment to reform by alternating regimes, class inequalities in an adversarial, elitist, and autonomous legal system—all undermined the reform at critical junctures.

In practice, limited tenure reform has led to the eviction of countless sharecropping tillers and the erosion of sharecropping opportunities for would-be tillers. These consequences represent the interactive effects of conceptual flaws in the policy logic of the model and the ambivalent, often contradictory, political will behind land reform in the region. Politically, the fact that some tenants, typically not the least secure or most exploited, have gained security and status vis-à-vis some landlords, has deprived nascent peasant movements of local leadership through a weaker form of the *embourgeoisement* dynamics. The policy logic supporting tenure reform—the presumed economic defects of share tenancy, and the political consequences of rack-renting and tenurial insecurity—is equally supportive of a land-to-the-tiller reform which abolishes tenancy altogether and avoids the administrative costs of continuous intervention and regulation. Indeed, there has been perceptible movement in this direction in official policy logic, but the political and normative configurations necessary to support so logical, yet radical, a policy have not developed extensively in the subcontinent.

3

Peasant Democracy, Tenure Reform, and the Liberal State: Ceylon's Paddy Lands Act

"Theory is grey, but life is eternally green."
—*Philip Gunawardena, Minister of Agriculture*

The reasons for the failure of the limited tenure reform policy model to achieve even its limited goals were examined in the previous chapter. There is little empirical ambiguity on this point; wherever the tenant was originally in the weakest position, and thus in most need of legislative protection, the legislation was minimally effective, and often counterproductive.[1] From this point, widely recognized in South Asia, policy thinking has led to a number of different conclusions.

One possible conclusion is that the inherent power imbalance of the landlord–tenant relationship inevitably vitiates external policy initiatives to redistribute power and income in favor of the tenant. An official report from Delhi in 1968, considered in detail below, concluded that "so long as the direct landlord–tenant relationship subsists, provisions for security of tenure and regulation of rent are not effective in practice." The logical implication would seem to be a land-to-the-tiller policy, abolishing landlordism and making cultivators the owners of the land they till. This option has figured importantly in policy thinking, as will be explored in subsequent chapters; but it is immediately evident that political realities render the planners' policy logic irrelevant in most situations. Land to the tiller is a direct attack on private property and seems to presuppose an organized and militant peasantry, a revolutionary situation, or some extraordinary concentration of power, perhaps from outside the indigenous political system (as in Japan and Taiwan).

---

1. As elaborated in chapter 2, the distinction between socially powerless tenants-at-will and tenants of high caste, or with large holdings, etc., is crucial in any generalization; cf. Daniel and Alice Thorner (1965: 149); India (1976: XV: 57–58); P. C. Joshi (1975: 98–99). For a treatment of these dynamics in one of the more successful tenure reforms, Maharashtra (1974); Desai (1971). Though it is impossible to verify the figure and difficult to understand its basis, official Indian documents (e.g., India, 1970) state that 82 percent of India's tenants remain without security of tenure after decades of tenure reform.

Moreover, divergent lines of thinking from both left and right converge in recognizing that land to the tiller aggravates the basic problem of transformation in an agrarian society–namely, the vast numbers of tiny peasant producers deeply attached to their private plots but unable to organize agriculture rationally or to live very well on those plots. But whether or not the policy is, from a transformational viewpoint, an agro-economic and social-political cul-de-sac, the hard political facts would force consideration of other options in most situations.

Daniel Thorner (1956: 82) seriously argued that "saying and doing nothing" is preferable to token reform when the political and administrative conditions do not permit an effective, comprehensive agrarian reform. This option has not been practicable in most of the subcontinent. In India, constitutional directives for improving the lot of the disadvantaged and decades of Congress rhetoric on agrarian reform militate against Thorner's suggestion. The pervasive use of land-reform slogans in electoral politics and regime-legitimating symbolic manipulations, as well as the strength of peasant organizations or threat of rural violence in some areas, likewise rule out saying and doing nothing. The result has been theorizing on new institutional forms to correct structural defects *other than those* inherent in the landlord–tenant production relationship.

After exploring the dilemma of new institutional forms to remove such defects, this chapter treats a serious transformational conceptualization of land reform which retains the landlord–tenant organization of production but introduces countervailing institutional innovations—the Paddy Lands Act in Ceylon. The case is particularly important because, stripped of its transformational inspirations and innovations, the Paddy Lands Act became in practice a limited tenure reform, concretely illustrating the general propositions discussed in the preceding chapter. The reform was no sham; carefully conceived and energetically applied, it allows more rigorous analysis of the limits and possibilities of effective tenure reform in the liberal state.

Tenure Reform and Participatory Democracy: The Institutional Conundrum

The failures of both tenure reform and ceiling legislation to improve substantially the condition of the agrarian underclass in India were well known and documented by the mid-1960s. One possible response, well established in international policy literature and previous Indian policy logic, was a turning away from purely bureaucratic mechanisms in favor of local democratic bodies. The Second Five Year Plan had specifically recommended that *panchayati raj* (local government, village council) institutions become involved in land-reform implementation, especially in the maintenance of land records, determination of surplus land, regulation of common land, and protection of tenants from unlawful eviction.

This had been the recommendation of the important Congress Agrarian Reforms Committee (1949) as well, but had not been implemented. Moreover, an international planning model suggested the necessity of local involvement, as illustrated by the ECAFE conference held in Bangkok in 1960, on the "Relationship between Land Reforms and Community Development."[2]

Exemplifying these concerns, a study team was appointed under the Land Reforms Implementation Committee of the National Development Council. The group was charged with studying the feasibility of involving *panchayati raj* and community development institutions in land reform and the desirability of organizing the tenantry, "who are likely to be victimized as a result of land reform measures," into "articulate and informed interest groups" (India, 1968: appendix 1, 34).

The study group found that a major obstacle to implementation of land reforms was the absence or inadequacy of land records and the inability of the administration to cope with this problem (p. 4 and passim). The policy logic of local involvement seems unexceptionable: though land records may be dated, false, easily manipulated, or absent altogether, the actual tenurial situation as it exists on the ground will be known to local agriculturalists or can be quickly determined. Moreover, some tenurial regulations can be enforced *only* through intimate, timely contact with the parties involved—what share of production costs does a given landlord bear and what share of the output does he take? In such matters, particularly in the absence of rent receipts or written tenurial contracts, even the best administrative apparatus cannot be expected to intervene judiciously. And in a situation in which a single change in the records can destroy a tenant's prima facie evidence for legal rights, and in which personalistic considerations, corruption, and coercion are likely to influence individual cases, an independent local review or appeal process seems a priori indispensable.

In spite of the apparent logic of the case for popular institutional involvement, the study group concluded that no statutory powers should be given local institutions for enforcing land reform; at most, such institutions could perform advisory or "watch-dog" functions, without possessing any real power (pp. 27–29). These recommendations reflect in part the professional bias of high-level administrators, who wrote the report; disdain for the petty squabbling and factionalism of local (or national) politics is a common attitude of professional administrators. Faith in basic democratic premises—that ordinary people can handle their own affairs—is notably weak. Moreover, the institutional prerogatives of the administration are threatened by any increase in popular involvement.

2. For the impact of United Nations studies and recommendations on reactivation of interest in popular participation in land reform, see India (1968: 7–8); United Nations (1970: 208, 238). An academic study which supports the paradigm is Montgomery (1972).

Nevertheless, the study team did present some strong arguments against popular participation.

First, local democracy is more a planners' assumption than a social fact; *panchayati raj* institutions have uneven levels of development, and do not exist at all in some areas. More importantly: "in many areas Panchayati Raj bodies today are dominated by landed interests, interests of the moneylenders, higher castes, etc. . . . Thus constituted, these bodies cannot be expected to safeguard the interests of the rural tenantry comprising mainly the weaker sectors of the community" (p. 23).

This conclusion is neither surprising nor moot. As land control is traditionally the center of village power and status, one would expect village bodies to represent landed interests disproportionately. The study team suggested that *panchayats* could be given land-reform duties only after "effective and adequate representation of the weaker sections of the community" was ensured. The institutional means of accomplishing this formidable task were not specified. Ironically, land reforms themselves are often posited as the means for ensuring the success of local democratic institutions by breaking dependency relations, but it is land reform that could not be implemented, evidently, without local democratic institutions. The Chinese Communist Party had come to a similar conclusion after long experience; redistribution of land was considered a necessary precondition for local self-government: a village congress could be formed only in those villages in which the land reform had been successfully completed.[3]

One alternative to involvement of local government could be official efforts to organize the tenantry, as suggested in the study team's terms of reference. The study team, however, concluded that this option was ill-advised: "If rural tenantry are organized into interest groups, it is likely to increase factions in the villages; it might also prove hostile to the existing machinery which is maintaining land records" (p. 29). Even though it was recognized that such machinery was frequently an obstacle to effective land reform, there was fear that organization of the tenantry qua interest group would "needlessly expose the administration to avoidable conflicts with political parties and other peasant organizations." In short, ordinary administrative procedures, however ineffective, should not be supplemented by the formation of new interest groups because of the disruption to ordinary administrative institutions that would result. The assumption that genuine land reforms can occur without conflict and disruption is a curious one; moreover, the report does not question the feasibility or mechanisms for "organizing the tenantry," but merely concludes that to do so is undesirable.

3. For an account of Communist Party directives and implementation in one village, Hinton (1966: 272–73).

The resultant policy dilemma is acute: if consciousness and organization of depressed agrarian classes are necessary for implementation
of policy, by what *policy* mechanisms can these conditions be created?
By 1972 the concern over agrarian unrest had grown dramatically in Indian policy circles. The Task Force on Agrarian Relations (the Appu
Commission) noted continuing victimization and eviction of sharecroppers, as the local administration was coopted or cowed by landed interests. In a marked escalation from "articulate and informed interest groups,"
the report stated that "politicization of the poor peasantry on militant
lines is a prerequisite for any successful legislative-administrative action
for conferring rights and privileges on them."[4] The ineffectiveness of ordinary measures for effecting land reforms received a prominent place in
the justifications given by Indira Gandhi for imposition of a national
emergency and suspension of important liberal processes in June of 1975,
but still there was no concrete strategy for using policy measures to organize (or "politicize") the "poor peasantry" either "on militant lines" or
into "articulate and informed interest groups."[5]

But if official means of organizing and politicizing the rural poor to
aid in implementing reform are difficult to imagine, the issue of local
democracy presents an even more complex policy conundrum. The complexity results from the interdependency of tenurial reform and local participation. Some tenurial systems are more conducive to participatory
democracy than others. It is clear that rural dependents have not always
been politically free agents. In his study of rural conditions of the North-
west Frontier Province in Pakistan, Herbert Albrecht (1974: 200 ff.) noted
an important distinction between "owner-operator villages," characterized by a land tenure system dominated by self-cultivating owners, and
"landlord-tenant-laborer villages." In the owner-operator villages, the
economic independence of cultivators was reflected in political-social independence. Village matters were decided democratically, and representatives to the *Jirga* (council) were elected, though "usually the larger owner-
operators are elected." Albrecht (p. 203) argued that the political success
of larger farmers was not simply a reflection of land control, as "total
status" was determined by "public service" as well. Significant land
ownership was evidently a necessary, but not sufficient, condition for local leadership. The limited power of the landed elite in these villages was
attributed to tenurial pluralism; since owner-operators owned a high per-

4. India (1973); *Economic and Political Weekly* (Bombay), May 19, 1973, p. 895. For
a review of the documents reflecting a growing consensus on the necessity of nonofficial
involvement in land-reform implementation, *The Report of the National Commission on
Agriculture* (India, 1976: XV: 79–91).

5. Official spokesmen, when pressed on this point, admitted that no institutional
mechanisms had been planned; there was reliance instead on a new "atmosphere" of awareness among the rural masses and a new commitment in the bureaucracy, both supposedly
created by the Emergency; cf. Finance Minister C. Subramaniam's speech in the Lok Sabha
(Parliament), August 4, 1975, reprinted in India (n.d.: 64–84, esp. 73).

centage of the village land, village dependents (craftsmen, servants, laborers, etc.) did not face a tight oligopsony of landlords, and thus had more social and political independence. In landlord–tenant–laborer villages, the dependence of most villagers on a small landlord class for employment and house sites circumscribed the dependents' freedom of action. The village studies of Hamza Alavi (1971) and Saghir Ahmad (1977: 91–126) corroborate these familiar dynamics of dependence in Pakistan's Punjab.

The relationship between land reform and local democracy thus runs in two directions and presents a paradox. As dependent variable, land reform in South Asia has been hampered by the absence of local-level participatory institutions to ensure effective implementation. As independent variable, land reform can be seen as a necessary condition for the effective development of such local institutions. It is this latter relationship which has evoked policy thinking on the necessity of breaking rural dependency ties, primarily based on land, in order to make free political agents of tenants and the rural poor.

The tactical problem for land-reform theorists is thus set. If a land tenure structure characterized by abject dependency relations allows local landed elites to dominate local politics, decentralization and local participation are likely to enhance the power of local elites (cf. Bell, 1974). That result is unlikely to improve prospects for land-reform implementation. The remainder of this chapter explores this policy dilemma, and innovative responses to it, in the conception and execution of the Paddy Lands Act in Ceylon.

The particular case introduces further complications in the argument, but one general conclusion about tenure reform and local democracy seems clear: each presupposes the other if either is to be effective; as a result, neither has been fully successful. It is from this conclusion that an added impetus is given to land-to-the-tiller models. Daniel Thorner (1956: 82) argued simply: "Put land in the hands of those who are working it and you crack the existing concentration of power." The Paddy Lands Act in Ceylon seriously attempted to regulate production relations through the establishment of official and popular institutions in order to "crack the existing concentration of power" *without* putting land into the hands of those who were working it, and largely failed.

Transformational Tenure Reform: The Paddy Lands Act in Ceylon

The Paddy Lands Act presents something of a paradox in tenure reforms. Though created by a Marxist minister of agriculture whose vision was clearly a transformation of the peasant paddy sector along collectivist lines, the act in redistributive content follows the conservative tenure reform model—reduction of rent and security of tenure. In order to explain this apparent paradox, it is necessary to explore a Marxist paradigm of rural land relations and to differentiate clearly strategy and tactics in agrarian policy.

The minister of agriculture, Philip Gunawardena, faced a complex political situation after the Mahajana Eksath Peramuna (MEP) coalition of which his small Marxist party was a part came to power in 1956. The minister considered land reform necessary on the grounds of both productivity and social justice.[6] Yields in the paddy sector were low, and the cultivators impoverished, conditions dramatically presented in Sarkar and Tambiah's *The Disintegrating Village* (1957) and the Government of Ceylon's *Report of Kandyan Peasantry Commission* (1951). The 1953 Paddy Lands Act, a classical laissez-faire tenure reform, had been an unmitigated failure, abandoned by the government.[7] The 1956 MEP coalition itself covered a broad range of social bases and ideologies, from rural populist left to conservative landed interests, and had no coherent economic or agrarian philosophy; tenure reform was not a part of the election manifesto.[8]

Given the constellation of political forces in the coalition, it was clear that no radical land reform would be supported by the Cabinet or parliamentary group. The orthodox left was in the opposition and represented almost entirely nonagricultural working-class interests; its outlook was urban (cf. Kearney, 1971). Rural mobilization to support land reform was minimal; the peasantry had not been organized by either the urban left or a nationalist independence movement. The partial exception was the plantation proletariat, but having been disenfranchised soon after Independence and separated by ethnic hostilities and religious tradition from the Sinhalese peasantry, the Tamil laborers did not offer a potential ally.[9] Moreover, the demands of the Kandyan peasantry for ex-

6. For the provisions of the draft, and the policy thinking behind them, I rely primarily on the explanation of G. V. S. de Silva, personal secretary to Gunawardena. The post was accepted with the understanding that de Silva would draft an agrarian reform. The parliamentary debates on the bill, and later on the act, its amendments, and implementation, corroborate and deepen information from this primary source. Gunawardena acknowledged in Parliament in 1961 the critical role of de Silva in drafting the bill; Ceylon, *PD*, vol. 42 (1961), col. 7229. As Mr. Gunawardena was no longer living when I was doing research in Sri Lanka, I am deeply indebted to Mr. de Silva for his help in understanding the policy model. The exposition in the text is corroborated by Peiris (1976) and Gold (1977: chap. 3).

7. Herring (1972/74); Gold (1977: chap. 2). The failures of the act were important in the minister's formulation of the 1958 bill.

8. See Denzil Pieris (1958); Wriggins (1960: 326–66); Herring (1972/74: 119–23); Peiris (1976). Marshall Singer collected data which corroborate the conventional wisdom: "the overwhelming majority of the [political] elite own at least some land" (1964: 85). On the politics of the MEP coalition, Wilson (1974), pp. 153–58, 199–200, and passim.

9. For a moving treatment of the acute isolation and suffering of the "Indian" estate laborers, Vellupillai (1970). Jeffery Paige, in *Agrarian Revolution: Social Movements and Export Agriculture in the Underdeveloped World* (1975), presents a systematic argument for the divergence between the economic interests and typical political involvement of plantation laborers, on the one hand, and those of peasant proprietors, on the other, though his treatment of Ceylon's plantation sector in particular is flawed.

pansion of village lands would threaten the employment position of hill-country estate laborers. No political party had an extensive rural cadre network, and the paddy villages themselves were notably lacking in both local democratic institutions and class-based organizations such as peasant associations. Population pressure on the paddy lands was extreme; the median size of holding in the early 1950s was 0.82 acres, and the mean size of paddy holding was 1.17 acres (Ceylon, 1952, *Survey of Landlessness*: 7, 28).

The tenurial structure likewise produced a vector sum of forces which offered very little net support for a land-to-the-tiller policy. Most paddy cultivators had plots so small as to necessitate nonagricultural employment for some family members, and a very broad range of nonagriculturalists owned paddy land. Rather than presenting a confrontation between relatively few huge landlords and vast numbers of landless tenants, the rural social structure in the 1950s represented the cumulative impact of the forces of early commercialization and extreme population pressure. *The Economic Survey of Rural Ceylon* (1950–51) found that 26 percent of all *agricultural* families owned no land and another 16 percent owned less than 0.5 acres. These figures exclude the landless "Indian" (Tamil) estate workers, the bulk of the agrarian proletariat. In contrast to the very large percentage of agricultural families who owned no agricultural land, well over half of the *nonagricultural* families owned land, overwhelmingly in small pieces of less than 2 acres each (Ceylon, 1954: 28 ff.). These nonagricultural petty landowners covered a range of occupations, as illustrated in table 3.1.

Agriculturalists were a minority of all landowners, and about one-third of the land was tilled by tenants.[10] Traders (and boutique-keepers)

Table 3.1: Distribution of Landowning Families by Occupation (Ceylon, 1950–51)

Occupation	Percentage of Landowners	Status of Agricultural Families	Percent
Agriculture	40	Owner-cultivator	35
Trade	7	Tenant-cultivator	18
Handicraft	5	Agricultural laborer*	45
Labor (nonagricultural)	17	Landlord	2
Other	31		
Total	100		100

*Agricultural laborers exclusive of "estate" labor (largely Tamil).
SOURCE: *Final Report of the Economic Survey of Rural Ceylon* (Ceylon, 1954).

10. As in India, the exact extent of tenancy is difficult to determine, even prior to The Paddy Lands Act. Part of the difficulty lies in the peculiarity of the land-tenure system of some areas in the Eastern Province (see n. 31 below). A second difficulty is that tenancy was technically illegal on land in colonization schemes under the terms of the Land Devel-

constituted a significant category of landowners. Particularly interesting is the high percentage of proletarian landowners. By definition, these workers received most of their income from nonagricultural labor, yet owned land. The typical case was probably of the family plot becoming too small to support all the offspring of a family, some of whom took up manual labor while retaining a share of the holding. Such proletarianization of the peasantry, a phenomenon given great importance by Lenin, creates potential resistance in the working class to radical land reform, as some workers are petty rentiers or part-time owner-cultivators.

The significant group in table 3.1 is that labeled "Other"—fully 31 percent of the landowners. This category includes many small groups, including the occupations of "teaching and subordinate government service." The large size of this sector is a function of the early development of an activist, penetrating state in Ceylon, and the power of these two groups in the villages is well documented, representing a weighty opposition to abolition of the rentier system. Land ownership represented almost 40 percent of the total property assets of families in this category (author's calculations from Ceylon, 1954: 42). Of equal social and political importance is the fact that the "Other" category includes village religious functionaries, a significant source of opposition to the Paddy Lands Bill (Peiris, 1976: 33; Gold, 1977: 52–54).

We get a sense of the social composition of this petty rentier class from conservative speeches in Parliament in opposition to the Paddy Lands Bill. One United National Party member characterized "95 percent" of the owners in Kandyan areas as "lower middle class people: . . . take, for instance, the schoolmaster, the ayurvedic physician, the registrar, the retired government servant, the pensioner" (Ceylon, *PD*, vol. 30 [1957: col. 1948]). Sarkar and Tambiah's 1957 village study confirms that portrait. Of the village paddy land owned by outsiders, salaried classes owned 35 percent of the land; priests, plantation owners, and businessmen also figured heavily. Of the resident village rentiers, 31 percent were of the "salaried classes," mostly teachers, clerks, engineers, and so on. The salaried rentiers were found to be increasing their ownership of paddy land. Resident noncultivating owners held one-fourth of the village paddy land.[11]

---

opment Ordinance, though all reports indicate sharecropping as a common, legally unrecognized, tenure in the schemes (e.g., *PD* vol. 30 [1957: col. 2508]). Gold (1977: 62) reports that government officials instructed colonists to distort land records to preserve the "fantasy" of the absence of tenancy. The 1946 Census showed only 25.9 percent of the paddy holdings as tenanted, but as Sanderatne (1972b) argues, this is certainly an underestimate. The Department of Agrarian Services estimated in 1958 that about 40 percent of the paddy *area* was tenanted. Determination of the extent of tenancy after the Paddy Lands Act became even more problematic because of false registration of landlords as owner-cultivators to evade the law. For further discussion of underestimation of the extent of tenancy, Peiris (1976: 24).

11. Sarkar and Tambiah (1957: 14–18). More recent systematic confirmation of this phenomenon can be found in ARTI (1974), pt. 1, pp. 28–31; pt. 2, pp. 29–32.

Because the activist social base of the MEP coalition was the rural middle-class, frequently led by traditional and modern rural intelligentsia—teachers, ayurvedic physicians, Buddhist monks—the potential support for a radical agrarian reform was very weak indeed.[12] In fact, opposition to land reform within the governing coalition figured heavily in diluting drafts of the Paddy Lands Act.

The agrarian structure and its local political morphology, as well as the balance of political power in Colombo, thus made a land-to-the-tiller reform tactically impossible. In addition to the formidable political obstacles facing the minister, were his own strategic doubts about the desirability of such a reform in terms of the potential *embourgeoisement.* Gunawardena had visited China and had been tremendously impressed by the reorganization of agriculture there; his vision of the future of Ceylonese agriculture was clearly collectivist. The creation of still more marginal proprietors he took to be a poor idea in both political and economic terms. Politically, such a move would increase the dominance of petit bourgeois ideology and resistance to eventual collectivization, which he considered essential in Ceylon's agroeconomic situation. Gunawardena stated flatly in Parliament: "I am not a believer in peasant proprietorship, because I do not think that the prosperity of agriculture in this country can be built on peasant proprietorship" (Ceylon, *PD*, vol. 30 [1957: col. 2454]).

Though it was tactically impossible to end the rentier exploitation of tenants, it did seem possible to introduce comprehensive measures which would lessen that exploitation while strengthening tenants politically and economically vis-à-vis landlords but not foreclosing the option of eventual collectivization of agriculture. The *content* of the resulting reform did resemble the limited tenure-reform model, but it is important to remember that even the Chinese Communist Party supported for tactical reasons the "double reduction" model of limited land reform—reduction of rent and of interest—to ameliorate tenants' conditions and aid in mobilization when a more radical agrarian program was politically impractical and tactically undesirable.[13] Moreover, the measures of the minister's draft which supplemented limited tenure reform were the core of the strategy. These measures represented a unique response to the structural features of rural society which have thwarted other attempts

12. The most systematic attempt to delineate the social class of political leaders in the period is Singer (1964), pp. 85, 139, 142, and passim. It is clear from Singer's data, and from every other source, that landownership was a significant source of income and prestige for the political elite; cf. Peiris (1958: 1–18). Our information about the mass base of the new coalition is much scantier, but anthropological and other sources support the presentations of Wriggins (1960: 326–66); Jupp (1978: 62–68).

13. For specific policy thinking and directives, see Mao Tse-tung (1967), 1:23–63; 3:131–35, 247–52; 4:71–74, 201–02. For historical placing of the party's land reform, Chesneaux (1973: 101–48); Belden (1970: chap. 7 and passim).

at tenure reform. The reform's failures thus deserve detailed consideration.

The Minister's World-View and Parliamentary Politics

The core of the perceptual paradigm which spawned the 1958 Paddy Lands Bill held that landlord–tenant relations are conflictual class relations based on unequal power and unequal exchange. As a result, neither a laissez-faire policy nor reliance on ordinary bureaucracy would suffice to improve the status of tenants. Not only Gunawardena, but also leftist leaders in the opposition, emphasized that tenurial rights could be guaranteed only through extraordinary means.[14] The understanding was that, except in the very few areas where tenants were politicized, a combination of landlord coercion and the "feudal" attitudes of deference on the part of tenants would defeat redistributive measures.

This perception differed dramatically from that informing the liberal 1953 Paddy Lands Act, and was in marked contrast to views of those opposing the 1958 bill. One Member of Parliament, in attacking Gunawardena's view of rural Ceylon, explained (*PD*, vol. 30 [1957: col. 2391 ff.]): "In my village there is amity and peace between the owner and the tenant. They depend on the owner for their feudal ceremonies, marriage ceremonies, etc."

Another member interjected: "That is slavery; serfdom." The reply was: "It is not serfdom. It is cooperative companionship. . . . Even in time of drought they will be helped by the owners. They advance money for two years and three years and also rice to keep them going."

Another landlord Member of Parliament, Sir Razik Fareed, argued that the attack on landlords was unwarranted: landlords, he said, live on manors and oppress peasants; in Ceylon, there were no such things (with the acknowledged exception of one owner of 4,000 acres of paddy in the Eastern Province who exploited Muslim tenants). In the Member's view, landlords were not exploiting tenants but helping them. In contrast to the minister's views on tenants' being forced to *pay* excessive rents, Sir Razik Fareed cited his own practice: "I give . . . half the harvest." The perceptual difference here is wide—the difference between a tenant being deprived of the product of his labor and a landlord generously giving one-half of *his* harvest—although the empirical fact is exactly the same, a half-share tenancy arrangement.

The perception that "there are no landlords in Ceylon" had two aspects. The meaning was first that *landlord* connotes exploitation, and this characterization did not fit the close personal, paternalistic character of owner–tenant relations in Ceylon. Second, *landlord* connotes a person of great power. But Sir Razik Fareed illustrated the character of "land-

14. E.g., *PD*, vol. 11 (1951: col. 277); vol. 30 (1957: cols. 2009, 2016, 2431).

lordism" in Ceylon by stating that he had given his chauffeur an acre of land. The chauffeur then rented out the land and lived in Colombo. The Member noted that there were countless similar cases; the data on land-ownership cited earlier demonstrate that he was right.

But despite the personalistic ties between owners and tenants, and the extremely differentiated social character of the rentier class, the minister framed the Paddy Lands Bill with the assumptions (a) that there would be conflict between owners and tenants, and (b) that because of the structural power imbalance, tenants would be victimized. These perceptions were translated into concrete compensatory measures. The unequal relationship between owners and tenants was explicitly recognized as multiplex, as being more than a land tenure contract in the narrow sense.

The minister and his associates, particularly Mr. G. V. S. de Silva, prepared a draft incorporating this policy logic. This draft is crucial to understanding the policy model; the final bill and act reflect compromises forced on the minister by conservative political leaders, compromises which Gunawardena felt "castrated" the act (PD, vol. 42 [1961: col. 7223]).

The conception was relatively simple. Since abolition of landlordism was politically impossible and strategically undesirable, tenants were to be assured security of tenure and reduced rents. Although the provision was little understood in practice, the rental limit was not simply a reduction in the share owned by tenants, but was a statutory amount (which varied by area) or one-fourth of the crop, whichever was less. In theory, the tenant would receive the economic advantages of a fixed rent and the traditional security of reduced rents in bad years. The cultivator could theoretically invest with the assurance that after paying a fixed rent, the total increment of product would accrue to him, with the added security of a reduced rent if yields were low. In the minister's draft, the rental limits were extremely low; political compromises between draft and act significantly raised the legal rent ceiling.

Realizing that reductions in rent could not be enforced unless tenants were protected from threats of eviction, the draft allowed for immediate restoration of evicted tenants on the land pending an inquiry—the presumption was in favor of the tenant, the burden of proof on the landlord. This provision, very similar to that of Kerala's contemporaneous draft agrarian reform (by which the minister was influenced), was deleted because of conservative political pressure; opponents claimed the provision was a corruption of normal legal process (with its clear presumption in favor of property).[15] The ultimate impact of this deletion was devastating.

15. For sources of draft provisions, see n. 6 above. Also PD, vol. 37 (1958: col. 709 ff.); vol. 42 (1961: col 7223 ff.).

The important institutional innovation—termed the "heart" of the Paddy Lands Act by the minister—was provision for elected Cultivation Committees. The multifunctional committees were in part responses to precisely that dilemma noted in the first section of this chapter—the absence of village-level democratic institutions or associations of cultivators; simultaneously, their various mandated functions responded to the reality and complexity of the tenants' dependency ties to owners. Because of the paradigmatic emphasis on a structural conflict of interests and inequality in power between economic classes, the draft excluded noncultivating owners from the committees altogether. The logic was that inclusion of landlords would intimidate tenants and cripple the committees' implementation of the redistributive measures (Ceylon, *PD*, vol. 42 [1961: 7241, 7222]). This provision likewise had to be compromised, the final act providing only that cultivators make up no less than three-fourths of the members of the Cultivation Committee. This compromise, too, had a serious impact on implementation.

The same conflictual paradigm prompted the draft's authors to assign the cultivation committees intermediary functions; they were empowered to collect rents, loan payments, and other charges from cultivators, and to pay these to designated recipients. This provision theoretically would allow tight control of the amount of rent (and interest, which was also regulated) actually paid by the cultivator. Moreover, the intervening body of cultivators would discourage the direct intimidation of tenants by landlords which is common in unequal dyadic relationships.

The cultivation committees were also to provide a number of services that could be considered substitutes for the individual and collective traditional functions of landowners and the village elite. For example, they were to develop and maintain irrigation works, serve as a conduit for cultivator grievances to the authorities, mediate disputes, ensure the supply of working capital, fertilizers, implements, and so on (Ceylon, 1958: sec. 36). These provisions explicitly recognized the multiplex character of relations between owners and cultivators, and sought to encourage cultivator initiative in collectively organizing functions previously performed by their superordinates. Another critical function was the preparation and maintenance of a register of paddy lands and cultivators; tenure reforms have frequently foundered because they failed to compensate for the absence of local records or their corruptibility.

Two additional provisions in the broader plan of the minister of agriculture addressed the peculiar problems of the patron-client character of production relations. First, credit was considered a crucial nexus of tenant dependence, and measures were proposed to create collective responsibility for institutional loan repayment and to reorganize institutional credit facilities; the existing cooperative societies were considered to be excessively bureaucratic and dominated by local elites. Second, recognizing the crucial role of landlords in providing a source of financial security as a hedge against crop failures, the minister proposed comprehensive measures for crop insurance. These supplemental measures evoked fierce political opposition and could not be fully implemented.[16]

Gunawardena termed the cultivation committees the "seeds of the new society." Not only were the traditional functions of landlords and village elites to be largely assumed by them, but new functions of a transformational sort were added. The committees were to organize the cooperative, communal aspects of paddy cultivation and were empowered to hold land under special conditions and to prepare schemes for the consolidation of holdings and the establishment of collective farms and to fix the wages of agricultural laborers. The provision for collective farms, though acknowledged by Gunawardena to be more aspirational than realistic, provoked virulent attacks on the bill, including references to Soviet totalitarianism, the destruction of rural harmony and stability, and the charge that the act would "pervert the minds and morals of the rural community" (Peiris, 1976: 33). These attacks on the bill and the minister precipitated a governmental crisis. The prime minister supported the minister of agriculture on most issues, but opposition in the cabinet and government parliamentary group was strong enough to force Gunawardena to resign from the cabinet.[17]

The second major institutional innovation was the creation of a new Department of Agrarian Services, which had as its first responsibility implementation of the Paddy Lands Act. In addition, the department acquired a number of auxiliary functions in strengthening the Cultivation Committees, channeling agricultural inputs and irrigation contracts to the committees, dispensing credit, and so on. When a political compromise forced the minister to include landlords on the committees, Gunawardena expected officials of the department to take an activist stance to safeguard tenants' interests.

The conceptualization of land rights and cultivation responsibilities in the act is complex. Tenancy rights were made heritable, permanent, and impartible. Thus the unit of ownership could continue to subdivide, while the unit of cultivation was protected from fragmentation and parcelization. The separation of ownership and cultivation rights also, in theory, facilitates the transition to collectivism. One scholar has noted the resulting curious position of landlords—the rentier was relieved of

16. *PD*, vol. 30 (1957: col. 1897); Wilson (1974: 143–44). On the inadequacies of crop insurance, Sanderatne (1969).

17. The parliamentary debates of the period contain much of the conflict, especially, *PD*, Senate, vol 11 (1957: cols. 823 ff.). Accounts of the Cabinet dispute were leaked to the press and carried in *Ceylon Daily News*, November 13 and 14, 1957. Opposition also built around the allegation that Gunawardena meant to use the cultivation committees as a rural base for his political ambitions. cf. Wilson (1974: 199–200), on the "Cabinet Strike"; Jupp (1978: 76–77, 65–68, 10); Gold (1977: 30–31).

all land rights other than receiving rent—and questioned the utility of retaining nonfunctional landlords as rent-receivers (Sanderatne, 1972b: 133). As explained in this section, there were good reasons, paradigmatic and political, for retaining the owner–tenant structure in the paddy sector, but it is interesting to note that while land reforms in other parts of South Asia were seeking to make the parasitic rentier a functioning landlord, the Paddy Lands Act was reducing the landlord, who often did provide production services, to the position of functionless rentier. Gunawardena's logic was that emancipation of the tenant and the emergence of cultivator-controlled local institutions necessitated the breaking of dependency ties created by landlord provision of working capital, security insurance, credit, and diffuse brokerage functions.

Politics, Embedded Production Relations, and Implementation

In theory, the Paddy Lands Act of 1958, even in its compromised form, addressed most of the structural obstacles which have defeated tenure reform in other settings—the embedded character of production relations, the lack of land records, the absence of tenant interest groups and local democratic institutions. However, as Gunawardena himself admitted, "theory is grey, but life is eternally green" (Ceylon, *PD*, vol. 37 [1958: col. 709]).

Political Will and Uncertainty

Timing is critical to any land reform. Even with its safeguards, the act necessarily presupposed that tenants would undertake an activist role. They had to bear the brunt of breaking long-standing tradition, the *ande* half-share tenancy, thus violating important norms of the dependency relation. Moreover, the class sympathies of the owner-cultivators were not clear; for the cultivation committees to act consistently as guardians of tenant rights, the tenants would be forced to take an active political role, as they were outnumbered in most areas. Such an activist role requires that tenants be certain they cannot be evicted by an angry landlord and that they can otherwise obtain crucial services provided by patrons if patrons withdraw them. Without this security, quiescence would be more prudent. Moreover, without an active tenantry, the possibility of elite co-optation of the cultivation committees and corruption of land records increases; once the list of cultivators is corrupted, a challenge becomes difficult, as only registered cultivators can vote for members of the committees that revise the records.

Given this imperative, the Paddy Lands Act was jeopardized by circumstances. First, as a result of political compromises, the act was to be administered sequentially; full implementation was to begin in only two districts, gradually extending across the island. Thus, early failures could demoralize tenants in other districts and tilt the balance against activism. Second, the cabinet crisis and isolation of Gunawardena as a Marxist in a non-Marxist coalition government left the act with an unstable political base. When Gunawardena was forced from the Cabinet, largely because of agrarian reform issues, the act passed into the hands of those who did not share its vision. Gunawardena himself charged: "This is a 'landlord Government,' it is not interested in working the Paddy Lands Act properly" (Ceylon, *PD*, vol. 37 [1958: col. 714]).

Land reform in any parliamentary system is likely to suffer from changes in government, as tenants, owners, and officials cannot be certain of the depth and vigor of political support for implementation of an act. The Paddy Lands Act was especially vulnerable in this respect, as continuous intervention and supervision were central to the policy logic.

The discontinuities and instabilities in the national political system during the history of the Paddy Lands Act were particularly striking. The bill itself was hotly disputed within the government, caused a cabinet crisis, and was opposed by the conservative wing of the coalition from its incpetion.[18] The exit of Gunawardena's tiny Marxist party from the government caused the two Marxist parties in the opposition to withdraw their "qualified support" from the MEP government. Soon after, the prime minister was assassinated and extreme political instability followed. Although the act was to be administered by the new Department of Agrarian Services and thus had some institutional support despite changes in regime, when the department faced debilitating legal problems in the early years, the government demonstrated its lack of political commitment to the act by failing to make necessary amendments.

The personal exit of Gunawardena from the Cabinet was especially damaging to the new act. His eventual successor was Felix Bandaranaike, whose views on land relations were quite different. Whereas Gunawardena had spoken of the act in terms of "abolishing feudal relations" and planting the seeds of a collectivist rural society, Bandaranaike, as minister of agriculture and lands, stated that the "sole object" of the act was "to increase production of paddy in this country" (Ceylon, *PD*, vol. 56 [1964: col. 1257]).

The creation of a new organization to implement the reform contrasts favorably with the Indian and Pakistani practice of relegating tenurial reform to existing land-revenue machinery. By all accounts, the Department of Agrarian Services took its mandate seriously and began implementing the act with enthusiasm. As a crude measure of commitment, we should note that the early violence in Hambantota district, the

18. Herring (1972/74: 120); for the SLFP agriculture minister's view, *Daily Mirror* October 5, 1973; also Pieris (1958: 14). The minister of lands in 1957, C. P. de Silva, termed the Paddy Lands Act "diabolical" and more insidious than Soviet land reforms. Gunawardena added fuel to the fire with vitriolic attacks on his opponents, for example, terming the landlords "feudal rubbish" (Peiris, 1976: 34).

first in which the act was implemented, was directed against officers of the department as well as against tenants.[19] The priorities of the department in implementation suggest the same: during the first five years of the act, 3,125 applications were filed by landowners for permission to evict tenants to take up self-cultivation as allowed conditionally in the act; only 341 cases were acted upon and, of these, permission was granted in only 56 cases (*CAR*, RCAS [1962–63: KK 72]).

However, since departmental orders for restoration of evicted tenants proved unenforceable because of court rulings, and under threat of eviction tenants refrained from initiating cases of unlawful rent exaction, the department began to shift its energies to other mandated functions such as provision of credit, minor irrigation, and so on. These priorities, which stressed the production and physical input side of the act rather than the redistributive and transformational, also reflected the change in political impetus behind agrarian reform following the departure of Gunawardena and the dissolution of the MEP government.

Risk and Tenant Rationality in Implementation

In order to make the case that tenants might lose more than they would gain by taking advantage of the rental reduction in the act, it is necessary to establish just what the cultivator stood to lose. Eviction is a threat only if the alternatives are less desirable; it becomes a serious threat only in those agrodemographic situations in which tenants need landlords more than landlords need tenants. Evidence from village-level studies indicates that this was the case, at least in much of Ceylon.

Sarkar and Tambiah's village study in the Central Province (1957) indicated an average size of holding of 0.48 acres of paddy. Five percent of the households owned almost one-half of the land, whereas two-thirds of the households were landless. Over half of the cultivators were sharecroppers; the institution of *madaran*, a fee—often competitive—paid to the landlord each season for access to a plot, reflected the extreme competition for land (cf. Ceylon, 1955). Traditionally paid in betel and plantains, the charge had been commuted to cash and represented about 8 percent of the tenants' net income.[20] The extreme poverty of some cultivators was reflected in the *karu-ande* system of tenure, in which the tenant provided no inputs other than labor; the owner received three-fourths of the gross produce. In addition to payment of *madaran* and rent, sharecroppers supplied unpaid labor on the owner's land or compound for the privilege of tilling.

These conditions illustrate one extreme of tenant dependence on owners arising from a high worker–land ratio, unemployment, and a sig-

---

19. *Ceylon Administration Reports* (hereafter *CAR*), *Report of the Government Agent, Hambantota*, 1958, A 649–50. A similar conclusion is reached by Gold (1977: 85–86).

20. My calculation from data given by Sarkar and Tambiah (1957: 23).

nificant pool of landless people eager to obtain any opportunity for security. Many landlords, on the other hand, had secure incomes from other sources (salaries, business, etc.); given the competition for land, tenants were easy to replace. Thus the threat of eviction, simply from the perspective of loss of income, could not be taken lightly.

But because an *ande* relationship is embedded in a complex social and economic matrix, the tenant typically risks more than loss of income by opposing the landlord. To develop a sense of the rationality of tenant action in demanding legislated benefits, it is necessary to add these risks to the more obvious, and considerable, costs incurred—legal fees, travel expenses, lost work-time, bribes, and so on. Then all these costs must be weighted by the likelihood of success, as perceived by the tenant, in initiating action against an owner.

Nimal Sanderatne has insightfully advanced this line of reasoning with regard to the Paddy Lands Act. He noted that landlords often provided working capital and draft power, as well as employment outside the paddy sector for the cultivator and his family, and that some tenants viewed the customary tenurial terms as a moral obligation which could not be dissolved by passage of a law in Colombo. Most importantly:

> The landlord-tenant relationships are not impersonal contractual relationships and may have existed for generations among the landlord and tenant families. It may not be considered morally justifiable to break such an agreement for the sole purpose of obtaining what might in any case be an uncertain economic advantage: once a tenant breaks the long-standing relationship, to whom can he turn when he needs a recommendation for his son's employment, or who of importance would grace his children's weddings? If he were in dire need who would come to his rescue, especially when anyone else he could turn to might be closely related or associated with the landlord?[21]

Several points in this analysis require comment. In the paddy sector, the landlord–tenant nexus was often not only personal in nature but frequently a kinship relation. *Ande* tenancies were sometimes given to cement marriages, build alliances, attach loyal followers, aid impoverished kin, and evidently were not typically experienced as class relations or as primarily economic-contractual, at least in most areas.[22] The depen-

21. Sanderatne (1972b: 126–27); based on his own fieldwork, and Sarkar and Tambiah (1957). ARTI studies (1974, 1975) indicate regional variation in the production services provided by landlords, from minimal to extensive contributions. The act almost certainly contributed to drying up landlord contributions. Gold (1977: 189) attributes the significant decline in the share of rural credit provided by landlords—from 8 percent in 1957 to 0.7 percent in 1969—to this phenomenon; Harriss (1977: 157) concurs.

22. This conclusion emerges from the best anthropological literature on Sri Lanka, studies of implementation of the act, and my own field experience (1973). Major anthropological works include Yalman (1967); Leach (1961); Obeyesekere (1967: esp. 215, 226); Ryan (1958: esp. 24); Brow (1980). In addition to Sanderatne's work, there is Wimaladharma and Clifford (1973: 6–11 and personal communication); Raza (1970: 9); Gold (1977: 162). Gerald

dence of tenants on landlords for both productive inputs and services and additional employment, necessitated by the tiny holdings, is well documented in village studies. Sanderatne correctly assumes that tenants act in terms of calculations that posit a post-reform world essentially the same as the pre-reform world—a world in which it will still be necessary to depend on men of wealth and influence for production needs, emergency aid, social security, brokerage with the larger society, and derivative social status (the gracing of marriages, etc.). This assumption is critical; any reform in which the tenant must take the initiative *and bear the risks* of dissolving patron–client ties must be accompanied by measures which will convince him that the post-reform rural world will be different.

The extra-economic relations between owners and tenants suggest why tenants may not always demand radical land reform or even press for limited legislated benefits. The dimension of security and certainty is crucial, particularly when life is near bare subsistence.[23] In investigating landlord-tenant relations in Sri Lanka, Paul Casperz (1973: 8) asked some tenants why they did not seek their own lands via a government distribution program. He was answered: "Anyway, it is perhaps better if we stay here. At least we know these big people and they look after us. All that we now have we get from them. If their lands were also taken away, then there would be no one to help us."

It is difficult for tenants to conceive of a world in which outside help would be unnecessary. The state represents an uncertain and unreliable source of services, *even if* it promises to replace those of the patron. Moreover, some of the more important material services of patrons, such as emergency and consumption loans, are typically beyond the scope of state policy. The alienation of a patron may thus entail greater costs than the benefits which can be reasonably expected from the reform proce-

---

Peiris (1976: 35–37) concludes from his survey of village-level evidence that *ande* tenancies predominantly took patron–client or kinship forms and were typically not experienced in class-conflictual terms, but he adds the important qualification that tenancy systems in some areas (Hambantota, Kegalla) were characterized by overt conflict (cf. Dias and Wickremanayake, 1977). Brow's (1980) account stresses the tension between mutuality and dominance existing simultaneously at the material and ideological levels in *ande* relations.

23. For a general argument that security and risk-avoidance are central to peasant politics, economics, and ideology, see Scott (1976). The refutation in Popkin (1979) is only partially successful: the empirical observation of risk-accepting behavior by peasants does not refute the argument that the most marginal and insecure of the peasantry may prefer risk-avoiding arrangements; such behavior may, under certain circumstances, be perfectly "rational" in Popkin's terms, as illustrated in the argument in the text concerning tenure reform. Because Popkin fails adequately to appreciate class differentiation within the peasantry, he underemphasizes the importance of security-seeking behavior on the part of some sections of the rural populace even as more secure peasants exhibit significant risk-taking tendencies. Moreover, dimensionality is critical: risk-averse behavior with regard to potential loss of access to the means of production may easily coexist with risk- accepting behavior in relation to a single crop or investment.

dures; the rationality of initiating action to receive reform benefits in the existing institutional framework then becomes moot. But then the question arises: why should tenants believe or disbelieve that the reform will deliver its promised benefits? The operation of the Paddy Lands Act offers instructive suggestions.

Implementation: The Courts versus the Paddy Lands Act

From the tenant's perspective, the early years of implementation did not induce confidence. The act immediately produced large-scale evictions of tenants; the task of restoring these tenants fell to the Department of Agrarian Services. It began investigations enthusiastically, but immediately encountered severe legal difficulties. First, the courts ruled invalid all cultivation committees that did not have exactly twelve members. Landlords boycotted meetings and elections, invalidating the committees in early court rulings. This problem was finally addressed by an amending act (no. 61 of 1961), but contributed to early disillusionment with the reform.

The courts also dealt the act a serious blow by questioning the definition of *eviction*. The act did not define the term; the courts construed *evict* to mean "to forcibly and physically eject a tenant from the paddy field."[24] The more usual practice—simply refusing the tenant permission to till the land he had been tilling—was not construed as eviction. Because the cultivation committees in the districts where the act fully applied were charged with issuing vacating orders to landlords who had illegally evicted tenants, this ruling, combined with the ruling that many committees were illegally constituted, prevented restoration of evicted tenants. In the original conception, the courts were to have had no part in adjudicating disputes under the act; special administrative machinery was provided instead. But the courts ruled that it was within their power to take up any case de novo, even a decision by the Board of Review, the body intended to be the final arbiter under the act. Other adverse court rulings included a very strict definition of *tenant cultivator*, a construction so narrow that one Member of Parliament remarked sarcastically, "there is no tenant cultivator in the island, and no tenant cultivator has been evicted" (Ceylon, *PD*, vol. 42/2 [1961: 7182]).

The courts had a cumulatively debilitating effect on implementation. In Hambantota district, the first in which the act was applied, landlords were able to force tenants from the land with hired thugs but could not be prosecuted because of court rulings. Proceedings for the restoration of evicted tenants dragged on in the courts for years. Moreover, the time and energy of cultivation committees and officials of the depart-

24. *PD*, vol. 42, no. 2 (1961: col. 7182); *Administration Reports* of the Department of Agrarian Services. cf. Gold (1977: 95–96); Peiris (1976: 48); ARTI (1979: 41).

ment were expended on new elections to satisfy the courts and on long legal proceedings against (often superior) landlords' lawyers, often in courts presided over by landlord-judges (Gold, 1977: 89–94). Legally valid cultivation committees could not be formed in parts of Hambantota district because most landowners were absentees and could not serve on them. Rural courts deprived the functioning committees of their only source of revenue (the "acreage levy" of Rs 6 per acre) by refusing to prosecute defaulters. The long and incomprehensible court battles discouraged tenants. The Member of Parliament for the Tissamaharama constituency described the general effect of the legislation in the district as "great demoralization in the countryside and chaos in the field of cultivation."[25]

The 1961 amendment corrected several legal problems, such as the definitions of *cultivator* and *evict*, and provided for substitutions to fill vacancies on cultivation committees. But a great deal of damage had been done, and new problems emerged. In Hambantota district, the cultivation committees were plagued by lack of funds and were unable to hire competent secretaries. The one-year tenure of office was arguably wasteful, as elections consumed time and disrupted continuity; the three-year term in the original draft had been compromised in deference to conservative political forces.

Philip Gunawardena had worried that his agrarian measures would succeed only if supported by the full weight of government; this support, he charged, had not been given the act during the two "caretaker" governments nor under the Sri Lanka Freedom Party. This argument rings true. Though Gunawardena prepared a long list of amendments to correct technical flaws in the act, and the commissioner of agrarian services did the same in 1959, the government took a laissez-faire stance toward implementation, allowing the courts to vitiate major provisions, thus crippling the cultivation committees. Effective amendments were urgently needed but not made. Gunawardena noted that confidence in the act was fundamental to its success, as tenants had to be convinced that they could trust and rely on the state, that they had to exercise power and not fear the landlords. The former minister believed that much had been achieved in 1958 "by sheer propaganda," but that subsequently tenant confidence understandably waned (Ceylon, *PD*, vol. 42/2 [1961: cols. 7227, 7239]).

Implementation of the act began on March 1, 1958. By December of 1959 there had been 14,500 complaints of eviction (*CAR*, RCAS [1959: KK 49 ff.]). Restoring the tenants wrongfully evicted required that the department force landlords to vacate the land. In the original draft, the tenant would have been restored immediately, pending investigation. In the event, the presumption in favor of property in the legal system forced

25. *PD*, vol. 42/2 (1961: cols. 7187, 7192–93, 7197, 7226). Interviews with officers of the department who served in the district during this period, as well as administration reports of the Government Agent for the district, confirm this account.

the department (or cultivation committees) to go to court to force land-lords to restore tenants. Thus, even tenants who won their cases in the departmental inquiry, and were judged to have been illegally evicted, had to await resolution of court battles before being reinstated as tenants. These court proceedings often took years. In addition, as Martin Gold (1977: chap. 7) correctly emphasizes, the local police proved to be a major impediment to the protection of tenants' rights.

Though landlords were legally prohibited from charging excess rents or evicting tenants except under certain restricted conditions, both in-fractions were common. The department attempted prosecution of twenty-five landlords during the first year and failed to convict in every case (*CAR*, RCAS [1959: KK 50]). The Government Agent for Hambantota re-ported that evictions in the district continued to increase yearly, reaching 1,130 reported in 1960 (*CAR*, RGA [1960–61: A 13]). Political instability affected tenants, landlords, and officials. The Government Agent, Galle, noted that "the working of the Paddy Lands Act was impeded by unset-tled political conditions and uncertainty about the future of the Act" (*CAR*, RGA [1960–61: A 11]).

The commissioner of agrarian services, in his report for 1960–61, noted the failure of the new cultivation committees to receive legitimacy or function effectively, and worried that the widespread publicity of im-plementation failures had made it virtually impossible to extend imple-mentation; owners had already seen how ineffectual were the punitive provisions. At the time of the report, the department had ordered resto-ration of 6,263 tenants, but actual possession had been restored in only 1,995 cases, and most of these through "persuasion and amicable agree-ment" rather than court proceedings. Because the security of tenure pro-visions could not be enforced, the rental provisions proved infructuous. The Department had received no rental complaints, presumably, the Commissioner felt, because tenants feared eviction (*CAR*, RCAS [1960–61; KK 50–51]).

The failure of both the department and the cultivation committees to protect tenants from eviction or restore evicted tenants was one vi-tiating factor; another was the failure of the new institutional forms to take up the collective and individual functions of the landlord class as patrons and village leaders. The cultivation committees were caught in a vicious circle—lack of funds and legal difficulties prevented them from performing effectively, and this failure induced cultivators to withhold funds and commitment, perpetuating the ineffectiveness of the commit-tees. Agricultural credit, a crucial link between owner and tenant in many areas, was not effectively institutionalized so that cultivators could de-pend on cooperative or government sources; the total amount of official credit fluctuated widely over the years. In the six districts in which the act was being fully implemented, between 1958–59 and 1959–60 insti-tutional credit volume fell by Rs 1.7 million (*CAR*, RCAS [1960–61; KK

37]). Supplemental measures such as crop insurance likewise remained irrelevant to the situation of most tenant cultivators. Under these conditions, the estrangement of a landlord patron was clearly risky.

An amendment in 1961 solved important legal problems, but in 1963 lower courts began refusing to recognize restoration orders issued by the department and challenged its legal right to issue such orders. The Supreme Court upheld the lower courts, dealing a nearly fatal blow to the implementation of the redistributive measures in the act. This legal difficulty was not rectified until 1970.

A second major amendment to the act was passed in 1964 under the SLFP government. Curiously, in the debate on that amendment, several conservative Members, including Dudley Senanayake, author of the 1953 Paddy Lands Act, urged an end to the administrative headaches and disruption (all the "politics and law" was hard on the cultivator, as one Member said) by making *ande* cultivators owners of their lands. Surprisingly, Felix Dias Bandaranaike, as minister of agriculture, agreed and said he would prepare a scheme to do so (Ceylon, *PD*, vol. 60 [1965: cols. 1303–33; 1483]). The government subsequently changed, and though there were references to such a scheme in the governor's Speech from the Throne in following years, there was evidently no serious political force behind the proposal. Undoubtedly some of the impetus for suggesting this alternative came from the evident impracticability and large recurring cost of continuous supervision and intervention in tenant-landlord relations. But, even with compensation, a land-to-the-tiller scheme would have been politically unattractive to the major parties, given the size and political importance of the class of small paddy rentiers.

The Paddy Lands (Amendment) Act No. 11 of 1964 was meant to correct severe enforcement lacunae and restore confidence in the act and its new institutions. A survey conducted that year by the department showed that landlords were continuing to collect the traditional half-share rent in violation of the law and threatening eviction if tenants did not comply. Moreover, the study found a large number of unreported evictions; the situation was even worse than official statistics indicated (*CAR*, RCAS [1963–64: KK 35, 61–64]). Despite the new amendment, the annual rate of restoration of evicted tenants remained stagnant: by September of 1966 evictions had officially reached 31,181; only 5,301 evicted tenants had been restored. The unofficial number of evictions was, of course, much higher. In the Speech from the Throne in both 1965 and 1966, the intention to transfer ownership rights to tenants was declared. Although the gesture was almost certainly only symbolic, it probably added to the pressure to evict tenants; the number of recorded evictions in 1966 was double that of 1965.[26]

26. *CAR, Report of the Commissioner of Agrarian Services* (hereafter *RCAS*), 1963–64, KK 64. The discrepancy in dates is due to delays in publication of reports.

The measure in the 1964 amendment that evoked the greatest dispute was a change to prohibit agricultural laborers from voting in elections for cultivation committees. The committees had the statutory power to fix the wages of laborers, but the minister of agriculture felt that the laborers did not have "a permanent and abiding interest in any paddy land" (Ceylon, *PD*, vol. 56 [1964: col. 1263]). Gunawardena argued in vain for inclusion of the laborers. Another change with potential impact on implementation was a provision making the paddy-land registers prima facie evidence for their contents. To the extent that these registers had been corrupted in the early years of implementation, the cause of victimized tenants was formally set back by the amendment.

Despite the amendments of 1961 and 1964, implementation of tenancy provisions had reached "a stalemate" by 1968 because of unresolved legal difficulties. The department awaited a Supreme Court decision for new impetus in implementation (*CAR*, RCAS [1967–68: KK 49]). In his report to the joint FAO–ECAFE–ILO Seminar on the Implementation of Land Reform in Asia and the Far East in 1969, the Commissioner of Agrarian Services noted that the reduction of the rice ration in 1966 had increased profitability of paddy cultivation, and thus renewed landlord interest—and resulted in a new wave of evictions of tenants (Ceylon, 1969). As previously, the department was able to do very little, as its restoration orders were not recognized by the courts. The courts had ruled that the department and the Board of Review were not institutions of the judiciary and thus were not empowered to make judicial decisions, forcing the department to suspend action on 3,052 cases.

Noting that court decisions had "cast a gloom" over tenants and cultivation committees, the UNP's minister for agriculture, Mr. Banda, introduced an amendment in 1969 purportedly to save the act and restore confidence in it (Ceylon, *PD*, vol. 88 [1969: col. 2380 ff.]). Curiously, Mr. Banda had delivered the opposition UNP's speech against the Paddy Lands bill when it was first introduced (Herring, 1972/74: 119). The minister observed that at every large gathering of farmers, the question of restoration of evicted tenants was raised. The cultivators found it incomprehensible that, even after strict compliance with the law, tenants could not be reinstated on their plots (Ceylon, *PD*, vol. 88 [1959: col. 2390]).

The minister's amendment, the Paddy Lands (Special Provisions) Act No. 2 of 1970, in theory freed the Department of Agrarian Services from the legal difficulties that had been blocking restoration of illegally evicted tenants. During the course of the year 1,171 new cases of eviction were recorded, bringing the total to 40,069 cases since the enforcement of the act (*CAR*, RCAS [1969–70: KK 33]). For assessing tenant rationality in accepting violations of the act, we can look to the record up to the date of the amendment. The department had made inquiries into about 88 percent of the 40,069 cases of *recorded* evictions. In all, 7,547 tenants had been restored either through mutual agreement or departmental orders. Thus only 18.8 percent of the recorded evictions had been rectified, and only after long delays (years in some cases); the odds did not favor tenant initiative. A total of 5,549 tenants, or 13.8 percent of the evicted cultivators, withdrew complaints "as petitioners lost interest." Moreover, of the 35,102 total cases decided, 38.3 percent of the tenant complaints were dismissed.[27] These odds were further lengthened by the uncertainty and delays in restoration even when the department ruled in the tenant's favor.

Taken together, the petitions withdrawn and the complaints dismissed constituted more than half of the total reported evictions. Some of the eviction complaints were probably unwarranted, but the department was convinced that reported evictions represented only a fraction of the actual total. Certainly the delays and uncertainty of restoration, and the costs involved, prevented many tenants from filing complaints.[28] The 1970 amendment in theory rectified the restoration problem. However, by June of 1973, the number of recorded evictions had reached 46,635; the yearly rate of evictions thus remained high—higher, in fact, than for the year 1970. More than half of the cases decided (51.4 percent) went against the tenant.[29] Restoration remained an uncertain and delay-strewn process. And because the security of tenure provisions remained uncertain in enforcement, many tenants, fearing eviction, continued to pay illegal rents.[30] A study by a senior member of the department in 1975 indicated that rent control remained ineffective and that fewer than one-fourth of the evicted tenants had been reinstated (Peiris, 1976: 43).

It was difficult, of course, to convince tenants that the odds had been changed sufficiently to justify new initiatives; but more than confidence was involved. Under threat of eviction or in ignorance of provisions, many bona fide tenant cultivators had not been listed on the village-level Paddy Lands Register. Thus a primary source of evidence, legally prima facie evidence, was already biased against the actual cultivators, seriously weakening their chances in administrative inquiries. Landowners had great incentive to register themselves as cultivators, recording the tenant as a laborer, for then the actual cultivator had no rights to security of tenure or a statutory share of the crop. There is no doubt that this phenomenon was widespread.

Although there are areas where a cultivation committee's records

27. *CAR, RCAS* (1969–70: KK 46); my calculations from table 4. It is not clear on what terms "voluntary settlements" were made. Some tenants were reinstated by owners after agreeing to pay traditional rents and to drop charges.

28. Wimaladharma and Clifford (1973: 11) reported that *none* of the evicted tenants in their village study had reported the eviction to authorities. Similar accounts of unreported evictions appear in ARTI (1979: 55); Sanderatne (1974b: 362); Gold (1977: 143, 145). My fieldwork in Hambantota and Batticaloa districts in 1973 supports these findings.

29. Data supplied by the Department of Agrarian Services; my calculations.

30. Interviews with the Senior Assistant Commissioner of Agrarian Services, November 1973 and field officers with experience in various districts.

accurately reflect the tenurial situation, there is decisive evidence of general corruption of the registers. One example will illustrate the dynamics: an owner of both tea and paddy land who was losing some tea estates under the 1972 ceiling legislation decided to intensify paddy operations. He planned to evict his paddy sharecroppers (on tank-fed land in Anaradhapura district) and replace them with wage labor, which was more profitable (especially since the recent increase in paddy prices). The cultivators were paying the traditional (and illegal) half-share rent and could easily be evicted as "they are only village folk"; their names had not been entered in the paddy register in anticipation of the need to evict them (interview, December 1973, Kandy District).

The landowner in this example was not a great landlord, but owned only thirteen acres of paddy; moreover, he was not a resident of the village where the land is located. Yet even this absentee rentier found it possible to circumvent the law by having himself recorded as "cultivator" on the lands. The same phenomenon was discovered by Sanderatne in his field investigations of implementation, though he noted that it was the *resident* landowner who was more likely to succeed in circumventing the law (1974b: 367). I. K. Weerawardena (Ceylon, 1971a: 3, 6), an officer of the Department of Agrarian Services, came to the same conclusion in his study. Wimaladharma and Clifford (1973: 8, 11) discovered the practice in their study in the North Central Province. In Batticaloa district, I found that even Muslim women in purdah were recorded as cultivators.[31] False registration of landlords as cultivators was discovered more recently in a study of villages in Colombo and Kegalle districts (ARTI, 1979: 65). Even the late prime minister, S. W. R. D. Bandaranaike, was listed as a paddy cultivator on his ancestral land in village records, though he stated that this was an unintended error when the point was raised in Parliament.[32]

The Cultivation Committees: "Seeds of a New Society"?

The cultivation committees faced formidable obstacles from the beginning—institutional innovation is inherently difficult. But the evidence

31. Noncultivating men are recorded as cultivators as well, but it is particularly revealing that women in purdah (seclusion) are registered as paddy cultivators. The peculiar tenurial structure of the district exacerbates the problem. Owners engage *mullaikaran* or "watchers," who attend the fields all season and supervise labor gangs hired for peak-season operations. The owners are mockingly known as "postcard cultivators," as their supervision is often limited to sending a postcard ordering the watcher to commence cultivation. The watcher falls somewhere between a tenant and an attached farm laborer, typically receiving both a wage and a crop share, but is not eligible to vote for or serve on cultivation committees. Watchers not only occupy uncertain legal status, and thus find it difficult to challenge their exclusion from the village registers, but fear doing so because of debt dependency and personal ties to owners. Author's field investigations, Batticaloa district, 1973.

32. *PD*, vol. 33 (1958: col. 109). N. M. Perera raises other examples of the same phenomenon in this exchange.

indicates that an additional handicap, one perhaps sufficient to cripple the innovation, was the crisis of confidence engendered by early legal setbacks (Ceylon, 1966; Perera, 1970: 26–30). In many ways the policy model, and even the more restricted act, provided an open-ended role for the cultivators in reorganizing paddy production collectively; measured against this potentiality, the failure is clear, though in other ways the committees proved useful.

The cultivation committees succeeded to varying degrees. Some of the prescribed functions ran afoul of the prerogatives of other departments and the provisions of other laws (irrigation, for example). Enforcement powers of the committees were plagued by adverse court rulings. Everywhere, the committees had severe difficulties in raising funds; without funds, little could be done, and since little was done, it was difficult to convince cultivators to contribute funds so that something could be done (Ceylon, 1971a: 4–6; 1966). The lack of funds made it difficult for the committees to retain qualified staff, and in itself reflected the lack of local commitment to the committees and the inability of the new institutions to enforce their levies. Of the almost fourteen million rupees due as acreage levy in the year of the 1970 amendment, only 2 million rupees, or about 14 percent of the total due, was collected.[33] Even in the best years, collections did not exceed one-third of the levy.

The institutional initiative of the reform was clearly blunted by early legal difficulties that discouraged and disillusioned cultivators, but there were other serious problems. The policy model itself seems to have assumed more latent collective spirit than exists in the villages, at least under prevailing conditions, though more favorable circumstances might have evoked more response.[34] The inclusion of landlords on the committees, a political compromise forced on the minister, led to open conflict in some areas; factional disputes and landlord obstruction were widely reported as causes for organizational difficulties.[35]

The tenurial structure of paddy cultivation also contributed obstacles, though these are hard to assess rigorously. One official with long field-level experience explained that the cultivation committees were particularly inactive in areas where the cultivators had so little land that they were only part-time farmers and thus took little interest in organizations in the paddy sector.[36] For Ceylon as a whole, 41 percent of all

---

33. Calculations from *CAR, RCAS* (1969–70: KK 45); cf. Gold (1977: 101–05).

34. The contentious argument that a great deal of latent collective spirit exists in the villages is made nicely by Hewavitharana (1971).

35. Narayanaswamy (1973: 4); ARTI (1977: 18); ARTI (1979: 66–67, 44); Gold (1977: 111–12). Parliamentary debates also provide examples of landlord obstruction of the committees. Gunawardena's position in Ceylon, *PD*, vol. 37 (1959: col. 709 ff.) and vol. 42 (1961: col. 7222).

36. Interview, November 1973, Colombo. Data necessary to test this proposition do not exist.

paddy holdings were less than one acre in 1962.[37] On all dwarf farms of less than one acre, only 31.9 percent of the operators were full-time cultivators. Significantly, 53.1 percent of these dwarf farmers received the major part of their income from nonagricultural sources.[38] By 1972, the percentage of paddy farmers with less than one acre had reached 65 percent (Ceylon, 1971c). The logic of individual and collective action would suggest that such farmers might not find it worthwhile to commit time, energy, or resources to the cultivation committees.

The cultivation committees did not succeed in the transformational or redistributive functions assigned them in the policy logic. As suggested in the opening section of this chapter, a large part of the failure lay in the inability to resolve a central tension created by attempts toward decentralization and local participatory democracy in a stratified society characterized by embedded production relations. There is decisive evidence that local elites were able to dominate cultivation committees (ARTI, 1977: 18; Gold, 1977: 111–12; Peiris, 1976: 46; ARTI, 1979: 44, 66–67) and indeed some evidence that landlords continued to manipulate committees even after being excluded from them (in 1964) through dependent tenants (ARTI, 1979: 43). There is no evidence that cultivation committees were able to effect a lowering of rents generally, though there are regional exceptions to the half-share *ande* arrangement. Nor were the committees successful in protecting tenants from eviction, registering all tenants in the area, or restoring evicted tenants.

These outcomes were confirmed in a study by the Agrarian Research and Training Institute of paddy cultivation in five representative districts in 1975 which found continued widespread violations of the rental limits; 35 percent of the tenants felt that their tenancies were insecure (ARTI, 1975, pt. 6: 16). The meaning of tenurial "security" for the remaining tenants is problematic; as a study by the same organization concluded (ARTI, 1979: 51): "Generally, the Ambana tenant was relatively secure in tenancy, even though this security was the result of their servility and not through their ability to assert themselves." The tenants in that study continued to pay illegal rents; some provided unpaid labor to landlords; many feared eviction. Evicted tenants had been unable to be reinstated, and a significant minority (a majority in one of the two villages) remained unregistered; "voluntary" surrenders of tenancy often occurred under the threat of economic and social sanctions [ibid.: 54–55, 59–60, 64, 100]) The study concluded that among the many obstacles to gaining new rights, the failure of tenants to identify themselves consciously as a class greatly facilitated landlord dominance, individually and collectively. But as this chapter emphasizes, organized opposition to landlord dominance, however collectively rational and necessary for real

37. Calculations from table 2, pp. 56, 62, in Ceylon, *Census of Agriculture, 1962*, vol. 3.

38. Ibid., vol. 1, p. 33, table 3.

tenure reform, runs counter to the logic of individual quiescence, given the social framework in which production relations are typically embedded.

As in most tenancy reforms, the evidence about effectiveness is mixed, depending largely on local tenurial conditions, and the social-political matrix within which production relations exist.[39] That tenants with greater local social, economic, or—often—physical strength or kinship connections were able to take advantage of the provisions of the Paddy Lands Act is not disputed. Indeed, the emergence of a cash market for tenancy rights (Gold, 1977: 151, 179; Herring, 1977b) and subletting of established tenancies[40] illustrate, somewhat ironically, that the act has created new property rights for some tenants, though hardly in keeping with the objectives of the policy logic. What seems clear, however, is that the act failed to guarantee the redistributive benefits for those sharecroppers originally most in need of them.

Despite the failure of the cultivation committees to transform the paddy sector as envisioned by Gunawardena, there were successes in performing functions of a different kind. The major successes of the committees were in those areas in which no radical departure from existing patterns was required and in which state expenditures were available to encourage participation (minor irrigation works, in particular) (Gold, 1977:

39. Decisive aggregate data on success of the act do not exist. Gerald Peiris (1976) argues that the act was most ineffective in the Kandyan areas; Gold (1977: 187) concurs and attributes this to the more "feudal" attitudes of deference of tenants in these areas, as contrasted to the coastal southwest, where caste animosities and greater political awareness contribute to tenant assertiveness. The five-district ARTI study (1974, 1975) offers some support for this conclusion, but regional exceptions to the illegal half-share rental norm can be misleading. For example, only a minority of tenants in Hambantota district reported illegal rents, but subtenancies are common there, landlords are typically absentee, and tenants lose a large share of the crop, in addition to rent, to gambarayas (middlemen, originally landlords' agents) for various services on extortionate terms (Herring, 1977b; Harriss, 1977: 157; Dias and Wickremanayake, 1977). A later ARTI study (1979) indicated extreme ineffectiveness of the act in sample villages in both Colombo and Kandy districts. Gold's own data (p. 176) indicate primarily a wet-zone–dry-zone difference in the level of rent and offer some support for the Kandyan phenomenon he identifies, though the pattern is mixed and the data, originating from Cultivation Committees, are suspect. A survey by the Central Bank of Ceylon (1969: 18) in 1966–67 found estimated mean rental shares within legal limits in only three of the eighteen districts reported. One of the three (Galle) supports Gold's argument concerning political organization and consciousness; relatively low rents in the other two districts are obviously not due to these factors and almost certainly reflect agroclimatic conditions. Though data on both scores are unreliable, Gold (p. 187) argues, probably correctly, that rent control has been more effective in areas where relatively fewer evictions were reported.

40. Such subtenants in Hambantota district, where I did field research in 1973, were called "atha yata" cultivators—literally, "under the hand" in the sense of the English "under the thumb," meaning dependent and subservient (Herring, 1977b: 139; cf. Dias and Wickremanayake, 1977; Gold, 1977: 164).

116; Peiris, 1976: 45; Raza, 1970). Though important for development, these linkage and distributive functions in some ways undermined the aspirational and transformational aspects of the policy model. Paddy laborers, the most depressed agrarian class, were eventually excluded from any participation related to the committees. The committees became arenas for factional and political disputes, landlord obstructionism, and landlord–tenant conflict rather than organs of a collectivist transformation of agriculture. Ironically, as resources were channeled from the state to the committees, local elites were in some cases able to use the "seeds of the new society,"via patronage dependency, as mechanisms for reinforcing the old.

Citing these antidemocratic features and administrative incapacities, the minister of agriculture in 1973, Hector Kobbekaduwa, introduced the Agricultural Lands Bill; the major provisions were to include agricultural lands other than paddy lands under the basic provisions of the Paddy Lands Act and to replace the elected cultivation committees with appointed ones. Parliamentary debate on the bill stressed continuing evictions on paddy lands. The minister argued that the committees could not be effective under existing conditions of bitter factionalism and conflict in the villages. The primary motives of the minister were almost certainly somewhat different, of course; the appointment power would be an important resource for political patronage.[41] But his analysis has force: popularly elected bodies cannot effectively reconstruct the village power structure if they themselves represent the unreconstructed power structure. Nor can villages characterized by conflict and distrust consistently elect local bodies of any real authority. Moreover, the government argued that appointive powers and greater political penetration of local developmental institutions were necessary to translate the government's mandate into effective policy implementation.

New local institutions for developing agriculture multiplied in the 1973–77 period, and the authority and responsibility of cultivation committees became blurred and disputed. The transformational vision was transferred to a different kind of land reform—experimentation with collective farms on land appropriated under the 1972 ceiling legislation—and the cultivation committees were integrated more securely into the regime's effort to control local bodies for political support (ARTI, 1979: 66–67, 83–85; ARTI, 1980: 40–41).

41. Speech reported on the Sri Lanka Broadcasting Company, October 4, 1973; also *Ceylon Daily News*, October 5, 1973. It was widely believed that the minister was broadening his appointment powers to build a rural political power base, as other ministers of agriculture and rural development had done. Indeed, some of the strongest opposition to the Paddy Lands Act originally was expressed in the fear that Gunawardena would use it to create a radical rural power base. There is evidence that the new appointed rural bodies were used for partisan and patronage ends in the mid-1970s (ARTI, 1977; ARTI, 1979).

After the overwhelming electoral victory of the United National Party in 1977, the new government moved immediately to dismantle the vertical political patronage network of the SLFP minister of agriculture, including the appointed agricultural productivity committees and cultivation committees. Appointed cooperative managers were likewise dismissed, sometimes being spontaneously beaten by local people for their high-handed and corrupt ways. These institutions, along with other appointed local bodies, were widely perceived as political tools of the SLFP, mechanisms for rewarding supporters and victimizing opponents. Land-reform institutions thus followed the pattern stressed by Robert Kearney (1973)—the increasing politicization of development processes in Sri Lanka. A recent study by the Agrarian Research and Training Institute (1979: 84) found that, with the change in governments in 1977, UNP partisans simply replaced SLFP partisans in local appointed bodies, with no improvement in the representation of the weaker sections of village society. As the major parties tend to be structurally isomorphic at the local level, this is not a surprising result.

A new Agrarian Services Act (no. 58 of 1979) is the most recent successor of the Paddy Lands Act; its provisions institutionalize the long political drift away from Gunawardena's vision, particularly with regard to cultivation committees. The original concept of village-level elected bodies of cultivators charged with a broad range of developmental, regulatory and conciliation functions has disappeared. The act provides instead for agrarian services committees, appointed by the Commissioner of Agrarian Services, of not more than fourteen persons; farmers are limited by statute to no more than six of these positions, evidently relegated to permanent minority status (part 5: section 43.3). The committees have vaguely defined functions as a conveyor belt for implementation of other provisions in the act, as directed by the commissioner, in addition to two important traditional functions: maintenance of land registers and collection of acreage levy. The act also provides for the appointment of cultivation officers (pt. 6: 55) who look to be a reincarnation of the traditional irrigation headmen (*vel vidane*) who were replaced by the cultivation committees in the Paddy Lands Act. The agrarian services committees are far removed from village society compared to the cultivation committees and seem likely to be dominated by officials rather than by farmers. The provisions for protection of tenants are little changed, though the problem of subtenancy is explicitly recognized (pt. 1: 5.9) and a formula for determination of rent ceilings somewhat less favorable to tenants is established (pt. 1: 17.2). Eviction complaints must go through the commissioner's staff, and appeals are to be heard by the Court of Appeals rather than by a special Paddy Lands Board of Review (pt. 1: 5). The vision of employing tenure-reform legislation for agrarian transformation has for the time being been abandoned.

Incrementalism and Tenure Reform: Costs and Limits

The ideal liberal incremental model of politics and policy is cybernetic—a sensitive political system responds to defects in on-going programs and corrects problems as they arise; though the path may be circuitous and progress slow, the original goal is ultimately reached. In contrast to tenure reforms in some parts of the subcontinent, the Paddy Lands Act was a serious program, not a symbolic sop to peasant unrest or electoral exigencies. The cybernetic potential was real: progress was extensively monitored and corrections continually legislated; feedback loops were in place and functioning. The act was amended in 1958, 1961, 1964, 1966, and 1970, extended to other agricultural lands, and fundamentally altered, in 1973 and 1979. The evidence from twenty years of enforcement allows several firm conclusions and raises serious doubts about the potentiality of the cybernetic-incremental process in the liberal state for effecting genuine land-tenure reform.

The policy logic of Gunawardena's model proved to be remarkably accurate. Those provisions deleted from the draft in the final legislation through political compromises forced on the minister by conservative forces inside and outside the government—crop insurance, adequate credit facilities, immediate restoration of evicted tenants, exclusion of landlords from the cultivation committees, and so on—proved crippling, as predicted and for the reasons specified in the policy logic. The ambivalent and contradictory political will behind the land reform was a direct consequence of the dynamics of electoral tactics and coalition-building typical of parliamentary democracies. Paddy tenants were only one group to be considered, and not an organized, articulate, or powerful group at that; concessions to the more powerful and equally numerous landed interests considerably vitiated the potential for effective redistributive policy. The vector sum of forces for and against reform was positive, but just barely so. The political will to pass and enact the Paddy Lands Bill was thus critically compromised; the act itself was, as Gunawardena said, "castrated" in the intragovernmental struggle over the draft. The crippling compromises of the final version represent those conflicts concretely: political birth defects.

But even the compromised act had more potential than was realized in practice. It is important to emphasize the role of the courts and changes in regime, and particularly the two in conjunction. Gunawardena's model presupposed enthusiastic and compensatory political support from above in order to generate tenant confidence and promote institutional innovation. But changes of regime raised questions about continued political commitment to the act and critically delayed necessary amendments, eroding tenant confidence. After the death of S. W. R. D. Bandaranaike and the exit of Gunawardena, the act fell into the hands of its original enemies; accordingly, its linkage and distributive functions were stressed over its redistributive and transformational aspects.

The most serious consequence of the ambivalent political commitment and changes of regime was failure to protect the implementation of the act from the courts. The independent judiciary, dominated by a body of law predicated on protection of existing property relations and strict separation of state powers, was thus allowed to contravene the intent of Parliament expressed in the act. This obstacle alone, which is a permanent structural feature of the liberal state, was sufficient to cripple implementation, though the act certainly faced other difficulties.

Implementation of the acts thus raises a serious question about the cybernetic-incremental model: the damage done in an incremental reform may prove cumulative and negate subsequent incremental attempts to achieve the original objectives. The early experience of unpunished evictions and delays in restoration of tenancy rights even to those tenants who were able to establish their cases, as well as corruption of the land records that serve as the basis for protecting other cultivators, undermined the confidence and dampened any potential enthusiasm of cultivators for the new institutional forms that were a hallmark of the act. This damage, too, was cumulative; without local support the institutions could not develop properly and, lacking adequate development, could not stimulate local commitment. Ambivalence and discontinuities in state support for the reform, as evidenced particularly by the failure to intervene quickly to save the act from the judiciary, allowed the corruption of land records and the de facto or de jure deprivation of tens of thousands of tenant families of both their traditional and newly legislated rights.

Despite energetic enforcement efforts by the Department of Agrarian Services, the tenant activism and involvement upon which the policy logic depended were not forthcoming. The department could not convince tenants that cultivation committees or its own officers could protect them from eviction; acquiescence in illegal, disadvantageous tenurial relationships remained an objectively rational (and common) tenant response. Nor could the department adequately explain to tenants why evictions went unpunished or why restoration was difficult. Without tenant activism, the department simply could not intervene and regulate effectively as it must in the classic tenure-reform policy model.

In sum, it seems that three central characteristics of the "politically developed" liberal state proved incompatible with effective tenure reform in Sri Lanka: (1) bargaining and compromise as process in producing legislation; (2) alteration of regimes between parties with meaningfully opposed ideologies and programs; and (3) an autonomous and independent judiciary.

Does this mean that tenure reform is impossible in the liberal state? The answer has to be no; one can conceive of circumstances in which Gunawardena's original draft might have been passed and regimes sympathetic to the rural poor retained power long enough to institutionalize the power of the cultivation committees. But such speculation ignores another kind of structural determination in the liberal state: the translation of the agrarian structure into democratic politics insured that the legislation would not be everything that tenants needed. The irony of tenure reform as policy is that half-a-loaf may in fact *not* be better than none; the compromised act produced a net deterioration in the situation of uncounted thousands of paddy tenants and changed nothing for others.

But if the Paddy Lands Act had many enemies, what of its friends? Ceylon's leftist parties were well-organized, articulate, and long established relative to other Ceylonese parties and relative to left forces in most of the subcontinent. What was their contribution to land reform?

The role of the established left was positive but limited by its social base and theory. The predictions of left parliamentarians from the debates on the Paddy Lands Bill beginning in 1951 were accurate; their suggestions, if heeded, would have improved the act's prospects. The left opposition supported Gunawardena's efforts to save key provisions of the draft and to correct defects in the act. But the efficacy of the left was severely restricted by the absence of class-based rural organizations or a network of rural cadres. The political morphology of Sri Lanka might have been different, of course, had the Tamil plantation proletariat not been disenfranchised at the beginning of the independent period, though the urban orientation of the left parties and the conflicting objective and perceived interests of plantation workers and paddy cultivators would certainly have prevented any automatic development of broad-based political support for agrarian reform.

Indeed, the Paddy Lands Act did not address the problems of the rural proletariat, the most disadvantaged agrarian class. Table 3.2 presents comparative data for the period when the Paddy Lands Act was being drafted. Paddy laborers were the poorest of all agrarian classes, and in the most precarious economic position—the highest ratio of debt to property or income and the slimmest margin between expenditures and income. Relative both to other classes in the paddy sector and to laborers in the plantation sector (excluding Tamils), the paddy laborer derived the least benefit and security from tilling the fields.

The tenure-reform model, even in the aspirational and innovative formulation of Ceylon's 1958 act, envisions improvement in the condition only of those tillers who have some hold on the land less tenuous than that of the field laborer. The reasons for excluding the laborers were partly political, partly paradigmatic. The Paddy Lands Act had to be sold politically as a measure to increase rice production or it could not have been sold at all. In the early 1950s, Ceylon was already beginning to feel the dislocation of having to import more than half the nation's rice requirements. A dominant policy paradigm (Ceylon, 1955) attributes low productivity to "tenurial defects," but the hiring of wage labor in paddy

Table 3.2 Comparative Economic Condition of Agrarian Classes in
Ceylon Prior to the Paddy Lands Act

| | Average Monthly: | | Property | Outstanding |
	Income	Expenditures	Value (Rupees)	Debt
Paddy landlord	168	141	11,496	210
Paddy owner-cultivator	110	93	4,058	108
Paddy tenant cultivator	95	86	1,409	86
Paddy laborer	58	57	847	85
Rubber laborer	81	78	1,147	26
Coconut laborer	64	59	1,171	64
Tea laborer	77	75	918	15
Unspecified agricultural laborer	74	73	1,247	57

SOURCE: *Final Report of the Economic Survey of Rural Ceylon*, Sessional Paper no. 11 of
1954, p. 42. These figures exclude estate-resident laborers (i.e., mostly non-citizen Tamils)
and have been rounded to the nearest rupee.

fields does not figure as a defect in the model. Politically, the paddy sector
was a zero sum game; any effort to reallocate a share of the social surplus
to field laborers would have been resisted by small owners and tenants
who were themselves poor, as well as by the rural elite. The solution to
"landlessness" in Ceylon was held to be the creation of new land for the
landless—the expensive colonization projects in the Dry Zone (cf. Farmer,
1957; Ellman, et al., 1976). The landless laborers remain an especially
"awkward class"—an embarrassment even to the more radical reformers
of South Asia, tillers whose claim on the land is even more tenuous than
that of the most insecure tenant, both in policy logic and village culture.

The measurable consequences of the Paddy Lands Act were perhaps
more unintended than intended: tenants were evicted, incorrect records
of production relations became established legal evidence, the cultivation committees floundered and eventually were dissolved. In conclusion, Ceylon's experience with a carefully planned and seriously implemented tenure-reform model seems to support the logic of land to the
tiller rather than tenure reform. In policy logic which appeared before the
1971 insurrection rerouted land reforms in Sri Lanka, the *Draft Agricultural Development Plan, 1971–1977*, agreed: "The landlord with his superior command of resources can always tilt the balance in his favor and
frustrate the objectives of the Paddy Lands Act. . . . The transfer of ownership to the tiller of the soil appears to be the only permanent solution
to the problem (Ceylon, n.d. III: para. 63)."

4 Land Ceilings in Pakistan: An Agrarian Bourgeois Revolution?

I can't nationalize the land. It's not possible. Tomorrow, if someone wants to do it, let him try. At the same time, I can't allow bigger estates to remain. I must cut them down so that production increases and the feudal power is eliminated.
—*Zulfikar Ali Bhutto, President of Pakistan*
Address to the Karachi Chamber of Commerce

A land-to-the-tiller reform eliminates landlords as a class and landlordism as a social institution. A tenure reform alters the relations between landlords and tenants, theoretically in the direction of more equitable distribution and improved efficiency. A ceiling-redistributive reform does neither, but takes land from large owners and redistributes it among the landless and land-poor. The ceiling may thus be seen as a simple redistributive measure—a response to the perceived inefficiency and injustice of a skewed distribution of holdings and the political consequences of both. But, as importantly, the policy logic of ceiling reform has included transformational goals as well—fundamental alterations in the agrarian structure. In Pakistan, the legitimation of land reforms has been transformational, though the reforms were not. The transformations involve the "eradication of feudalism," meaning essentially the creation of good landlords from bad, modern entrepreneurs from traditional parasites.

The ceiling-redistributive reform has become a common response to agrarian and regime crises in South Asia. It is a new response; unlike the intervention-regulatory tenure-reform model, the policy was not employed by colonial regimes. The normative model posits as unacceptable on a variety of grounds existing concentration of ownership of agricultural holdings and the social, economic, and political consequences of the vast disparities between large owners and the landless. The response is to set a ceiling above which agricultural land will be "resumed" by the state, with or without compensation, and subsequently redistributed among poor peasants or laborers.

Though ceilings in practice have been rather mild in their attack on the landed elites of South Asia, particularly in India and Pakistan, the normative principles underlying ceiling reform are quite radical. The legitimacy of those institutions and processes which produce and maintain skewed distributions of land is challenged. Central principles of capitalist legitimation—functional inequalities and unlimited accumulation of private property in the means of production—are questioned on grounds of justice, economic efficiency, and political democracy. There is, then, a paradox and contradiction in ceiling reform in capitalist societies in which the landed gentry retains disproportionate political power. The transformations posited in the policy logic—from feudal stagnation to entrepreneurial dynamism—seem essential, yet the means seem antithetical to the normative structure of a bourgeois society and to the politics of an agrarian society: attacks by the state on the private property of the gentry in favor of the landless. This paradox is reflected in the policy contradictions of ceiling reforms in the subcontinent.

The legislative acts which incorporate the ceiling model include the most important land reforms in the past twenty-five years. In Pakistan, the major land reforms have been ceilings, imposed first by Ayub Khan in 1959 and later by Zulfikar Ali Bhutto in 1972 (with further reductions in 1977). In Sri Lanka, the first ceiling legislation was the 1972 Land Reforms Law, the first land reform applied to the plantation sector of the economy and the first Act of the new republic. The 1975 amendment to that law extended the land reform to the estates of public companies, foreign and domestic, substantially nationalizing the plantation sector.

In India, ceiling legislation described as such has come piecemeal, as the constituent States have responded differentially to reformist urgings of the Center (urgings which have been more ambiguous than is commonly believed). But the major thrust of early land reforms in independent India, the "abolition of intermediaries" (particularly, in the titles of acts, zamindars), was functionally a ceiling-redistributive model; the intermediary was allowed to retain for personal use a limited area (khudkasht, etc.—the "home farm"), while the remainder was made the proprietary interest of the tenure holder immediately below the intermediary in the land-tenure hierarchy. The first round of ceiling legislation proper in India followed in the late 1950s and early 1960s. Though implementation varied from State to State, there was very little serious implementation of the acts. In the early 1970s, a new round of ceilings was urged upon the States by the Center following serious concern over rural violence in the late 1960s. More recently, implementation of ceilings and redistribution of surplus land to the rural poor were used as one justification for and priority of the state of emergency imposed in June of 1975 by Indira Gandhi.

The picture of rural society presupposed in the ceiling model varies with the agronomic and political situation, but several features differentiate the perceptions from those which inform the policy logic of tenure reform. Recognition of the structural power imbalance of rural society is central and is itself one of the justifications for reform. The agrarian system is viewed as unproductive, unjust, premodern in a pejorative sense, and inimical to rural democracy. Following the perception of systemic defects, the model posits need for systemic change, and is thus transformational. It should be stressed that the *form* of the model, the policy logic, is transformational; the actual policy and its impact reflect the vector sum of social forces—needs of particular regimes, class conflict, and the ordinary politics and administration of implementation. And whatever the policy logic of ceiling reforms, they tend to appear in times of political crisis.

Good Landlords and Bad Landlords, Parasites and Entrepreneurs[1]

Perhaps the most common adjective attached to "landlord" by advocates of land reform in political and planning documents is "parasitic." The clear implication is that landlords do not do whatever they should do in return for the share of the social surplus which they appropriate. The colonial rulers of South Asia distinguished between "good landlords," who invested in the land and provided services to tenants, and "bad landlords," who did neither.[2] Indeed, a major goal of colonial land policy was to create a class of progressive landlords patterned after the English gentry (cf. S. Ambirajan, 1978: chap. 5; Merillat, 1970: 15 and passim; Stokes, 1959). Nationalist thinking in British India elaborated and developed the critique of the bad landlord; the word *zamindar* (literally "landholder") came to *mean* the parasitic and collaborationist landlord. Jawaharlal Nehru argued in 1928: "To our misfortune, we have zamindars everywhere, and like a blight they have prevented all healthy growth."[3]

The criticism of bad landlords on social and economic grounds was based on the confluence of specific normative and empirical arguments; empirically, the landlords were held to be nonproductive, and normatively this nonproductive status delegitimized the landlord's claim to

1. This section closely follows Herring (1979b).
2. For a classic example, Malcolm Darling, *The Punjab Peasant in Prosperity and Debt* (1932: 270–71).
3. The word *zamindar* literally means "one who holds the land," but in political rhetoric came to mean a cateogry of proprietor created by British revenue reforms, a pure intermediary. The term was a land-revenue category, defining rights to agricultural income and tax obligations, not a structural-functional category such as "rentier." In the Permanent Settlement areas of India, the zamindars were indeed rentiers—sometimes absentee, sometimes not—but both in the *zamindari* areas and elsewhere there were categories of landholders not termed "zamindars" whose tenurial position was equivalent to that of the majority of the zamindars. To confuse matters more, "zamindar" in the Punjab, Sind, and other areas could mean anything from a great landlord to a small peasant proprietor (*kisan*). Confusing as the revenue terminology is, the tenurial structures were not so esoteric as is often believed, and the major agrarian classes can be fit into general functional categories—rentier, supervising landlord, owner-cultivator, mortgagee, protected tenant, tenant-at-will, etc.— and these categories are far more useful than the technical revenue terms. Nehru's remarks are cited by Congress theoretician H. D. Malaviya (1954: 20). On colonial property and revenue systems, Baden-Powell (1892), vol. 1, chap. 4–5.

privilege. In some formulations, nonproductive was escalated to counter-productive. Reflecting a major strand of leftist Congress thinking, Nehru asked rhetorically: "What does he (the *zamindar*) do to get his share or deserve it? Nothing at all or practically nothing. He just takes a big share in the produce—his rent—without helping in any way the work of pro-duction. He thus becomes a fifth wheel in the coach—not only unnec-essary, but an actual encumbrance, and a burden on the land" (Malaviya, 1954: 56). Nehru termed "the land problem" the "outstanding and over-whelming problem of India" and felt that the "feudal relics" obstructed not only agricultural but also industrial growth, and thus the fundamen-tal prospects of the new nation (ibid.: 55, 73; cf. Nehru, 1960: 290–96).

The same intellectual currents ran in Pakistan, though not so broad or deep. The Hari (sharecropper) Enquiry Committee of Sind (1947–48) quoted approvingly an unnamed American economist to the effect that "next to war, pestilence and famine, the worst thing that can happen to a rural community is absentee landlordism."[4] Indeed, this particular quo-tation had fairly wide currency in South Asian agrarian reform circles. But the core meaning of *absentee* did not necessarily denote physical absence from the land; the Hari Enquiry Committee noted: "Absentee landlordism can take two forms, namely, a landlord who does not reside on his lands and a landlord who, though he may reside on his lands, takes little or no interest in [their] management and development" (p. 19). The committee argued that such nonfunctioning landlords left the tenants without aid or direction and subjected them to harrassment by interme-diaries—the *kamgars* of Sind, for example—who managed the land and extracted rents.

The landlord who abdicates his responsibilities on the land forfeits his moral claim to privilege in this normative model. The Hari Enquiry Committee stated: "The advantageous position of the big land-owners in relation to the *haris* which they employ demands that all such zamindars in virtue of the privileges which they enjoy should take a personal and paternal interest and adopt an enlightened and progressive attitude in matters concerned with the welfare of their *haris*" (pp. 20–21). The good landlord of Sind was thought to be the zamindar "of sufficient enterprise and sense of duty to take a paternal interest in his *haris*." This analytical division of the landlord class foreshadowed subsequent official thinking. The West Pakistan Land Reforms Commission stated in 1959: "We admit that there are progressive landlords, but they are in a minority" (Paki-stan, 1959b: 19). This bifurcation, and the argument that not all landlords are parasitic, opened the possibility of land reforms with transforma-

---

4. Government of Sind, *Report of the Government Hari Enquiry Committee, 1947–48* (No date or place of publication is given; presumably Karachi), p. 19. This interesting report is in a curious way an apologia for the Sind zamindars, and a plea for their voluntary reform, written by a committee headed by a large zamindar. The *hari* is a sharecropper, a tenant-at-will.

tional aspects, designed to change undeserving landlords into deserving ones, which would avoid the political costs of a full confrontation with the landlord class as implied in the policy logic of land to the tiller.

The notion of what a landlord should do to deserve his share has varied over time. In the traditional setting, the "good landlord" provided a range of functions, as the landlord–tenant nexus was frequently of the patron–client form. The modern "good landlord" was not expected to perform the diffuse, personalistic noneconomic functions of a traditional patron, but *was* expected to provide such services as modern farm management, technical information, working capital, fixed capital improvements, and so on. The traditional good landlord was to be a patron, the modern good landlord, an entrepreneur.

The services of the traditional "good landlord" seem to have declined over time in South Asia for a number of reasons. Perhaps the cynical view has merit: as courts and a new administrative apparatus in the colonial period began to enforce contracts and uphold the landlords' property claims, the necessity of good patron–client relations diminished and with it the services provided by patrons.[5] Likewise, the extension of administrative systems (and political parties in some areas) into rural society obviated the need for some landlord services. In any event, at the time of independence, there was a feeling in both reformist and Marxist circles in South Asia that the traditional "good landlord" had become parastic and anachronistic. Consider, for example, the position of a leading Communist theoretician, E. M. S. Namboodiripad (1954: 19–20): "In mediaeval days, landlordism was a social, political, and cultural institution, as well as economic. But shorn of all these functions, the Malabar *janmis* [landlords] today are only dead corpses of their own forefathers." After figuring the total rent paid by tenants to landlords, he concluded: "If the payment of this amount goes hand in hand with some social service, rendered by the landlords as a class, it would be quite justified."

But contemporary landlords, "shorn of all these functions," the diffuse traditional social services, must justify their rent by providing economic services. Namboodiripad asked:

> But does it [the landlord class] justify its economic importance by performing any useful function in that sphere as does the entrepreneur in modern capitalist industry? Does it provide capital, either short-term or long-term, to the cultivator who needs it? Does it construct and improve irrigation sources and prevent the preventible drought? Does it carry on any research work to make agriculture up to date and scientific?

After concluding that the landlord class does not perform these economic functions, and certainly no longer has the social, cultural, political

5. For evidence that this was the case in Kerala State, Verghese (1970: 29, 41, and passim). For a treatment of similar phenomena in an adjoining region, Scott (1972). It should be added that consolidation of the state decreased the need for attachment to a patron for physical protection.

responsibilities of an earlier time, Namboodiripad argued for the abolition of landlordism. There is an interesting point in this conclusion;
Namboodiripad's Marxist vision of what modern landlords *should* do to
justify rents was the same as that in the avowedly capitalist planning
circles of Pakistan: large landowners must justify their privileges through
performance of modern, scientific, entrepreneurial functions. The dis-
agreement comes in what should be done: should the landlords be dispossessed or transformed?

Official policy logic in Pakistan has sought to justify land reforms
as policy tools, along with powerful economic incentives, to transform
the "feudal"[6] rent-receivers into progressive agricultural capitalists (while
simultaneously continuing the colonial policy of putting lands into the
hands of new potential entrepreneurs: civil servants and military officers,
for example). The "good landlord" is explicitly recognized as the rural
counterpart of the urban entrepreneur. This policy logic in important reformist and certain Marxist analyses converges: "feudal" relations on the
land, already disintegrating, must be thoroughly rooted out; the capitalist
revolution in agriculture is held to be a necessary historical stage and a
political imperative.

Land Ceilings in Pakistan: Justifying Redistribution

The justification for a ceiling-redistributive reform has as its core the
notion that existing concentrations of land are unjust. This argument is
buttressed by the claim that the landlord class came upon their wealth
by dubious or even illegitimate means. In elaboration, the argument is
often couched in terms of the scarcity of agricultural land and the pressure of population on the land, which produced oligopolistic control of
land resources with unfair consequences. The ceiling-redistributive model
thus has a double-edged justification: it seems unjust that the primary,
and limited, resource of rural society should be concentrated in the hands
of a tiny fraction of the population, however they obtained it; and it seems
unfair that some—the landless—should be reduced to the levels of poverty, hunger, and deprivation that result from the unequal distribution.
This double-edged argument is made in noneconomic terms as well: the
extreme concentration of land bestows inordinate political and social power

---

6. The word "feudal" should always be construed as surrounded by quotation marks,
though it is not always presented that way in the text. The question of whether or not one
can usefully apply the term "feudal" to South Asian agrarian configurations is debatable
and too complex to be addressed here. In political and planning usage in South Asia, the
term refers to something like the "bad landlords" discussed in this chapter (who are often
referred to simply as "feudals")—parasitic, backward landlords who exercise pervasive personal and oppressive social and political control over sharecroppers and other dependents.
For more detailed treatment in the Pakistani context, Herring (1979a: 520–25). Theoreticians in India have adopted the softening adjective *semi* and precipitated a lively debate on
"semifeudal" production relations.

on a few, whereas a great number—the landless—lack both social standing and political rights.

Economic efficiency also figures in the justification: the largest estates are too large for proper management and are less than optimally exploited. This argument, too, cuts two ways. Not only are the largest estates too large to be efficient, but the smallest farms are too small to be efficient; a redistribution creating economically sized small farms, it is argued, would increase production.[7]

The interaction of these factors was expressed by the West Pakistan Land Reforms Commission (1959) in arguing for ceiling legislation. After reviewing the statistics on land concentration, the commission noted:

> These statistics in themselves do not reflect the real situation. They do reveal vast disparities of wealth and incomes in the rural society, but disparities in wealth are not necessarily a social or economic evil in a system based on private ownership of means of production. It is the peculiar social, economic, and political consequences flowing from what amounts to an institutional monopoly of land in a primarily agrarian society, which is of key importance for our purposes, and we proceed to consider these consequential effects as they operate in the field of landlord-tenant relations and determine the attitudes and behaviours of both the landlord and the tenant. [Pakistan, 1959b: 14]

These effects are then listed (pp. 14–20). We may note here the extraordinary force given land-tenure variables in the policy logic. Socially, "those who do not own land are relegated to a socially inferior position with all the disabilities of that position." Economically, tenants are too impoverished to invest; landlords have wealth but lack incentives or initiative to invest. Moreover, tenant incentives are vitiated by rental exactions, and there are diseconomies of small scale. The net economic effect was held to be stagnation in total production and a decline in per capita production. Politically, "the right of franchise . . . becomes an idle weapon in the hands of many . . . as political power continues to remain with the privileged few." The political-economic fusion is explicit: "An individual may belong to a free society, but if he is economically dependent upon another he is seldom a free agent to exercise his political rights."

The policy logic of the committee is cogent, but there is a marked discrepancy between its acute analysis of the problem and the extent and type of response recommended. If the landlord–tenant organization of production results in microeconomic situations which decrease productivity (and the committee quotes Alfred Marshall to show that this is the case), then size alone is not the problem, and a ceiling is not the answer; a solution would require changing the microeconomic situation of tenants (reduction of rents, for example, a policy explicitly rejected) or vest-

7. For a paradigmatic treatment, Dorner, *Land Reform and Economic Development* (1972). There will be further elaboration of the economic logic in chapter 9.

ing land in the tiller. Likewise, if landlessness deprives an individual of fundamental social and political dignity and rights,[8] then sufficient surplus land must be appropriated to eradicate "economic dependence" through imposition of a very low ceiling and a radical redistribution; this solution the committee did not seriously consider.

The committee did not draw the logical conclusions from its inquiry; to have done so would have been an exercise in political futility. Indeed, the *justification* for a ceiling-redistributive reform provided the very reasons for the political impossibility of carrying it out: the powerlessness and dependence of the rural poor and the great concentrations of power—political, social, and economic—in the hands of the landed elite.

A second issue in the normative case for the ceiling-redistributive policy model is the legitimacy of the original mode of acquisition of the property. First, if the property was acquired in ways that are held to be illegitimate, the case for continued ownership of large estates is seriously weakened. Second, if the mode of acquisition was illegitimate, there is no case for compensating those whose land is appropriated. The position of such intermediaries as the Indian zamindars was weak for this reason. Their rights in land were considered illegitimate and antinational, as estates were acquired in return for service to the colonial state. The Agrarian Reforms Committee of the Muslim League, in a position later adopted in the *First Five Year Plan*, argued: "Landlordism in Pakistan is a historical accident which has already conferred vast advantages and profits on generations of its beneficiaries and it would be illogical to make it a justification for the conferment of further advantages" (Pakistan, 1956: 128). The Planning Board argued that the case for compensation of most landlords "would not bear any scrutiny," as their estates "would be found to have been acquired by dubious means or conferred by British rulers for loyal assistance given in establishing and consolidating their hold on this country" (ibid.: 129).

But how would one distinguish "dubious means" of land acquisition from other means? The dubious means that the Planning Board had in mind covered a variety of situations, but had in common their nonmarket character. Most of the great "feudal" estates were acquired through mechanisms other than market operations: physical force, grants for military or administrative service, official influence, and so on. The West Pakistan Land Reforms Commission noted that: "Governments preceding the British Rule 'found it convenient to secure the sword of the brave and the prayer of the pious man, to pacify the deposed chiefs and to reward powerful servants by assigning to them the Ruler's share of the produce of the land in particular villages or tracts'" (Pakistan, 1959b: 5). This strategy was of course continued by the British.

8. For treatment of these dynamics in rural Punjab, buttressing the policy logic, Alavi (1971); Saghir Ahmad (1977: esp. 91–126).

Logically, a number of policy responses to the agrarian defects speci-fied in this model were possible. The most direct response was a land-to-the-tiller policy. But there were important normative concerns, and over-whelming political constraints, which diverted the policy logic into other channels.

The Planning Board of Pakistan, in the *First Five Year Plan*, noted that East Pakistan had instituted a radical reform that "seeks to abolish the institution of landlordship." The board went to some lengths to jus-tify its own recommendation of preserving the existing social organiza-tion of production: "We do not advocate the drastic step of abolishing landownership in West Pakistan, as it will generate tensions and insta-bility and create a number of difficult problems. Private property is a recognized institution in the community because of the values it en-shrines for the individual and social development" (Pakistan, 1956: 128). The Land Reforms Commission established by Ayub Khan in 1958 reaf-firmed the position: "For the healthy growth of the economy it is essen-tial that private ownership of the means of production is accompanied by free competition and equal opportunities" (Pakistan, 1959b: 14–15). Given the prior acceptance of private property in land, "tenancy is inevitable." However:

> "There is nothing inherently wrong with the institution of tenancy, but if there is no proper adjustment in the terms of tenancy, production incentives are adversely affected." (ibid.: 15).

The normative basis of the ceiling model in Pakistan was thus: (*a*) private property is the legitimate organizing principle for society, partic-ularly because of its implications for individual development and politi-cal liberty: (*b*) radical reform entails serious social costs, particularly with regard to stability; (*c*) one dominant existing manifestation of private property in agriculture—i.e., landlordism—thus cannot be directly at-tacked or abolished, but must be transformed along lines congruent with modern, capitalist notions of efficiency and rationality.

The policy implications were certainly not laissez-faire, however. The rulers of Pakistan in the mid-1950s faced serious agrarian and polit-ical problems. One was the critical and deteriorating food situation, the result of agricultural stagnation.[9] Politically, the independent power of the great landlords had destabilized successive regimes and prevented consolidation of the state.[10] Socially, the abusive and oppressive practices

9. The *Second Five Year Plan* discussed the dislocations resulting from diversion of foreign exchange from other imports to food, cuts in the development program, and "serious distortion" of Plan priorities (Pakistan, 1960: 28).

10. This position is also taken by Bredo (1961: 270), who stresses the role of landlord intrigues and intransigence in the fall of regimes prior to Ayub Khan; cf. Feldman (1967: 60–61 and passim); Rounaq Jahan (1972: 56–57). For treatment of the political conflicts and instability of the period prior to martial law, and the role of landlords therein, Sayeed (1967:

of the "feudal" landlords offended the modernist legitimating themes of
the new nation and threatened rural unrest. Continuous intervention and
regulation in the peasant sector were rejected, but changes to facilitate
the modernization and rationalization of agriculture were considered imperative.

The tenant problem was a source of continuous official concern, but
there was a curious strain of policy logic which held that the tenant problem would wither away with the coming of agrarian capitalism. The
Planning Board concluded that protection of tenants by the government
was necessary in the *short run* because of landlord abuses—"the ugliness
of prevailing conditions"—but the policy conclusion was classically liberal. Through operation of the ceiling reforms, tenants would be freed
from the monopoly power of landlords and would gain "equality, opportunity, dignity, and freedom." Finally: "We hope that in course of time
their relations will come to approximate those prevailing in the industrially advanced countries" (Pakistan, 1956: 130).

The argument that once concentrations of land were broken up the
government's role in tenant–landlord affairs should revert to a laissez-
faire position was dominant in official policy thinking during the Ayub
period. After the reforms of 1959 supposedly achieved this equalization,
the Land Commission reported in 1966: "Tenants who do not discharge
their obligations . . . should have no sympathy and cannot be considered
worthy of protection from a Government, which is so much interested
in the restoration of normal relations between all classes of population
and increasing agricultural production" (Pakistan, 1966: 24).

The ceiling reforms were thus justified as moving toward those conditions presupposed by liberal capitalist ideology: contractual bargaining
among equals, just as it was presumed to be "in the industrially advanced
countries." When this was achieved, rural stability and harmony, as well
as agricultural growth, would characterize the agrarian system, and the
government could revert to its proper laissez-faire stance (including, as is
common but somewhat contradictory, an aggressive role in subsidizing
entrepreneurs).

The Logic of Setting the Ceiling: How Much Is Too Much?

The acreage limit imposed by the ceiling depends on the justification for
the measure and what it is meant to accomplish. This problem is complicated by the apparent incongruity between restriction or confiscation
of landed property and a laissez-faire or supportive policy toward industrial and commercial property. How can a case be made for land ceilings

---

60–92). Ayub Khan himself acknowledged the role of land reforms in diminishing the political power of the landlords in his autobiography (1967: 88).

in this context? The *First Five Year Plan* (Pakistan, 1956: 128) recognized the difficulty and stated:

> The argument is frequently advanced that if concentration of land ownership is undesirable and in conflict with the social policies of our country, so must also be concentrated of ownership of other forms of wealth—factories, urban property, industrial shares, government securities or cash. We consider that the ownership of land is clearly distinguished from other forms of wealth. Landowners who do not manage and cultivate the land themselves, with very few exceptions do little to increase its productivity. By contrast, the owners of most other forms of wealth are usually progressive and provide increasing employment by their activities. They serve an essential purpose in a dynamic economy.

Concentrations of wealth are thus justified if the result is dynamic economically, creating employment and increasing productivity. In agriculture, this distinction divides those who actively manage and supervise their lands from those who merely live on the rental income from them—or agricultural capitalists from "feudal" landlords, entrepreneurs from "social parasites."

But how is that line to be drawn? Total confiscation—the literal "abolition of feudalism" so frequently mentioned in planning documents—was ruled out both on normative grounds (as private property was an accepted first principle) and for political considerations.[11] Moreover, abolition of the great landlords would, in the official view, deprive rural areas of their "natural leadership." Thus the Planning Board recommended a ceiling of 150 acres of irrigated land, 300 acres semi-irrigated, and 450 acres rain-fed (*barani*). The logic was that this ceiling would provide "suitable units of management" for landowners willing to manage their own lands but would not discourage enterprise. Specific exemptions were recommended for what were arguably more capitalistic agricultural enterprises—plantations, orchards, and estates "already being cultivated with mechanical means" (Pakistan, 1956: 128).

Despite the cogent official logic establishing the case for a mild ceiling reform and redistribution, no purely political regime in Pakistan dared to move against the rural elite. Not until the onset of political immobilism and crisis, and the imposition of martial law, did the policy logic find its way into law. Almost immediately after seizing power in the coup of 1958, Ayub Khan appointed a commission to recommend land-reform measures. The Land Reforms Commission for West Pakistan, in setting the ceiling between 500 and 1,000 acres, noted that "looked at from the

11. The political power of the landlords in the 1950s in Pakistan is well established: Sayeed (1967: 15, 54–55, 114, 240, and passim); M. Shahid Alam (1973: 14–19); Pakistan (1966: 7); Sanderatne (1974a: 123 ff.). Mushtaq Ahmad (1970: 106–07, 236, 247 and passim) presents data on the overwhelming dominance of landlords numerically in both provincial and national legislatures.

point of view of social justice alone" the ceiling "will appear large" (Pakistan, 1959b: 30). This certainly seems possible, as more than three-fourths of the cultivators owned less than 15 acres at the time.[12] But considerations of social justice were tempered by other imperatives in the policy logic. Specifically, the commission (Pakistan, 1959b: 30) argued:

> [In] determining the extent of the ceiling, social justice has not been the only criterion before us. Even if we were to recommend a much lower ceiling than what we have suggested, the surplus land which would have become available for redistribution among landless tenants would have been too small to secure for each of them a subsistence farm unit. The ends of social justice, in the sense of securing land for the entire landless population, thus being almost unattainable, what we thought was prudent was to fix the ceiling at a level which will on the one hand eradicate the feudalistic elements from the existing tenure structure, and on the other, by causing the minimum disturbance of the social edifice lead to a harmonious changeover and at the same time, by providing incentives at all levels, conduce to greater production.[13]

Evidently, social justice was not taken to mean equality but rather the right of all farmers to own a subsistence holding; even such a restricted notion of justice was, however, unobtainable without setting a ceiling so low (at about 25 acres, by my rough calculations) that there would be "disturbance of the social edifice." In short, a lower ceiling was politically impracticable. But aside from the political situation, the commission argued that the goal of the land reform, the modernization of agriculture, would be frustrated by a low ceiling:

> We are also anxious that farming as a profession should remain sufficiently lucrative to attract and engage suitable talent on a wholetime basis. It should provide to those engaged in it a standard of living which will compare favorably with that obtainable in other professions. Above all it should offer opportunities for enterprise and leadership which, through precept and example will be capable of influencing rural life and which will

---

12. There exist no exact data. The 1960 *Census of Agriculture* gives no data at all on ownership patterns, only on *operated* size of holding. The Land Reforms Commission compiled existing data on owners but not on landless tenants or laborers. Calculations from their *Report* (1959b), appendix 1, show that 64.4 percent of all owners owned less than 5 acres, 93.1 percent owned less than 25 acres. Altogether, the owners of less than 5 acres owned about as much land as the owners who held more than 500 acres, though the latter consituted only 0.12 percent of the total number of owners. Pure (totally landless) tenants constituted 34 percent of all rural households in 1972, and landless laborers about 12 percent. The percentage of pure tenants was certainly higher in the 1950s preceding the Ayub reform. The figure in the text is thus an estimate but certainly no exaggeration, and probably understates the inequality in land ownership.

13. There was, however, dissent on the commission; Ghulam Ishaque Khan argued for lower, but substantial, ceilings more in line with the recommendations of the Muslim League's Agrarian Reforms Committee *Report* (1949).

provide a point of contact between rural conservatism and ignorance and modern ideas and technology.[14]

So convinced was the Ayub regime of the disincentive effects of a low ceiling, that the existing ceiling in East Pakistan (now Bangladesh) was *raised* at the same time that a ceiling was imposed on West Pakistan, a marked departure from the tendency of ceilings to be progressively lowered over time throughout South Asia.

The conceptualization of the Ayub period was remarkably similar to the British colonial model of a modernizing gentry leading a backward peasantry to agricultural modernity. The reference group is the top of the rural elite, men whose style of life, tastes, and needs preclude occupations in agriculture except under conditions of substantial rewards considerably greater than those available to the peasant farmer.

The 1959 ceiling reform had avowedly political as well as economic objectives; as in most land reforms, political tactics were dominant. A genuine laying of the groundwork for rural democracy through land reform, freeing dependent tenants from their overlords, would have been possible only if the ceiling had been set very low, allowing a great deal of land to be redistributed and converting most tenants into owners. Such a low ceiling was politically, economically, and normatively unacceptable. But there were other political objectives in the reform logic. An official report published while Ayub Khan was still in power stated that "the reforms were considered by him to be an absolute necessity for the survival of the system" (Pakistan, 1966: 7–8). In announcing his reforms, Ayub Khan himself stressed their role in creating a politically stable society. The concern for the stability of the system was not so much fear of the political consequences of landlessness and discontent among the rural poor, as was the case in ceiling legislation in India and Sri Lanka in the early 1970s, but a recognition that the great "feudal" lords wielded so much political power that an integrated and stable center was an impossibility. To break those concentrations of power through an attack on their landed base was an acknowledged part of the land reforms (cf. Burki, 1980: 41).

With its very high ceiling and numerous loopholes (exemptions, gift and transfer provisions, etc.), the 1959 land reform (Marital Law Regulation 64)[15] did not fundamentally alter the agrarian structure even in theory. Indeed, official publications justifying the reform stated that "even the landlords have benefited from these reforms . . . the Reforms Scheme has

14. Pakistan (1959b: 30). The point was also emphasized to me by Mr. I. U. Khan, a member of both Ayub Khan's commission and Bhutto's counterpart (Rawalpindi, March, 1974).

15. Pakistan, *The Gazette of Pakistan Extraordinary*, Martial Law Regulation no. 64, Notification no. 181/89, March 3, 1959, p. 297. Exemptions from the ceiling are contained in part 3. Akram (1973: 60–66) for rules promulgated under the regulation.

not reduced their economic or personal status." The basis for this position is the official claim that the reforms forced landlords to intensify production, adding that the feudal lords could not have been happy with their "habits of a drone" (Pakistan, 1966: 25).

Empirical assessment of the official claim that the ceiling forced modernization on reluctant feudals is problematic. Certainly some large owners have modernized, participating fully in the explosive tractor-tubewell and "green revolution" technological changes of the mid-1960s. But other, far more powerful, factors were simultaneously at work, primarily the extremely favorable terms on which agricultural capital was provided, including both direct and indirect subsidies (exchange rates, credit terms, price supports, etc.)[16] and the absence of an agricultural income tax. The independent effect of Ayub's mild land reform is virtually impossible to assess, but clearly it was not decisive. Indeed, the most aggressive entrepreneurs in Pakistan's surge of agricultural development in the 1960s were not the great feudal lords, but rather the medium-sized owners of between 12.5 and 150 acres.[17]

Despite the contrary argument presented in earlier planning documents, compensation was paid to the relatively few landlords who were unable to evade the ceiling. Compensation was paid at ten times the rental value, capitalized, on a graduated scale inversely proportional to size of holding; this was held to represent the "economic" or market value.[18] Because of the various loopholes, only 1,902,788 acres were resumed (about 3.9 percent of the land owned), representing about one-fourth of the land in holdings larger than 500 acres each.[19] But these figures exaggerate the actual impact; because owners were allowed to select the area they would retain, a great deal of land resumed, and for which compensation was paid, was waste. In many cases, this was a boon to the landlords.[20] Only

16. For a thorough treatment, Kaneda (1969); also, Gotsch (1971); Griffin (1974: 221 ff.); Alavi (1976).

17. This argument is based on calculations from Pakistan, "Report of the Committee on Farm Mechanization," officially unpublished (Islamabad, 1970), p. 60 and passim. For a detailed explanation of the logic, Herring and Kennedy (1979). Shahid Burki (1977; 1980: 43) reaches a similar conclusion but exaggerates the role of Ayub Khan's land reform. For evidence of participation of smaller farmers in aspects of the "green revolution" in Pakistan, Azam (1973).

18. For the compensation provisions, Martial Law Regulation no. 64, part 4; Akram (1970; 67 ff.); for rules, Pakistan (1960: 13).

19. My calculations, data from Pakistan (1966: appendix 1); Pakistan (1959b: appendix 1).

20. One of the largest landlords of Mardan told me that his family benefited from the 1959 reforms, as did many large owners he knew, by discarding unwanted waste, with compensation from the government. This same owner lost some good land under the 1972 ceiling law; since all the political parties promised land reforms, he did not take the PPP pledge seriously and had not bothered to make anticipatory transfers, as is usually done (interview January, 1975). Official publications from the period also claim that "even the landlords" benefited from the land reform.

43.2 percent of the total resumed area was cultivated land; only 28.2 percent was tenanted land. Despite the negligible benefit to tenants, the burden on the public treasury was significant.[21]

Tenants who received land—and there are great discrepancies in official claims as to the number benefited—had to pay for it, thus considerably weakening the redistributive impact. Since the tenants purchased the land at Rs 8 per Produce Index Unit, and the landlord received from Rs 1 to Rs 5 per Produce Index Unit compensation at what was considered the market value, it seems that the "abolition of feudalism" was no bargain for the few beneficiaries.[22] One official report noted that some tenants were paying installments to the government as new owners and simultaneously paying rent to the landlord, still considering themselves "vassals" (Pakistan, 1966: 18). Tenants were frequently given holdings well below the official "subsistence" level, thus permitting no complete break in dependency relations with village landlords. Moreover, there is clear evidence of fraud and coercion operating at the village level to deprive even those tenants officially counted as beneficiaries from benefiting.[23] Though academic treatments of the Ayub period usually accept the government estimate of between 150,000 and 200,000 tenant beneficiaries, that figure is extremely misleading.[24] The 1959 reform was more a forced sale of marginal land by some landlords to some tenants than a genuine redistribution of wealth or alteration of agrarian structure.

Though compensation to landlords blunted the 1959 reform's redistributive impact and was contrary to earlier official policy logic, the Ayub

21. Total compensation due landlords was Rs 89,180,674; interest payments came to Rs 3,346,669 annually (Pakistan, 1966: appendix G).

22. Pakistan (1966: 13 and appendix H). The payments were, however, spread over twenty-five years, representing a considerable financial boon to tenants because of the subsequent inflation.

23. In the village studied by Saghir Ahmad (1977: 38–39), of forty-one recorded recipients of land under the reform provisions, only two were actually owners of the land; local landlords had threatened or bullied other tenants into not accepting land or relinquishing it once accepted, utilizing control of irrigation water, other tenants and various diffuse pressures. Moreover, the land distributed was allocated in such small parcels (well under the official guidelines) that recipients were still dependent on landlords for employment. Similar dynamics operated during the Bhutto period, but the extent is unknown.

24. It is known that not all recorded beneficiaries benefited, or for that matter even existed. More important, even the official figures of 622,199 acres of land sold to 150,000 tenants yield little more than 4 acres per family, one-third the official "subsistence" holding. If tenants had in fact bought the land in "subsistence" plots of 12.5 acres each (larger in Sind and Baluchistan), just under 50,000 pure tenant families could have received land. But these calculations ignore land *quality*. Tenants in the aggregate owed Rs 44,736,806, or about 5,592,101 Produce Index Units of land (at Rs 8 per PIU), or about 9 Produce Index Units per acre. This calculation indicates that landlords lost only their most unproductive land: land which averages 9 PIU's per acre can only be called marginal; far more than 4 acres of such land would be required to provide a family with even an impoverished existence. Double-cropped irrigated land in the canal colonies could have a rating of 120, for example; the lowest possible rating is 5 PIU.

regime considered it necessary because "expropriation without compensation would shatter the nation's faith in the institution of private property and enterprise, around which the country's economy was largely built" (Pakistan, 1966: 13). Ironically, it was thus difficult even in theory to root out feudalism because of the regime's firm commitment to capitalism.

Bhutto's Land Reforms: The Opening Round

In sharp contrast to the ascent to power by military coup and the subsequent long technocratic, openly procapitalist rule of Ayub Khan, Zulfikar Ali Bhutto came to power through electoral success and mass mobilization characterized by vitriolic attacks on landlords and capitalists.[25] Bhutto promised "Islamic socialism," dignity, and justice to Pakistan's poor. Early in his tenure in office, President Bhutto announced that his agrarian reforms were the first priority of his avowedly populist regime. Almost seven years later, the martial-law regime of Zia-ul-Haq issued a White Paper on the performance of Bhutto's government (which Zia ended with a coup in July of 1977) charging that the land reforms were, in practice, yet another example of the Bhutto government's cynical posturing and manipulation, favoritism and victimization, corruption and abuse of power. The irony is that a centerpiece of Bhutto's program for the "salvation" of Pakistan should appear in a White Paper which attempted to add legitimacy to the execution of the ex-prime minister.[26]

The potency attributed to agrarian reform by Mr. Bhutto in rhetoric was extraordinary. The reforms were to restore "dignity" and "self-respect" to the oppressed rural masses and provide for their "salvation," to crush the power—economic and political—of an "opulent feudal class," and to facilitate the modernization of agriculture, the core of the national economy (Pakistan, 1972a). Given this analysis, and the social ferment at the base of the Bhutto regime, one might expect dramatic shifts in the conceptualization of land reforms. Yet the Bhutto period exhibited remarkable continuities in policy logic and reform practice, demonstrating how little had changed in elite politics despite the stirring rhetoric and mass mobilization that accompanied the fall of Ayub Khan and the eventual success of Bhutto's Pakistan People's Party (PPP).

In introducing his own land reforms in 1972, President Bhutto termed

25. E.g., *Election Manifesto of Pakistan People's Party, 1970*; Zulfikar Ali Bhutto, *Let the People Judge* (1969). For a systematic analysis of the rural base of PPP support, Frankel and Von Vorys (1972). For a broader analysis of Bhutto's bases of political support, Feroz Ahmed (1973); Hasan Askari Rizvi (1973); Burki (1980). The following sections follow Herring (1979a).

26. Pakistan, *White Paper on the Performance of the Bhutto Regime* (1979), vol. 4. Bhutto's title changed from president to prime minister under the 1973 Constitution, but with no noticeable change in political power.

Ayub Khan's 1959 reforms "a subterfuge," designed "to fool the people in the name of reform" with "all manner of concessions" to "buttress and pamper the landed aristocracy and fatten the favored few." This description is rather accurate. Bhutto's reforms were touted as a means for effecting "the eradication of the curse of feudalism and man's unjust overlordship of the good earth." The agrarian system, which Bhutto termed "oppressive" and "iniquitous," was to be transformed in such a way that the "life and fortunes of the common man" would be affected by the land reform more than by any other measure contemplated by the regime (Pakistan, 1972a: 1–2).

In Bhutto's view, the 1959 reforms had eradicated neither feudalism nor oppression because of the concessions made to landed elites. The remaining concentrations had "stunted the growth of a just and harmonious social order"; moreover, it was still the case that "millions of those who produce the wealth of the nation struggle helplessly at a miserable level of existence" (ibid). From a leader maintaining this position, one would expect radical land reforms. In fact, the Martial Law Regulation 115 of 1972 was primarily another ceiling law; it reduced the existing ceiling by about two-thirds, with no compensation to former owners. The concentrations of land wealth considered acceptable were substantial relative to the situation of most rural Pakistanis. The ceiling remained high relative to average holdings: with 89 percent of all operated holdings smaller than 25 acres in 1972, and 43 percent under 7.5 acres, the ceiling varied nominally between 150 and 300 acres, with a much higher de facto ceiling.[27]

The unwillingness to impose a ceiling closer to the average size of holding (about 13 acres) reflects both the (perceived) political constraints facing the regime, and Bhutto's own ambivalence concerning agrarian reform.[28] But the mild nature of the attack on landed wealth also represents an important continuity in the policy model of gentlemen-farmer capitalists as the vanguard of an agricultural revolution. President Bhutto explained that of the several factors which went into setting the ceiling, the "prime one" was that "agriculture should continue to be an attractive and profitable vocation." He continued:

> The size of holding should permit maximum benefit of investment to enable productivity to increase. Enterprising and enlightened farmers

27. Pakistan, *Census of Agriculture 1972* (1975a), vol. 1, table 1. Herring and Chaudhry (1974) for a discussion and calculation of operative ceilings.

28. In an interview for *Stern*, June 15, 1972, President Bhutto stated: "I can't nationalize the land. It's not possible. Tomorrow, if someone wants to do it, let him try." Also, Esposito (1973); Sanderatne (1974a). As Burki (1980) correctly argues, Bhutto's PPP contained distinct right and left factions. Had Bhutto aligned himself firmly with the left instead of purging it, as he eventually did, the political potential for radical land reform might have been greater.

should continue to live on the land and give agriculture the sense of purpose it deserves. For these compelling reasons, we are following exactly the same principle for the enlightened entrepreneur. We are as much against the ignorant and tyrannical landlord as we are against the robber barons of industry. We are as much for the creative and humane land-owner as we are for a productive and conscientious owner of industry. [Pakistan, 1972a: 2]

In explaining his land reforms to industrialists in Karachi, Bhutto struck the same note. The ceiling was necessary to break up concentrations of wealth and redistribute some land, but "at the same time, we have tried to preserve the incentives for the continuation of agriculture as an attractive and profitable vocation for the enterprising and the enlightened farmers" (Pakistan, 1972b: vol. II, 157).

The policy logic is straightforward, and shows marked continuity with the agrarian entrepreneurial model of Ayub Khan and the progressive gentry model of colonial administrations with which Ayub's vision so clearly resonated. The operative notion of social justice allows concentration of wealth in land, just as in industry, provided that the owners are "humane," "enlightened," and "enterprising." A very low ceiling, the logic runs, would not be conducive to agricultural progress because it would not attract—indeed would discourage—modern entrepreneurs; the maximum farm-size must allow a standard of living comparable to that afforded by alternatives available to the representatives of the stratum which presumably produces agricultural entrepreneurs, a stratum accustomed to high levels of income and privilege. The symbolic expression of the entrepreneurial landlord is the tractor, and, significantly, the 1972 ceiling allowed an exemption averaging 50 acres per holding above the ceiling for purchase of a tractor or tubewell.[29]

The main thrust of Bhutto's attack on parasitic landlordism was his ceiling reform; as before, the policy logic held that "feudals" who lost land would of necessity intensify production to compensate. The tenancy reforms included in the 1972 legislation in theory exerted additional pressure on backward landlords to modernize.[30] Before considering those tenancy reforms, however, it is necessary to analyze the policy logic of ceiling reforms as a tool for creating an entrepreneurial gentry from traditional landlords. What was the operative meaning of the "feudalism" that was the object of so much political vilification, and how effective could land ceilings be in eradicating or transforming it?

29. Herring and Chaudhry (1974: 250) for calculations and discussion.
30. Interview for *Stern* in Pakistan (1972b: 2: 193). Bhutto's statement was in response to the interviewer's question about the possibility of a decline in production resulting from the land reforms. It appears from his statements on the subject that Bhutto did not fully believe the conventional wisdom of the economic benefits of land redistribution. The regime's vigorous encouragement of farm mechanization and the prohibition of partition of land in MLR 115 confirm the view that the prime minister was not a believer in the superiority of very small-scale peasant agriculture.

Land Ceilings and the Eradication of Feudalism

The connection between enforcement of a ceiling on land ownership and an attack on feudalism (by any definition of the term) is problematic. A ceiling affects landowners selectively according to size of holding. But feudalism as a social system is unlikely to be neatly delimited by any criterion so narrow as size of farm, particularly in a modernizing agrarian sector. That is, there is no necessary connection between size of holding and the character of relations—economic, political, and social—between owner and cultivator, at least beyond certain rather flexible technological constraints. Thus, wherever the ceiling is set, it may pass over a number of "feudal" landlords with small holdings while simultaneously disturbing a number of large entrepreneurial farmers, a class explicitly favored by successive Pakistani regimes, including Bhutto's.

The use of the ceiling reform as the focal point of the attack on feudalism is therefore curious but quite consistent with Pakistani precedents. In official parlance and political rhetoric in Pakistan, "feudalism" has meant the existence of functionally irrelevant, nonprogressive landlordism; in this sense, the rhetorical attack on feudalism in planning documents is as old as the Pakistani state. But such documents in Pakistan were careful to distinguish, as had British colonial policy thinking, between parasitic feudal landlords and progressive agricultural capitalists, the latter deserving encouragement and support rather than eradication. Mr. Bhutto's policy logic followed exactly the same lines. Indeed, his 1972 ceiling was about the same as that suggested in the *First Five Year Plan*, and for almost exactly the same reasons; the ceiling had to be set low enough to break up the massive estates of feudal lords (and provide for redistribution of confiscated lands—an important symbolic objective), but could not be set so low as to discourage progressive agricultural entrepreneurs.

A relatively high land ceiling, by allowing some concentration of landed wealth, was considered a necessary, but far from sufficient, condition for the growth of a progressive capitalist farmer class. The more powerful incentives to capitalist farmers were subsidies to agricultural capital. But exactly what was being attacked as feudal? The most nearly feudal holdings in a narrow legal sense—the *jagirs*, or grants of land from the precolonial and colonial state for service (often military), were finally eliminated in the 1959 reform, but the estates affected were not extensive—316,930 acres in all, of which only 43,390 acres were farmed by tenants.[31] If a narrow economic structural criterion is applied, it is possible to distinguish (superficially) capitalist farming from feudal landlordism by the presence of wage labor in the former and sharecropping, labor-rents, and corvée (*begar*) in the latter. But *begar* was legally abolished in

---

31. Pakistan (1966: appendix 1). The NWFP and the Punjab had in law abolished *jagirdari* earlier.

the 1959 reforms, and Bhutto's reforms (while reiterating that prohibition) not only allowed continuation of sharecropping but institutionalized that mode of organizing production. There was no strong objection in Bhutto's policy logic to share tenancy: indeed, the president announced that his reforms "lay down the foundations of a relationship of honour and mutual benefit between the landowner and the tenant" (Pakistan, 1972a: 2).

Evidently, then, feudalism can be eradicated and still leave behind the landlord–tenant social organization of rural society. Indeed, the landlord–tenant nexus, with proper adjustments and good (enterprising) landlords, was considered potentially conducive to both social justice and productivity. Significantly, the two goals were linked conceptually; in President Bhutto's words: "The relations between land-owners and tenants have caused grave anxiety to the country and our people. There has been strife and bitterness causing serious problems affecting agricultural production and social harmony (ibid.: 4; cf. Pakistan, 1972b: 173). Share tenancy was not to be eliminated but rationalized and stripped of arbitrary abuses. In no sense were the feudal lords to be eliminated; their holdings were to be sized down, but provisions for transfers of land and an individual (rather than family) unit for calculating the retainable area assured the "feudal" owners of very large post-reform holdings even if the legislation were administered effectively.

That the modernization and rationalization of the agricultural core of the economy should be addressed in part through land reforms does not surprise the student of agrarian change; what does at first seem peculiar is that modernization should be built on the ancient social organization of landlords and tenants. But this seemingly structural incongruity is by no means novel, nor unique to Pakistan. Lenin, for example, termed this pattern of agrarian development via land reform the "Prussian model," leading to Junker capitalism, as opposed to the American or English models (1962: vol. 13, 238–42). Barrington Moore, Jr., makes a similar distinction and traces the origins of German fascism to this form of the capitalist agricultural revolution from above (1968: 420, 424, 460–61).

Important features of Bhutto's reforms follow Lenin's "Prussian model" in facilitating mechanization and modernization while retaining the sharecropping organization of production. An important strain of economic policy logic has indicted share tenancy for frustrating agricultural modernization and rationalization; Bhutto's reform mandated changes in production relations which in theory reduce the drag of tenancy on dynamism within the traditional landlord–tenant system.

The usual objections to share tenancy on the grounds of efficiency assume that the tenant is responsible for fixed-capital improvements and supply of working capital, and that the low marginal return on investment (a consequence of the share rent) and poverty of the cultivator combine to reduce efficiency and thwart technical change. The rentier is essentially passive and the tenant is not up to the task. But in the Pakistani model, the landowner has been given every incentive to invest in fixed capital—both through the effective absence of rent control[32] and through the numerous subsidies granted owners for fixed capital. Bhutto's reforms granted the tenants security of tenure and mandated that working capital expenses must be shared equally between tenant and landlord, in theory eliminating the disincentive problem of low marginal returns to the tenant's investment.[33] Moreover, a major item of working capital—expenditure for seeds—was legally made the responsibility of the landlord alone. As gentry are assumed to have more scientific inclinations, education, and extension contacts than sharecroppers, the provision would facilitate (again in theory) employment of the best-quality seed and appropriate varieties. Increased responsibility for working capital investment should simultaneously encourage functionally absentee landlords to take a greater interest in production.

In economic terms, "feudalism" has connoted absentee (whether geographically or functionally) landlordism of a parasitic and nonprogressive sort. But in our common understanding of the term, and in usage in Pakistan, feudalism has important extraeconomic dimensions, the core of which seems to be the exercise of social and political control over the peasantry and concentrations of political power largely independent of the state. Bhutto spoke of the system in terms of "oppression," "servitude," and "the overriding authority of the Tribal Sardars, the Waderas and Maliks." The PPP founding principles and manifesto were quite open about the necessity of breaking the political power of the great landlords. Themes of social oppression and loss of dignity imposed on the tenantry

32. In theory, the tenancy acts of the early 1950s are in force, but these acts have never been seriously enforced and are construed to apply *only to ground rent*. Installation of a tubewell, for example, will allow the landowner to increase his share of the gross output by treating the increment as return to supply of working capital (water) rather than an increase in "rent." The same has been done with tractors. Thus, even if limits on ground rent could be enforced (and there is no mechanism to do so), the modernization of agriculture renders limitation of ground rent per se increasingly irrelevant.

33. Assuming the output is shared 50-50, as are the input costs. This removes all neoclassical constraints on share-tenant efficiency except the return to labor, which remains less than it would be under ownership conditions. However, with increases in labor productivity through fixed and working capital investment, and the absence of off-farm labor opportunities, this theoretical constraint may prove irrelevant on the ground. The tenancy reform section contains no provision for enforcing rent control, allowing landowners to invest and raise de facto rents accordingly. There are instances in which landlords have installed tubewells and purchased tractors and thereby increased their share of the gross produce to two-thirds or three-fourths. At this end of the rent spectrum, the sharecropper is as much a laborer on a piece-rate basis as a tenant, as all capital is provided by the owner.

(particularly the *haris*) run throughout Bhutto's public pronouncements on land reform.[34]

A skewed distribution of land ownership would not necessarily yield the abject social, political, and economic dependence described by official reports; small holders may be influenced by large owners, but the total dependence that results from lack of independent access to the means of production would not characterize the agrarian system. Likewise, tenurial defects associated with low productivity are related, not to the large size of the owners' holdings, but to extreme competition for limited opportunities on the land, producing high rents and insecure tenure. There is the possibility—as illustrated by more densely populated areas of South Asia such as Sri Lanka, Kerala, or Bangladesh—of the social, economic, and political evils mentioned in ceiling models existing without any significant concentration of land in huge holdings. Certainly the available technology, combined with the extremely large size of many estates, historically made sharecropping the most likely organization of production in Pakistan, but it is less clear that a ceiling on holdings would eliminate the evils attributed to share tenancy. Indeed, the vast majority of Pakistan's share tenants operate holdings owned by landlords of a relatively small size, far below the ceiling limits of the Ayub Khan or Bhutto reforms (Pakistan, 1975a: vol. 1, table 7).

If this analysis is accurate, an attack on "feudalism" requires severing the connection between control of land and control of people; there are two obvious land-reform responses. The most obvious measure would be a land-to-the-tiller reform in which tenants are deemed owners of the land they till, abolishing landlordism with a stroke. With complementary reforms in the supply of working capital, marketing services, local administration, and so on, such reforms would arguably stand a good chance of eradicating "feudal" social and political relations. A less direct method of attacking the extraeconomic manifestations of landlordism would be to impose an extremely low ceiling, somewhere near the average size of holding (about 13 acres in Pakistan). Such a low ceiling would allow, in theory, continuation of "feudal" (rentier) economic relations on a petty scale, but would largely eliminate the political power base of the great landlords. Social and political oppression of dependent tenants could continue, but no single landlord could exercise such control over more than two or three families, nor so easily defy the state apparatus.

34. The oppression of the sharecropper was one of the themes in the Address to the Nation (March 1, 1972) that introduced the 1972 reforms. At public meetings Bhutto often reiterated his pledge that the oppression of the *haris* had come to an end with his reforms. The *sanad*, or deed, given tenants who received land, read in part: "You stand free today." This was the theme of a speech at Thatta (Sind) (reported in *Dawn*, January 3, 1975): *haris* who receive land would not only benefit economically but would feel strong enough to fight tyranny and injustice.

However, neither a land-to-the-tiller policy nor a radical land redistribution has ever been a serious possibility in Pakistan. Even if Bhutto's PPP had not in part been composed of powerful landed interests, the political capacity to carry out so fundamental a restructuring of the agrarian sector could have been generated only by mass mobilization of revolutionary proportions, a tack rejected by the regime.[35]

Agrarian Structure and Ceiling Reforms: Where Are the Feudals?

Before considering the impact of Bhutto's reforms on the agrarian structure, it is necessary, though difficult, to outline that structure on the eve of the reforms. We have census data for 1972, but the census is a poor mirror for agrarian structure. First, and most obviously, landowners knew that agrarian reforms were coming; since the Ayub reforms, prudent landed families had been transferring and partitioning land—often only for the records—in order to escape further reforms. The PPP's founding principles spoke of radical agrarian reform, and other political parties promised land reform as well. Indeed, in announcing his reforms President Bhutto noted that "landowners have been feverishly transferring land on an extensive scale and in a manner designed to defeat land reforms" (Pakistan, 1972a: 5). Thus, precisely because there is a threat of land reform, the actual impact of a land reform becomes difficult to assess; the data simply do not reflect reality on the ground. Moreover, existing data frequently do not fit the size categories of ceiling measures, informal tenure arrangements go unrecorded, some geographical areas are excluded, and a host of other difficulties appear upon close scrutiny. An instructive illustration of the complexity is the long and tortured attempt by Herring and Chaudhry (1974: 250–55) to estimate the actual land area available for confiscation and redistribution under the 1972 reforms (cf. F. Ahmed, 1972).

The extent of "feudalism" is thus difficult to determine even in the problematic, superficial sense of size of holding, as operationalized in the reform legislation. The 1972 Census of Agriculture shows 16,163 private farms in excess of 150 acres, representing less than 0.5 percent of the farms covered in the census. Such farms covered 9 percent of the farm area and 5 percent of the cultivated area. The ratio of uncultivated to cultivated land was thus quite high on the large holdings; whereas cul-

35. In the interview for *Stern* cited above, Bhutto went on to say that, although it is impossible to "nationalize the land," still: "The world doesn't come to an end with one reform. If that reform is successful, on that you can build other reforms. But no one can sweep the boards clean in one go." The text does *not* imply that either Bhutto or Ayub Khan was inclined toward radical land reform, but that both considered it politically impossible, explicitly recognizing the political power of landed interests.

tivated area constituted 83 percent of farm area for all holdings taken together, for the largest farms that figure was only 46 percent.[36]

But not all of these large farms (averaging 277.3 acres each, of which only 128 acres were cultivated) can be called feudal, even by the roughest of criteria. Indeed, 9 percent of the large farms were controlled and operated by tenants, another 28 percent by owner-cum-tenants. Moreover, about one-third of the land held by large nonowning operators was leased in through a sharecropping arrangement; some of the feudals were sharecroppers (Pakistan, 1975a: vol. 1, tables 5, 6). For the large agriculturalists who were owners, leasing out land on a sharecropping basis was not the dominant organization of production. These large owners reported that 79 percent of their area was operated by themselves, 21 percent by tenants; only 12 percent of the total area of large estates was sharecropped. This figure is particularly interesting when compared with the organization of production on smaller holdings. The farmers most likely to lease out their holding to sharecroppers were those in the size category of 7.5 to 12.5 acres. Beyond that size, the tendency to lease out land to sharecroppers is *inversely* related to size of holding, with the largest owners being the least likely to engage in this "feudal" practice.[37]

Again, the data must be treated cautiously. Moreover, some areas of Pakistan were omitted from the census (the Mari Bugti subdivision of Baluchistan, all of Gilgit, Swat, Chitral, Malakand, etc.) and, indeed, these areas would be expected to produce large concentrations of genuine feudals. But for the agricultural heartland of Pakistan, it is clear that a ceiling on land ownership is a curious way to catch a feudal, if by feudal we mean, at a bare minimum, the use of sharecroppers to cultivate the owner's estate.

Lenin considered wage labor to be the fundamental characteristic of capitalist agriculture. Of all Pakistani farms in 1972, 30.1 percent employed casual wage labor; of the largest farms, 50.6 percent employed casual labor. Clearly capitalism, as defined by the rough structural criterion of use of wage labor, is well established on the largest holdings. With regard to permanent hired labor the situation is more ambiguous. The "hired hand" was certainly a fixture of capitalist agriculture in the West, and may be so in Pakistan, but we know that, historically, workers have been attached to estates through debt bondage and serflike relations. Census data do not, of course, distinguish between feudal and capitalist

---

36. Pakistan (1975a: vol. 1, table 1). It is not clear, however, whether that difference is evidence of feudal indifference or simply an indication that large holdings contain a greater percentage of uncultivable land. Large owners do report a larger percentage of "unculturable waste" (table 14), but the definition of "culturable" is problematic, and the difference is not sufficient to explain all of the variation in intensity of land use.

37. Ibid., table 7. Regional disaggregation does not reverse the argument, though large owners in the NWFP are much more likely, in the Punjab much less likely, to lease out land to sharecroppers, compared to the national mean.

forms of permanent labor. The largest farms are more likely than smaller ones to report such laborers; more than 45 percent of the largest farms reported permanent laborers, an average of more than five workers per household reporting. But, more significantly, these large farms reported more *family* farm workers, by almost 50 percent, than permanent hired workers, suggesting a structure that could hardly be called feudal.[38]

Thus, in terms of the social organization of production, very large estates seem more, rather than less, capitalistic than smaller farms. But what of the technical characteristics of production? The census allows comparison of farms according to relative adoption of certain modern agricultural practices. (Mechanization is an inappropriate measure because of the existence of economies of scale, though mechanized farming is certainly the *symbol* of progressive agriculture in South Asia.) The census recorded use of "plant protection measures" (pesticides) and chemical fertilizers. Since these practices are neutral to scale, or nearly perfectly divisible, their employment serves as a reasonable indicator of modern agriculture.

The data in table 4.1 demonstrate that not all land in large holdings is farmed in primitive ways. Indeed, in terms of percentage of cropped area treated with fertilizers and pesticides, the largest holdings are the most modern.[39] However, the percentage of large farms utilizing fertilizers falls well below the national mean, close to that of the dwarf "farms." Taken in conjunction, these indications corroborate a central theme of this chapter: size of holding is not an adequate proxy for organization of production in either the technical or social sense. Many large holders are indeed extremely "backward" in agricultural technique; others are at the forefront of Pakistan's agricultural modernization.[40]

Having considered the top of the agrarian hierarchy, we may turn briefly to the bottom. A land ceiling, and the case for redistribution, can

38. *Census of Agriculture 1972*, vol. 1, tables 60, 61. There may be reporting biases, and problems of different meanings of family "worker," but one would expect that truly "feudal" families would *not* exaggerate the extent of family participation in agricultural work. The presence of so many family farmworkers on the large estates more probably suggests the rich peasant or capitalist farmer organization of production than feudalism. Tractorization has been crucial in inducing greater family participation on the large farms.

39. Disaggregation by province does not refute this argument. Indeed, in Sind, a stronghold of feudalism in popular perception and political rhetoric, the relationship holds even more strongly. The percentages of farms using fertilizer and pesticides were highest on large estates in Sind, much higher than the national average (*Census*, tables 53, 54). The NWFP is the exact opposite; very few large-estate owners use fertilizer. The Punjab shows little variability by size of holding, as does Baluchistan, where modern techniques are extremely rare.

40. "Modern" and "backward" are temporal, not normative, designations; modern energy-intensive agriculture may very well be inappropriate in a developmental sense, despite its high productivity. The mistaken use of holding size as a proxy for social organization of production is evident not only in the policy logic but in many academic treatments, e.g., Burki (1976, 1980).

Table 4.1: Indicators of Technical and Social Organization of
            Production by Size of Holding (Pakistan, 1972)

Size of Holding	Percentage of Farms Using Fertilizers	Percentage of Cropped Area Fertilized	Percentage of Cropped area Treated with Pesticides	Percentage of Farms Employing Casual Labor
"Feudals" (greater than 150 acres)	39	49	7	51
Dwarf (less than one acre)	34	35	2	10
Modal farm size (7.5–12.5 acres)	55	43	2	33
All farms	52	43	2	30

SOURCE: *Pakistan Census of Agriculture* 1972, vol. 1, tables 53, 54, 60.

be interpreted only with reference to the position of the majority of rural people; from that perspective, Bhutto's attack on landed wealth was quite moderate. About two-thirds (67 percent) of Pakistan's farm families operate less than the officially designated "subsistence" holding (12.5 acres), tilling less than one-third (30 percent) of the farm area. Almost half of Pakistan's farmers (43 percent) till less than 7.5 acres and in the aggregate operate only 12 percent of the farm area on holdings averaging 3.75 acres each. Totally landless tenant families constitute 34 percent of the farm households; another 24 percent rent at least some of the land they operate. The exact number of pure agricultural laborers is unknown, but is probably about 12 percent of the rural population.[41] The policy logic of ceiling reforms in Pakistan has addressed the top of the agrarian structure; little attention has been paid to the bottom of that structure, where most of the people—and the most intractable problems of production and justice—are located.

Implementation and Structural Change

Bhutto's 1972 reforms provided a number of levers to alter the agrarian system. The ceiling would attack the largest concentrations of landed wealth, considered the stronghold of feudalism. Tenancy reforms would benefit sharecroppers economically and would strengthen tenants politically and socially. Redistribution of land would free some tenants from the landlord's yoke entirely, creating politically independent yeoman

41. Data from 1972 *Census*, vol. 1, tables 1, 3. "Subsistence holding" is an official designation and is agroeconomically meaningless. The percentage of landless laborers is from data collected by the Agricultural Census Organization in 1972, as yet unpublished, and seems reasonable in light of population census data, though certain publications of international development organizations place the percentage much higher.

farmers in place of the socially oppressed and economically exploited sharecroppers. To what extent did implementation of the reforms effect these changes?

When translated into law, the reforms deviated somewhat from the principles of the PPP election manifesto. The de jure ceiling was set at 150 acres of irrigated land (or the equivalent), or 300 acres of unirrigated land, though the de facto ceiling (calculated in terms of Produce Index Units) was considerably higher, particularly for farmers who purchased tubewells or tractors to take advantage of the bonus provision (Herring and Chaudhry, 1974: 264, 274; Sufian, 1972: 9). The relatively high ceiling would seem to be a political compromise in favor of large owners, but even so, it represented a significant reduction of Ayub's ceiling. Moreover, the manifesto's provision for compensation to landowners was deleted; land in excess of the ceiling was to be confiscated. On paper, in theory, some very powerful landowners, whether feudal or capitalist, would be severely hurt by implementation.

It goes without saying that there were many slips between the law and the land, between legislation and implementation. Shaikh Rashid, minister for land reforms and chairman of the Federal Land Commission, spoke of "primeval forces" unleashed by feudal landlords "fighting last ditch battles recklessly" to halt implementation. The minister acknowledged that the regime's political capacity to carry through the reforms was questionable; resistance came not merely from opposition parties but also from "some quarters of a reformist government."[42]

The first obstacle to implementation of the ceiling was not, however, pitched battles with primeval forces, but the rather mundane maneuvers of landlords to evade the law. Land was concealed, records were altered, forgeries made.[43] Shaikh Rashid (Pakistan, 1977: 3) acknowledged that even before the promulgation of the reforms landowners were "feverishly" transferring land to evade the ceiling. The Land Commission was thus given the authority to determine whether or not the intent of certain land transfers was evasion of the ceiling law and the power to void such transfers.[44] Obviously such determinations were extremely problematic.[45]

42. Shaikh Muhammad Rashid, "Land Reforms—The Dawn of a New Era," mimeographed paper (Rawalpindi: 1977). Similar implications can be drawn from the minister's public and private statements regarding implementation.

43. I encountered numerous instances through investigations in 1974–75. For documented examples, *White Paper on Performance of the Bhutto Regime* (Pakistan, 1979: 4: 13–25).

44. Pakistan, Martial Law Regulation 115 (*Gazette of Pakistan, Extraordinary*, March 11, 1972, pp. 291–300), pt. 3, sec. 7.

45. The criteria established for evaluating transfers resemble those of market capitalism rather than the norms of feudal society. For a transaction to be valid, the recipient must have paid "adequate consideration," operationally defined as reasonable market value, and must be able to offer evidence of active management of the land. Revenue Department

The first level of evasion was not alteration of transfer records in fraudulent ways, however, but simple refusal to file a declaration of land ownership (required of every owner with land equal to the ceiling). About 1,200 owners had been caught for having failed to do so by the end of Bhutto's reign. Federal inspection teams appointed in each province discovered 3,265 cases of evidence of fraudulent transfers. The overturning of such cases resulted in an additional 483,691 acres of land being resumed by the commission, an average of 169 acres per case.[46]

Amid the evasion and ambiguities, can we determine the extent of implementation of the 1972 ceiling? Official aggregate data are available and are presented in table 4.2, but the official picture is misleading. First, there are no data indicating the *quality* of land resumed and redistributed. The legislation allowed owners to choose the land to be retained; thus the worst land was surrendered to the government. Second, widespread fraud at the local level corrupted the official statistics. For example, land was distributed in the name of bogus tenants though in fact it was retained by landlords; land was forcibly taken back from tenants by landlords and their thugs, and so on.[47] Ironically, these malpractices were almost certainly concentrated in the most "feudal" areas. There is no way to determine the aggregate effect of such distortions. Thus the official figures must be taken as the upper limit of land redistribution, with the gap between reality and data varying with local political and administrative conditions.

The data in table 4.2 illustrate the limited aggregate effect of the ceiling provision. Even using the census estimate of operated farm area, which is an understatement, the area redistributed during the Bhutto regime came to only 2.5 percent of the total farm area. The effect of land distribution on sharecroppers was limited by the relatively high ceiling and the provision allowing owners to keep their best land, discarding the waste; less than 10 percent of the country's pure tenant families received land according to official data (which overstate the case). As noted previously, most sharecroppers hold their land from small owners, not great feudal lords; about 85 percent of the pure tenants held land from owners of less than 25 acres.

In terms of regional differences, the NWFP (Sarhad) and Baluchistan

officials demanded to see record entries, receipts, and changes in bank accounts to reflect purported sales, as well as evidence of active management such as cultivation or direction of cultivation, payment of wages, cesses, water rates, taxes, etc. In those cases rejected, it was on this point of active possession that most fraudulent claims broke down. This account is based on interviews with Revenue Department officers and members of the Federal Land Commission, and case files from administrative hearings and appeals; cf. Qayyum (1977).

46. Data from Federal Land Commission. Cf. Pakistan (1977).

47. In addition to evidence of such cited in notes 43 and 45 above during the Bhutto reforms, there is solid evidence of the same phenomenon in the Ayub reforms, and no reason to believe that implementation dynamics fundamentally changed in the interim.

Table 4.2: Progress Officially Claimed in Implementation of Ceiling Reforms during the Bhutto Period

	Area Appropriated (1,000 acres)	Area Redistributed (1,000 acres)	Land Redistributed as Percentage of Total Operated Area*	Number of Families Receiving Land	Recipients as Percentage of all Totally Landless Tenants**
Jan. 1974					
(MLR 115)	787	285	0.6	35,000	2.7
Jan. 1975					
(MLR 115)	882.9	426	0.9	51,225	4.0
Sept. 1976					
(MLR 115)	(1,148.4)	(682.8)			
(MLR 64)	(1,094.8)	(491.6)			
Total	2,243.2	1,148.4	2.3	117,412	9.1
May 1977					
(MLR 115)	(1,731.6)	(725)			
(MLR 64)	(1,094.8)	(498)			
Total	2,826.4	1,223	2.5	119,182	9.2

*Of 49,206,552 acres reported in the 1972 Census of Agriculture. Revenue Department figures show much more land in operation. Using Census figures thus inflates the percentage of total area affected.

**Of 1,296,468 tenant families in the Census, an underestimate of the total. Only pure, landless tenants are included here, not owner-cum-tenants (who constituted 24 percent of farm families in 1972).

SOURCE: Federal Land Commission.

showed significantly higher percentages of farm land redistributed and tenants benefited. Interpolating between census data and unpublished government sources, I put the number of peasants receiving land in the NWFP at about one-third of the total number of landless tenants in the province. Almost 12 percent of the total farm area in the province was confiscated and about three-fourths of that redistributed. These figures reinforce the popular interpretation of implementation of land reforms in the province as tactical politics in the struggle of the Bhutto regime against the National Awami Party (a party composed of and supported by powerful Sarhad landlords), which staunchly opposed Bhutto's centralization of power.

Data from Baluchistan are of course extremely suspect. However, if we are to evaluate the prime minister's claim to have been waging war against the feudal *sardar* (tribal chief) system of Baluchistan, it is important that the largest amount of land confiscated under MLR 115 in any province was taken in Baluchistan, though that province has less than 10 percent of Pakistan's farm area. About 10 percent of the farm land in the province was expropriated, and the officially claimed beneficiaries constituted more than 36 percent of the landless tenants in the province. Moreover, a special regulation, MLR 117, redistributed additional land in the Pat Feeder area of Baluchistan amounting to half a million acres. Again, as with the NWFP, this outcome is understandable if we view land reform as a political instrument for winning support of the masses in politically hostile territory while simultaneously weakening the local opposition power elite, primarily the great landed families.[48]

Tenancy Reform

Because of peculiarities of Pakistan's agrarian structure—the concentration of most tenants on land owned by relatively small holders—the ceiling mechanism, even under ideal conditions of implementation, would have limited capacity to ameliorate the social, economic, and political disabilities suffered by sharecroppers. The tenancy reform sections of Bhutto's 1972 legislation prohibiting eviction of tenants (except under

48. This point is reinforced by considering the province-wide distribution of land confiscated by the Federal Land Commission in exercise of *suo moto* revisional powers. Of the 567,835 acres of fraudulently concealed land discovered and seized, 37 percent was in Baluchistan. Another 23 percent of the land so confiscated was in the NWFP, whereas the Punjab, with most of the farm area, contributed only 7 percent. The other claim to land redistribution made by the regime was in the erstwhile "princely states" of Dir, Swat, and Chitral; about forty thousand families in those areas were settled on land withdrawn from the ex-rulers and other landlords. If substantiated, such a redistribution would arguably constitute a very real attack on something like real feudalism, but would have little impact on the structure of Pakistan's agrarian economy. Frederick Barth, in his celebrated study of the Swat Pathans (1959), explicitly terms the system "feudal." Data from the Federal Land Commission.

explicitly stated and restricted conditions) in theory removed the land-lord's most potent control mechanism—the power to deprive a peasant of security and livelihood.

Enforcement of this crucial protection for tenants is problematic, however. First, the reforms offer no new means of enforcing rental controls. If rents can be increased at the owner's whim, protection from eviction becomes irrelevant. Yet there is no historical precedent for successful control of sharecropping rents in Pakistan. The tenancy acts of the early 1950s regulated rents, typically limiting the owner's share to no more than 40 percent of the gross produce, but the legislation remained a dead letter.[49] No serious analyst has argued that these earlier tenancy laws were effectively enforced; in fact, the 1972 census confirms widespread violation. Of the sharecropping contracts reported, 80.5 percent specified the owner's share as one-half. In 3.5 percent of the contracts, the owner's share was two-thirds, and in 16,907 contracts (0.7 percent), more than two-thirds (Pakistan, 1975a: vol. 1, table 8). Moreover, some of the highest share rents obtain in areas not covered by the census (Barth, 1959: chap. 5).

Enforcement responsibilities for Bhutto's tenancy regulations fall directly on the Revenue Department, a bureaucracy known for characteristics which do not auger well for effective implementation. At the local level, the revenue machinery is more an organ of society than of the state, and thus is of dubious value in enforcing laws contrary to the interests and wishes of local landed elites. The lower levels of that bureaucracy are mired in petty corruption and abuse of power.[50] President Bhutto himself referred to the system of the Revenue Department as "decadent," characterized by "corruption, mischief, vendettas, ... harassment" (Pakistan, 1972a: 6). Curiously, the revenue machinery had already proved totally incapable of enforcing earlier tenancy reforms when Bhutto handed it the new responsibilities.[51]

To what extent have the tenancy reforms succeeded in preventing tenant evictions and forcing landlords to assume a specified (and preponderant) share of production costs? It is impossible to answer this question without extensive field surveys, but the likelihood of effective enforcement seems negligible. Significantly, the government has no systematic method of monitoring, much less enforcing, the regulations on input costs,

49. Akhter Hamed Khan (1973); Mushtaq Ahmad (1970: 184 ff.). Shafi Niaz (1959: 10), a member of the Land Reforms Commission, concurs. A later study for the government authored by Niaz (1965: 28–30) confirmed that the tenancy acts produced dynamics and results similar to those elaborated in chapter 2. For summary of land tenures and legal provisions in the early period, Cheema (1954).

50. Herring and Chaudhry (1974: 271) present the argument and sources; for a vivid account, Punjab (1938: 11 ff.).

51. In fairness to the Revenue Department, political interests representing landlords controlled the Pakistani state in the 1950s, were hostile to what Ayub Khan (1967: 87) termed "even the very mild reforms" of 1952, and were able to scuttle reform initiatives.

just as it cannot monitor or enforce terms of rental contracts. Indeed, the task is mind-boggling—intervention in and regulation of millions of complex tenancy contracts seem virtually impossible administratively in rural Pakistan. Likewise, evictions come to the attention of the Revenue Department only if tenants take the initiative to bring adversary court proceedings. That particular arena is, of course, not particularly conducive to the effective struggle of the poor and weak against the wealthy, influential, and well-connected, as argued in chapters 2 and 3.

Thus no one, including the government, has a firm idea of how many tenants have been evicted by landlords illegally. The Zia regime's *White Paper* on the Bhutto government claims that tenant evictions *increased* after the land reform (Pakistan, 1979: vol. 4, 24). This claim is not unreasonable; the reaction to tenancy legislation by landlords historically in South Asia has been to alter records, changing tenants into "laborers" or "servants," or to evict tenants to avoid the problem altogether. Studies of tractorization in Pakistan find that large owners do not experience difficulty in evicting tenants in order to mechanize.[52] It is unlikely that a law from Islamabad would dramatically alter that customary situation, which is likely to be different only in those few areas in which tenants are well organized, individually well connected, or otherwise locally powerful.[53] The multiplication of such areas is likely, in part because of the further development of political and social consciousness among tenants in rural Pakistan, augmented by the land reform itself, which would predict increased militance in resisting evictions.[54] Indeed, there is evidence that the Bhutto regime became quite concerned about the implications of the hornets' nest it had stirred up by promising security and justice to the sharecroppers.[55]

---

52. E.g., the controversial study for the World Bank by McInerney and Donaldson (1973). An unpublished study by the Agricultural Development Bank of Pakistan (1974) also documents widespread tenant evictions during mechanization. My conversations with landlords in 1974–75 confirm the general view: if there was need to be rid of a tenant, there was no real problem in doing so. Comparisons between 1960 and 1972 show a marked decline in percentage of farm area operated by tenants reported in the census. Cf. Herring and Kennedy (1979); Burki (1980: 158–59).

53. Alavi (1971) gives an example of effective resistance organized by Rajput farmers in the area he studied, though local conditions were rather special.

54. This was a theme of Bhutto's speech in Thatta (Sind), reported in *Dawn* (January 3, 1975) as well as of his reply to a delegation of landlords who complained of abusive peasants and underground movements (*Pakistan Times*, January 26, 1974). Cf. *Pakistan Forum* 2, nos. 9–10 (June–July 1972): 19 ff.

55. Addressing a gathering at Nawabshah (Sind), Bhutto admonished peasants that (in the press reporter's words) "if instead of working harder they just kept running after the Prime Minister and other Government leaders with complaints of ejectments and non-availability of seed, the peasants would achieve nothing" *Pakistan Times* (January 18, 1974). Subsequently the government expressed concern about the failure of landlord–tenant relations to "stabilize" after the promulgation of the land reforms: Pakistan (draft), "Report to the Agricultural Enquiry Committee," typescript (Islamabad: June 1975).

Officially recorded complaints of unlawful eviction are almost certainly only the tip of a much larger iceberg. Given the social and administrative structure of rural Pakistan, the purely rational response to eviction would probably be quiescence. By the last month of the regime, official complaints of eviction totaled 19,324, more than 83 percent of which were in the Punjab (reinforcing the common perception that Punjabi tenants are far less intimidated by their landlords than are those of Sind, for example). Most of those cases were processed, and 13,747 tenants, or over 70 percent of the cases decided, were granted restoration orders (though the actual reinstatement of the tenant on the land remained problematic). Prosecution of landlords was ordered in 247 cases, but only 6 cases ended in conviction. The quick resolution of ejectment cases and the high percentage of decisions in favor of tenants compared favorably with experience in other parts of the subcontinent, but it must be emphasized that only a fraction of the total number of evictions came to court and no landlords were actually punished for illegal eviction of tenants. Moreover, the energy behind implementation of the tenancy reforms came largely from the personal interest of the prime minister, and particularly of Shaikh Rashid, in cases of this sort; under a less sympathetic regime, the ability of tenants to win ejectment cases, and their willingness to bring such cases, would arguably deteriorate.[56]

The Second Round of Ceilings and Other Antifeudal Measures

A "second round" of ceilings was announced by Prime Minister Bhutto on January 7, 1977. The ordinance significantly reduced the ceiling (by one-third) to 100 acres of irrigated land or 200 acres of unirrigated land. Unlike MLR 115, however, the new legislation provided for compensation at the rate of Rs 30 per Produce Index Unit. The compensation must have come as a relief to the feudals presumably still reeling from the blows of 1972, but the confiscatory element in the new law was significant, as the compensation fell far short of the market price of land.[57]

Bhutto had promised, in May of 1972, that MLR 115 was the final reduction of the ceiling and that "no further changes in land ceilings will be made" (Pakistan, 1972b: vol. 2, 157). The motive behind the second round was clearly tactical and political. The reforms were pushed through the National Assembly on the final day before dissolution for the elec-

56. Data from Federal Land Commission. Reinstatement of evicted tenants, even after courts ordered restoration, proved a major obstacle to implementation of Ceylon's Paddy Lands Act; inability to restore tenants quickly and the uncertainty surrounding restoration proceedings prevented many of the evicted tenants from going to court and discouraged most from demanding newly legislated legal rights, as explained in chapter 3.

57. Pakistan, *Ordinance No. II of 1977.* An estimate of the ratio of compensation to market value by a senior revenue officer is one-third. Market prices are so inconsistently related to Produce Index Units that any estimate is only approximate.

tions. The PPP had played heavily on the symbolism of land reforms as evidence of the party's commitment to the common people and to a redistributive populism. It is thus not surprising that a new round of land reforms, accompanied by introduction of a graduated agricultural income tax on larger farmers and exemption of small farmers from the land-revenue tax, should appear on the eve of an important election campaign.

The last round of reforms was heralded by banner headlines proclaiming: "New Deal for Farmers: Feudal System Comes to an End." The manipulation of symbols resembled that of the 1972 reforms. Landlords were threatened with stiff penal sanctions and forfeiture of property for evasion of the new law (though no one, to my knowledge, had been punished for violation of the earlier law, despite widely acknowledged evasion). The reforms promised social justice as demanded by the "ideology of Pakistan" (invoking the Quaid-e-Azam) and by the requirements of modern agriculture. Bhutto excoriated other politicians who talked of land reform for "dangling promises, raising bogus slogans, faking a concern for the poor only in order to achieve their selfish political ambitions."[58]

The prime minister defended his reforms—designed to eliminate the last "vestiges of a feudal order in our society"—as "socially just and historically inevitable." There was the familiar concern with "balance," ensuring that the needs of agriculture were met while simultaneously providing more land for the landless and further leveling rural inequalities. References in the speech also made clear, however, the sense in which the reforms were a preemptive strike, stealing a march on opposition political parties which planned to promise land reforms in their election manifestos.

As with earlier reforms, the rhetoric outran potentiality. If the 1977 ceiling were to be enforced, not very many owners, nor very much land, would be affected. According to land-revenue data collected immediately prior to promulgation of the ordinance (and indeed collected to gauge the net impact of the reforms), 46,831 owners possessed land in excess of 100 acres but less than 150 acres, and 56,254 owners possessed holdings greater than 150 acres. These 103,085 owners (a number vastly greater than that suggested by the census)[59] would be allowed to retain in the aggregate 10,308,500 acres of irrigated land or 20,617,000 acres of unirrigated land. The actual amount possessed by the two groups together was 15,039,922

58. The text was printed in *Pakistan Times* (January 6, 1977). Oddly enough, considering the obvious mass political appeal of the address, the prime minister spoke in convoluted and polished English, elaborating the main points only afterward in Urdu.

59. Revenue data on land holdings, aggregated from village records, reflect individual rather than family ownership units. Subdivision of land for the records occurs legitimately because of family property divisions and less legitimately for evasion of ceiling reforms, though the operational farm unit frequently remains intact. This phenomenon renders the two census reports (1960 and 1972) noncomparable, as the methodology was changed in 1972.

acres, of which only 3,430,045 acres was irrigated. Moreover, 6,157,488 acres of that total, more than one-third, was uncultivated, and almost certainly contained a high percentage of wasteland. Since owners are allowed by law to choose the land to be retained within the ceiling, very little cultivable land would change hands even if the new law were rigorously enforced.

This result was to be expected; landowners were aware that land ceilings might be lowered. Though Bhutto at times promised an end to ceiling legislation, at other times he mentioned future reductions in the ceiling. Cultivators had for some time been redistributing land among kin, selling land, and making adjustments to avoid losing land should the ceiling be lowered.

Although the second round of ceilings would yield very little land in the aggregate, there are important regional variations. Large owners of Sind and the Punjab would be virtually unaffected by the new ceiling. However, landowners in the NWFP stood to lose a great deal of land should the ceiling be enforced. Census data for Baluchistan suggest the same conclusion.[60] This regionally differentiated impact of the new ceiling offered potential opportunities to attack "feudal" political enemies in the two rebellious provinces while simultaneously avoiding serious confrontation with the politically important gentry of the Punjab and Sind, areas of PPP electoral strength. In this case "anti-feudal" measures and the tactical interests of the regime coincided.

Bhutto was unable to implement his second ceiling. The violence of the election and postelection periods precluded serious attention to land reform. After the coup in July of 1977, the military regime instructed the Land Commission to proceed with implementation of the ceiling, but the future of the second round later became uncertain.

Other last-minute measures taken by the Bhutto regime illustrate a similar appeal to the rural poor. On December 18, 1976, a "National Charter for Peasants" was promulgated, mandating that all cultivable land which vests in the state, if not reserved for some public purpose, will be distributed among landless cultivators and farmers with less than a "subsistence holding."[61] Cultivating tenants would be given first priority.

60. I have used unpublished Revenue Department data on holdings wherever possible in this section because it was collected in 1976, four years after the census, and presumably reflects operation of the 1972 reforms. However, Revenue Department data for Baluchistan are internally inconsistent and obviously inaccurate. The census data for Baluchistan suffer from the omission of the Mari Bugti area, but addition of that area would strengthen the case in the text. It is reasonable to use the data to judge the politics of reform because they constitute the information, whether accurate or inaccurate, which the prime minister had before him in making policy decisions and were collected for just that purpose.

61. In signing the National Charter, Bhutto said, "All power to the peasants. May Allah bless them and their children" *Pakistan Affairs* (January 1, 1977). There are regional differences in the officially designated "subsistence holding"—12.5 acres in the NWFP and Punjab, 16 acres in Sind, and 32 acres in Baluchistan.

Moreover, all tenants on state lands would be granted ownership rights. Such a policy, if enforced, has potential significance because the aggregate area made available through ceiling reforms has been small and of poor quality. Moreover, if enforced, the policy would counteract the tendency for state lands to fall into the hands of powerful and wealthy, often nonagricultural, individuals.[62]

Bhutto's final attack on the feudal system included a dramatic revision of the agricultural tax system. The traditional land-revenue tax is imposed on each acre of cultivated land and is thus regressive, though relatively light in incidence. The real burden on the cultivators is the oppressive and corrupt revenue bureaucracy at the local level. Bhutto's revisions exempted from the tax all farmers with holdings under 25 (irrigated) acres; the land revenue was to be replaced by a progressive income tax. The government claimed that the reform would exempt 95 percent of the peasantry from taxation.[63]

Like the 1972 ceiling act, the agricultural income ordinance contains incentives for modernization and mechanization. The law allows full deduction of the cost of tractors, agricultural machinery and implements, tubewells, leveling, and land development, as well as current expenses, in the year in which the costs are incurred. Because agricultural income is almost impossible to monitor, a simplified accounting system tied to Produce Index Units was proposed. Taken together, the deduction allowances and simplified accounting procedures provide real tax incentives to invest in agriculture. The accounting procedure, in the selection of a mechanism for translating PIU ratings of land into income, would necessarily involve discrimination among large farmers, rewarding the most productive and penalizing—perhaps ruining—those with low productivity.[64] Those feudal landlords who escaped eradication through three

62. The Revenue Department estimated that 3,471,531 acres of culturable land was available for distribution under the National Charter. This figure, though only a fraction of that claimed by Bhutto's spokesmen, represents about twice that made available through ceiling reforms. Of the total, only 559,968 acres are irrigated, however. That area would allow about 44,000 tenants to become owners, assuming distribution in "subsistence" plots. If all the "culturable" land is indeed cultivable, and were distributed, about six times that number of tenants could be given subsistence farms, representing about one-fifth of the pure tenants of the country.

63. Pakistan, *Ordinance No. III of 1977*. For the finance minister's explanation, *Pakistan Affairs* (February 1, 1972); *Pakistan Economist* (November 29, 1975), p. 14.

64. Sections 1 and 2 of the *Ordinance*. The accounting procedure proposed would estimate income as a multiple of the Produce Index Unit rating of the land. The setting of that ratio is the source of the differential impact of the tax, since productivity even on comparable land varies significantly. The mechanism could be set to allow inefficient producers a moderate tax rate (leaving efficient producers with lightly taxed profits) or to tax the profits of efficient producers at a moderate level, imposing a very heavy tax burden on inefficient producers (the backward feudals, presumably). I have excluded consideration of Bhutto's other attack on feudal landlords—the abolition by statute of "feudal dues"—for lack of reliable information about the impact.

rounds of ceiling reforms were again being nudged into the role of agricultural entrepreneurs, just as they were being integrated politically into the PPP for the election campaign.[65] Though the issue is now moot, it seems that Bhutto's changes in tax policy held at least as much potential as the ceiling reforms for the conversion of feudals into entrepreneurs, and reflected similar policy logic.

The Bourgeois Revolution and the Eradication of Feudalism

Official justifications of land reform in Pakistan have taken an unambiguous position on the necessity of eradicating "feudalism" and replacing it with an agriculture organized around private property and material incentives, dominated by modern entrepreneurs. This sounds very much like a bourgeois revolution. Should we take the official rhetoric seriously? We can usefully approach this question by asking a prior one: what is it that those who have sought to transform Pakistan into a thoroughly capitalist society, devoid of feudal residues, have found objectionable in the agrarian system? Though this question will be considered more broadly in chapter 8, it is important to conclude the discussion of land reforms in Pakistan with a brief treatment of the issue.

Economically, in Pakistan feudalism has connoted traditional parasitic landlordism and, by implication, agricultural stagnation. As the core of the national economy is agricultural, and the state of agriculture directly affects the lives of most Pakistanis, concern for rationalizing and modernizing production in rural areas has been a policy problem for ruling elites since Independence. No regime in Pakistan can long endure if the granaries are empty. Nor can broad national economic development be contemplated without the foreign exchange earned by agricultural exports (primarily cotton and *basmati* rice). Moreover, the necessity to expend scarce foreign exchange on imported food limits developmental choices and resources. To the extent that inefficient and primitive means of exploiting the land persist on "feudal" estates, the economic development interests of those classes which control the national state are threatened. In Pakistan, this imperative became manifest as the new nation changed from a food-surplus to a food-deficit area in the First Five Year Plan period; the resulting dislocations seriously upset national planning processes.

65. A critical analysis of the Bhutto land reforms in terms of the regime's social base by the president of the Mazdoor–Kisan (Worker-Peasant) Party, Ishaque Mohammad, was published in *Punjab Punch* (March 19 and 26, 1972) and reprinted in *Pakistan Forum* 3; no. 2 (December 1972). For a discussion of how great landlord families entered Bhutto's PPP, based on extensive fieldwork, Jones (1978). Feroze Ahmed, in *Pakistan Forum* 2:9–10 (June–July 1972), presents an account of PPP factions and the government's turning against the rural left. On the prominence of landlords as PPP candidates in the election of 1977, see Burki (1980: 56); *Pakistan Progressive* 2, no. 2 (May–June 1978), pp. 8–14.

"Feudal" economic relations also deprive the state, and dominant political groups, of opportunities for integration and penetration of the rural economy. The traditional landlord mediates economically between tenants and market in a functional parallel to political mediation through patron–client networks. Opportunities for suppliers of working and fixed capital, niches for urban and rural capitalists, are denied not only by the economic stagnation of "feudalism," but also by its mediating function vis-à-vis inputs and marketing. Moreover, a stagnant agricultural sector deprives the regime of flexibility in extracting tax resources. Vigorous economic development in rural areas, on the other hand, produces effective demand both for new consumption goods and for new agricultural inputs, creating new markets and marketing niches, new channels for extracting surplus from rural producers.

Beyond these economic imperatives, in the policy logic of land reforms in Pakistan there was a great deal about "feudalism" that needed eradicating. Politically, the concentration of power in the hands of great landed families has tied the hands of Pakistani regimes, preventing political centralization and integration. Ayub Khan acknowledged the role of his land reforms in addressing that chronic problem. The PPP as a mass populist party was originally, in part, an effort to circumvent dependence on entrenched rural power brokers. Once in power, a pressing political problem was the inability to exercise central governmental control in Baluchistan and the NWFP. There the meaning of *feudal* was quite clear to Mr. Bhutto, and indeed the land reforms of 1972 and 1977 struck hardest at the large landowners of those provinces. Likewise, the strategic position of the NWFP and the crucial natural resources of Baluchistan (along with the traumatic separation of Bangladesh) undoubtedly sharpened Bhutto's concern for national integration, political penetration, and political stability. One may wonder how eager the prime minister would have been to eradicate the feudal system if all the *khans* and *sardars* had lined up politically with the PPP, but in the event, critical regime objectives were blocked by powerful chiefs whose traditional relations to both state and following may usefully be termed feudal. There the eradication of feudalism was both a regime-specific and strategic political desideratum.[66]

Socially, in Pakistani policy circles feudalism has meant the presence of "tyrannical" and "oppressive" landlords. Abusive conditions in

66. On the analytical utility of applying the term *feudal* to social configurations in the areas adjoining Afghanistan and Iran, cf. Herring (1979a: 515–17). For an official treatment of how the writ of the central government did not apply in Baluchistan as of 1974, Pakistan, "White Paper on Baluchistan," *Dawn* (October 20, 1974). On Baluchistan's social system, we have the field notes of Robert Pehrson (1966) compiled and organized by Frederick Barth. Barth's own classic (1959) argues that Pathan social organization was indeed "feudal." The fusion of political and economic power is suggested linguistically in the term *khan*, which means both landlord and chief in the region. For a more recent treatment of these areas, Embree, ed. (1977).

the social relations of production are conducive neither to economic efficiency nor to political stability, and are offensive to the legitimating
ideology of a market economy and democratic polity—free labor and cit-
izenship.

The anwer to our question is then: yes, the land reforms may be
considered a part of the process of completing, invigorating, and facilitating the bourgeois revolution, contributing to the elimination of those
political, economic, and social vestiges which are antithetical to a na-
tionally consolidated bourgeois society, economy, and polity. But the reforms must also, more decisively, be analyzed in terms of tactical imperatives. These functions were clear during the Bhutto regime—generating
powerful symbols, retaining the allegiance of the PPP Left, attacking political opponents and regional satraps, attempting to coopt peasant discontent, stealing a march on other political parties that threatened to use
the same symbols in a countermobilization of the rural have-nots. The
tactical and strategic imperatives are of course complementary—a regime must manage the short-term struggles to retain power in order to
achieve long-range strategic goals.

But if agrarian reforms are potentially such powerful weapons in the
bourgeois revolution, why were they wielded so meekly by regimes openly
committed to creating and protecting a "progressive and enlightened"
capitalist economy in agriculture as in industry? The answer has both
tactical and strategic elements.

Strategically, a problem is posed by structural characteristics of the
rural economy: "feudal" and capitalist relations are inextricably inter-
twined in Pakistan's agriculture. In an important sense, the bourgeois
revolution in land relations was begun under colonial auspices (cf. Alavi,
1973); capitalism is firmly installed in rural Pakistan, though often operating through traditional, precapitalist social organizations of production such as sharecropping. Large estates in Pakistan show more characteristics of modern capitalist farming than do smaller farms—extensive
use of wage labor, modern inputs and machinery, and so on—primarily
because of easier access to heavily subsidized credit and capital and surplus farm income. Landed families have roots and branches in both economies, modern and traditional, "feudal" and capitalist; the analytically
distinct categories interpenetrate on the ground. Thus any radical land
redistribution, or a land-to-the-tiller policy, would, like harsh cancer
treatments, root out feudal residues in agriculture, but only at the expense of damaging the healthy capitalist tissue in which it is embedded.
Bhutto's public statements on the level of the ceiling reiterated the earlier policy logic of reforms in Pakistan: a very low ceiling would discourage exactly that class of agrarian entrepreneurs on which he felt the future of Pakistan's agriculture depended.

But if these strategic concerns mitigated the attack on feudalism
via land reform, tactical political constraints played a more proximate

and determinate role. Whether feudal, capitalist, or some permutation of these, the landowning gentry of rural Pakistan wields local political power; it is hard to imagine any regime—in the absence of agrarian revolution—governing long without their support. Given this constraint, and the economic and symbolic imperatives facing Pakistani regimes, the land reforms have been tactically astute. The great landed families were neither eradicated nor permanently alienated, but were given strong cues as to their appropriate role and behavior, both politically and economically. Bhutto's reforms were more serious than those of Ayub Khan, and yet the powerful landed families of Sind and the Punjab found themselves able to support (and join) the PPP in increasing numbers after the reforms.[67] Bhutto's second round of ceiling reforms would have affected very few landlords in the provinces of PPP strength—the Punjab and Sind—but would have attacked quite a few recalcitrant "feudals" in rebellious Baluchistan and the NWFP. But Bhutto's land reforms, like the agrarian measures of previous regimes, were not intended to *eradicate* feudals so much as to nudge them into the fold—the fold being comprised of progressive, enlightened gentry who invest in the land and do not arbitrarily abuse their tenants, who fulfill their traditional paternalistic obligations toward the less privileged, and who may be tempted to throw their considerable political weight behind the regime in order to protect their privileges and to ward off future, perhaps more serious, attempts at their eradication.

67. The wide discretionary power exercised in the implementation of ceiling reforms, particularly after Bhutto's politicization and purge of the bureaucracy, arguably encouraged the great landed families to cast their lots with the probable winner in the elections. Burki's (1980: pt. 3) argument that the alienation of urban constituencies, particularly the middle class, led Bhutto to cultivate links with rural power brokers for the election is consistent with the argument in the text and resonates with the political thrust of the Peasants' Charter, elimination of land taxes for small holders, and new ceilings just before the election, particularly if the landlords understood that evasion of the new ceilings would be easier from within the governing party and had redistributed lands in anticipation of further reforms in any event. For documentation of the widely recognized use of land reforms during the Bhutto period as a resource in "ordinary politics" (rewarding supporters, punishing enemies), Pakistan, *White Paper on the Performance of the Bhutto Regime* (1979) 4:10–16.

5 Transformational Logic and Ordinary Politics: Land Ceilings in India and Sri Lanka

I shall be failing in my duty, if just for the sake of political advancement, or for winning cheap applause from Land Reform enthusiasts, I do not in utmost humility raise my voice . . . against a policy which is destined to give death knell to any chances of modernization in farming, and keep agriculture forever in primitive stage and make it the monopoly of illiterate, ignorant and poverty-stricken class of people by turning out of this profession men of intelligence, enterprise and ambition who wish to settle on land not as parasitic type of landlords but as progressive and enterprising farmers.
—Sardar Lal Singh, Member of Parliament and Member, Panel on Land Reforms, Indian Planning Commission

Both of Pakistan's ceiling-redistributive reforms were martial law regulations; both were produced in circumstances which may usefully be termed political crises, despite the obvious ambiguity presented by the word *crisis*. Ayub Khan's coup ended a period of extraordinary political immobilism and came at a time of declining agricultural output per capita; among his first acts and top priorities was the land reform. Zulfikar Ali Bhutto took power in a truncated Pakistan after the national trauma of civil war in Bangladesh. Bhutto's electoral base was geographically narrow and arguably shallow; the 1972 land reforms were part of a dramatic bid for legitimacy and support for the new regime. In both cases, political power was concentrated; single individuals had the power to alter or abort agrarian reforms.

Ceiling reforms in India and Sri Lanka, by contrast, have been the products of political systems characterized by institutionalized dispersion of political power. In India, as in Pakistan, early political and planning documents prescribed and defended appropriation and redistribution of land in transformational terms, mandated by considerations of distributive justice, economic rationality, and "social harmony." But as the plea from Sardar Lal Singh which introduces this chapter so clearly illustrates, neither the normative nor the empirical case for land redistribution went unchallenged. The resultant political conflicts yielded a vector sum weakly in favor of ceiling reform, but with sufficient opposition to gut the reforms of any serious transformational impact. Nevertheless, two decades of ceiling debates and legislation have firmly established the concept of land ceilings and redistribution, as well as progressively lower ceilings, aided in part by widening perceptions of agrarian crisis and broader redistributive political-symbolic imperatives.

In Sri Lanka the connection between crisis and land reform was direct and immediate. In contrast to India and Pakistan, land ceilings were not legislated until the 1971 rural insurrection jolted the government into action. The curious result is that a far greater percentage of Sri Lanka's agricultural land was affected by the precipitous 1972 ceiling than by progressive rounds of ceiling reforms in India and Pakistan in the two decades since the late 1950s.

Land Ceilings in India: Zamindars and Progressive Farmers

The failures of land reforms in India are among the best-documented in the world. The Indian state, in distinct contrast to that of Pakistan, has extensively monitored its efforts at land reform, periodically constituting committees and task forces to study the issue. The center of gravity of these reports is bluntly critical. As the Planning Commission's Task Force on Agrarian Relations stated in 1973: "In no sphere of public activity in our country since Independence has the hiatus between precept and practice, between policy pronouncements and actual execution, been as great as in the domain of land reform" (India, 1973: 7).

One cause of this unquestionable hiatus is located in political structure. India's political system is federal and land reform is a State prerogative; the Center can plan agrarian strategy, but individual States determine the actual policy; the gulf has been wide between Central plans and State programs of land reform, with great variations among States depending on the local political conditions and agrarian configuration.[1] State-level political power has, with important exceptions, remained more closely tied to the agrarian power structure, hence more responsive to landed elites, than is the case in national politics.

The resistance of conservative State-level political and administrative elites to Central directives on land reform is well understood and rightfully emphasized. What is less understood, and underemphasized, is the ambiguity in the Central directives; the political conflict that surrounds land reforms has by no means been resolved in Delhi. The issue of ceiling legislation has been particularly conflictual: what is the justi-

---

1. For an excellent overview, Merillat (1970). Representative recent official documents reiterating the themes of numerous studies include India (1973), (1974: 42–45), (1976: vol. 15, chaps. 66.4, 66.5). Some general propositions for explaining State differences are found in Hart and Herring (1977). Along with the exceptionalism of States with strong leftist movements, other variations appear for special historical reasons (e.g., Kashmir); see Kotovsky (1964: 114–16), Thorner (1956: chap. 3).

fication for redistributing India's land wealth and, by implication, restructuring rural India?

There has been great concern in Indian policy logic, on both ethical and economic grounds, that the good and deserving landlords be separated from the parasitic and undeserving. It is useful to consider Indian ceiling reforms as coming in three waves: first, the "abolition of intermediaries" in the early 1950s was an explicit attack on the bad landlords, attempting to size down their estates, free their tenants from social and political oppression, and create entrepreneurs from parasites. The second round was ceiling legislation of the more usual sort, with uniform ceilings regardless of the title of the landowner; these reforms came in the late 1950s, early 1960s, and were universally recognized as failures. The third round coincided with the surge of redistributive political initiatives of Indira Gandhi's *garibi hatao* ("abolish poverty") period in the early 1970s and received added impetus from growing concern about peasant violence and "land grabs" organized by the Left.

The first round of land redistribution was the "abolition of intermediaries." The term "intermediary" is a functional one and denotes a position in the agrarian structure between the state and the cultivator. Such intermediaries mediated rental exactions from direct producers and exercised broad local powers of "overlordship," as well, under colonial rule (Baden-Powell, 1892: vol. 1, chap. 4, 5). The titles of the intermediaries varied—*zamindars, inamdars, jagirdars,* and so on—though the word *zamindar* (literally "landholder") is frequently used as the generic term. The *zamindars* came to be, linguistically, the very symbol of the bad landlord—not only nonproductive, parasitic, and "feudal," but antinational and collaborationist, having acquired and retained their privileged landholding status through unjustifiable means. Jawaharlal Nehru heaped scorn on the *taluqdars* and *zamindars* of Avadh, terming them "the spoilt child of the British Government" . . . "physically and intellectually degenerate" . . . who had "outlived their day." Congress theoretician H. D. Malaviya expressed the core of elite nationalist sentiment when he claimed that "the zamindars literally functioned economically as the native garrisons of an alien imperialism."[2] Moreover, the "semifeudal" zamindars were seen as responsible for India's agricultural backwardness (India, 1976: vol. 15, 17, 47–50).

The normative argument for zamindar (etc.) abolition was thus quite simple: the mode of acquisition of the land rights had been unacceptable and the failure to perform productive functions on the land ruled out possible legitimization of status in the independent period. The "abolition" acts which addressed this problem typically appropriated all lands

2. Malaviya (1954: 46), wrote as Secretary, Economic and Political Research Department, All-India Congress Committee; Nehru's remarks, p. 6. For more on the issue, see the opening section of chap. 4; Thorner (1956: 17 and passim); Nehru (1960: 290 ff.); India (1976: vol. 15, 65.2).

of the zamindar except the "home farm" (*khudkasht*, etc.), which the zamindar was allowed to retain and farm. The state compensated the former owner and vested what were effectively ownership rights in the former intermediary's tenants. Only those areas of India with technically intermediary tenures, about 40 percent of the total area, were affected by the reforms.

The treatment of intermediary abolition as ceiling reform is unorthodox but useful. The major deviation from classic ceiling reforms is simply that the ceiling is variable and particularistic rather than uniform, as are the norms for redistributing postreform rights in land, following the main lines of the traditional land-tenure hierarchy. Ground rent as an institution was not attacked or abolished; old owners ("intermediaries") were allowed to retain large amounts of land for "self-cultivation," which often meant continuation of sharecropping, and new owners (former superior tenants) were—in fact if not in law—free to engage sharecroppers as well. Many zamindars, large and small, were wiped out, but the center of the policy should be seen as a variable ceiling, depending on the individual *zamindari* tenurial configuration, which did not mandate changes in the social organization of production. The reforms did not assure that *cultivators* would obtain land nor that new proprietors would not function as parasitic rentiers.

Despite the fact that Land to the Tiller was one of the major slogans for mobilizing the peasantry in the anticolonial struggle, the slogan itself always had divergent interpretations; the abolition of intermediaries was justified in terms of securing land for the tillers, but the effects were as ambivalent as the interpretations of the slogan. The summary of effects in the draft *Fifth Five Year Plan* (India, 1974: 43) is accurate: "With the abolition of intermediary interests the ownership of land became more broad-based and the erst-while superior tenants acquired a higher social status." The position of erstwhile inferior tenants was little affected, except negatively through waves of evictions of sharecroppers on the "home farms" and increased landlord reluctance to establish new formal, secure tenancies.[3] Angus Maddison (1971: 105–06) captured the process nicely with a graphic metaphor:

> The rural structure is still like an onion with many layers. The British peeled off one layer. Zamindar abolition peeled off another. This time, as under the British, all the benefits have been absorbed by the next two or three layers. . . . But the sharecroppers and laborers are still squeezed to a

---

3. The National Commission on Agriculture (1976: vol. 15, 56 and passim) noted that *zamindari* abolition produced an "unprecedented wave" of evictions of tenants. Gunnar Myrdal (1968: vol. 2, 1309) commented: "Put bluntly . . . the abolition of intermediaries in India and Pakistan was not intended to give land to those who actually till it" (Cf. Geof Wood [1973] for a treatment of northern Bihar State). For a summary of regional case studies, Kotovsky (1959: chaps. 2, 3). An official State-by-State analysis of impact, with rejoinders from State governments, is India (1966b).

sub-human margin of subsistence as they were under the Moghuls.

Because of the massive compensation payments to ex-intermediaries and the tortuous administrative process involved in the reforms, the abolition of intermediaries was extremely costly to the state. The belief that zamindars were inimical to economic development was one justification for bearing that cost, but it must also be emphasized that the intermediaries had under "indirect rule" been intermediaries in the political structure as well as the economic, thus representing a significant obstacle to the new state's programs for political penetration and integration in the rural areas.

Despite the strength of nationalist feeling against the zamindars, legislation at the State level was slow, filled with loopholes, entangled in tedious litigation, and allowed major sections of the rentier class to continue as rentiers, though on smaller areas, with compensation for the rights surrendered.[4] Consensus in nationalist circles on the evils of *zamindari* control of the rural economy was relatively easy, as a central theme of nationalist analysis of what was wrong with rural India centered on colonial land policy, the most vulnerable symbol of which was the zamindar. Moreover, the relatively prosperous peasant castes which strongly supported the Congress movement stood to gain from the vesting of intermediary rights in superior tenants (cf. Neale, 1962: 256). But what of the large landowners who supported the nationalist movement or had accumulated land through means other than collaboration with the British?

This question was not settled in the highest policy circles, and as a result the often-mentioned Central initiatives in land reform were more qualified than is usually recognized.[5] Though the important 1949 *Report of the Congress Agrarian Reforms Committee* (often referred to as the Kumarappa committee, after its chairman) contained an explicit model of the use of ceiling legislation to transform the agrarian sector, and argued its case forcefully, the report was not unanimous and certainly did not reflect the consensus of the Congress Party. Opposition to the recommendations of that report surfaced both at the Center and in the States. But the report was extremely influential, in some ways prophetic, and deserves extended comment. Indeed, the model presented, a very low ceiling combined with a land-to-the-tiller policy, is closely approximated

4. The study of Bihar by Jannuzi (1974) treats the loopholes, political opposition, and delays common in other States, though Bihar is an extreme case. For India's largest state, Walter C. Neale (1962: chap. 13). The Planning Commission estimates that 20 million "tenants" were brought into direct contact with the State through the abolition of intermediaries. Compensation payments came to 6.7 billion rupees (India, 1974: 42).

5. An example of the frequently posed dichotomy between progressive Central initiatives and conservative State policy is Jannuzi (1974). For a critical treatment of State legislation and variations therein by a leader of the peasant movement in India, Bhowani Sen (1955: chap. 4).

by the contemporary Karala reforms that will be considered in subsequent chapters.

The Report of the Congress Agrarian Reforms Committee (1949)

The report presented a view of rural society which necessitated transformation. The land-tenure structure was seen as an obstacle to appropriate economic, political, and social goals of a modern state. The view of rural dynamics and obstacles to change seems strikingly accurate; it is the efficient causation in the model which raises serious questions.

In economic terms, the report argued that large holdings in India were inefficient, whereas small (but not dwarf) farms were efficient. The solution was a scaling down of large farms to upgrade dwarf farms and rehabilitate the landless. The empirical argument for redistribution was based on tables showing output by size of holding in the United States, Denmark, Switzerland, and England (AICC, 1949: 22 ff.). In every case, gross output per acre was higher on small farms. The committee used these data to argue for a ceiling on ownership and the economic viability of a society of small farmers.

The committee envisaged three kinds of postreform private agricultural holdings (ibid.: 8). First, the "economic holding" was that amount of land necessary to provide a "reasonable standard of living to the cultivator" and "full employment to a family of normal size and at least to a pair of bullocks." The "basic holding" was smaller than an economic holding, yet not so small as to be "palpably uneconomic." The basic holding could be rehabilitated through various government programs, but would not in itself provide full employment (nor, presumably, "a reasonable standard of living"). The "optimum holding" was to be the largest allowed by law, the ceiling level. The committee suggested a ceiling of three times the economic size, varying in acre measurement according to agronomic characteristics of different regions.

The threefold differentiation left two classes of people to be considered—the landless and the cultivators of holdings so small as to be "palpably uneconomic." Presumably, these classes would live primarily by agricultural wage labor. Land in excess of the ceiling was to be used to provide "cooperative joint farming" and experimental collective farming opportunities. The committee envisioned the cooperative farms as creatures of the village community and warned against "giant cooperatives in which the individual may lose his individuality." Reflecting a strain of thought important in nationalist ideology, the committee rejected the Western laissez-faire market model ("the clash of interests of uncoordinated individuals") which resulted from "the decay of the village community," and argued that agricultural development could not be left to "the individual peasant" (ibid.: 9, 36, 43).

The model of land ownership was thus not the purely market one in which the entire "bundle of rights" is vested in any private individual, but one in which rights in land are "shared between the community and the tiller." For example, because land was legitimately the "owner's" only so long as he used it, uncultivated land was to revert to the "village community" (ibid.: 10).

The final recommendations of the committee present a model of rural society that is a blend of traditional, perhaps romantic, Gandhian notions of the "village community" and egalitarian impulses, combined with particular notions of economic efficiency. In arguing for collective local responsibility for enforcing efficient land use, the committee cited for justification (p. 41) both the ancient Hindu Laws of Manu and the 1947 Agriculture Act of Great Britain.[6] The ideal was clearly small-plot peasant proprietorship within a communal village context. Bigness per se was suspect: large-scale cooperatives and large-scale private capitalist farms were both explicitly rejected. The village community was to restore traditional (perhaps mythical) guarantees of economic security and to ensure the just and efficient distribution and use of village land. The rejection of bigness, and the strong belief in decentralization, extended to the state itself. The ideal was local self-government based on a revitalized village society, the necessary preconditions for which included thorough land reforms (ibid.: 22, 43, and passim).

The view of the rural world which underlies the committee's position was one that has been confirmed in empirical studies of land-reform implementation throughout South Asia. The administrative machinery of the state was seen as inadequate, not only because of the absence of land records or written lease agreements, but also because of the "illiteracy of the cultivating class," the "dishonesty of the land-owning peasantry," and the "corruption of officials" (ibid.: 49). Given this model of the way the rural world works, and the normative and practical objections to highly centralized, authoritarian bureaucracy, the mechanism for effecting land reforms had to be the "village community" itself. The irony is that the village community invoked by the committee could be reconstituted only after the implementation of land reforms, and thus could hardly serve as the efficient cause mechanism for realizing those reforms, as argued at length in chapter 3.

Dissent and Ambiguity on Ceilings

The vision of the Congress Agrarian Reforms Committee was not primarily punitive, as was much of the argument for *zamindari* abolition,

6. This line of argument, including the reference to the British legislation of 1947, was reflected in Sri Lanka's Agricultural Productivity Law, discussed below. For a treatment of the egalitarian strands of Gandhi's thoughts on political economy (which were, however, frequently contradicted by conservative positions on concrete issues), see Francine Frankel (1978: chap. 1).

but had positive transformational elements: the surplus land was to be used to create cooperatives to provide models for Indian rural development and to rehabilitate marginal small farmers. Along with the land-to-the-tiller component of the reform, the ceiling was to serve the regeneration of village society and self-government. Necessarily, the ceiling was quite low; though no acreage figures were given, it would arguably have ranged between 6 acres in productive paddy areas to 30–40 acres in infertile rain-fed areas, based on a rough calculation of the economic holding.[7]

The basic world-view of the model—the normative arguments about acceptable degrees of inequality in land ownership, the productivity argument, the vision of the future or rural India, the evaluation of alternative possibilities for more limited reform—was by no means widely shared. The Congress did not formally adopt a resolution committing the party to the committee's recommendations (Malaviya, 1954: 83). In the largest State, the Uttar Pradesh Zamindari Abolition Committee rejected a ceiling-redistributive measure after agreeing to *zamindari* abolition.[8] Congress Party resolutions on national agrarian policy other than abolition of intermediaries were vague and avoided the ceiling issue.[9]

The economic case for the ceiling model by no means went unchallenged. Indeed, the draft *First Five Year Plan* rejected ceilings as too costly to implement and contrary to productivity imperatives in agriculture. Daniel Thorner, one of the most astute foreign observers of early land reforms in India, argued (1956: 60–61) that the final version of the *First Five Year Plan* adopted a ceiling recommendation only because the Congress had suffered electoral defeats to parties promising more radical land reforms (cf. Kotovsky, 1959: 86–87).

The ceiling case made by the Congress Agrarian Reforms Committee was challenged by important organs of government. In an official publication of the Ministry of Food and Agriculture in 1955, when ceilings were supposedly official policy as enunciated in the *First Five Year Plan*, it was noted that the ceiling question in recent years had been the subject of "heated controversy."[10] That publication hedged even on the issue of intermediaries, arguing that absentee landlords were in reality no different from absentee owners in industry (stockholders), and could not be condemned unless land resources were being inefficiently utilized. Moreover, landlordism "was a situation acquiesced in by society" (India, 1955: vol. 6, xlix). In contrast to the position of the Congress Agrarian Reforms

7. My estimation, simply to give orders of magnitude. For evidence that this range is reasonable, A. M. Khusro (1973).

8. Thorner (1956: 56); AICC (1949: 24). A ceiling of 30 acres was placed on the acquisition of *future* holdings, however.

9. The major policy statements are contained in Malaviya (1954: 78–95). Cf. India (1976: vol. 15, 65.2).

10. India (1955, vol. 6: xlviii). Daniel Thorner (1956: 63, 70) stressed the notable lack of commitment to the ceiling concept in the Agriculture Ministry. Serious differences between the ministry and the planning commission have continued.

Committee, which held that the transfer by landlords of use rights to tenants constituted surrender of a claim on the land in favor of the tenant, the Agriculture Ministry held that resumption of land from tenants by landlords for self-cultivation was justifiable (ibid.: xlix).

The argument in favor of ceilings was presented by the Agriculture Ministry as primarily moral—the constitutional imperatives of equality, security, and the right to work. Economic considerations seemed to argue against ceilings, as there would be little advantage to the economy to compensate for "penalizing those few who had begun to apply advanced methods of production to agriculture on areas sufficient to permit optimum use of modern machinery and other resources." In short, from production and modernization perspectives, ceilings were "an unwise and retrograde step." Also noted in opposition to the ceiling were the inadequacy of land records, the massive administrative costs, and the possibility that those not benefited by the redistribution would develop a "new sense of dissatisfaction" (ibid.: xlix).

In tracing the history of the ceiling issue in the Five Year Plans, Wolf Ladejinsky (1972a) noted that the primary justification was inevitably in terms of "public interest" or "social justice," and seemed to carry no conviction that redistribution would either relieve the problem of landlessness to a significant extent or increase productivity. Land ceilings were also a part of the flirtation with cooperative farming as a means of achieving "socialism" in rural India, echoing refrains from the Congress Agrarian Reforms Committee. The Second Plan, in particular, stressed cooperation. The efficient causation was double-edged. Ceilings and redistribution were seen as necessary conditions for cooperative farming because "cooperation thrives best in homogeneous groups in which there are no large inequalities" (ibid.: 402; cf. Krishna, 1961). Second, land distributed to the landless could be worked cooperatively. But the commitment to cooperative farming was shallow and theoretical. Ladejinsky noted that "the character of the cooperative farms established in the wake of the ceilings was nothing as envisaged: those farms are essentially dummy institutions created by the big owners as one of the means to evade the basic provisions of the land reforms" (1972a: 402).

The normative case against the "intermediaries" had been clear; it was believed that the mode of acquisition of rights had been illegitimate and that no productive function was performed, thus the rental income was not justified. The case of ordinary landlords was different. The conscience of the Congress, Mahatma Gandhi, while conceding the parasitic nature of landlordism as usually practiced, stated that he would not be a party to dispossessing the "propertied classes," nor did he think the people of India in a referendum would vote for expropriation.[11]

11. Gandhi (1970: 33, 35, 40–41), originally in *Amrita Bazaar Patrika*, August 2, 1934. Gandhi explicitly rejected a structuralist view of exploitation: "I do not believe that the capitalists and landlords are all exploiters by an inherent necessity" (p. 41).

The normative case *against* land ceilings thus had modern techno-cratic strands—individuals should not be deprived of their investment so long as it is used efficiently—and traditional Gandhian aspects—the feel-ing that expropriation was a violent, unacceptable method of dealing with a problem that could be handled through moral suasion. Indeed, the *bhoodan* (land gift) and later *gramdan* (village gift) movements were be-gun by Gandhians who saw the solution to the problem of landlessness in organized appeals to the conscience of large owners voluntarily to give a part of their land to the less fortunate.[12]

Though it was relatively easy to build a normative consensus against the zamindars for their "feudal" repression of the peasantry, antinational collaboration, parasitism, and so on, the same kind of moral outrage could not be raised against large landowners in general. Culturally, even the large landlords were often peasants, poor relative to urban elites and to world standards of landed elites. Why was their wealth to be confiscated and redistributed while that of urban businessmen, speculators, black marketeers, slumlords, and so on, was to be protected? Didn't the large landowners other than feudal zamindars carry the seeds of modern Indian agriculture?

A central issue in the debate over land ceilings was thus their trans-formational potential: would such reforms turn parasitic landlords (who had few defenders) into modern entrepreneurs, as policy logic in Pakistan had held, or simply ruin agriculture by creating disincentives for the ca-pable and industrious? The zamindars were almost by definition inimical to the modernization of agriculture, and though it was hoped that com-pensation provided through *zamindari* abolition would facilitate new in-vestment on the land, there was no guarantee. Ceiling reform thus pre-sented the same dilemma in India as in Pakistan: how could the unhealthy, "feudal" elements be excised without harming the fragile modern capi-talist tissues that were just beginning to form? Sardar Lal Singh, a Mem-ber of Parliament and progressive farmer himself, as well as a member of the Planning Commission's Panel on Land Reforms, expressed the ques-tion forcefully: "Let there be elimination of feudal landlords or those of parasitic type but why expell from agricultural profession enterprising and progressive agriculturalists . . . who can provide necessary leadership in rural areas? Ceiling at [a] low level will drive away men of intelligence, ambition, business enterprise and capital from farming" (India, 1959: 123, 125). A ceiling attacks large holdings, some of which may be feudal and parasitic, others modern and enterprising; a mechanism for differentiat-ing the good landlords from the bad was clearly needed.

A compromise that recognized the fears of those who saw ceilings

12. For a treatment of the intellectual roots of the movement, Tennyson (1955); for a critical appraisal, Jannuzi (1974: chap. 7, 93 ff.). Though Jannuzi and others are justifiably critical of the impact, the results are actually rather impressive when compared to formal ceiling legislation, which was backed by the full resources of the state.

as antithetical to a modern, dynamic agriculture and yet separated deserving from undeserving landlords was to legislate exemptions from the
ceiling for capitalist farms. The *Second Five Year Plan* recommended, and
most States adopted, exemptions from the ceiling for large farms that
were "efficient" or "mechanized" or were characterized by "heavy investment" or constituted "a compact block" (as opposed to the far-flung,
chaotic, tenanted parcels of "feudal" estates). Types of agriculture which
are typically organized along capitalist lines were also recommended for
exemption: cattle-breeding and dairy farms, sugarcane farms owned by
sugar factories, orchards, plantations (India, 1959: 105–06; India, 1956:
196–97; Kotovsky, 1964: 105). But even this compromise failed to quiet
concerns about the economic wisdom of ceilings; simultaneously, political opposition to the normative basis of so direct an attack on private
property remained strong.

Considering the ambiguity as to the value of a ceiling at the Center,
and the resistance from the States where local landed elites were well
represented politically, it is not surprising that planning directives from
Delhi were, in general, translated haltingly and imperfectly into legislation at the State level and implemented with little enthusiasm. Moreover, with a weak and contradictory political will behind ceiling reform,
the obstacles produced by local power structures discussed at length in
chapter 2 generated dynamics which vitiated implementation: bureaucratic lethargy and collusion, distortion of land records, hostility from
the courts, the absence of organized activism among potential beneficiaries, and so on. The aggregate results were negligible, and ceilings were
neglected in policy strategy until 1970, exemplifying what the National
Commission on Agriculture termed "colossal drift" and a "perversion"
of earlier commitments (India, 1976: vol. 15, 81).

In conjunction with Indira Gandhi's populist pledge to "abolish
poverty" and stirred by increased official concern about rural violence
(including the 1969 "land grab" agitation led by the right Communist
Party), the Congress leadership established in September of 1970 the
Central Land Reforms Committee to draft recommendations for a national ceiling policy (Hart and Herring, 1977: 264–66). The results of ceiling reform up to that time were officially termed "meager." The poor
result was attributed to "the high ceiling level, large number of exemptions from the law, mala fide transfers and partitions, and poor implementation" (India, 1974: 43). From the operation of ceiling laws in all the
States, only one million hectares of land had been declared surplus, and
only 0.53 million hectares distributed to the landless. The former figure
represents less than 0.7 percent of the net sown area, the latter 0.38 percent.[13]

13. Calculations from India, Ministry of Agriculture, *Indian Agriculture in Brief*,
(New Delhi, May 1973), p. 32.

In August of 1971, the committee made its recommendations. In its report, published in May 1972, the urgency of new agrarian reforms was explained in terms of the dramatic increase in landlessness and growing tensions in rural areas, exacerbated by technological change that accentuated income differentials.[14] The earlier (1971) recommendations included a ceiling of "10–18 acres of perenially irrigated land or land capable of growing two crops." This recommendation was later compromised to allow higher limits to farmers with private irrigation, evidently through the efforts of the "progressive farmer" lobby and their sympathizers within the Agriculture Ministry. Compensation was recommended, but below market value. The actual legislation of new ceilings had to await State action.[15]

Implementation prospects were bleak, at least in most States. The draft *Fifth Five Year Plan* summarized the formidable obstacles, and these problems are precisely those identified in previous chapters: the "absence of strong peasants organizations," "legal hurdles," corrupt local revenue officials, the absence of "dynamic, firm and unambiguous political direction," lack of accurate land records, and so on (India, 1974: 44–45). The *Plan*, echoing the Central Land Reforms Committee, called for "mass campaigns" and "people's involvement" in every facet of reform. But, as noted previously and dramatically illustrated by the experience of the cultivation committees in Sri Lanka, the policy means to such an end are by no means clear. The draft *Plan*, in discussing the organizations of rural poor that were to energize implementation, admits: "Such organizations cannot, however, be built up simply by issuing executive orders" (ibid.: 45). Likewise, Prime Minister Gandhi told the Chief Ministers' Conference on Land Reforms (1972) that there is "no point in competing in proposing radical measures," for "where is the organizational structure and administrative set-up to implement a more radical policy?" (Ladejinsky, 1972b: A 129).

The evident failure of ordinary administration to effect redistributive reforms in rural areas was one of the justifications used by Indira Gandhi for the extraordinary powers assumed under the Emergency in 1975. The history of land reforms in India suggests that Mrs. Gandhi was correct in her argument that extraordinary measures were necessary to effect land reforms; what is less clear is whether the extraordinary measures employed generally succeeded. The pace of implementation of

---

14. The *Report* was published in *Socialist India*, July 8 and 15, 1972. Cf. Ladejinsky (1972b).

15. Ladejinsky (1972b); also, "Land Ceiling and the New Farm Entrepreneur," *EPW* 7, no. 19 (May 6, 1972): 915–16; *Mainstream*, May 13, 1972. Ladejinsky was pessimistic about prospects. In support of his position, see "Chief Minister's 'No' to Land Reform," *EPW* October 3, 1970, p. 1629; for examples of state level resistance, *The Hindu*, May 3, 1972 and *EPW* January 22, 1972, p. 828, January 8, 1972, p. 736. For a detailed account of the politics of one state's reaction to the central directives, Hart and Herring (1977: 264–69).

ceiling-redistributive reforms was accelerated by the introduction of "summary" procedures, with the usual regional variations, but very little dent was made in the gap between promise and practice. Moreover, redistributive measures undertaken during the Emergency so incensed village oligarchies, particularly when "untouchable" communitites were benefited, that incidents of class/caste repression—murder, rape, burnings, dispossession of land and housesites—frequently followed.[16]

The historical commitment to land reforms in India, however compromised, was a commitment from the ruling Congress Party. With Congress no longer assured of dominance at the Center or in the States, the future of land ceilings is even more clouded. Some State-level discussion of raising ceilings appeared during the Janata interregnum. Moreover, the conflict at the Center between the Planning Commission and the Agriculture Ministry on ceilings continues. The Agriculture Ministry argues that what is left to be done in ceiling reform is minimal; there is little surplus left to appropriate and redistribute. The Planning Commission disputes the assumptions and methodology of the Agriculture Ministry; relying on different data, it projects as much as 21.24 million acres of available land given *present* ceilings compared to the ministry's 4.2 million-acre estimate. Lower ceilings and elimination of loopholes and fraud could, of course, greatly magnify either figure.[17]

Long debates on the "available surplus" miss the point, however. The problem is less in "declaring" land "surplus" than in the field-level problems of identifying stretches of land and transferring control. Even with new laws and the new administrative procedures so frequently discussed, actual appropriation and redistribution of land on a serious scale is unlikely; landed families have had two decades to redistribute their holdings in anticipation of ceiling legislation and have gone to great lengths to avoid possible losses.[18] Even though the ceiling continues to be lowered, the estimated surplus available for redistribution continues to shrink —from about 62 million acres in the late 1950s to the Agriculture Ministry's new low of 4.2 million acres. If that level is indeed the best that

16. There is a good summary of the new administrative measures in Frankel (1978: 551–52). The Indian press has commented extensively on the increased levels of caste / class violence and the roots of many of the attacks in land redistribution. In addition to press reports, there is evidence of the phenomenon in the report of the Bureau of Police Research and Development on "Atrocities against Harijans," *Hindustan Times*, August 11, 1980.

17. "Land Reform: False Passion," *EPW* 13, no. 20 (May 20, 1978): 826; "Land Reform: Concealing the Surplus," 12, no. 26 (July 1, 1978): 1051–52.

18. Kusum Nair (1962: 64) went to the heart of the problem by quoting an Andhra village schoolteacher: "You see, practically everyone has distributed any surplus land that he had already, though the ceiling legislation is yet to come. Today, almost nobody here will be found to possess, in his own name, more land than the proposed ceiling"; cf. Mencher (1975). Announcements of ceilings imposed on the family unit were followed in some areas by a wave of divorce actions (to double the ceiling by separating husband and wife).

can be expected, the potential for ceiling reforms identified by the Congress Agrarian Reforms Committee—to transform village India—is disappearing.

Ceiling Reform in Sri Lanka: Political Crisis and Economic Logic

In Sri Lanka, land redistribution did not receive the extensive official attention it did in India or Pakistan. Both the Muslim League and the Indian National Congress before Independence appointed committees to consider land reforms to transform the agrarian system. Numerous commissions afterward, and a great deal of high-level policy debate, surrounded the issue over the decades. In contrast, a dualism in policy logic and inquiry in Ceylon reflected the dualism of the agrarian economy: solutions to problems in the peasant sector were considered largely in isolation from the modern "estate" sector where land was concentrated in large holdings—the tea, rubber, and coconut plantations. Culturally and socially, that dualism is understandable, but the two sectors are inextricably linked in a dominant problem of Ceylon's economy: the peasant sector does not produce enough to feed the population and the foreign currency to import food is earned through sale of export crops from the plantations. Large holdings were not seen as stagnant and oppressive feudal remnants but as the most dynamic sector of the economy and, indeed, the reason for Ceylon's wealth relative to subcontinental neighbors.

The *Report of the Kandyan Peasantry Commission* (1951) painted a bleak picture of the conditions of smallholders in the uplands and did blame the commercial plantations, which cut off village expansion, appropriated commons and grazing lands, restricted *chena* (swidden) cultivation, and so on, but the problem was conceptualized primarily in terms of employment; the plantation sector had taken the Kandyan peasantry's land and state resources but provided no compensating employment (as plantation labor had been imported from India) (Ceylon, 1951: 9, 71–74). The problem of landlessness and underemployment could logically be met, given this analysis, by redistributing estate lands. But neither the Kandyan Peasantry Commission nor the Home Affairs Ministry's *Plan for the Rehabilitation of the Kandyan Peasantry* (Ceylon, 1956) recommended a redistributive land reform.

The political upheaval of 1956 produced new positions on land reform; the election manifesto of the populist Mahajana Eksath Peramuna (MEP) coalition promised nationalization of foreign-owned plantations (along with some basic industries). However, reflecting Ceylon's extraordinary international economic vulnerabilities, Prime Minister S. W. R. D. Bandaranaike rejected nationalizing the tea estates in 1957 as a plan that would "kill the goose that lays the golden eggs."[19] Instead, Ceylonese

---

19. Speech to planters, reported in Ceylon, *PD*, vol. 25 (1956–57: col. 2510).

political elites, as had the British before them, looked to development and recolonization of the land of the ancient kingdoms in the dry zone to solve the peasant problem in the populous wet zone. This extremely costly alternative was, significantly, financed largely by the "golden eggs" of the rich export-crop sector. As long as the plantation-centered economy was healthy, expensive colonization schemes were the preferred solution to population pressure and landlessness in the peasant sector.

Serious consideration of a ceiling-redistributive reform did not emerge until the victory of the leftist United Front coalition in 1970. By 1972, Sri Lanka had its first ceiling legislation; the Land Reform Law was the first act of the new Republic. Since no ceiling legislation had been proposed in the coalition's manifesto, it is widely believed that the land reform was a direct response to the rural insurrection of April 1971 (Sanderatne, 1972a: 8; ARTI, 1980: 17). Indeed, the minister of agriculture admitted as much, and the prime minister introduced the bill with an urgent "we are sitting on a volcano."[20] But the explanation must be more subtly developed; though the land reform was clearly a response to the Insurrection, the Insurrection was in part a response to the government's failure to effect land reform or other measures for the transformation of rural Sri Lanka.

The social forces represented by the United Front's overwhelming electoral victory in 1970 supported a broad range of redistributive and "socialist" policies. There was strong pressure for land reform within the ruling coalition, particularly from the leftist junior partners, the Ceylon Communist Party and the Trotskyite Lanka Sama Samaja Party (LSSP) prior to the Insurrection. The youth wing of the LSSP, in particular, supported low ceilings and wide-ranging redistribution. The coalition manifesto mentioned appropriation of neglected and marginal estate land for redistribution to relieve "acute landlessness," though this did not require a sharp break with existing policy or legislation.[21] As importantly, policy toward the plantation sector over two decades had evolved toward increasing state control and intervention (Abeysinghe, 1979: 50–51; Peiris, 1978: 611). Moreover, the normative logic of the land ceiling was paral-

20. The minister of agriculture and lands, in a speech to the National State Assembly reported in *The Sun* and *Ceylon Daily News* of August 19, 1972, attributed the Insurrection in part to rural landlessness, particularly as it affected the unemployed educated youth, and stated flatly: "We do not want to see another April 1971 in this country. That is why I pressed the Prime Minister to hasten legislation in regard to land reform." The prime minister's remarks in *Daily Mirror* (Colombo), June 6, 1972.

21. Existing legislation, such as the Estates Acquisition Act and Land Acquisition Act, were used to condemn parcels of estate land for state purchase. The United Front's election manifesto is reprinted in Ceylon Daily News, *Seventh Parliament of Ceylon: 1970* (Colombo, 1970), pp. 171–82. Positions of political parties on land reform from party publications, parliamentary debates, and personal interviews in Sri Lanka, 1973–74. The manifesto also called for abolition of "feudal" *nindagama* estates, though such tenures were more of symbolic than of economic importance.

leled in the Compulsory Savings Act (1971), the Ceiling on Income Act (1972), the Ceiling on Housing Property Act (1972), and other measures restricting property rights and accumulation.

The conclusive evidence that a serious land reform was being considered before the 1971 revolt was the appointment in October 1970 of a committee to make recommendations for land reforms in line with proposals in the election manifesto. This "shadow" form of the Land Reform Commission, composed of high-level permanent officials from various departments, was asked to consider measures for imposing a flexible ceiling on holdings, making paddy cultivators the owners of their plots, encouragement of cooperative ownership, and other matters (Ceylon, 1971c; cf. Perera, 1970: 35).

While the shadow Land Reform Commission was collecting data and preparing its report, the Insurrection erupted in April 1971. The revolt was in no sense a traditional jacquerie: the object of attack was the state, not landlords, and the demands were for social revolution. Nevertheless, the rural youth who for a brief time challenged the armed forces of the state did demand nationalization of the land, the uprooting of tea bushes to plant food, and redistribution of estate land, and occupied several estates. But the main thrust of the Janatha Vimukhti Peramuna's revolt should be seen as a rejection of the electoral and compromising path to socialism advocated by the establishment left parties in the government. The failure of that government to provide relief for the poverty and unemployment that plagued rural Sri Lanka strengthened the rebels' analysis that the only possible progressive transformation would come through armed insurrection.[22]

It is difficult to convey the political and social trauma caused by the revolt. The JVP forces were routed, but the Insurrection seemed to many of the nation's political elite to confirm the prediction of one Member of Parliament in 1956 that the Sinhalese educated youth were a "Frankenstein monster" created by a government which had led them to believe they would secure salaried employment, a monster that would eventually devour its creators (Ceylon, *PD*: vol. 25 [1956–57: col. 942]). Prime Minister Sirimavo Bandaranaike stressed that the Insurrection "instilled in us a new sense of urgency," captured in the metaphor of "sitting on a volcano" (*CDM*, June 6, 1972). The shape the land reform took, and the urgency with which it was enacted and implemented, concretely reflect the fear of discontent and unemployment of the rural educated young, which the insurrection dramatically manifested.

The policy logic in the recommendations of the shadow Land Reform Commission deals very little in questions of social justice; rather,

22. On the Insurrection, Halliday (1971); Jupp (1978: 293–95); Obeysekara (1973); Kearney (1973: 201–08); Kearney and Jiggins (1975); Alles (1979). On the ideology of the JVP, see the statement of its leader to the Ceylon Criminal Justice Commission (Wijeweera, 1975).

the concern is with providing employment and income to as many of the landless as is politically practicable. Much of the report is an exercise in the political arithmetic of land reform: how many can benefit at the expense of how many by setting the ceiling at one level or another? (see chap. 8). There is also extensive analysis of the "pressure for land reform," meaning the agronomic and demographic configuration of rural unemployment and underemployment. The question of productivity is relegated to the background—not only are the relevant data unavailable, but the commission flatly argued: "there is no scientific basis for fixing a ceiling on agricultural holdings" (unpublished *Draft Interim Report*, 1971: 16).

The imperatives of employment and practical politics figured importantly in every consideration made by the commission. Its terms of reference included specification of measures for vesting ownership rights in tenant cultivators. Indeed, the *Draft Agricultural Development Plan, 1971–77* argued that "the transfer of ownership to the tiller of the soil appears to be the only permanent solution to the problem" of regulation of tenurial terms (Ceylon, n.d., mimeo: III, 63). The commission argued that the empirical case was ambiguous: many "noted agricultural experts" argued that any disturbance of the tenurial situation would decrease productivity, but it was possible that tenants, once made owners, would produce higher yields. According any land-to-the-tiller policy low priority, the commission presented the probably decisive (political) argument against land to the tiller: "there will be no increase in employment and the process will harm as many small holders as the number of tenants it will benefit" (Ceylon, 1971c: 10). The data on agrarian structure presented in chapter 3 support that conclusion. Another reason for the lack of official concern about the paddy sector was the very small amount of land in large holdings; data assembled by the commission showed less than 10 percent of the total paddy land in holdings larger than 10 acres. Moreover, the commission made one particularly interesting point: the subsidized rice ration *in effect* gave every family the produce of one-fourth of an acre of paddy land free, without any redistribution of physical land (pp. 31, 1).

The response to the rural crisis which produced the "urgency" with which the commission worked was the Land Reform Law (No. 1 of 1972). Its introduction stated the objectives to be increased productivity and employment, which were to be the criteria employed in redistribution of land. The position was not that equity, or social justice, required a leveling of inequalities, though this concern was evident in the coalition's common program, but specifically that the twin crises of agricultural production and employment necessitated changes in landholding patterns. The ceiling was the first act of the new National State Assembly; the second act was the Agricultural Productivity Law, designed to insure that all land, of whatever size or tenure, be utilized to achieve "maximum productivity." The prime minister stated publicly in June of 1972: "I have introduced the land ceiling legislation not to rob people of their lands but to make these lands productive. These lands would be given to the landless to produce the food required by our country and not to be given as dowries" (*CDM*: June 15, 1972). The minister of agriculture stressed that a new concept was developing: land as a limited national resource must be utilized in ways which conform to social needs and thus must be socially determined (*TC*: June 11, 1972).

Through what mechanisms, by what policy logic, were the 1972 land reforms to attack the twin crises of food and unemployment? First, the shadow Land Reform Commission noted that productivity on many estates, particularly coconut estates, was disturbingly and unnecessarily low, a reflection of neglect and poor management (cf. ARTI, 1977). It was assumed that a smallholder, given an allotment of such land, would of necessity intensify production and perhaps (optimally) engage in subsidiary food production as well. The Agricultural Productivity Law went on to attack the problem of production on lands which remained in the owner's control; owners who did not personally cultivate the land were legally required to provide the capital and equipment necessary to enable the actual cultivator to achieve maximum efficiency.[23]

The food problem in Ceylon was chronic, though it was not to reach crisis proportions until 1973. Land use in the "estate" sector is crucially related to the food production in two ways. Most important, plantation-crop exports financed food imports. As the terms of international trade turned dramatically against Ceylon in the 1960s, the plantation sector had to produce more each year to maintain even a given level of food imports; providing for population growth imposed an extra burden. Shortfalls in foreign exchange earnings over the course of the 1960s led to short-term borrowing and a serious foreign debt burden which eventually rose to consume one-fifth of all export earnings.[24] Second, through intercropping and subsidiary production strategies (dairying, for example), the estate lands offered great potential for directly increasing food production.

The case for the employment-generating capacities of a redistribu-

23. *Agricultural Productivity Law*, pt. 1, 2 (2). The mechanism resembles Bhutto's 1972 tenancy reforms in Pakistan, attempting to legislate "good landlord" behavior. The practical difficulty was the ambiguity of the term "maximum efficiency," which left room for considerable discretion (and thus partisan considerations).

24. During the decade 1960–70, outstanding public debt had increased more than threefold and the budget deficit more than doubled. Foreign debt servicing consumed only 2 percent of foreign exchange earnings in 1965, 20.3 percent by 1975. The deterioration in the terms of trade was dramatic: though the economy was exporting substantially more in 1975 than in 1960, the real purchasing power of exports was about one-third the 1960 level. Data from *United Nations Statistical Yearbook* (1977: 518–25); Central Bank of Ceylon, *Annual Report* (yearly); IBRD, *Annual Reports*; ILO (1971), *Technical Papers* (sec. 24, table 1).

tive land reform has several component strands. In the simplest case, unemployed rural people can be given land which is not being cultivated at all, resulting in a direct and dramatic increase in employment (provided the land can be made productive). For land that has already been utilized, the policy logic depends on the propensity of smallholders to use land more intensively than large owners; a redistribution of land from large to small owners should thus have a positive net employment effect, particularly if the large owners are neither resident on the land nor agriculturalists by profession, situations common in Sri Lanka (e.g., ARTI, 1977). An important direct statement of this case was the two-volume report by the International Labour Office (1971), *Matching Employment Opportunities and Expectations: A Programme of Action for Ceylon.* The report argued that the case for a ceiling in terms of productivity and employment was strong on coconut and paddy lands, but weak on tea and rubber lands, primarily because of the alleged existence of economies of scale in the production of those two plantation crops.[25]

The policy logic of the reforms is thus plausible, but open to dispute (cf. Peiris, 1975). The Central Bank, for example, was worried that the effect in the short run might be to decrease total marketed surplus and thus aggravate rather than alleviate the food crisis. The shadow Land Reform Commission threw up its collective hands on the question of productivity and admitted that there was no "scientific basis" for setting the ceiling and that agricultural experts disagreed on the productivity effects of land reform. If the logic of the ILO team's 1971 report was accurate, redistribution would *decrease* productivity on large tea and rubber estates. Moreover, the ceiling in the critical paddy sector was set so high as to have virtually no impact on the structure of paddy-land holdings. Because of the ambiguity of the productivity case, the source of the ceiling reform and its specific provisions must be explained in political terms. The case for a ceiling in terms of employment is far more powerful, and indeed, the alleviation of rural unemployment in general became a central policy theme after the 1971 revolt dramatically illustrated the crisis. This imperative was reflected not only in the employment provisions of the land reform, but in a Five Year Plan that placed emphasis on the problem of unemployed youth,[26] the organizational linking of planning and employment in one ministry, and continuous expansion of public sector jobs.

25. ILO (1971), *Report,* 92–98; *Technical Papers,* 113–17. Nimal Fernando (1977) has correctly criticized the methodology of the ILO argument about productivity; many of the conclusions are not supported by hard evidence.

26. Ceylon (1971b). See, especially, the foreword by the prime minister. Estimates of the level of unemployment are problematic, but the phenomenon was unmistakably serious. The ILO report (1971, vol. 1, chap. 2) estimated that at least 14 percent of the labor force was *openly* unemployed. Underemployment was severe and dissatisfaction with jobs "inappropriate" to the level of education or expectations, widespread and bitter.

To the extent that any norm of social justice appeared in the ceiling policy logic, it was that of the welfare state. Minister of Agriculture and Lands Hector Kobbekaduwa explained to land-reform officials: "It is the duty of any Government to provide every citizen with an income that is socially equitable and emotionally satisfying" (ARTI, 1973). In its deliberations on appropriate ceilings and units of redistribution, the shadow Land Reform Commission sought to determine the size of holding necessary to provide an income of Rs 200 (later raised to Rs 300) per month, given intensive use and full employment of family labor.[27] The operative norm was that every citizen who does not find employment in other sectors should ideally have access to enough land to provide a certain minimum standard of living. The Secretary of the Ministry of Food and Agriculture stated that the specific monthly income target for land-reform beneficiaries was to offer young people a chance at farming that would compare favorably with a job of "0 level" educational qualification in the public sector (ARTI, 1973). The Rs 300 per month income standard was written into the ceiling law (pt. 2, sec. 25). This stipulation demonstrates both the concern of the regime with discontent among educated unemployed and the acceptance of an income floor determined by what the educated youth felt they deserved—the salary of a lower level public servant.

The ceiling was set at 50 acres, of which not more than 25 acres could be paddy land, per nuclear family, with provisions for transfers to adult offspring and to minor children when they come of age, raising the operative ceiling considerably. Compensation was to be fifteen times the "average annual profit" on plantation land, or ten times the average annual profit on paddy land, or the assessed value, whichever was greater. Exempted from the ceiling were lands of religious institutions (reflecting the political power of the Buddhist Sangha) and those of public companies, both local ("rupee firms") and foreign ("sterling firms"). Their exclusion from the 1972 ceiling exempted some of the finest estates, particularly tea estates, and limited the redistributive potential of the law (Fernando, 1977; Abeysinghe, 1979). The government justified these exemptions on grounds of productivity, but had other concerns as well; the shadow Land Reform Commission noted in an unpublished interim report:

> The Government has directed that all plantations owned by sterling and rupee companies should be exempted from the operation of the ceilings. This is partly because much of this land is worked by non-national labor and also because production is likely to fall if these viable commercial undertakings are fragmented . . . , but largely on account of the risks of international repercussions. [Ceylon, 1971c: 14]

27. Ceylon (1971c: 19). The area thus determined varied from 1–1.5 acres of well-drained irrigable land to 3–10 acres of rain-fed paddy or 2–5 acres of tea, rubber, or coconut, depending on agronomic characteristics.

The international repercussions were partly commercial, as the international tea trade (from which Ceylon received almost 70 percent of its foreign earnings) is centered in London. But there was a parallel concern for the opinion of the powerful international agencies, such as the International Monetary Fund and World Bank, and of the United States, an aid-giver with whom Ceylon had tangled previously on the issue of nationalization and compensation. By 1975, these fears had evidently subsided; the land reform was extended to the estates of public companies, foreign and domestic, through an amendment to the 1972 law (no. 39 of 1975). Compensation was to be paid, and sterling firms would receive hard currency. Through the amendment, an additional 417,957 acres of land, much of it prime, was appropriated, representing about 8 percent of the total agricultural area, including 40 percent of the tea acreage and 15 percent of the rubber acreage.

Nationalization of the estates in 1975 finally redeemed an SLFP manifesto pledge of 1956. It is difficult to say exactly why the government risked "killing the goose that lays the golden eggs." In part, there was clearly fear that the geese, frightened by land reforms, were holding back on egg production; investment and management suffered on some estates and were potentially troublesome throughout the plantation sector. Agreeing to pay compensation in hard currency strained the exchequer but mollified international objections. Moreover, diversification of tea markets, particularly to Pakistan and west Asia, reduced the concern for London's opinion.[28] In factional and political terms, the nationalization enhanced the power of the SLFP minister of agriculture vis-à-vis both party rivals and the LSSP minister of plantation industries. Nationalization also served important patronage functions, placing new jobs under the regime's control. The symbolic functions seem obvious for a regime claiming to be "socialist" and "anti-imperialist" but facing doubting challenges from the left. Indeed, nationalization of the estates answered a central criticism voiced by the revolutionary JVP. Likewise, nationalization of the estate sector symbolically redeemed the long-standing pledge to right the wrongs done to the Kandyan peasantry under colonial rule.

In structural terms, Sri Lanka's politics must be placed in the context of extreme dependence and vulnerability in the international political economy; the nation lives on the export of plantation crops. To take control of that sector potentially allows the state to plan rationally for

28. The Central Bank worried that productivity would decline on the large estates because of owners' fears of further land reforms; e.g., *Annual Report: 1974* (pp. 16–17). For data on the changing composition of tea exports, and an excellent discussion of the 1975 amendment, Fernando (1977). Political uncertainty about the future of foreign-owned plantations had mounted progressively since the promised nationalization in 1956. The minister of agriculture in 1972 pledged in Parliament to extend the land reforms to public companies (Peiris, 1978: 613–14). The minister of plantation industries stressed the connection between nationalization and maintaining or improving foreign exchange earnings (Abeysinghe, 1979: 51) at a time of mounting international deficits.

export diversification, investment (e.g., replanting), more efficient land use, employment, and so on, and to coordinate the national economy. These imperatives, and the potential of exercising considerable patronage power, face any regime in Sri Lanka; the defeat of the leftist parties in 1977 by the conservative United National Party has not reversed the ceiling reforms, despite significant reversals of other redistributive policies.

Ceiling Legislation and Agrarian Transformation

In an important Indian policy model, though not in practice, land ceilings figured as a means of transforming rural society toward a cooperative-centered land system. Large blocks of land seized through ceiling implementation were to be alienated to groups of cultivators for cooperative or even collective farms. The political commitment was diffuse, shallow, and ambivalent, however, and the strategy became irrelevant as the ceilings themselves were not seriously implemented.

Sri Lanka's ceiling did not figure as a part of a comprehensive transformational strategy, but rather as a response to an unemployment and legitimacy crisis, dramatized by a rural insurrection. The crisis was evident in the actual reform: the long delays, privileged loopholes, and political obstruction characteristic of Indian ceiling reforms were notably absent. The legislation was passed quickly and implemented with great speed and little detectable evasion. Eloquent testimony to effectiveness of implementation is the fact that the Land Reform Commission actually appropriated more land than had been projected as surplus.

Even though the ceiling imposed was higher than that demanded by the leftist members of the ruling coalition and recommended by the ILO and shadow LRC, the amount of land affected by the 1972 and 1975 reforms together offered significant potential for transforming the agrarian sector. This potential was greatest in the case of tea, the center of the national economy. The two reforms put under government control 63.1 percent of the total tea acreage of Sri Lanka, accounting for 80 percent of total production. Almost a third of the rubber-growing area (30.4 percent) and a tenth of the coconut area were appropriated. In the aggregate, about one-fourth of the land under commercial crops was appropriated, leaving, as Gerald Peiris stresses (1978: 624), the state as "almost the sole owner of large plantations." Because of the very high ceiling, paddy lands were virtually unaffected: only 3.3 percent of the land taken under the 1972 ceiling was paddy land and less than 2 percent of the nation's paddy acreage was appropriated. In comparison, ceiling reforms per se in India have fallen far below even the figure for the paddy sector.[29]

The *redistributive* impacts of the 1972 and 1975 reforms differed

29. Excluding the "abolition of intermediaries" in India. Data from the Land Reform Commission and the Central Bank's *Review of the Economy*, 1979.

considerably. Much of the land appropriated under the original ceiling was that of "bad landords"—underdeveloped, neglected, or uncultivated. The 1975 amendment appropriated largely professionally managed commercial estates, primarily tea, which offer far less scope for simple reorganization of production or employment creation. Under the 1972 ceiling alone, 563,400 acres were appropriated and reassigned. Even though almost a third of this land was uncultivated or jungle or waste, the redistributive potential was great. The question then arose: how should the land be allocated and utilized.

The question of strategy in disposing of the surplus land was serious; a general commitment to cooperative land management at the ideological level was contradicted by the problematic history of cooperatives at the practical level. At an orientation course for government officials implementing the reform, the chairman of the Land Reform Commission stated that each District Land Reform Authority would work out its own set of redistributive priorities. He noted that "at the policy level the cooperative form of management seems to be favored," but added that consumer cooperatives had proved impracticable and cooperative land management was even more difficult to institute (ARTI, 1973: 11). The discussion in this orientation course, attended by foreign experts, high-level officials, political leaders, and district administrators, reflected the range of hopes and fears about cooperatives; examples of both success and failure were presented. The conclusion was that local projects would depend on "political realities" and "political nuances," essentially meaning that the local MP (or shadow MP in opposition areas) would have a great deal of leeway. The surplus land would then in effect be available for institutional experimentation.

Flexibility and experimentation, as well as "political realities," were evident in the actual dispensation of surplus lands. More than half the total land alienated under the 1972 ceiling was allocated to cooperative (often de facto collective) organizations of various kinds. About 7 percent was assigned to government agricultural enterprises, primarily the State Plantation Corporation. The amount distributed to individual villagers was originally negligible, between 3 and 4 percent of the total. A much larger quantity of land was parceled out among various research institutes, government offices, Divisional Land Reform Authorities, and so on.[30]

The initial distribution of appropriated land thus departed from traditional means of satisfying the "land hunger" of poor families through allotment of individual small plots. The minister of agriculture termed

30. Data from Central Bank of Ceylon, *Annual Report 1974* (Colombo, 1975), table II(B)2. The text is influenced by the analysis of Nimal Fernando in a graduate seminar paper presented to me at the Land Tenure Center, University of Wisconsin, in 1975. For a presentation of the variety of authority and production arrangements on alienated land, see Ellman and Ratnaweera (1974); Abeysinghe (1979); Sanderatne (1977); ARTI (1979).

distribution of land in small farm allotments "unsuccessful, unscientific, unproductive" (ARTI, 1980: 20). Sri Lanka had been quite innovative in experimenting with cooperative farming (Youth Settlement Schemes, Cooperative Agricultural Projects, etc.), even before the land reform provided new resources (Sanderatne, 1977). Cooperative farms established on land alienated by the Land Reform Commission added to the institutional variability.

Ordinary politics at the local level has been important in preventing Indian ceiling legislation from appropriating very much land; in Sri Lanka, ordinary politics entered, not in the appropriation stage (though predictable minor distortions along partisan lines were reported), where the urgency of crisis dominated, but in the redistributive stage. A primary manifestation of this phenomenon was the establishment of Electorate Level Land Reform Cooperative Societies under the direction of local political leaders. A member of the Land Reform Commission acknowledged that the cooperatives "were a result of the pressure of politicians" and were utilized "by politicians for their personal gain or as seats of patronage," quickly becoming "hot beds of corruption and mismanagement."[31] Such cooperatives received about 185,000 acres of land from the Land Reform Commission. The commission recommended their closure as early as 1975 because of "rampant" mismanagement, but "the power of politicians prevailed" (Abeysinghe, 1979: 118).

A second manifestation of ordinary politics in the distribution program was the reversal of the official prejudice against alienation in tiny individual plots. Pressure for individual plot distribution was reinforced by the 1975 amendment, which stirred the expectation that the Kandyan peasantry was finally to be redeemed; by 1976, individual plot distribution was established policy (Peiris, 1978: 623). Pressure to increase the scale of small-plot allotment was evident just before the 1977 elections, for clearly political reasons (ARTI, 1980: 40). The logic of distribution reinforces a political interpretation of the process; contrary to the economic logic on income floors and minimum size of holding explained previously and written into the 1972 law, the actual distribution was in minuscule plots as small as 0.125 acres, suggesting the imperative of political arithmetic: to benefit as many families as possible whatever the economic consequences. An evaluation study of land alienation concluded that the plots were too small, too marginal, too widely dispersed, and the subsidiary support too meager to contribute significantly to either employment or production (ARTI, 1980: 41, 33, 39). Moreover, the criteria for selecting beneficiaries were shifted from an emphasis on agricultural experience to criteria favoring the educated unemployed youth (ibid.: 26), reflecting the common perception of the causes of the Insurrection.

31. Abeysinghe (1979: 117). For corroborating evidence, Peiris (1978: 626); ARTI (1980: 22); ARTI (1979: 26–27). Partisan considerations also figured heavily in the selection of beneficiaries in both cooperative and individual plot opportunities.

Altogether, perhaps 150,000 families received individual allotments, only 120,000 acres in the aggregate (ibid.: 23, 38); but if the results from the study can be generalized, the economic consequences were minimal (cf. Peiris, 1978: 621).

The succeeding UNP regime charged that the land reform was used for "political revenge," "corruption," and patronage (as land was "alienated to supporters, kith and kin") (Abeysinghe, 1979: 141). As in the critique of the cultivation committees and other agrarian institutions under the SLFP regime, there were charges of partisan irregularities, injustice, and victimization. The new government claimed that the dominant role of the state and cooperatives in land utilization denied the promise of land for landless individuals and expressed its commitment to individual plot distribution formally through the Land Grants (Special Provision) Act of 1979. By 1979, 12.11 percent of all land alienated had gone to individuals, though the large estates remained under state control (Sri Lanka, 1979: 37). Though there is evidence that the government charges of political manipulation of the land distribution process are accurate (ARTI, 1979: passim; ARTI, 1980; Abeysinghe, 1979:118, 141), there is little reason to believe that local politicians will resist the opportunity to carry on under the new regime, and some evidence they are doing so (ARTI, 1979: 84, 89).

The experience of the cooperatives and collectives is difficult to evaluate because the absence of systematic studies, the short time period, and wide local variations. There have been real successes and total failures, with problems varying from farm to farm. Problems of ethnicity and bureaucratism plagued some collectives; partisan politics and patronage appointments, others.[32] There were predictable "free rider" problems and difficulties with new incentive systems, poor management, and inadequate agricultural expertise among the youth. But the experiments were, in a real sense, not given a chance; as a member of the Land Reform Commission expressed it: "the creation of pockets of collectivized socialist groups" could not work in a "society which works on and accepts individualism and individual profits" (Abeysinghe, 1979: 102). Despite the large amount of land involved in the collective and cooperative farms, there was always an air of experimentation and uncertainty about their future, reflecting what Sanderatne called their isolation as "collective islands in a sea of private ownership."

The present UNP regime is committed neither to collective forms of production and ownership nor to transformation of the rural society in socialist directions and has largely substituted state control or individual

---

32. For an early, sensitive, and tentative analysis of successes, problems, and potential of the cooperative farms, Ellman and Ratnaweera (1974: chap. 5). Cf. Fernando (1977); Abeysinghe (1979: pt. 6); Sanderatne (1977); Peiris (1975: 87–89; 1978); ARTI (1977, 1979). Interviews with appointed estate managers in 1973 convinced me that the charges of partisan politics were accurate.

plots for cooperative management, demonstrating the vulnerability of social experimentation to electoral politics at the national level. The fundamental changes in consciousness and social organization necessary to
transform rural society along collectivist lines necessitate at a bare minimum a social consensus and long-standing political commitment to new
forms of property and production relations.

Regimes in Ceylon, regardless of political composition, have recognized the necessity of addressing the acute problem of landlessness in
the peasant sector. Likewise, periodic food crises focused the attention of
regimes—colonial and Ceylonese—on the necessity of raising aggregate
production. Ceylonese regimes have added to these concerns explicit recognition of the historical grievances of the Kandyan peasantry against the
plantation sector which usurped vast stretches of land, hemming in the
villages. The policy debate between left and right in Ceylon has often
been between redistributive and distributive models: land reforms vs. state-
subsidized development of new lands, as exemplified dramatically in 1956,
when the Ministry of Agriculture and Lands was split between two ide-
ologically opposed ministers at the last minute as a political compromise
(Herring, 1972/74).

The dominant policies for relieving landlessness in Ceylon's densely
populated wet zone were colonization of the empty dry zone at state expense and "village expansion" schemes on estate land at the margins of
crowded villages. These methods had an enormous impact in aggregate
terms and certainly reduced the pressure for redistributive reform historically. Figures given by the shadow Land Reform Commission show a
total of 1,305,557 acres of land to have been allocated under village expansion and colonization programs by 1969, representing more than one-
fourth of the total agricultural land in Sri Lanka. There had been 678,615
allotments made, a remarkable figure when one considers that the 1962
Census of Agriculture showed only 1,169,801 agricultural holdings in the
country.[33] The Commissioner of Agrarian Services figured that nearly 20
percent of the total rural population had benefited from settlement schemes
alone as of 1969 (Ceylon, 1969: 5). Such methods are, of course, less costly
in *political* terms than are redistributive reforms, at least so long as landed
elites retain significant political power.

The economic strain of the distributive policies was considerable,
however. Severe budgetary deficits, mounting foreign debt, and foreign
exchange crises cast doubts on the continued viability of colonization
schemes in the early 1970s (ARTI, 1973: 13), but international interest
may replace the foreign exchange earnings of the plantation sector as a
source of funding the expensive projects. The UNFAO and World Bank

---

33. Ceylon (1962: vol. 2, 23). Per capita agricultural land in the wet zone in 1962
was only 0.39 acres, compared to 9.56 acres in the dry zone (table 3).

financed studies of the Mahaweli (river) development project, and the bank is financing infrastructural work. Since the installation of the "open economy" UNP regime in 1977, foreign contributions for development have multiplied and the scope and implementation pace of the projects have dramatically increased.

Recolonization of the dry zone is a resurrection and transplantation of a decaying peasant society rather than a transformation. The land reforms of the United Front government offered transformational potential, but in practice that potential was largely denied. On estates seized under the 1975 amendment, there was virtually no change in production relations, but simply a change of authorities and managers (Fernando, 1977). That reform meant primarily a simple change in juridical ownership, the state replacing the private companies. In contrast, on some of the cooperatives and collectives formed on neglected or uncultivated land, fundamental structural and functional changes were effected in patterns of ownership, management, authority, and social relations, at least for a time. On other cooperatives, old relations of production and authority were reproduced. For the stateless Tamil laborers, both land reforms typically meant the exchange of one set of Sinhalese bosses for another, with some improvement in working conditions.[34]

It is tempting to conclude that ordinary politics and the insecurity induced by fluctuating commitment to agrarian transformation vitiated the potential of the redistributive reforms, as in the case of the Paddy Lands Act. This is certainly part of the story, but other factors contributed. The preference of landless agriculturalists for the security and autonomy of individual private plots, a phenomenon evident cross-culturally and historically, was important, especially in conjunction with the dynamics of ordinary politics and regime changes incorporating significant ideological shifts. It is difficult to guess the unrealized potential which could have been developed through reforms in the state apparatus and political institutions and gradual institutionalization of new forms of property and labor process. As in the case of the cultivation committees, individual rationality and social transformation were at odds; the rational individual preference in a reform process charged with partisan politics, corruption, mismanagement, and uncertainty would be clear title to a private plot—a reaffirmation of the existing property system over the cooperative. Like the experiment in peasant democracy, the experiment in large-scale movement away from the cul-de-sac of peasantist subdivision of tiny family plots has been abandoned in favor of state control. In both cases, the imposition of new institutional forms—of property, man-

---

34. De Mel's (1980: 11) study of attitudes of estate managers reports a feeling of diminished control of the labor process. Wages have increased, but price indices have recently become so unreliable that no statement about real wages can be made.

agement, and authority relations—failed, in part because of the absence of bottom-up support and mobilization, in part because of the character of state mechanisms which attempted to enforce changes from the top down.

SOUTH ASIA

AFGHANISTAN

JAMMU
AND
KASHMIR

HIMALAYAS

CHINA

Peshawar
Islamabad
JHELUM R.
CHENAB R.
Lahore
Quetta
SUTLEJ R.
INDUS R.

Srinigar
HIMACHAL
Am-
ritsar
Simla
PUNJAB
Chandigarh
HARYANA
Mussoorie

INDUS R.

PAKISTAN

Karachi

MILES

0   100   200   300   400   500

BRAHMAPUTRA R.

HIMALAYAS

NORTHEAST
FRONTIER AGENCY

New Delhi
UTTAR
PRADESH
Agra

NEPAL

Jaipur

RAJASTHAN

Lucknow

Kathmandu

SIKKIM
BHUTAN

BRAHMAPUTRA R.

NAGA-
LAND

ASSAM
Shillong

MANIPUR

Allahabad
Patna
BIHAR

Varanas

BANGLADESH
Dacca

TRIPURA

TROPIC OF
CANCER

GUJARAT

MADHYA PRADESH

WEST
BENGAL
Calcutta

Ahmadabad

Bhopal
NARBADA R.

INDIA

ORISSA
Bhubaneswar

Nagpur

MAHARASHTRA

Bombay

Poona

ARABIAN
SEA

GOA

KARNATAKA

Hyderabad
ANDHRA
KRISHNA R.
PRADESH

BAY
OF
BENGAL

N

Bangalore

Madras

KERALA

TAMILNADU

SRI LANKA

Trivandrum

Colombo

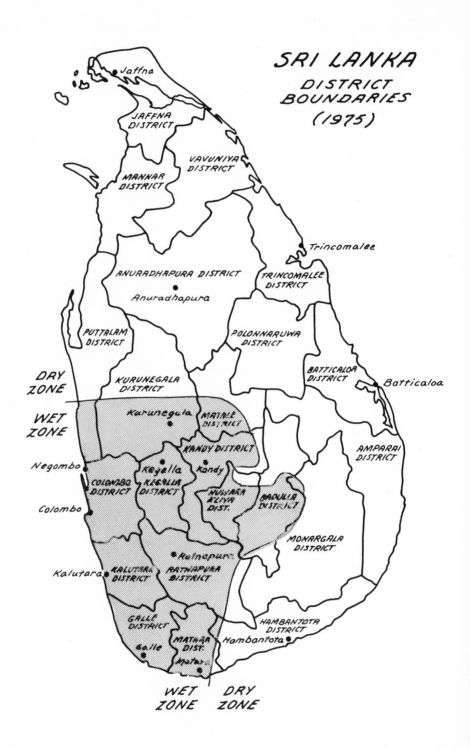

SRI LANKA
DISTRICT
BOUNDARIES
(1975)

Jaffna

JAFFNA
DISTRICT

VAVUNIYA
DISTRICT

MANNAR
DISTRICT

Trincomalee

ANURADHAPURA DISTRICT

TRINCOMALEE
DISTRICT

Anuradhapura

POLONNARUWA
DISTRICT

PUTTALAM
DISTRICT

BATTICALOA
DISTRICT

Batticaloa

DRY
ZONE

KURUNEGALA
DISTRICT

WET
ZONE

Kurunegala

MATALE
DISTRICT

AMPARAI
DISTRICT

KANDY DISTRICT

Negombo

Kegalla

Kandy

COLOMBO
DISTRICT

KEGALLA
DISTRICT

NUWARA
ELIYA
DIST.

BADULLA
DISTRICT

Colombo

MONARGALA
DISTRICT

Kalutara

KALUTARA
DISTRICT

RATNAPURA
DISTRICT

Ratnapura

GALLE
DISTRICT

HAMBANTOTA
DISTRICT

Galle

MATARA
DIST.

Hambantota

Matara

WET
ZONE

DRY
ZONE

PAKISTAN
REGIONS

MILES
0   100   200

U.S.S.R.

CHINA

Khorog

GILGIT

Gilgit

BALTISTAN

Pul-i-Khumri

North-West
Frontier

Kabul R.

Muzaffarabad

Kabul

Nowshera

AZAD
KASHMIR

Ghazni

Peshawar

Islamabad

AFGHANISTAN

Rawalpindi

Sargodha

Kandahar

Dera Ismail
Khan

Lahore

THE
PUNJAB

Lyallpur

Chaman

Quetta

Sahiwal

Sibi

Multan

Bahawalpur

Kalat

New Delhi

PAKISTAN

Indus R.

BALUCHISTAN

Sukkur

INDIA

IRAN

Khairpur

Bela

SIND

Pasni

Hyderabad

Karachi

ARABIAN
SEA

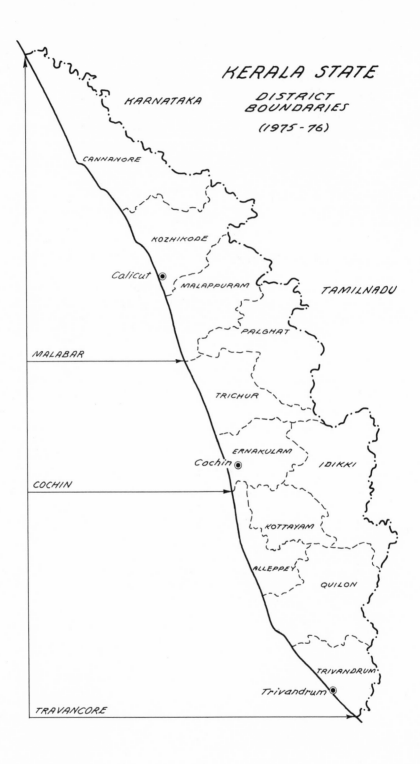

KERALA STATE

DISTRICT
BOUNDARIES

(1975 - 76)

KARNATAKA

CANNANORE

KOZHIKODE

Calicut

MALAPPURAM

TAMILNADU

PALGHAT

MALABAR

TRICHUR

ERNAKULAM

Cochin

IDIKKI

COCHIN

KOTTAYAM

ALLEPPEY

QUILON

TRIVANDRUM

Trivandrum

TRAVANCORE

6 The Logic of Land to the Tiller: The First Communist Ministry in Kerala

Lands and the fruits thereof are to belong to those who do the tilling, the tillers being defined as those who plough, harrow, sow, weed and harvest.
—Daniel Thorner

Social Justice and Land to the Tiller

Two important strands of policy logic have led to advocacy of land to the tiller. One strand is normative and related to notions of social justice; the other is empirical and practical, relating to observed failures in redistributing rights to or protecting the rights of tenants in a land-poor economy. The strands may converge, but need not.

The core of the normative position is that ground rent is in some sense illegitimate or unearned and serves no economic function. The legitimacy of the pure rentier is challenged from the Marxist perspective and in the justificatory framework of entrepreneurial capitalism—the normative rejection of parasitic landlordism. In addition to these modern currents, there are traditional and indigenous supports for the cultivator's claim to the fruits of cultivation. The Congress Agrarian Reforms Committee, in arguing for a land-to-the-tiller policy, quoted religious texts: "The King cannot give away the earth because it is not his exclusive property, but is common to all beings enjoying the fruits of their labor on it. It belongs to all alike."[1] Advocates of land to the tiller could find justification for the principle (though not the practice) in the Gandhian tradition as well. In 1937, Gandhi stated:

1. AICC (1949: 36). Hindu religious texts are, of course, not a reliable support for the principles advocated by the committee; the case of Islam is likewise ambiguous. Fazlur Rehman (1974: 36) has argued that in the early days of Islam there was sentiment against the "sleeping landlord"; if land could not be tilled by the owner, it should be let free of rent to whoever could till it. Rehman cites the Andalusian jurist Ibn Hazm as arguing that the Prophet meant all sharecropping and land rent to be forbidden by law. The point is that the "great traditions" of South Asia are less monolithically conservative than is often assumed and contain, in Mannheim's (1936) terms, both ideological and utopian themes, permitting divergent interpretations and political conflicts over rightful claim to cultural legitimation among opposed social forces. For an argument that the position in the text resonates across many agrarian systems across time, Jacoby (1971: 88).

Real socialism has been handed down to us by our ancestors who taught 'All land belongs to *Gopal.*' Where then is the boundary line? Man is the maker of that line and he can therefore unmake it. *Gopal* literally means shepherd; it also means God. In modern language it means the State, i.e., the people. That the land today does not belong to the people is too true. . . . Land and all property is his who will work it.[2]

The implication of these traditional arguments, as well as modern Marxian positions based on the understanding of production as a necessarily social process, is that agricultural land rightfully belongs to a community of producers. A ceiling is implied because no one is entitled to more land than the family can work, and with traditional technology the differences between any two cultivators will be small. The difference between the position adopted by the Congress Agrarian Reforms Committee and the socialist position, on the one hand, and explicitly bourgeois arguments for land to the tiller, on the other, lies in what is meant by "tiller." The differences in conceptualization are fundamental and have profound implications for land-reform policy.

Daniel Thorner (1956: 79) stated one position simply: "Lands and the fruits thereof are to belong to those who do the tilling, the tillers being defined as those who plough, harrow, sow, weed, and harvest." The Congress Agrarian Reforms Committee was equally straightforward: the only rights in land other than those of the state and village community should be for those engaged in "personal cultivation," meaning to "put in a minimum amount of physical labor and participate in actual agricultural operations." The only exceptions were to be widows, minors, and disabled persons; otherwise, the renting out of land was to be prohibited by law after a "period of transition" (AICC, 1949: 7).

The striking point in the committee's position, in contrast to modern capitalist notions, is the insistence that the tiller contribute physical labor to the production process. This requirement directly contradicts a fundamental principle of the traditional Indic agrarian social structure, sanctioned in ideology and cultural usage—namely, the explicit differentiation of functionaries who shared in the agricultural surplus but were excused, even prohibited, from working the land. Indeed, in a note of dissent to the majority report, two committee members argued that from antiquity Indic tradition had sanctioned separation of proprietary rights from cultivation responsibilities and that the Laws of Manu justified the institution of sharecropping (ibid.: 199). Likewise, the Uttar Pradesh Zamindary Abolition Committee decided that manual labor could not be used as a criterion for personal cultivation because high castes are prohibited from performing such activities (Thorner, 1956: 20–21).

In actual legislation on the subcontinent, "self-cultivation" has been

2. In Malaviya (1954: 69); for contradictory positions taken by Gandhi on the land question, Gandhi (1966: 233–40; 248–50); on Gandhi's conservative role vis-à-vis peasant movements, Dhanagre (1975).

defined as supervision of wage labor or cultivation through personal "servants," or landless "partners." It could be argued that these subtle legal maneuvers to permit noncultivating owners to be classified as "tillers" so as to conform to the land-to-the-tiller model are peculiarly Indic, necessitated by high caste prohibitions against agricultural labor. However, Lenin noted precisely this phenomenon in the reform programs of Russian liberals who idealized "toiler farming," where "toiler" meant simply an employer of agricultural labor, a small capitalist farmer.[3]

This distinction is crucial in terms of policy implications. If "tiller" means one who performs most of the farm labor, the implied ceiling and level of inequality are quite low. If "tiller" means one who hires and supervises wage labor, a high ceiling is normatively consistent with the model and the "tiller" is indistinguishable from a capitalist farmer. Thus the dominant policy logic has implied not "self-cultivation," implying exclusively small peasant farming, but rather small-scale capitalist farming, in which the "cultivator" bears the risk of cultivation by paying wages to laborers, investing working capital, and making managerial decisions. Curiously, it is frequently believed that a land-to-the-tiller reform is somehow "socialist." But conceptually a land-to-the-tiller reform could form a part of the bourgeois revolution in attacking parasitic "feudal" rentiers while legitimating the wage nexus as the dominant form of organizing agricultural production.

The normative position thus contains important ambiguities. For example, although it is easy to understand the productive function of a manager-supervisor on a large estate or where cropping patterns are complex and variable, what is the argument for property income of nontilling "cultivators" on very small plots employing traditional techniques on traditional crops? What is the place of the tilling laborers, as opposed to tenants who employ laborers, in a land-to-the-tiller reform: if the soil belongs to those who produce on it, what is the claim of the laborers?

The Economic and Practical Case

The policy logic of agrarian reform in South Asia has echoed a common theme: tenancy as a mode of organizing production has serious defects, whatever its normative basis as a distributive principle. The Congress Agrarian Reforms Committee (1949: 39) summarized the argument:

> It has been found by experience that unless land is owned by the tiller, his incentive to production does not reach the optimum point. Because of the absence of any guarantee that he would get the full benefit resulting from the improvement he has no desire to make any improvement in the land he cultivates. The improvement, if any, made by him will only enhance the

3. V. I. Lenin, "Mssrs. Bourgeois on 'Toiler Farming,'" *Selected Works* (1938: vol. 12, 283–87).

rate of rent which he has to pay even if he is allowed to enjoy security of tenure.

The committee noted that traditional remedies for production dis-incentives—tenure-reform legislation guaranteeing security of tenure, "reasonable rents," and compensation for improvements—would in theory remove most of these disincentives, but their inquiry also found that such laws were more often evaded than obeyed. The committee con-cluded that, under prevailing conditions, the only way to assure tenants of rights and production incentives was to make them owners.

The analysis in preceding chapters explains why the committee's conclusion was accurate and prophetic. Indeed, because of evictions and deterioration of patron–client relations, tenure reforms in practice have frequently worked to the net disadvantage of the weakest sections of the tenantry. The conditions which create the need for the reform—factors which produce the relatively weak bargaining position of the landless vis-à-vis the landed—are precisely those conditions which thwart imple-mentation. Moreover, even if the reform can be successfully imple-mented under certain conditions, the heavy administrative costs are re-curring, and exogenous factors frequently renew the pressure for violation of the law: technological change, improved produce prices, and other fac-tors create new incentives for increasing rents and evicting tenant-culti-vators.

The logical conclusion would seem to be the elimination of the landlord–tenant dyad altogether or adoption of a laissez-faire stance to-ward tenurial relations. But the laissez-faire option has become increas-ingly unacceptable both on political and ideological-symbolic grounds and because of the economic critiques of tenancy.

In theory, a land-to-the-tiller reform would eliminate both the con-tinuous failure of tenancy reform and the necessity of policing tenurial relations. It was probably the sheer frustration of constantly patching and mending the Paddy Lands Act which produced the widely shared conclu-sion, expressed in Ceylon's *Draft Agricultural Development Plan, 1971–1977*, that because of the unequal power of landlords and tenants, "the transfer of ownership to the tiller of the soil appears to be the only per-manent solution to the problem" (Ceylon, n.d.: III, 63). In India, the *Draft Fifth Five Year Plan* (1974–79) recited the dismal history of legislative attempts to protect tenants and concluded: "The logic of development in the field of land reform lies in the right of ownership being conferred on all tenants" (India, 1974: 43).

In broad historical terms, we can conceptualize this "logic of devel-opment" as progressive additions over time to the "bundle of rights" pos-sessed by tenants in a given piece of land. The progression has included security of land-use rights, a right to a statutory share of the crop, protec-tion from traditional arbitrary fees and labor levies, the right to pass on the tenancy to heirs, specification of landlord obligations in provision of working capital, even the right to mortgage tenancy claims. Together, these rights constitute something very close to full ownership. Thus, conceptually, the final step is a small one, adding another right to the bundle, the right to appropriate return to the land factor of production (ground rent); but in practice the step is a radical one, creating a totally new relationship on the land through elimination of a rent-receiving class from agriculture. For this reason, a seemingly incremental, logical extension of tenure reform is radical, controversial, and politically explosive.

The ambiguity of the meaning of *tiller* is central to an understanding of land reforms in Kerala, the only Indian state to abolish the landlord-tenant nexus in a serious way.[4] The remainder of this chapter explores the formulation and legislation of a land-to-the-tiller reform by the first Communist Party government (1957–59), the dismissal of that government by Delhi, and substitute reforms promulgated by the Congress Party.

Kerala's Agrarian Structure and Land to the Tiller

The land-tenure system of Kerala is frequently called the most bewildering in India, a maze of intermediary rights, esoteric usufructuary mortgage tenures, complex subinfeudation. Daniel Thorner (1956: 35) recognized the intricacy but offered a useful simplification: "a many-tiered edifice of interests in the land—janmies, kanamdars, verumpattamdars—rests on a mass of landless laborers known as Cherumas, Pulayas, or Poliyars."

This observation brings out two important points. First, though *janmies* were landlords in the usual sense, *kanamdars* were superior tenants, *verumpattamdars*, tenants-at-will. If these classes depended on a mass of landless laborers for cultivation in the fields, does a land-to-the-tiller reform mean land to the tenants or land to the laborers? Who are the tillers?

Second, Thorner's designations emphasize that the laborers belonged to distinct castelike groupings, many originally of slave status and

4. The *Bombay Tenancy Act, 1948,* as amended in 1955, did provide for compulsory vesting of the landlord's rights in tenants, but only for "protected" tenants after the weakest sector of the tenancy had been dispossessed. Moreover, in practice, about half of even the tenants who remained after the dispossession failed to become owners in the Maharashtra portion of Bombay State because of evictions, nonpayment of compensation, etc. In the Gujarat section of Bombay State, of 32 lakh acres held by tenants, only 14 lakh acres were purchased by 1966. The result was that tenants who failed to purchase ownership rights were made more insecure than previously. In addition to the discussion in chapter 2, see Dandekar and Khudanpur (1957); India (1966b: 8, 59); India (1970: 78, 92–94); Desai (1971); Maharashtra (1974); Wunderlich (1964). Nevertheless, the reforms did establish a substantial section of the better-placed tenantry on the land and were thus important in subsequent politics (Hart and Herring, 1977).

most "untouchable." Caste and class tend to coincide in most agrarian structures in India, though there is fluidity and complexity.[5] In Kerala, the confluence was direct and decisive. In the legendary origin of Kerala, a mythological hero caused the sea to withdraw and gave the land to imported Brahmans; their descendents are the Namboodiris; their original dependents, the contemporary Nairs (Ayyar, 1966: 1; Namboodiripad, 1968: 13–14). These two castes—the Namboodiri Brahmans and Nair chieftains—traditionally controlled almost all the land, either directly or through vast temple holdings (Kerala, 1968: 11). Cultivation of the land was performed by very low caste or "untouchable" communities.

Though there had been a marked historical decline of some of the great aristocratic lineages and a rise of other communities, such as the commercial Syrian Christians, Ezhavas, and Muslims by the early 1950s, the land-tenure structure remained roughly parallel to the social-ritual status structure. The major landholding communities continued to be of relatively high caste. Relative to percentage in the population, Nairs, Namboodiris, high-caste intermediaries, and high status Syrian Christians were clearly advantaged by the distribution of land in the mid-1950s. Muslims as a whole owned a greater percentage of the land in Malabar than their percentage of the population, though landholding within the community was quite skewed. The groups which owned very little of the land both absolutely and relative to their percentage of the population were the Hindu "untouchables" and outcaste groups which had converted to Christianity (Varghese, 1970: 100 ff., 190–91).

The rentier class in Kerala in the 1950s was quite small numerically but politically powerful and of high social ranking. Landlords were primarily Syrian Christians, Nairs, Namboodiri Brahmans, as well as Muslims in Malabar. Hindu and Christian "untouchable" groups were virtually unrepresented in the landlord class (ibid.: 195). Thus, though the tenurial and social structures are extremely complex, high social standing has generally been associated with a right to income from the land without working it, whereas those of the lowest social status have traditionally worked the land without owning it. Originally the lowest social orders, what Aiyappan termed the "self castes," were tied to the land as slaves or serfs of the higher orders, a structural configuration which persisted into the early postcolonial period (Cochin, 1949: 336 ff.; India, 1962: 30 ff.; Namboodiripad, 1968: 86; Aiyappan, 1965).

The close parallel between the class system and the social status system is one important explanation for the markedly successful mobilization of the rural poor under leftist auspices. Likewise, agrarian structural variables—extreme pressure on the land and a very large landless

5. For an analytical treatment, André Béteille (1974: 35–116). An excellent compendium is "Caste and Class in India," *EPW* 14, nos. 7–8 (February 1979); on Kevala, P. Sivanandan, pp. 475–80, in that volume.

population, producing rack-renting and tenurial insecurity—contributed, particularly in conjunction with agrarian policies of the colonial state and tactical responses by the left. The agrarian movement was strongest in Malabar, where tenurial insecurity created by colonial land policy and communal hostilities produced periodic peasant uprisings of serious proportions, culminating in the Mappilla Rebellion of 1921. Landlordism in Kerala was inextricably tied to a social system that imposed disabilities and indignities on the lowest orders which were extreme, severe, and rigid even by Indian standards. Opposition to the landlordism was thus inextricably linked to general social reform and attracted a broader social base than the tenantry who could expect to gain from the early demands for tenure reform espoused by the left. In Malabar in particular, opposition to landlordism was structurally linked to deeply felt communal grievances among the Muslims (who were an absolute majority in large sections of Malabar). As importantly, the nationalist movement in Malabar necessarily included opposition to landlords and their agents who utilized the colonial state to enforce their power.[6]

But social indignities, communal hostilities, nationalist ferment, and tenurial insecurity do not necessarily produce an effective radical agrarian movement. The colonial state created an important ecological niche—recognizing the tenurial roots of agrarian "outrages" but making only token and halting responses in the form of concessions to the top stratum of the tenantry. The left made demands for broadening and extending feeble and inadequate legislation such as the Malabar Tenancy Act of 1929 important foci for mobilization, integrated with anticolonial and social reform programs. They worked at first within the Congress movement and later split from the Congress when it refused to back increasingly radical agrarian demands. Moreover, the left took its program to the rural poor while not ignoring the small industrial working class, in marked contrast to communist movements in other parts of the subcontinent. Patient, painful organizing and extraordinary personal sacrifices by leaders and cadres eventually produced one of the strongest, though unevenly developed, communist movements in the region.[7]

6. For more on colonial responses, see chapter 2. This compressed summary does not do justice to the complexity of the Communist movement in Malabar; see Hart and Herring (1977); Hardgrave (1977); Pannikar (1979); Radhakrishnan (1980); Paulini (1978: 105–215); Koshy (1976: 51–59; 110–18). On the interpenetration of class issues, caste issues, agrarian change, and broader social movements in the politics of depressed communities in Kerala, Saradamoni (1980). Christians constituted slightly more than one-fifth of Kerala's population, Muslims slightly less; both communities exhibit marked internal stratification by class and status.

7. For accounts by two of the most important Communist leaders in the state, E. M. S. Namboodiripad (1976) and A. K. Gopalan (1973). For a literary/historical account which provides insight into the local dynamics, Niranjana, *The Stars Shine Brightly: Saga of the Kayyoor Martyrs*, translated from the Kannada (*Chirasmarane*) by Tejaswini Niranjana (New Delhi: People's Publishing House, 1977).

Kerala represented the agrarian crisis of India in acute form when the present state was created; in 1956–57, per capita net sown area was 0.38 acres, the lowest of all states, compared to an all-India average of 1.09 acres.[8] As illustrated in table 6.1, Kerala had a much lower percentage of peasant proprietors than the rest of India, and consequently larger percentages of tenants and laborers and a relatively larger rentier class.

Regional differences in tenurial structure were pronounced and politically important. Travancore, the southern third of present-day Kerala, more nearly approximated a peasant proprietor system, with relatively low percentages of tenants and landless laborers. This tenurial structure evolved through distribution of government land and colonization of a frontier in the nineteenth century and the relatively pro-tenant policies of the Maharaja (Varghese, 1970: 47 ff.; Koshy, 1976: 118 ff.). Whereas owner-cultivators constituted the largest agrarian class in Travancore historically, in Malabar and Cochin landless laborers and tenants were the largest agrarian classes. Cochin, the central section of contemporary Kerala, was also under "indirect" colonial rule, but the royal rulers followed land policies less favorable to the tenantry than those of Travancore. Malabar, the northern section of contemporary Kerala, was under direct colonial rule as part of the Madras presidency, and represented the archetypal agrarian system in disintegration, characterized by tenant evictions, rack-renting, and rural rebellion.[9] Table 6.2 presents data on regional differences from one important study.

Table 6.1: Agrarian Structures: Kerala and India, 1951

	Percentage of Agricultural Households	
Occupational Class	Kerala	India
1. Owners (cultivators of land wholly or mainly owned)	35.3	67.8
2. Tenants (cultivators of land wholly or mainly unowned)	23.1	12.6
3. Agricultural laborers	39.2	17.9
4. Noncultivating rentiers	2.4	1.8
	Acres	
Per capita net sown area	0.38	1.09

SOURCE: Calculations from India (1962) *Agricultural Labor in India: Report of the Second Enquiry*, vol. 7, p. 9.

8. India (1962: 9–11). The extreme population density and consequent population pressure per acre were partially compensated by higher average productivity and the importance of commercial crops that provided rural processing employment (though at abysmally low wages)—coir, cashews, toddy, etc. Cf. Hart and Herring (1977: 239–50).

9. Varghese (1970: 19–138); Namboodiripad (1968: 57–99). For more detailed analysis, Shea (1959: 94–170); Karat (1973); Radhakrishnan (1980).

Table 6.2: Agrarian Structure of Kerala, 1957–1958

| | Percentage of Agricultural Population | | | |
Tenurial Status	Travancore	Cochin	Malabar	Kuttanad[10]
Landless laborer	13	19	12	41
Owner-cultivator	56	29	10	18
Tenant-cultivator	25	50	75	35
Mortgagee	3	—	—	—
Rentier	1	2	3	6
Mortgagor	2	—	—	—

SOURCE: T. C. Varghese, *Agrarian Change and Economic Consequences* (1970: 161).

Table 6.3: Agrarian Livelihoods in Kerala, 1957–1958

| | Percentage of Agricultural Households | | |
Main Source of Income	Travancore	Cochin	Malabar
Agricultural labor	37	48	39
Tenant cultivation	21	20	47
Owner cultivation	41	30	10
Rents	1	2	2
	Acres		
Agricultural land per capita	0.49	0.29	0.43

SOURCE: T. C. Varghese, *Agrarian Change and Economic Consequences* (1970: 199, 201).

The figures in table 6.2 illustrate the numerical dominance of ten-ants and laborers but do not reflect the full importance of agricultural labor as an occupation. Because holdings are extremely small, a large per-centage of "owner-cultivators" and "tenant-cultivators" must depend on agricultural labor for their livelihood, as demonstrated in table 6.3.

Even in the relatively owner-cultivator dominated Travancore area, more than a third of the agricultural families depended on field labor for their main source of income. Such pressure naturally permitted the ex-action of onerous terms of exchange by landlords from tenants, as com-petition among the landless for tenancies was extreme. The *Report of the Agrarian Problem Enquiry Committee* (Cochin, 1949: 3) found that rents varied between one-half and three-fourths of the gross yield and that landlords were able to collect to the last cent even in bad years. The committee observed "rack-renting," precisely defined as a situation in which tenants, after paying cultivation expenses and rent, received no return at all for managing the land and often received no return for their

10. Kuttanad is the small but crucial "rice bowl" of Kerala, reclaimed from lowland lakes and swamps by the polder method in central coastal Kerala. It is a traditional center of capitalist agriculture, labor agitation, extremely large holdings, and the political base of the Kerala Congress. Cf. Kerala (1971); V. R. Pillai and P. G. K. Panikar (1965).

labor, incurring debt to pay the rent (cf. Koshy: 1976, 65–69). As early as
the late nineteenth century, one British observer noted that South Malabar "has earned the unenviable reputation of being the most rack-rented
country on the face of the earth" (Varghese, 1970: 78). The Malabar Tenancy Committee in 1940 debated whether or not to reduce ground rent
statutorily from two-thirds to one-half of the crop.[11]

The concentration of land in the hands of a few numerically small
communities and competition in the agrarian underclass for access to the
means of production bid up rents, reduced security of tenure, and created
classes of agricultural laborers differentiated by employment security. An
official study in Cochin in 1949 noted that the emancipation of laborers
from slavery in 1911 had effected no improvement in their material condition; many continued to be tied to the land through debt bondage. Above
the bonded laborer class were the "dependent laborers," who attached
themselves to the landowners at lower than the market wage rate in return for security of employment; by tradition, landowners did not let
their own laborers starve. "Day laborers" faced extreme insecurity of employment but received higher daily wages.[12] The material consequences
were severe. A Malayalam saying related that the laborer lived on man-
goes and jackfruit in one season, plant leaves in another, and "here and
there" in another. The "here and there" period was one of "partial starvation" that was physically evident. The laborers survived because they
were willing to eat "tapioca, root vegetables, game of the woods and
field rats."[13]

A survey of conditions of laborers in Kerala in 1956–57 showed that
though debt bondage was less prevalent than previously, the debt nexus
was still important; of attached laborer families, 91 percent were indebted; among casual laborers, 77 percent were indebted (India, 1962: 62).
Agrarian underemployment remained severe, and was worse in Kerala
than in any other Indian State (ibid.: 22). The situation of the laborers
had deteriorated in Kerala between 1950–51 and 1956–57, and had deteriorated more than in other parts of India; the decrease in per capita cer-
eal consumption was put at 50 percent.[14] Moreover, the percentage of

11. Reported by Namboodiripad (1968: 92) who was a member of the committee.
The reduction was rejected on the grounds that lower rent would not allow the landlord a
reasonable return on investment.

12. Cochin (1949: 337–40). Similar conditions were found in other parts of the state;
see Government of Travancore-Cochin, *Report of The Minimum Wages Committee for Employment in Agriculture* (1956: 9 and passim).

13. Cochin (1949: 341). Such dietary practices did nothing to enhance the social-
ritual standing of the laborer communities in a rigidly orthodox Hindu society; the very
poor, because they are very poor, are forced into ritually "unclean" practices, confirming
their status as unclean.

14. India (1962: 55–56). There were also decreases in per capita consumption of pul-
ses, sugar, oils, meat, fish, and eggs, though these made up a small percentage of caloric
intake.

laborer families with per capita annual expenditures of Rs 100 or less increased from 27 to 42 percent. The reason for deterioration in living standards was a decline in days of available employment per family; the consequence was that expenditures for the average family exceeded income, resulting in an increase in the percentage of families indebted (India, 1962: 49, 57, 60).

We may conclude this section with the question with which it began: who are the tillers? If the entire edifice of land rights and agricultural production rested on field laborers, whose employment was both insecure and inadequate, how would land to the tiller be conceptualized?

Land to the Tiller in Kerala: The Communists' Policy Logic

The important *Report of the Congress Agrarian Reforms Committee* has been used extensively to illustrate very sophisticated policy thinking on agrarian reform. Ironically, the policy model in the report did not become operative under any Congress regime but was closely approximated by the reforms of the Communist Party of India in Kerala. More ironically, the legislation of land to the tiller in accordance with Congress guidelines was a major issue in Congress opposition to the elected Communist ministry and its eventual dismissal by the Congress government in Delhi.

The Communist government took office in 1957, having emphasized radical land reforms in the election campaign and having done best electorally in areas where poor peasants and laborers were concentrated. It moved immediately to stabilize the agrarian situation, proclaiming the Stay of Eviction Proceedings Ordinance within a week to protect tenants and laborers with huts on landlords' lands (*kudikidappukars*) from eviction until comprehensive agrarian reforms could be framed. Drafting of these reforms began almost immediately under the direction of the revenue minister, Ms. K. R. Goury, in consultation with Delhi's Planning Commission. The finished draft was widely circulated to elicit popular response and to publicize the government's intentions.[15]

The government was in a delicate position. It was committed to radical land reform both on programmatic grounds and because the agrarian poor constituted the bulk of its mass base, yet was constrained by the necessity of working with a liberal constitutional framework with an elitist bureaucracy and court system.[16] Moreover, there was virulent op-

15. For an account of a Communist peasant organizer and parliamentarian, Gopalan (1959: 102 ff.). The chief minister's account, Namboodiripad (1959; 1968: 210–15; 1974: 54). Also Koshy (1976: 211–16); Chander (1973: 188–91); Paulini (1978: 231–35).

16. The Communist Party of India adopted the policy of land to the tiller and militant mobilization of the peasantry for an eventual agrarian revolution, much as in the Chinese model, at the Second Congress in 1948. The policy document was *On the Agrarian Question in India* (1949), published the same year as the *Report of the Congress Agrarian Reforms Committee*. Later, in May 1950, the Central Committee corrected what Namboodiripad has termed "crude 'leftism'" and argued that the main struggle should be against

position to Communist rule among certain communities and the government rested on a two-vote majority in the Assembly. These conditions dictated a cautious course, with careful attention to the political sensitivites of Delhi. The government had to prove its bona fides by working "within the system," which it recognized as hostile to radical change, and yet deliver some relief to its socially oppressed consistuency (Namboodiripad, 1968: 215).

The draft Agrarian Relations Bill steered this middle course. E. M. S. Namboodiripad, the chief minister from 1957 to 1959, has stated (1974: 43) that the party's aim in land reform was modest—to carry out policies announced by the Congress Central government but unimplemented by Congress State governments (cf. Leiten, 1979). The drafting of the bill went slowly, partly because of its public circulation to elicit popular opinion. The chief minister had written in 1952 that reform details must be left to the "innate, revolutionary common sense of the peasants themselves, organized in their own associations and committees" (Namboodiripad, 1952: 52). The draft set the parameters of the reform but provided for popular participation in adjusting implementation to local conditions. These parameters encompassed the major demands of the State's largest peasant association but went beyond those demands in important respects (T. K. Oommen, 1975: 1575).

The mechanics of the bill were as follows: first, fixity of tenure was to be conferred on a wide variety of holders of tenancylike rights in land. Recognizing that landlords had anticipated the reform, it was provided that all cultivating tenants, "irrespective of the deed or document held by the landlord," could claim fixity of tenure.[17] Certain deeds of surrender executed after the ministry took power were presumed to have been exacted under duress and invalidated. As importantly, cultivators were permitted to produce evidence that they were cultivating tenants even though described as agents or servants in documents; this provision permitted suspension of measures in the Evidence Act.

Landlords were allowed to resume land for personal cultivation under extremely limited conditions; tenants from whom land was resumed were entitled to compensation, and tenants could not be left with less

---

feudalism in agriculture, necessitating an alliance of laborers, tenants, small owners, and even rich peasants and progressive landlords. See P. C. Joshi (1975: 38); Namboodiripad, *On the Agrarian Question in India* (1952). Namboodiripad's conclusion was that the Party had erred in two ways: (a) in not sufficiently emphasizing expressed peasant demands and initiatives in land reform, and (b) in isolating the Party from the broad peasant masses through excessively "left" demands (specifically, alienating landowning farmers). This tactical reinterpretation parallels the party's movement away from explicitly revolutionary programs toward collaboration with a broader spectrum of "antifeudal" and democratic social forces and toward electoral politics.

17. Kerala (1961), chap. 1, para. 50. This act is a modified version of the Communist ministry's original but can be used as a reference for the original, except in those specific provisions altered by the Congress–PSP government.

than a subsistence holding, unless the owner held less than 5 acres. The special problems of these small owners were recognized; tribunals were to determine on a case-by-case basis the equity claims of small landlords and their tenants. Arrears of rent were dramatically reduced, particularly for small tenants. Provisions were set for establishing "fair rent" on all lands, varying between one-sixth to one-twelfth of the gross produce on dry lands and one-fourth to one-sixth on wet lands.

After fair rents had been established and fixity of tenure conferred, there was to be a "Peasants' Day" on which all cultivating tenants were deemed to have purchased their holdings, extinguishing the landlords' and intermediaries' rights in the land and vesting these rights in the government. The government was then to collect compensation from the tenants in annual installments and pay the landlords; compensation was set at sixteen times the fair rent for small owners, less for large.

Although these provisions would abolish rentier landlordism, it is not clear that they would establish land to the tiller. "Cultivating" tenants were to be made owners, but "cultivating" was defined to include supervision of hired labor, a rather surprising provision. The finance minister (later chief minister), C. Achutha Menon (1958: 20), wrote in his commentary on the bill:

> If the slogan, "Land to the Tiller," is to have any meaning, it is the person who actually cultivates the land either with his own labour or the labour of the members of his family who ought to get the benefit of land legislation. We have extended this a little and also included a person who personally supervises cultivation, although not doing actual manual labor, because we thought it was necessary in the interests of production to encourage such people also.

This does not seem a sufficient explanation; more important is the argument from Namboodiripad that the correct *tactical* line in that historical situation was an attack on feudalism. For this purpose, all nonfeudal classes could be rallied behind an agrarian reform. The cutting point was that only those who undertook the risk of cultivation could benefit from the reform. Namboodiripad considered the distinction between "parasitic" feudal landlords and "entrepreneurial" capitalist landlords critical, and argued that the former had to be destroyed, the latter encouraged: "capitalism in agriculture, like capitalism in industry, is an advance on the present situation in a semi-colonial, semi-feudal country."[18]

A second major compromise in the reform was the provision for compensation (at well below market value), both to former landlords and

18. Namboodiripad (1952: 27, 49, 61) makes a careful distinction between the types of exploitation practiced by the two kinds of landlords, capitalist and feudal. Both were held to be exploiters, but through different modes of appropriation and with different consequences for productivity and technical change. Cf. Lieten (1979: 29–31).

to owners who lost land through operation of the ceiling. The chief minister had been acerbically critical of Congress governments for compensating the *zamindars*, arguing that compensation severely restricted the
investment resources of poor tenants (Namboodiripad, 1952: 37). The
compensation compromise was inevitable, however, given the intent of
the government to work within the constitutional framework of the Republic of India; outright confiscation would almost certainly have been
ruled ultra vires of the Constitution.[19]

The bill included a ceiling on holdings. Considering the extremely
large number of landless and land-poor agriculturalists, the ceiling was
rather high, though by far the lowest in India at the time. The ceiling was
set at 15 acres of double-crop paddy or its equivalent, that is, 22.5 acres
of single-crop land, 15 acres of garden land, or 30 acres of dry land. The
limit was raised for large families, but could in no case exceed 25 acres
of double-cropped land or its equivalent. Exemptions from the ceiling
were allowed for public, religious, or charitable institutions (a concession
to Delhi) and for plantations.

The rather high ceiling and the exemption of the plantation sector
reflected the party's position that capitalism in agriculture must be encouraged in a semifeudal economy: Namboodiripad (1952: 49–50) argued:

> the lands of all feudal landlords without regard to the size of their holdings
> shall be taken over, as this is the crucial point in a programme of breaking
> the back of feudalism. As a capitalist landlords . . . a certain restriction of
> upper limit will have to be put on their holdings, taking care, however, that
> this limit is put at a sufficiently high level to enable them to carry on effi-
> cient cultivation. Finally, as regards rich peasants, no restriction at all should
> be put at this stage. . . .

The logic of good landlords, bad landlords, parasites, and entrepreneurs in the context of land ceilings sounds a familiar note. It is not
irrelevant, of course, that, as the party admits, rich peasants, middle
peasants, and even capitalist landlords are heavily represented in its peasant association and cadres, especially in comparison with the representation of poor peasants and laborers.[20] The reform provisions reflect an

19. Achutha Menon (1958: 40–41) calculated the purchase price for tenants as roughly
between one-third and one-half the market value of the land, depending on the crop; compensation to the landlords would be less in most cases, depending on size of holding.

20. Data on class origins of members collected by the CPI(M) were published in
Economic and Political Weekly April 22, 1970, p. 670. On the changing class base of activists in the agrarian movement, which increasingly incorporated poor peasants and landless
laborers, Radhakrishnan (1980). The CPI(M), which retained the more radical elements of
the agrarian movement after the split of the Communist Party in 1964, has explicitly recognized that the reliance on relatively privileged agrarian classes among activists constitutes a serious problem: Communist Party of India (Marxist), *Central Committee Resolution on Certain Agrarian Issues and an Explanatory Note by P. Sundarayya* (New Delhi,
1973), p. 2 of the *Note* and passim (cf. Krishnaji, 1979: 519–19). My fieldwork in Palghat

analysis of both the historical stage of development and the constraints of working within a federal system. The constraints of electoral politics were also in evidence; more radical options would have threatened the fragile unity of the agrarian movement. Achutha Menon admitted that the government had to steer a middle course between two positions— one, more prevalent in Malabar, favoring absolute commitment to the tenant's right in land, the other, more prevalent in Travancore, favoring the rights of established property in land.[21]

The strategic priority of attacking the social base of "feudalism" significantly influenced the policy logic. Namboodiripad noted that there were two possible strategies in an extremely land-poor economy. The meager amount of surplus land available could be redistributed to give economic holdings to a small percentage of the landless, leaving the rest in an unchanged and depressed situation, or it could be distributed equally, providing much less than an economic holding to all claimants. Namboodiripad's reasoning (1952: 50) suggested the latter: the equal distribution of land, even if in miniscule plots, would give the recipients "the economic prerequisite to build a free life—life unfettered by feudal shackles." Though there was also an expressed preference for distribution of surplus land in blocks for cooperative farming, that preference was more aspirational than realistic; the basic thrust of the party's logic was to mitigate dependence in the agrarian underclass to the greatest extent possible, primarily on the lines of individual peasant plots (Menon, 1958: 43).

This reasoning is more important for insight into the 1969 reform than for explaining the abortive 1959 bill. Namboodiripad could not have meant real economic freedom, of course; it was admitted that the plots distributed would be far below the "economic" level. What was meant was the security of a housesite and small plot to lessen the abject dependence of the totally landless on landowners. Following the same logic, the Agrarian Relations Bill made special provisions for laborers who held housesites and miniscule garden plots at the sufferance of landlords. Landlords had permitted these laborers, the *kudikidappukars*, to con-

---

district in 1980, as yet unpublished, suggests that the problem still exists and that the party remains concerned about it; cf. Mencher (1978); T. K. Oommen (1971); Krishnaji (1979).

21. Menon (1958: 23). Chander (1973: 213) argues that the reversal of the earlier radical position on compensation resulted from the fear of isolating the party in an adventurist position. Public positions taken by Namboodiripad, and especially the conservative thrust of Achutha Menon's commentary on the Agrarian Relations Bill, support that analysis. The smallholder provisions reflect the ambivalence. Owners of less than five acres of double-crop paddy, or its equivalent, were not subject to the general provisions of the bill; relations between tenants and smallholders were to be subject to "conciliation proceedings" to consider the relative economic positions of the parties. But in Kerala's agrarian structure, such "smallholders" were often quite privileged relative to the majority, and so many holdings were "small" that the reform's redistributive potential was blunted; in Travancore–Cochin, Menon estimated that 96 percent of the farms were in the hands of "smallholders."

struct huts on their land, originally as a means of securing attached labor and preventing theft of crops. The hutment dwellers had been granted security of tenure (of housesites) in earlier legislation, but with little effect.[22] The 1959 bill gave the *kudikidappukars* heritable security of tenure, discharged arrears of rent, and limited future rental payments to Rs 6 per year. Effective security of tenure was to aid the landless laborers in resisting domination by their traditional masters.

Beyond these measures, little was done in the bill for the laborers. The government knew that very little land would be available from operation of the ceiling. Achutha Menon (1958: 48–49) argued that with per capita land availability at only one-third of an acre, no land redistribution could significantly aid the laborers; the only relief was through provisions in the bill "to secure to them the right to live in a house of their own unmolested by the landlord or his *goondas* or the police."

Reform Logic and Embourgeoisement

As the landless laborers constituted a critical rural support base for the Communists, it seems curious that more was not done for them through land reform. Yet there may have been an understanding among followers, as among leaders, that very little *could* be done. Kathleen Gough related the following incident from a Kerala village in 1964: "I asked a wretchedly poor Irava coolie woman why she voted for the Communists. Had they helped her in any way? She answered soberly, 'Nobody really helps us. But we feel that the Communists are thinking of us. They are friendly, and have good hearts.'"[23]

Equally curious is the fact that a Communist regime would promote the creation of more "petit-bourgeois agrarians" (as Lenin termed the class) through land reform. Given that sufficient land is not available for creating the good life in peasant terms for any significant proportion of the laborers, should the regime not promote collective or state farms to improve the situation of both laborers and agriculture? Is a society of miniscule capital-starved fragmented plots a rational objective? More pragmatically, though the short-run effect of the reform might well be, as Namboodiripad believed, to strengthen the party, is the long-term effect not precisely the opposite; is *embourgeoisement* even on a tiny, almost parodied, scale not contrary to the party's goals of uniting the rural masses for revolutionary change?

22. Cochin (1949: 130–31). Many *kudikidappukars* were previously smallholders and tenants ruined by the depression. As landlords customarily owned all land in the villages, it was their traditional obligation to provide housesites. The *Report* notes that *kudikidappukars* received lower than prevailing wages for labor and frequently agreed to sign documents renouncing rights to the housesites guaranteed by legislation (appendix 22: 214).

23. Gough (1965: typescript reprint, 7). *Irava* (Ezhava) is a low-caste grouping in the traditional hierarchy but not now considered "untouchable."

These are serious questions; Namboodiripad himself, writing in 1954, stated that, of course, the eventual objective was collectivization of small holdings, voluntarily. He felt that the Congress Agrarian Reforms Committee had erred in recommending "bureaucratic collectivization," an official-dominated plan for cooperatives. However:

> Those who are serious about carrying out agrarian reform should ... depend not so much on the merits and demerits of particular schemes of land reform as on the question of which scheme or schemes are those that have been evolved and are being implemented by the mass of peasants. It may be that the mass of peasantry would like to have a particular scheme of land reforms which, from a scientific point of view, is not so good as some other scheme worked out by certain intellectuals; that, however, should not lead any revolutionary, who is serious about carrying out real agrarian reform, to the rejection of the scheme evolved by the peasants themselves, based on their own experience and understanding.[24]

This perspective has the weight of evidence in its favor: elaborate plans concocted without reference to the needs and demands of the peasantry have proved notably infructuous. The demands of the organized peasantry, particularly the *karshaka sangham*, historically came from those who already had some quasi-proprietary rights in land which they sought to expand (cf. Radhakrishnan, 1980). Laborers, on the other hand, though desirous of obtaining land, have pressed for more proletarian demands—wages, hours, working conditions, security of employment. The government took specific steps, other than security of home and garden sites, to meet these needs and demands—for example, the "new police policy," the appointment of a committee to set minimum wages for agricultural laborers, and the formation of the Industrial Relations Committee, which included representatives of laborers, cultivators, and government.

However, wages are not the only issue of importance to the huge class of laborers. The *Report of the Agrarian Problems Enquiry Committee* examined in detail the relations of debt-bondage, patron–client, or serflike ties between owners and various categories of laborers. The laborers' inability to bargain freely with owners and improve their standard of living was attributed to the "four fears": insecurity of employment, fear of losing priority of employment in the slack season, fear of eviction from housesites, and "fear of recall of loans which can never be repaid" (Cochin, 1949: 338). The Agrarian Relations Bill addressed the housesite issue, as did the police policy. The Agricultural Debt Relief Bill provided for scaling down debts and reducing interest rates, though more radical measures preferred by the government were dropped in the belief that Delhi would deny approval (Namboodiripad, 1959: 43).

The other two fears are analagous to insecurity of tenure for tenants

---

24. E. M. S. Namboodiripad (1954: 74, 80; quotation from 81). For a more recent CPI analysis with the same thrust, *Yojana* 16, no. 13 (1972: 506–07).

and have been objects of agitation by the agrarian labor unions. These needs were addressed much later in the Kerala Agricultural Workers Bill (introduced in 1972 and passed in 1974), which provides for priority in employment and permanency for laborers. The earlier reforms as a whole attempted to establish freedom from patron dominance, freedom from police suppression of wage struggles, a minimum wage and machinery to adjudicate demands on wages, hours, and working conditions. These measures, combined with organizational work, have resulted in the largest gains in wages of agrarian workers relative to productivity anywhere in India.[25]

The policy logic of the first Communist ministry recognized the political and economic undesirability of *embourgeoisement* of radical agrarian classes, but vesting land in the tenants was the only possible response to long-standing popular demands and decades of agitations on the past of the peasantry (particularly in Malabar) and was central to the strategic requirements of eliminating the feudal residues of parasitic landlordism. The reform logic recognized and addressed the interests of agricultural laborers qua rural proletarians, not as aspiring peasant proprietors; the demands of the tenants, who already held tenuous propertylike rights in land, were granted. The policy logic of the agrarian reforms thus formally recognized the structural division in the left agrarian movement; the attack on feudal landlordism was objectively and subjectively in the interests of both laborers and tenants. Landlordism was widely perceived as a system of social oppression that prevented both laborers and poor peasants from increasing their share of the agrarian surplus. With rental exactions abolished, the tenants were to share their surplus with laborers through wage increases. But would the tenants, who would remain poor and would reasonably be expected to use the surplus to improve their own standard of living, share with the laborers, or would they, rather, operate on the basis of their class interest as "petit-bourgeois agrarians," resisting the organized demands of the laborers? These issues were left unresolved and remained central to leftist politics, necessitating new strategies for uniting the agrarian poor.

Administration and Politics: Government as an "Instrument of Struggle"

Land reforms were central in the politics of the first Communist government. The chief minister termed the drafting of the bill the most significant accomplishment of twenty-eight months of rule (Namboodiripad, 1974: 54). Support for and opposition to the bill was a political reflection of the agrarian structure. The Karshaka Sangham (peasant association) at

25. "Wages and Incomes of the Weaker Sectors in Rural India," Special Issue of *Indian Journal of Agricultural Economics* (1974) pp. 83 ff.; P. K. Bardhan (1973).

the State level and as a pressure group within the Communist Party locally was a powerful force in shaping the bill. Within the Communist Party, the more radical demands came from the Malabar representatives as compared to the Travancore-Cochin groups; Malabar had historically been the center of tenurial disintegration and peasant activism. Opposition came from the Congress Party, and particularly from the Nair Service Society, a high-caste organization representing groups with significant landed interests, and the Christian churches, the elite of which were significant owners of plantations and *kayal* (polder) paddy estates.[26]

The Agrarian Relations Bill was passed by the Legislative Assembly on June 10, 1959. Within forty-eight hours, a "direct action" was launched against the government by the groups which had most strenuously opposed the land reform. There were certain other issues, the Education Bill especially, but the agrarian policy of the Communists was critical. Namboodiripad himself attributed the direct action to opposition to the land reform in particular.[27] Agitations were specifically aimed at bringing down the government; activists organized large-scale civil disobedience and urged supporters to "paralyze the administration." The tactics were partially successful; after considerable vacillation in Delhi, the Center intervened, dismissed the government, and imposed President's Rule on the grounds that the law-and-order situation was out of control. Although the Agrarian Relations Bill had been passed by the Assembly, it had not received presidential assent, and thus was not law.

In the following elections, the Communist Party not only retained but improved its percentage of the popular vote, polling nearly a million more votes.[28] However, with the opposition parties united and entering into electoral arrangements against them, the Communists received only a fraction of their previous seats in the Assembly. A Congress-Praja Socialist Party ministry was formed; the new government revised and passed the Agrarian Relations Bill again; it was signed into law January 21, 1961.

The act passed by the Congress-led ministry was significantly compromised through concessions to landed interests. The definition of "smallholder" was enlarged to benefit more owners at the expense of tenants. Additional concessions were made to plantation owners and religious, charitable, and educational trusts. The rights of *kudikidappukars*

26. Chander (1973: 220–29) provides a succinct summary of the parties and their social bases. Although class-disaggregated voting data are not available, the ecological analysis of Krishna Murthy and Rao (1968) of differential support bases for the parties is consistent with the analysis in the text.

27. Namboodiripad (1959: 42–47). For analysis that corroborates the chief minister's position, Chander (1973: 325–26). On the "Liberation Struggle" against the Communists, Fic (1970: chap. 5); Koshy (1976: 229–32).

28. The Communist Party's percentage of the popular vote increased from just over 35 percent to just over 39 percent. For a summary of electoral politics of the period, Hardgrave (1973). Election results in India, Election Commission, *Report on the General Election to the Kerala Legislative Assembly* (Delhi, 1965).

were restricted, and evicted tenants scheduled for rehabilitation in the Communist draft were excluded from benefits. The elected representatives to the Land Board and Land Tribunals were placed government nominees and bureaucrats (T. K. Oommen, 1975: 1577–78; Paulini, 1978: 258–60).

The Agrarian Relations Act never became a fully operational land reform; crucial provisions were struck down by the Supreme Court (1961) and the Kerala High Court (1963).[29] However, the act did have an impact on the agrarian politics of the State. Landowners organized and evicted tenants; the agrarian poor likewise organized and militantly demanded newly legislated rights. After the fall of the Communist ministry, the left and peasant organizations used the Agrarian Relations Bill as a rallying point; massive demonstrations were held against the diluting of the provisions by the Congress government.[30]

These historical outcomes raise significant questions about the role of a revolutionary party in a parliamentary system. An important analysis within the Communist Party in Kerala held that the electoral process could not being fundamental change or real relief for the propertyless masses because the organs of state power at the Center were in the hands of a bourgeois–landlord coalition.[31] The purpose of gaining electoral office was to use the admittedly limited resources and power of the government to relieve the immediate oppression of the people as much as possible and to utilize the public arena for mobilizing and politicizing them. E. M. S. Namboodiripad argued that despite the serious structural limitations, leftist governments could "consolidate" popular forces, facilitate "the polarization of socio-political forces," and, most importantly, could be used as "instruments of struggle in the hands of the people" (1974: 92, 94).

Concretely, one of the most important manifestations of this position was the "new police policy," based on the understanding that in a bourgeois state the police are an instrument of repression used against labor on behalf of property.[32] The government's new police policy was to limit police responsibility to apprehending "ordinary criminals"—those who commit common criminal offenses. The police were explicitly prohibited from interfering in agrarian or industrial labor disputes except when lives were threatened (Namboodiripad, 1959: 10–14).

Since workers dramatically outnumber owners, the effect of the po-

29. Kerala, *Synopsis of the Proceedings of the Kerala Legislative Assembly*, ser. 4, no. 4-I-63, January 9, 1963; no. 5-I-63, January 10, 1963; *The Kerala Law Times* (Ernakulam), 1972 *KLT* 702; Chander (1973: 235).

30. For an account by a leader of that mobilization, A. K. Gopalan (1973: chap. 27); cf. Paulini (1978: 238–66); Koshy (1976: 218–32); T. K. Oommen (1975: 1577–78); Chander (1973: 263–65).

31. Namboodiripad (1974: 92) states that the party has "no illusions" about the potential of the "parliamentary path." Cf. Gopalan (1973: 263; 284–85); Hardgrave (1973).

32. Enunciated in Namboodiripad's speech to the Legislative Assembly, July 23, 1957. Reprinted in Indian Commission of Jurists (1960), appendix E.

lice policy was to enhance the power of labor vis-à-vis property. T. K. Oommen's detailed study (1971) of Alleppey district, a nerve center of radical agrarian movements, shows that laborers were indeed able to improve their position in relation to landowners during the Communist ministry, despite previous failures (cf. Lieten, 1979). Oommen's work strongly suggests that the Communist strategy was successful, at least in Alleppey district, as the provision of external allies to the agrarian underclass accelerated the breakdown of patron–client ties through an increase in the militance and consciousness of depressed classes.[33]

An account of incidents of agrarian (and other) confrontations and violence during the Communist ministry was compiled by a committee of the Indian Commission of Jurists (1960). Those incidents show clearly how landowners who had traditionally depended on the police to enforce their property rights were denied the use of police during the Communist period,[34] and support Oommen's analysis of the mobilization of laborers during the period. The committee charged that the Communists used the executive power to "render nugatory the provisions of the law" by maneuvering around the established courts and judicial procedures; specifically, Communist "cells" allegedly exercised more power than the courts during the period (pp. 88–91, 97).

The impact of courts on land reform has been destructive in South Asia. The Agrarian Relations Bill explicitly removed from the purview of the courts adjudication on most matters, allocating that function to the Land Board and Land Tribunals. The use of party "cells" in administration raises a complex issue. A stated objective of the ministry was to democratize administration. A. K. Gopalan, a peasant organizer and party elder, argued that both the judiciary and the administrative corps were, because of their status as a "privileged caste" and the legal presumption in favor of property in a bourgeois society, likely to obstruct fundamental change (1959: 96). In response, the ministry established advisory committees to monitor and assist administration; all parties were to be represented, and the committees were eventually to be converted to elected bodies with executive powers (ibid.: 114; Namboodiripad, 1959: 25–36).

Chief Minister Namboodiripad argued that the strength of government officials—"efficiency in carrying out clear orders according to rules"—becomes a weakness when administrative tasks necessitate securing the people's cooperation; the advisory committees were to elicit popular par-

33. Kathleen Gough (1965) also points to the effects of land legislation in the breakdown of harmonious agrarian relations and the further development of class tensions in the period 1957–64; landlords, as well as tenants and laborers, initiated the breakdown of harmonious relations. Cf. Alexander (1975).

34. Indian Commission of Jurists (1960), especially pp. 45–56. The *Report* is clearly biased against the government, and labels party cadres "desperadoes" and "goondas." Nevertheless, the interviews and accounts present a useful source for understanding the "new police policy" and agarian conflict.

ticipation in such tasks. Namboodiripad claimed that the Communist Party did not monopolize the committees, but rather allowed more representation to opposition parties than their percentage of the popular vote, despite the fact that previous governments, including the Center, had excluded Communists from administrative positions (1959: 26, 35).

Whatever the validity of the charges and countercharges, it would not be surprising if the committees were used in partisan ways, given the norms of ordinary politics; nor would it be surprising if the Communist Party dominated the committees, since the Communists had the most organized, extensive, disciplined, and active cadre network in most areas. What is important is the model of efficient causation implied.

A major conclusion of analyses of agrarian reform is that ordinary administration has not been effective. Although sharp lines are usually drawn between policy and implementation and adjudication, the lines are artificial. Theoretically sound policy can be rendered meaingless by administrative indifference and a vigorous administration can be hamstrung by the courts, as the long history of the Paddy Lands Act in Ceylon demonstrated. Namboodiripad rejected the attitude of administrators that they should be protected from interference on the part of politicians and ordinary people, that implementation was their special function, whereas popular will was to be expressed only through legislators as representatives of the people. The chief minister instead concurred in the *Report of the Kerala Administrative Reforms Committee:* "it is difficult to draw a line between policy and implementation and say where one ends and the other begins. Moreover, it is proper implementation that makes policy significant. The Minister who is constitutionally responsible for all the executive actions of his Department has to ensure that the policy laid down by him is properly implemented" (Namboodiripad, 1959: 31).

In the field of agrarian reform, the legislating of policy and handing it over to the administration for implementation does not satisfy the constitutional responsibility of executing policy. The first Communist ministry did not have a chance to implement its agrarian reform, but the policy model did provide for novel forms of nonofficial participation. Moreover, the government's overall strategy included specific plans for vesting more powers in the *panchayats* and *panchayat samitis.* If government was to be an "instrument of struggle in the hands of the people," the prevailing structures of the state, as well as the norms of political participation, had to be radically changed; Delhi proved unwilling to allow either.

The Congress Interlude: Reformist Land Reform

After the dismissal of the Communist ministry in 1959, the Agrarian Relations Bill was passed in a weakened form by the Congress–PSP coalition but subsequently nullified by the courts. The Congress ministry almost certainly could have saved the act by having it included on the Ninth Schedule of the Constitution, affording it protection from the courts. Delhi was agreeable, but the government preferred to pass its own legislation, which was then included on the Ninth Schedule.[35]

The *Kerala Land Reforms Act, 1964*, eliminated the core of the Communist reform; instead of the compulsory vesting of landlord rights in the government for transfer to the tenants, the legislation provided a laissez-faire enabling provision—tenants and landlords could work out purchase schemes mutually through the land tribunals (Section 54). In effect, the abolition of landlordism was temporarily removed from the State's agenda; a traditional tenure reform replaced land to the tiller. Rents were fixed, though at higher levels than in the Communist bill, and security of tenure was mandated. A ceiling was fixed, varying between 15 and 36 "ordinary" acres. Exemptions from the ceiling were allowed for commercial estates, religious and charitable institutions, all plantations and spice gardens, dairy and cattle-breeding farms, the capital-intensive Kuttanad *kayal* lands, and other such enterprises that were deemed to be in the "public interest." Voluntary transfers of land were allowed on the basis of "natural love and affection," partition, and to a religious, charitable, or educational foundation.[36]

The entire opposition except the Muslim League walked out of the Assembly when the bill was introduced. It is clear that the landed groups within the Congress Party were able to have their demands incorporated into the legislation, seriously undermining its redistributive impact. Some Congress legislators, primarily Ezhavas, urged retention of the Agrarian Relations Act rather than the new legislation but acquiesced in the majority decision. Though the Communist Party demanded that the bill be circulated to elicit public opinion, the government refused. The opposition then refused to cooperate in legislating the new provisions, and massive protests were organized in opposition to them.[37]

The Congress Party's agrarian reform logic was curiously nonconflictual; it held that reform must not attack one section of rural society

35. Chander (1973: 236–40). My interviews with senior officials in the Planning Commission and Agriculture Ministry in Delhi (1979) support the contention of leftists in the Assembly that the Center was willing to include the revised act on the Ninth Schedule. The communists, and their mass organizations, mobilized against dilution of the original act but then supported even the weaker 1961 version as superior to what the Congress, pressured by landed interests within, was planning as a substitute. On the importance of inclusion of land reforms on the Ninth Schedule, see the discussion in the following chapter.

36. For more detailed discussion of the act, M. A. Oommen (1971). A commentary, including court rulings, written by a land tribunal is Gangadharan (1974).

37. *Synopsis of the Proceedings of the Kerala Legislative Assembly*, 1962 to 1964. Party affiliations and occupational background of legislators from Kerala (1962). Cf. Chander (1973: 249, 264–77); Paulini (1978: 250–70).

to the advantage of others, but rather must protect the interests of all groups.[38] The assumption of a fundamental harmony of interests in society is diametrically opposed to the Communist conception of land reform as a weapon of one class against another, with its explicit recognition of the conflict inherent in benefiting depressed groups in a nearly zero-sum game. The Congress model, by assuming that all interests could be protected during the reform, made significant concessions to landowners, basing the reform on the familiar laissez-faire, voluntaristic premises of the tenure-reform model and entrusting it to "ordinary administration."

Given the lack of redistributive intent evident in framing the law, the importance of landed communities in the ruling party, the laissez-faire conceptualization of the reform, and the political instability following its enactment, little redistributive impact could be expected. High-ranking officials of the Revenue Department, which was to administer the reforms, agreed that there was no serious political will behind the act.[39]

The major source for evaluating the impact of the reform is the *Land Reforms Survey* of 1966. The conclusions confirm the general picture of evasion and victimization in tenure reform presented in chapter 2. Landlords found many and ingenious ways to evade the law. For example, the year 1965 showed a curious sharp increase in the rate of creation of tenancies. The *Survey* report attributed this odd fact to the compliance of tenants, through landlord "persuasion, pressure or coercion," in accepting new tenancies which were in law null and void, making tenants ineligible for benefits under the act (Kerala, 1968: 73). Another common means of evading the tenancy provisions was a mortgage arrangement, which was in effect a concealed tenancy. Since the draft bill did not recognize mortgages as tenancies, this practice was especially widespread between 1962 and 1964, during which period 84 percent of the total area mortgaged over the ten year period 1957–66 was mortgaged.[40]

Tenants ignored the "fixity of tenure" provisions; only 3.12 percent of the tenants surveyed had gone through official channels and successfully obtained legal documentation. Over 91 percent felt that the land-

38. Based on debates in *KLA*, 1962–64; for example, 5-I-62 (March 5, 1962); 14-I-62 (March 20, 1962).

39. Interviews with Revenue Department officers in Kerala, 1974, 1979–80. The *Administration Reports* of the department indicate the same, as does the minimal commitment of personnel.

40. Kerala (1968: 84). Mr. A. K. K. Nambiar, former Secretary to the Revenue Ministry, explained that these mortages were mere formalities, concealing a structural relationship that was tenant–landlord. The 1969 amending act, which Nambiar helped draft, corrected this problem by "deeming" the mortgages tenancies. Interview, Cochin, December 24, 1974.

lord agreed to their continuance on the plot and did not apply for fixity (Kerala, 1968: table 11.1). Although these cases appear in official documents as secure tenancies, in fact the only security was a "mutual agreement" between owner and tenant. Since most tenancies were *verumpattom* (at will), and most *verumpattom* tenancies oral, the Congress reform accomplished virtually nothing in improving security of tenure. The *Survey* found no instances of "unlawful" eviction, though the report stated "on the whole the results of the survey on these aspects cannot be claimed to be quite reliable." There had been 4,742 cases of lawful eviction through the courts in the two years in which the act had operated.[41]

A Planning Commission study of implementation confirms this conclusion. The study found that tenants enjoyed security of tenure in those areas in which they were well organized; elsewhere, villagers and even lower-level revenue officials were unaware of key provisions of the reform. Moreover, there were virtually no usable land records, and tenants were typically not entered in the records (India, 1966b: 68, 71).

Section 54 of the act gave tenants the opportunity to purchase ownership rights from landlords. As of the time of *Survey*, no purchase had been made under this enabling provision, although tenants did purchase some land from landlords, in the aggregate less than 1 percent of the leased area. Those few tenants who brought land did not receive outstanding bargains. The average price paid by tenants who purchased land between 1957 and 1963 was Rs 604 per acre; following the reform, for the period 1964–66, the average price paid was Rs 1,550 per acre.[42]

The reasons given by tenants for not purchasing land varied; in the largest number of cases, 42 percent of the total, tenants expressed ignorance of eligibility. This situation is certainly understandable given the low priority accorded to agrarian reform by the government. Another 19 percent of the tenants listed "desire to maintain good relations with landlord." Significantly, only 1.5 percent of the tenants mentioned "fear of landlords," probably reflecting the strength of peasant associations and rural-based left mobilization in the state. Included in the "other reasons" category (37 percent of the cases) were financial incapacity, "indifference," aversion to litigation, and satisfaction with tenant status (Kerala, 1968: appendix table 30).

A "fair rent" provision in the act fixed rates higher than those of the Communist legislation, but still lower than the "contract rent." The *Survey* found that fair rent had been fixed on only 2.2 percent of the leased plots surveyed. More than a fifth of the tenants expressed igno-

41. Kerala (1968: 47). One reason the report was not satisfied with the evidence on eviction is presumably that the survey covered only landholders and thus excluded anyone whose rights had been terminated.

42. Kerala (1968: 89) and calculations from table 11.2. Prices are in nominal terms; adjustment for inflation would not change the order of magnitude.

rance of the provision, whereas almost half reported "satisfaction" with the prevailing rents (ibid.: 95). It is difficult to interpret the latter figure; tenants were often quite poor people, for whom rent was a major drain on income. It is likely that the "desire to maintain good relations with landlords," mentioned previously, and concern for security of tenure contributed to this curious satisfaction.

Provisions for scaling down arrears of rent by one-fourth likewise evoked little tenant response; over 70 percent of the tenants who owed arrears of rent did not attempt to have them reduced. One reason was that a lump sum equaling three-fourths of the arrears had to be paid within six months; about a third of the tenants lacked the necessary financial resources for this. As in other cases, a large number of tenants took no action because of ignorance of the law, desire to avoid litigation, or "indifference" (ibid.: 99).

The *Survey* found that about 25,000 households possessed land in excess of 15 acres. However, because there were an average of three family units (or unmarried adults) per household, 83 percent of these households possessed no resumable land under the law. Moreover, 24 percent of the households surveyed were protected from the ceiling because of the plantation and spice garden exemptions. Thus only 114,800 ordinary acres, or about 2.5 percent of the operated area was estimated to be resumable surplus (ibid.: 98–99). Appropriation, or even accurate location, of this land was problematic, however. The 1964 act, like the Agrarian Relations Act, "prompted hectic sales and transfers" of land (ibid.: 79). The data on land transfers for the decade 1957 to 1966 clearly show that landlords reacted to serious political consideration of land reform with a variety of transfer mechanisms, including partition and transfer of tenancies, and that such activity declined when the prospect of land reforms became less imminent, as when the Communist ministry was dismissed in 1959 and when the Supreme Court struck down the Agrarian Relations Act in 1961.[43] The question of evasion became irrelevant in the short run, however, since the government chose not to bring the ceiling provisions into force (India, 1966b: 69).

The 1964 Congress land reforms replicated the all-India experience with tenure reform and ceilings; virtually nothing was accomplished. In the six years of operation of the act, only 3,565 tenants had filed petitions for fixation of fair rent. More tenants were legally evicted than were officially granted fixity. Only 1,820 tenants had applied for purchase of landlords' rights. No land was appropriated under the ceiling provisions, and none redistributed. Both tenants and officials recognized the act as a

43. Kerala (1968: tables 10.1, 10.2, 10.3). Of the total area subjected to partition in the decade 1957–66, 52 percent was partitioned in the single year 1960 (when the revised Agrarian Relations Act was passed by the assembly) and 27 percent in 1964, when the Kerala Land Reforms Act became law.

dead letter.[44] The contrast to the 1969 legislation which replaced it could not have been greater.

The Congress ministry which legislated these reforms fell in 1964. Kerala was under President's Rule until elections in 1967 finally produced a viable government—the United Front coalition led by the left wing of the Communist Party. The Communist Party had split in 1964 over a variety of issues; the faction with the more consistently left analysis and tactical line retained the great majority of the party cadres and mass base, particularly the agrarian base (Hardgrave, 1973; Paulini, 1978: 272–73). The left group, known as the Communist Party of India (Marxist), or CPI(M), (or often, simply "Marxists") contributed the chief minister to the government—E. M. S. Namboodiripad. The right faction, now known as the Communist Party of India, or CPI, was a much smaller partner in the coalition.

The United Front government began drafting comprehensive agrarian reform, again under the direction of Ms. K. R. Goury, CPI(M), the revenue minister. The 1964 act was theoretically in force, and the new legislation was technically an amendment to the 1964 act but was in effect a drastic revision of that law. It was finally passed by the legislature in the fall of 1969. Immediately thereafter, the government collapsed and was replaced by a new coalition led by the Communist Party of India; the CPI(M) led the opposition. Though the 1969 reform was formulated by a CPI(M)-dominated government, it came into effect on January 1, 1970, under a CPI-led coalition, with the CPI(M) the largest opposition party. This unique political situation of competition between the two communist parties, which had been united in formulating the 1959 reforms, significantly influenced the politics of effecting land to the tiller over the subsequent decade.

44. Kerala, *Administration Report, Land Board and Land Tribunals* for 1969–70 (1972: iii, v, 21).

7 The Politics of Land to the Tiller: The United Front's Reforms in Kerala

"Why should I plough when I can get another man to plough for me?"
—*Bihari landowner to Kusum Nair*

The second land-to-the-tiller reform was legislated in Kerala in 1969, under virtually the same leadership as the abortive 1959 reforms. Before examining that legislation and its implementation, it is important to explore the agrarian configuration which the policy addressed. The central question remains the problematic conceptualization of "tiller" in Kerala's agrarian system.

Agrarian Structure: Who Are the Tillers?

The best source for examining the agrarian structure which faced the United Front Ministry in 1967 is the Kerala *Land Reforms Survey*, a stratified random sample of 3,475 households throughout the State conducted in 1966–67.[1] Reflecting the very early and extensive commercialization of agriculture, the plantation sector is extremely important in the economy of Kerala, but plantations have been excluded from land reforms by both communist and noncommunist regimes on grounds of economies of scale and fear of dispersal of the trained work force. As in Ceylon until 1972, land reforms have essentially been confined to the peasant sector. The peasant sector is heavily dependent on paddy, coconut, and tapioca; these crops together accounted for 64 percent of the cropped area in 1966. The pressure of population on land was extreme; Kerala had the highest density of population of any state in India and about 91 percent of the cultivable area was already sown. Cultivable land per capita was estimated at 0.32 acres, less than one-third the figure for India as a whole (Kerala, 1968/76: 3–7).

The *Survey* sampled only households which held some recognized

---

1. Kerala (1968/76). For discussion of problems in landholding data in Kerala, United Nations (1975: chap. 5).

rights in land, however marginal. As before, the use of landholding cate-gories obscures the numerical importance of agricultural laborers as a class. As developed below, a large percentage of landholders with minus-cule holdings received most of their income from agricultural wage labor. Table 7.1 presents important characteristics of the agrarian structure.

The data in Table 7.1 illustrate concretely the complexity of the agrarian class configuration and the problem of identifying tillers. Al-though the Kerala reforms, like most reforms in the region, identify ben-eficiaries primarily in terms of the formal relation to the property sys-tem—tenants vs. landlords, for example—it is clear that in Kerala, as emphasized more generally in chapter 2, there are tenants and tenants. The *Survey* divided the tenantry into two strata—*kudiyirrippu* and "other tenants." *Kudi* means "hut" in Malayalam; *kudiyirippu* tenants are those who leased a housesite and some land from landowners. Such tenants constituted almost half of all tenants, and owned virtually no land, leas-ing in more than 99 percent of the land they possessed. Their annual income was far below that of "other tenants" and owner-cultivators; 71.2 percent held less than one acre. Given the size of holding and average income, we may infer that most of these tenants derived most of their income from performing agricultural wage labor.[2] However, there was significant inequality within the stratum: the 1 percent who held more than ten acres possessed almost 10 percent of the area held by *kudiyi-rippu* tenants.

The "other tenants" exhibited more mixed-class characteristics. Their average income was 63 percent higher than that of *kudiyirippu* tenants and indeed 15.7 percent higher than that of owner-cultivators. These tenants owned 31.7 percent of the land they operated, and some were large operators in the Kerala context: 15.5 percent operated more than five acres, and these households possessed almost 60 percent of the area operated by the stratum. The "other tenant" stratum thus contained a number of relatively privileged cultivators in the Kerala context: less than 1 percent (0.8) held more than 25 acres but accounted for 12 percent of the land operated by farmers of the category. More significantly, "other tenants," though little more than half of all tenants, controlled more than 95 percent of the land held by tenants (Kerala, 1968/76: tables 7.8, 9.1).

The stratification within the tenantry was replicated among the landlords. Although the landlord class constituted only 2.3 percent of the households with interests in land, these households owned 37 percent of the total agricultural land. Most landlords were small owners; the few large landlords possessed the bulk of the land. Fully 12 percent of the landlords owned less than one acre; 70 percent owned less than 10 acres,

---

2. Kerala (1968/76: table 7.7). In my intensive study of two villages in Palghat dis-trict in 1979–80, *kudiyirippu* tenants were uniformly known not as "tenants" (*kudiyan*) but as wage laborers (*koolikaran*), as the tiny size of their holdings necessitated wage labor for a livelihood.

Table 7.1: Kerala's Agrarian Structure at the Time of the United Front Government

Class	Percentage of Landholding Families	Percentage Possessing Less than One Acre	Average Annual Income (Rs)	Leased-in Area as Percentage of Operated Area	Percentage of Class Belonging to Wealthiest Stratum*	Percentage of Class Belonging to Poorest Stratum*
Landlords	2.3	1.2	4,039	17.8	18.9	7.4
Owner-cultivators	40.6	65.1	1,601	0.0	3.0	38.1
Kudiyirippu tenants	21.8	71.2	1,137	99.1	1.2	55.7
"Other tenants"	23.1	43.1	1,893	68.3	33.2	43.1
(Total Tenants)	(44.9)	(56.7)	(1,526)	(83.3)	(34.4)	(49.2)
Kudikidappukars	12.2	100.0	869	—	0.0	71.4
All Classes	100.0	59.7	1,526	42.60	2.7	43.9

*Wealthiest stratum includes households reporting annual income greater than Rs 6,000 (approx. 1967 US $750); poorest stratum, those households reporting less than Rs 1,000 (approx. 1967 US $125).
SOURCE: *Land Reforms Survey* (Kerala, 1968/76) tables 7.1, 7.7, 7.8, 8.1, 9.1, 7.5, and p. 51; part 3, calculations from tables 1, 2. Figures for Total Tenants in columns 2, 3, 4, and 6 are weighted means.

though they held in the aggregate only 12 percent of the land owned by landlords. Landlords with 25 acres or more constituted only 13 percent of the landlord class, but owned 74 percent of the land owned by landlords. As importantly, landlords leased *in* 17.8 percent of the land they possessed. Leasing in was especially characteristic of the top strata; whereas only 6.8 percent of the smallest landlords leased in land, 45 percent of the largest landlords (owning more than 25 acres) did so (Kerala, 1968/76: tables 7.4, 7.5).

It is thus difficult to equate tenurial position with relative wealth and poverty, privilege and deprivation. Another way to emphasize this point is to examine the richest and poorest strata in terms of class composition. Although a section of the landlord class was quite wealthy, the majority had incomes of less than Rs 3,000. Only 18.9 percent of the landlords fell into the highest income category, compared to 3 percent of the owner-cultivators, 1.2 percent of the *kudiyirippu* tenants, and, significantly, 33.2 percent of the "other tenants." None of the landless *kudikidappukars* fell into the wealthiest category; 71.4 percent of that class belonged to the poorest stratum, a percentage markedly above that of other agrarian classes, as reflected in the very low average income.

Together, these characteristics of the agrarian system mean that the vesting of tenanted lands in the leasee, regardless of the class and stratum of the leasee, would benefit a large number of agriculturalists of relatively high position in the agrarian hierarchy. Indeed, "other tenants" stand out as a category for having by far the highest percentage of households in the wealthiest stratum, though a very high percentage belonged to the poorest.[3] The percentage of leased-in area among large holders (those possessing more than 15 acres per household) varied between 35.7 and 51.3 percent. As importantly, the concentration of tenants in the smallest holding size category means that the vesting of tenancy rights in tenure-holders without any alteration of the size distribution of holdings below the ceiling would leave the bulk of the beneficiaries with miniscule holdings and thus in continuing poverty, though unburdened of rental exactions. Land to the tiller as conceptualized by the government would thus have a class-differentiated impact; though the aggregate measure of inequality in landholdings would be reduced, there would be regional variation (cf. United Nations, 1975: 69–70), and the poorest, precisely because their poverty reflected control of very little land, would benefit less than some of the wealthy.

A further ambiguity for conceptualization of a land-to-the-tiller reform is that landholders of all classes were not necessarily agriculturalists. Many of them were involved in agriculture only partially, intermit-

---

3. There is an obvious irony in terming the top strata "wealthy," an irony bitterly noted by larger farmers, but the wealth is real relative to the rural poor. The survey definition of "landlord" includes any household that leased out land and is thus not strictly comparable to earlier studies which employ a primary-income source criterion.

tently, or tangentially. Of all households with interests in land, a minority, 42 percent, were primarily agriculturalists; the remaining 58 percent received most of their income from nonagricultural sources (Kerala, 1968/ 76: pt. 3, table 2). The *Land Reform Survey* also asked how many individuals in each household were "actually engaged in agriculture." Only 24.5 percent of the landholding families had at least one member engaged in agriculture. The *Survey* concluded that a large majority of the landholding households were not engaged in agriculture, even in a supervisory function on their own lands. This was true even of the smallest holdings; many of the smallest holders take other employment but retain title to the land and arrange for its cultivation by others.

It is well known that cultivators in Kerala with substantial interests in land, and even many with insubstantial interests, depended heavily on the laborers to cultivate their fields (Krishnaji, 1979; Mencher, 1978; Herring, 1980). The latest available Farm Management Study, conducted one year before the *Survey*, indicates that even on the smallest farms (less than 1 acre), family labor constituted an average of only 47 percent of total labor; the remainder was hired. The percentage of hired labor to total increased with size of holding: for farms between 2.5 and 5 acres, the percentage of hired labor was 76 percent; on farms larger than 25 acres, 97 percent (India, 1972a: table 4.11). Capitalist agriculture was well established in Kerala, and the policy means of separating tenants who were victims of "feudalism" from tenants who were small-scale operatives of capitalism were by no means clear.

The reasons for the predominance of nonagricultural income varied from farm to farm, depending on the different opportunities and pressures facing various groups of cultivators. These opportunities, in turn, depended on such factors as location, education, caste, political connections, access to capital, and so on. The central point is that possession of land in Kerala, on whatever terms, across the size spectrum, did not necessarily imply work on the land; the separation between landholding and agricultural work was a distinct feature of the agrarian system. But if landholders did not cultivate the land, who did? The *Survey* noted quite accurately that of all the agrarian classes with rights in land, those with the most marginal rights, the *kudikidappukars*, "are more intimately related with land and agriculture than any other category of agricultural households." The report concluded, with Daniel Thorner, that the landless laborers were thus "the real tillers of the soil."[4] In 1971, agricultural laborers were the largest single occupational category in the state, 30.69 percent of those employed; the second largest category, cultivators, accounted for 17.8 percent. Agricultural laborers outnumbered the culti-

---

4. Kerala (1968/76: 61). Not all *kudikidappukars* were purely agricultural laborers; some were workers in agroindustries intermittently, a small percentage, industrial laborers. Nor were all agricultural laborers hutment dwellers, as some owned tiny plots. But the two categories overlap considerably.

vators significantly, 1.9 million laborers to 1.1 million cultivators (India, 1971: 146).

Data on concentration of holdings demonstrate that a land ceiling could be an effective redistributive tool in Kerala but would have to be extremely low. Holdings of less than 5 acres in 1966–67 constituted 92 percent of the total but only 51 percent of the area; the 8 percent of the holdings above 5 acres accounted for 49 percent of the area (and controlled 44.4 percent of the leased area, including 61.8 percent of the leased wetlands). The average size of holding was 1.01 acres in the former case and 11.05 acres in the latter. Moreover, most of the very large holdings were plantations (Kerala, 1968/76: tables 8.1, 8.8). In 1972 almost half of all landholders (46.9 percent) held less than 0.5 acres and operated only 8 percent of the area (Kerala, 1973a: typescript, 212).

In sum the high ratio of landless households to landed, widespread unemployment, the extreme concentration of peasants in tiny size categories, and the advanced state of modernization of the economy—rates of literacy, nonagricultural employment, and commercialization of agriculture among the highest in the region—have together produced an extreme disjuncture between ownership of land and labor on the land that crosses the categories of class and size.[5] Owners of most of Kerala's farms need more than agriculture to support their families adequately and abjure labor in the fields by hiring those who own virtually nothing. Though the landlord–tenant system was equated with "feudalism" in the policy logic, in fact distinct privileged strata within the landholding class, including landlords, leased land. On a majority of tenanted holdings, tenancy was indeed part of a configuration of abject poverty and dependence, but such tenants controlled a disproportionately small percentage of the tenanted area. Most of the tenanted *land* was held as a property form which was part of a configuration of relative privilege—privilege not relative to the urban middle class, but relative to the numerically dominant rural poor. That privilege was to control the labor process and appropriate labor's product, albeit on a small scale and with results which left most of the controllers of land no great margin, yet far better off than the laborers.

The United Front's Land Reform: The Policy Logic

Following two years of President's Rule after the inconclusive 1965 elections, a United Front was formed to contest the 1967 elections. The Front included the CPI(M), the CPI, three socialist parties, the Muslim League, and an agrarian party led by a radical Catholic priest. The parties agreed

5. The early and extensive commercialization of agriculture was related to Kerala's early incorporation into the world spice trade (cf. Varghese, 1970). On current demographic and economic patterns in the State, Hart and Herring (1977: 239–50); United Nations (1975: chaps. 1, 6, 9, 11).

on a "minimum program," a chief component of which was land reform, in order to defeat the Congress, which had secured more votes than any other party in 1965, one-third of the total. The strategy succeeded; though the Congress slightly increased its percentage of the popular vote, it was virtually eliminated from power in the Assembly, with only 9 of 133 seats. The United Front received a scant majority of the votes, and 113 of 133 Assembly seats; by far the largest number of votes for the coalition were for the CPI(M). Only the Congress and the Marxists, of the thirteen parties contesting, received over 10 percent of the popular vote, with 35.4 and 23.5 percent, respectively. E. M. S. Namboodiripad again became chief minister.[6]

Upon assuming office in 1967, the government moved quickly to protect tenants and *kudikidappukars*, as in 1957; experience suggested that the Front's election victory would induce countermeasures by landed classes. The Stay of Eviction Proceedings Ordinance was issued, and proceedings for recovery of rent and for "shifting" of the laborers' housesites were stayed as well. There were provisions for cancellation of forced sales of land for recovery of debts.[7] These stop-gap measures were to serve until comprehensive legislation could be drafted.

The drafting was again under the direction of Ms. K. R. Goury, the CPI(M) revenue minister. The drafting went slowly; the 1959 experience recommended both extraordinary caution and construction of an airtight reform with scrupulous attention to constitutional and legal questions. The presence of the conservative Muslim League in the coalition introduced political reasons for caution, but it should be stressed that the fate of the Agrarian Relations Act imposed formidable drafting problems— the legislation had to be flawless. Moreover, the complicated legal maneuvers of owners, such as "mortgaging" land to tenants, obtaining misleading documents regarding tenurial status, and so on, introduced drafting complications. In addition to these constraints, the government faced an immediate crisis in procurement and distribution of food because of extreme nation-wide shortages.[8]

When K. R. Goury introduced the bill, technically an amendment to the largely unimplemented 1964 act, to the Assembly in August of 1968, she stressed that the core of the reform, the abolition of landlordism, would prove effective because the burden of proof was being shifted from the tenant to the landlord; instead of a cultivator being forced to

6. Data from Kerala (1977a). The Marxist percentage of the popular vote does not reflect the party's full strength, as the party ceded a number of its strongholds to alliance partners and consequently contested fewer seats. On the politics of the period, Hardgrave (1973); Paulini (1978); Hart and Herring (1977).

7. Kerala, *Administration Report, 1967–68, Land Board and Land Tribunals* (1969: 337 ff.).

8. Interviews with A. K. K. Nambiar, Secretary to the Revenue Ministry, who had a major role in drafting the bill and was later head of the Task Force on Land Reforms, and the revenue minister (December 1974).

prove tenancy status, the landlord who disagreed was required to prove the opposite.[9] Once the tenants were recognized, the bill provided for compulsory vesting of the rights of landlords and intermediaries in the government for eventual transfer to cultivating tenants.[10]

The policy model was thus essentially the same as that of the 1959 act, with elaboration of the "deemed tenant" concept. New categories of cultivators were deemed tenants to cover those legal fictions created by landlords attempting to evade the earlier laws. In addition, cultivators "honestly believing (themselves) to be tenants" were to be deemed tenants, as well as "certain persons occupying lands under leases granted by incompetent persons." These curious provisions were necessitated by landlords' creating invalid lease documents by having a minor of the family sign the deed.

A variety of customary categories of sharecroppers—*sambalapat-tamdars, varamdars, odachartudars,* and so on—were presumed to be tenants unless the landowner could prove that the cultivator had not undertaken any risk of cultivation. In recognition of the practice of landlords of obtaining documents from sharecroppers stating that the cultivator was a servant, agent, or something other than a tenant, certain documents were rendered inadmissable as evidence. To summarize a very complex piece of law, the act provided for a broad range of cultivators, whatever their formal-legal or customary designation, to be deemed tenants if they bore the risk of cultivation. Cultivation was defined, as in the 1959 law, to include supervision of wage labor.

The criteria for "cultivation" and "risk of cultivation" are clearly those of capitalist agriculture. The ambiguity of the agricultural role and dependence on wage labor of all categories of "cultivators"—tenants, owners, landlords—in the concrete tenurial structure of Kerala underlines the importance of this conceptual point. Curiously, contribution of land alone or labor alone would not qualify the contributor as a cultivator, whereas contribution of working capital alone (wages and farm inputs) would define the contributor as a cultivator entitled to land ownership.

As in the 1959 reform, the right to resume land from tenants by landlords for personal cultivation was permitted but severely restricted. No land whatsoever could be resumed from *kudiyirippukars,* who constituted half of all tenants, nor from a tenant who was a member of a Scheduled Caste ("untouchables") or Scheduled Tribe. Moreover, any re-

9. Kerala, *Synopsis of the Proceedings of the Kerala Legislative Assembly,* series 4 (Trivandrum), II:6:68 (August 26, 1968). Hereafter *KLA.* The first number in the citation is the legislative session; the second, the meeting; the third, the year.

10. For the CPI revenue minister's account, K. T. Jacob (1972). For provisions, including administrative *Rules* (Kerala, 1977c). For legal commentary by a land tribunal, Gangadharan (1970). The law is *The Kerala Land Reforms (Amendment) Act* (no. 35 of 1969), gazetted December 17, 1969.

sumption right lapsed six months after the effective date of the act.[11] Any tenant from whom land was resumed was entitled to compensation for improvements made on the land or a solatium equal to two years' gross produce, whichever was greater. The tenant was also allowed to choose the area to be retained after resumption. Altogether, the resumption provisions were quite favorable to cultivating tenants but did make concessions to smallholders who wished to cultivate their own land (section 20). To compensate for the negative effects of the 1964 act, there were provisions for restoration of certain tenants who lost possession on or after the effective date of that act.

After determination of tenancy, a fair rent well below the contract rent was to be set for different types of land (section 27). The importance of these provisions is sometimes overlooked, as the main thrust of the act was to abolish rent altogether. But the compensation owed to landlords and the purchase price paid by tenants to the state depend on the level of rent fixed; thus the reductions are significant.

Once tenants were officially established on their holdings, and fair rents fixed, landlords' rights were to be vested in the state. The title, right, and interest in the land, free of any encumbrances created by the landlord, were then to be assigned to the cultivating tenant, provided that such assignment did not increase the tenant's holding beyond the ceiling limit (section 72B). Compensation to the landlord was to be paid by the government, at sixteen times the fair rent, plus other considerations on some lands. The compensation was to be paid to the government by new owners in installments, reduced if paid in a lump sum. Failure to pay the installments did not prejudice ownership rights; defaults would become recoverable as arrears of land revenue. Arrears of rent were significantly scaled down; a tenant holding less than 5 acres could pay no more than one year's rent to discharge all arrears, and larger tenants, no more than three years' rent. The creation of future tenancies was prohibited and such tenancies rendered invalid; the landlord–tenant organization of production was statutorily ended (sections 72L, 73, 74).

The rights of *kudikidappukars* were significantly expanded by the amending act. Security of tenure was granted and *kudikidappus* (hutsites) were made heritable. Arrears of rent, if any, were reduced to no more than one year's rent; future annual rent was set at very low rates (less than two days' wages in rural areas). Customary or mutually agreed existing rights enjoyed by the *kudikidappukars* could not be abridged.[12]

11. Sections 14–18. Landlords were allowed to resume 0.2 acres for residential construction, for extension of "places of public worship" (a concession to Delhi), and other minor exceptions were allowed. Though seemingly innocuous and fair, these provisions did allow for some abuse during implementation.

12. Section 79. There was some confusion on this point, as legislators pointed out that the customary position of the *kudikidappukar* was akin to that of a serf or slave, but only traditional rights, not traditional obligations, were protected; the latter had been prohibited in other legislation.

More importantly, the *kudikidappukar* was granted the right to purchase the plot at 25 percent of the market value. One half of this purchase price was to be paid by the government from the Kudikidappukars' Benefit Fund. The balance was spread over twelve annual installments.

The ceiling set by the legislation was rather high considering the acute pressure on the land, but was the lowest in the subcontinent region. The ceiling ranged from five standard acres (6 to 7.5 ordinary acres) for a single adult to an absolute maximum of 20 ordinary acres for a very large family. In an attempt to repair some of the damage done by the 1964 act, certain voluntary land transfers were invalidated retroactively. Compensation was to be paid the owners for appropriated land; surplus land was to be redistributed to the landless.[13] Exemptions from the ceiling remained but were reduced. Plantations remained exempt, but the definition of plantation was narrowed, subjecting a number of previously exempt lands to the ceiling—for example, pepper, areca, cashew, coconut, and so on, as well as the *kayal* (polder paddy) lands typically owned in large blocks in Kuttanad.

Curiously, despite Namboodiripad's insistence that no scheme of land reform can be implemented from above, but must involve the peasants themselves, implementation was entrusted to the Revenue Department. One explanation given by a drafter of the legislation is that K. R. Goury, as president of the State peasant association, provided a direct channel for peasant demands. Moreover, the bill was circulated to elicit public opinion. But these popular inputs apply to the formulation of provisions not to their implementation. A more important explanation for the deviation from Namboodiripad's insistence that the peasantry be directly involved is the federal structure within which the government was operating. Early in its tenure, in April 1967, the government issued orders to enable popular committees to help uncover corruption and advise on local conditions in food distribution and paddy procurement, and so on. These Civil Supplies popular committees were opposed by the Congress Party and challenged in the courts. The government attempted to give statutory powers to the committees and applied to the Center for permission to issue an ordinance; it was denied (Jayaraj, 1974).

It is likely that the Center would have likewise vetoed statutory powers for popular committees for land reforms at that time. Indeed, Delhi's Central Study Team, which investigated the advisability of popular involvement in land reforms, issued a report in 1968 rejecting the idea (India, 1968). In defending the bill in the Assembly, Revenue Minister Goury explained that the land tribunals were to be revenue officers in

13. Sections 82–96. Section 96 gives priorities for redistribution. Applicants must be landless or possess less than one acre. First priority was to kudikidappukars resident on the land, then landless agricultural laborers, and then smallholders and landlords who were not allowed to resume any land. One-half of the land was to be reserved for scheduled castes and tribes and similar "socially and economically backward classes."

accordance with a Central directive to that effect (*KLA*: II:23:69). Moreover, the courts proved to be hostile to the concept of popular committees.

Failure to include popular participation institutionally in the implementation process represents a major departure from the earlier logic
of the Marxist leadership, as well as a major compromise with what the
left wing of the party denounced as "Constitutional niceties." Although
this compromise was the most serious departure from earlier theory, other
major concessions were made to constitutional requirements or the preferences of the Center: annuities to religious and other trusts, other
concessions to religious bodies, and payment of compensation to dispossessed landlords and owners. A final constraint from Delhi was financial;
effective administration, compensation payments, and land-development
credit for so extensive a reform would place heavy financial burdens on
an already poor State, but the Center was unwilling to make major financial concessions (M. A. Oommen, 1975: 71–76).

The United Front's Land Reform: Politics

Introduced in the Assembly in August of 1968, the bill was not passed
until October of 1969. There were thus long delays during both the drafting and legislating stages of the reforms. These delays were the subject
of heated political controversy. Delays in passage of the act were attributed by the government to the Center and by the Congress opposition to
the United Front itself.

The revenue minister responded to this criticism by noting that the
Center, after receiving the bill in August, made no response at all until
she stated publicly that the bill would become law. In February of 1969,
the Center finally responded, terming the fair rent and other provisions
"arbitrary and unreasonable." Even if the Center was not blocking the
bill for political reasons to embarrass the government (as was charged by
the left) (*KLA*: II:18:69), some delays were inevitable, as five separate
ministries in Delhi had to examine and approve land reforms. But the
Center found it possible to approve the 1964 Congress-backed legislation
in a mere three weeks. Moreover, it is also quite clear that there was
serious ambivalence at the Center as to the desirability of radical land
reform, as well as considerable hostility to communist State governments.

The Assembly debates on the bill replicated the patterns of support
and opposition, and paradigms of agrarian reform, which emerged in consideration of earlier reforms. There were attacks from the left on issues
of compensation and, especially, the tedious complexity of the bill. Some
leftist MLA's argued that a popular measure should be expressed in simple,
concise phrases that everyone could understand rather than in tortuous
and esoteric legal jargon. The obvious answer—that any bill radically de-

parting from legal norms and precedents would be unacceptable to the Law Ministry in Delhi and would be vitiated by court rulings—did not convince some legislators, who argued that "Constitutional niceties" had replaced the first priority of legislating the clear will of the people.[14]

These leftist positions are extremely important for understanding the subsequent politics of implementation. One radical MLA worried that the bill seemed to assume that "winning the rights of the people depended on the ability of legal experts." Another argued that the coalition had been elected to "do social justice," not to worry about the Constitution. Another worried that the legal complexities would result in poor cultivators' being dragged into court with crippling delays and disruption. Events later proved these worries to be well founded.

Positions taken by Congress legislators again demonstrated opposition to radical agrarian reform. Indeed, the Chief Whip of the Congress Legislative Party (who later sided with Indira Gandhi's faction in the Congress split) termed the bill even more injurious to agriculture than the 1964 reform (which his party had legislated). He argued that the agrarian reform was nothing more than a bid for "cheap popularity" (KLA: II:6:68). Congress legislators expressed the same preference for distributive over redistributive policy logic examined earlier. Rather than perceiving an essentially zero-sum agrarian situation, in which some classes could be benefited only at the expense of others, they argued that the government should provide housesites and land for the rural poor without disturbing the holdings of landed groups. The leader of the Congress legislative party, and later Home Minister during implementation of the act, K. Karunakaran, stated that the Congress Party supported any bill giving land to the tiller, but that the legislation at hand was "robbing Peter to pay Paul" (KLA: II:9:68).

Members of the Kerala Congress (a primarily Syrian Christian splinter party representing landed interests) in particular argued for higher ceilings, more compensation, exemption of kayal lands and coconut plantations, and so on. The Congress Party leader Karunakaran argued for a higher ceiling, more concessions to small landowners and plantations, and questioned some of the deemed tenancy provisions. The public position of the important Muslim League was generally supportive of the reform, but with reservations. Members of these three parties expressed concern about the kudikidappukar provisions, fearing that "rank trespassers" would gain rights in land at the expense of owners (KLA: II:14:69; 21:69).

The positions were thus fundamentally opposed. The government proposed the abolition of the rentier class and rent as an institution, whereas the more conservative forces, including the Congress leadership,

14. KLA, II:6:68 (August 26). Party affiliation and background information on MLA's for this period is from Kerala, Kerala Legislative Assembly Who's Who (1968). Information for the post–United Front period is from the 1972 edition.

opposed radical redistribution, preferring instead a distributive reform involving government waste and forest lands and mere regulation of tenancies. The Marxists' stated objective was the same as in 1957–to legislate benefits for as many of the rural poor as possible within the limits of
the federal structure and Constitution. But within the CPI(M), both national and local leftist forces urged the government to cease placating
conservative elements in the coalition, legal scholars, and the Center.
They urged that a truly radical land reform be legislated; if struck down
by Delhi or the courts, the situation would dramatically illustrate to the
people the impossibility of fundamental change within the existing
structure of power. The analysis was that there was more potential for
politicizing and mobilizing the rural masses in an abortive radical reform
that in meticulous compliance with existing constraints (cf. Hardgrave,
1973).

In retrospect, the leftist analysis appears compelling; however, the
CPI(M) leadership took the strictly parliamentary path on land reform.
That stance strained party cohesion and contributed to the formation of
leftist splinter groups, but there was more than the question of radical
land reform versus legalistic, constrained land reform. One group argued
against redistribution of land to the landless altogether. Their analysis
posited, as had Philip Guanawardena in 1956 in Ceylon, a danger in the
embourgeoisement of the poor peasantry, creating a conservative class in
the place of a revolutionary one. The prevailing analysis held that the
reform measures gave the rural underclass more security and thus potential for militant action and in any case were necessary to meet the expressed needs and demands of the majority of the rural population. Moreover, the consciousness of the peasantry had not yet reached a stage that
would allow voluntary collectivization. In her final speech before passage
of the act, K. R. Goury stated that the provisions were by no means the
final word or a real solution to the agrarian crisis, but did offer important
relief to tenants and kudikidappukars.[15]

Shortly after the passage of the 1969 land reform, the United Front
government fell on a vote of no confidence. Various charges were made
by the component parties, but the fundamental cause was that the constituent parties had been united more in opposition to the Congress than
in genuine commitment to a common program; partisan differences
eventually produced open splits, defections, and finally the fall of the
ministry (cf. Hardgrave, 1970; 1973). Assembly debates prior to the government's fall revolved around recurring themes. The other parties charged
the CPI(M) with behaving imperiously, adopting a "big brother" attitude
toward the other parties and ignoring their opinions. There were the usual
charges of favoritism, corruption, and partisan administrative decisions.

15. KLA, II:27:69; author's interview with K. R. Goury, Trivandrum, December 1974.
For a similar CPI analysis, Yojana (1972). On splits and factions in the CPI(M), cf. Hardgrave
(1973).

It was specifically charged that the CPI(M) had politicized distribution of land, rewarding its supporters, and had also politicized the police on partisan lines [KLA, II:27:69]. The Marxists responded that the CPI had been conspiring with the Congress from the beginning to sink the coalition, a charge made more credible by subsequent events. The CPI(M) also charged the crucial Muslim League block with opportunism and lack of commitment to the United Front's left program, in particular the land reform. There is evidence that these charges were accurate.[16]

After the fall of the ministry, Achutha Menon of the CPI welded together a second United Front (often called the "mini-front") without the Marxists. His government rested on informal Congress support as well as on the Kerala Congress. The CPI(M) analysis was that such a coalition could not possibly carry out radical land reforms because of the landed interests and ideologies it represented. When the act came into effect, on January 1, 1970, it was under a government which had not been primarily responsible for drafting it, and which depended on parties which had opposed it.

The CPI(M) was thus placed in an awkward political position. If it cooperated in implementing a land reform that had been formulated by its leadership, it would be supporting a government to which the party had serious objections. Opposition to the government, on the other hand, could jeopardize the land reform, assuming that the government was seriously committed to the act (and on this point the party had serious doubts). There were also questions of ordinary politics. The CPI(M) felt it deserved credit for formulating an effective and radical land reform, but saw that credit potentially accruing to the "anti-people," CPI-led government. Moreover, the party feared that the reforms would be used to dilute its support base and build that of its political opponents.

Throughout 1969 there had been serious incidents of agrarian violence. Clashes between landlords and laborers occurred, as well as between laborers of rival parties. There were charges that the police were not protecting landowners or supporters of opposition parties; owners in Kuttanad threatened to leave land fallow in protest.[17] The atmosphere of partisan and class confrontation carried over into the implementation phase. The Marxists felt that their legacy, and the primary hope for implementation of the reform, was the raising of the consciousness of the potential beneficiaries of the 1969 act. After the fall of the United Front government, a CPI(M) member of the Assembly stated: "If for nothing else the previous government had to be credited that they at least had

16. Positions taken in the Assembly from 1962 to 1974 and information from interviews with Revenue Department officers in 1974 support the CPI(M) charges.

17. *The Hindu*, March 3 and 29, April 23, 1969; *KLA*, I:34:69; II:10–14:69; Paulini (1978: 297). A. K. Gopalan (1973: 289) argued that the fall of the ministry produced attacks by landowners on the landless, leading to the Marxists' decision to implement the land reform without waiting for state initiatives.

been able to rouse the dumb millions . . . and to kindle in them a new zest in life and courage to fight and win their rightful claims" (*KLA*, I:27:70).

Political Conflict and Implementation

The "mini-front" coalition assumed office on November 1, 1969, supported from outside by the Congress. The debate on the governor's speech in January 1970 centered largely on the bona fides of the government in implementing the land reforms (*KLA*, I:2–3:70). The Marxists charged that the government was adopting a "go slow" policy in implementation to avoid alienating landed interests in the Kerala Congress, Congress, and Muslim League on whom it depended. The government charged the Marxists with refusing to give it a chance to implement the reform, and with adopting an obstructionist and agitational approach aimed simply at bringing down the government. The CPI(M) was charged specifically with urging *kudikidappukars* and tenants to take the law into their own hands without regard for the legal rights of owners or procedures established by the law.[18]

Before the effective date of reforms, a mass meeting attended by about 15,000 delegates from both the peasant association and agricultural laborers' union met in Alleppey district under Marxist auspices. The resolutions adopted urged action that went beyond the technical provisions (though perhaps not the spirit) of the act: (1) *kudikidappukars* should pay no rent to owners; (2) all excess land should be forcibly occupied; (3) *kudikidappukars* should fence 0.1 acres around their huts and begin taking the yields from the land; (4) all steps by the government, courts, police, and landlords to prevent these actions should be resisted.[19]

Official claims to the contrary notwithstanding, the movement attracted mass participation. In Alleppey district alone, 25,000 activists were accused in cases related to the agitation in the first five months of 1970. Of the 4,881 persons actually arrested for "encroachment," almost all were CPI(M) members or sympathizers. All of the arrested were laborers, with the exception of 32 landowners. The Marxists claimed that nearly a hundred activists were killed.[20] The fact that the CPI(M) was leading militant actions before the effective date of the law undermines the par-

18. For presentation of the CPI position, Balaram (1973) especially pp. 51 ff. Balaram, who has been a minister in Menon's government, presents the arguments against the CPI(M) during the first United Front as well.

19. T. K. Oommen (1975: 1579); E. M. S. Namboodiripad, "Peasants and Agricultural Laborers: Allies in a Common Struggle," *Peasant and Labour* (Journal of the All-India Kisan Sabha) 3, no. 1 (January–February 1974); Koshy (1976: 241–24); A. K. Gopalan (1973: 289).

20. T. K. Oommen (1975: 1579). E. M. S. Namboodiripad, "Kerala Peasants Implement Programme of Struggle for Land and Wages," *Peasant and Labour* 3, no. 6 (August–September 1974: 12); K. Mathew Kurian, "The Struggle," *Seminar* (April 1971: 27).

ty's claim that the agitations were a response to mala fides on the part of the government in implementing the reform. Moreover, the actions agreed to in the Alleppey resolution seem to contradict the scrupulously legal-istic model of land reform adhered to by the party when it was in power; all of the resolutions contravene specific provisions in the law.

Implementation of the land reform thus began in an atmosphere of confrontation and severe partisan animosities. The month of January witnessed major incidences of violence, some on a very large scale, typi-cally between owners and laborers, between local laborers and outsiders (over priority of employment, etc.) and between laborers of different po-litical affiliations. The violence extended even into the chambers of the Legislative Assembly (KLA, I:14:70).

The lines of conflict were set. The Marxists argued that the meager success in implementation claimed by the government was the result of a de facto land reform being carried out through mass action. The govern-ment charged that the Marxists were encouraging trespass and violence, thwarting reform. The Marxists argued that the CPI was taking credit for their reform; the CPI answered that the Marxists were trying to take credit for a reform which they were in effect sabotaging.

The important aspect of this political debate is that all sides as-sumed that a radical land reform was something meritorious, not a polit-ical liability. Long and intensive politicization had translated the tenurial structure into effective redistributive political forces. Robert Hardgrave noted that, remarkably, "even the right wing Kerala Congress went along with land reform implementation" (1973: 174). Although this character-ization is misleading, it is significant that the Kerala Congress, which opposed virtually all measures of the new act, felt compelled to wax elo-quent on the virtues of the legislation and its commitment to land re-form. This public profession of support by a party whose constituents were engaged in obstruction of and noncompliance with the reforms also supports the CPI(M) charge that the "mini-front" rested on support of groups which were not committed to the land reform, and underlines the universal political recognition in Kerala that the agrarian underclass must be answered.

The "public zeal" which met the new act contrasted sharply with response to the 1964 act. During the first three months of the act, 146,884 applications for purchase of kudikidappu were filed.[21] The response of kudikidappukars to the new legislation directly reflects a level of aware-ness and consciousness notably absent under previous regimes, as mani-fest in the widespread ignorance of and indifference to the 1964 act. In Alleppey district, long a center of militant organization by agricultural

21. Kerala, *Administration Reports, Land Board and Land Tribunals* (1969–70: iv). There were 27,995 applications from tenants for ownership in these three months, almost ten times the number from six years of operation of the 1964 act.

laborers, 50 percent more applications were filed in three months of operation of the 1969 act than in three years of the 1964 legislation.[22]

In May of 1970, the CPI(M)-led peasant association again urged agitation by *kudidappukars* to gain their hut sites. T. K. Oommen has argued that in Alleppey district, the Marxists were able to convince the
laborers to seize hut sites without going through legal channels because
the legal procedures were necessarily slow and because the rural poor had
had long experience of unresponsive treatment from the bureaucracy (1975:
1579). (Moreover, direct action obviated the purchase price requirement.)
Oommen's data from the district collector and figures from the Land Board
diverge, but agree on one point: the percentage of hutment dwellers benefited through the legal process was a very small percentage of the total.
Formal legal procedures would necessarily take a great deal of time.

One reason *kudikidappukars* were not willing to wait for the formal procedures is that delay often means denial of rights in a land reform.
The new reforms prompted illegal eviction or harrassment of hutment
dwellers by landlords, *goondas*, and police. Once evicted, a laborer would
face a long, expensive, and uncertain struggle to regain the house and
garden site. The CPI(M) argument that the landless would not gain their
rights without mass agitations and direct action was by no means un-
founded.

But frequently voiced criticisms of the speed of implementation as
reflected in terms of numbers of cases ignore a fundamental point: as of
January 1, 1970, landlordism was in effect terminated. Tenants were no
longer liable for rent and became de facto proprietors unless challenged
by owners. Moreover, since payments for ownership rights did not begin
until formal application was made, the tenants, now paying neither rent
nor installments, had little incentive to apply.

The first session of the Legislative Assembly in 1970 ended on a
motion of no confidence that failed by five votes. The government called
elections to mobilize support for its policies. The top priorities, as stated
in the governor's address, were implementation of the land reform and
industrialization (*KLA*, I:3:70).

The elections produced new alliances. The most significant change
was the formal alliance between the Congress faction loyal to Mrs. Gandhi—the Congress (R)—and the CPI, two socialist parties and the Muslim League in a new United Front. The far right united in a Democratic
Front, composed of Swatantra, Jana Sangh, Congress (0), and the Kerala
Congress. The CPI(M) led a People's Democratic Front which included
three splinter socialist parties and a small agrarian party. The United Front
won a clear majority of the seats, though with only a plurality of the
votes. The largest number of votes, by a wide margin, went to the CPI(M),

22. Implementation data from Kerala (1968/76: XI); *Administration Reports, Land
Board and Land Tribunals* (1969–70). On the agrarian movement in Alleppey, T. K. Oommen (1971); Mencher (1978).

followed by the Congress (R), and, at a distance, the CPI. The Democratic Front was virtually blanked, except for the regionally powerful Kerala Congress. Achutha Menon remained chief minister; the CPI revenue minister lost his seat and was replaced by Baby John of the Revolutionary Socialist Party.

The new government faced charges of brutal suppression of agrarian agitations and charged in turn that there was a growing Naxalite (agrarian revolutionary) threat to the state. Concern with land-reform implementation received additional impetus from violence between laborers and owners, which disrupted production. But the most serious land-reform problems were adverse court rulings which crippled implementation.

Judicial Philosophy and Land to the Tiller

The judicial system, because of its procedural rules, precedent-based methodology, social character and ideology, has been a major obstacle to land reforms throughout South Asia. The 1969 law removed most issues from the civil courts' jurisdiction. But, as in the Paddy Lands Act in Ceylon, the courts had an impact far beyond that intended by the legislators; major decisions invalidated sections of the act, and stay orders and interpretations advantageous to landowners became common. Adverse court rulings hampered every phase of implementation, necessitating appeals, amendments, and long delays. The operative philosophy of the courts in general, particularly the High Court, was clearly incongruent with the intent of the legislation.

The definition of eviction, for example, was crucial to the effective operation of the tenancy provisions. The courts first ruled that "voluntary surrenders" could not be considered evictions (while admitting that coercion was often involved). Likewise, eviction was construed as necessarily involving "force or compulsion," although the simplest method of evicting a tenant is to refuse renewal of the seasonal tenancy agreement. The courts also ruled against popular participation in land distribution, arguing: "The very association of an extraneous body such as a popular committee with the discharge of the statutory functions of the Tribunal is noxious and strongly to be deprecated" (Gangadharan, 1970: 50, 56, 132).

During 1970, the High Court of Kerala delivered several major judgments which crippled implementation. The rulings are extraordinary in their logic and are concrete evidence of the artificiality of the judicial-legislative-executive division of functions in effecting a thorough land reform.

In August of 1970, the court struck down several provisions of the act and strongly implied that, though it could not rule on the important "deemed tenant" provision at the time, it would rule that any encouragement of "trespass" would not be afforded protection as a measure of agrarian reform and would be struck down.[23] Predictably, in October of 1970 the court got its chance in a case involving a cultivator on Hindu temple lands. As the 1969 act had not yet been included on the Ninth Schedule of the Constitution, its only constitutional protection was Article 31A, which protects agrarian reforms from challenge on the grounds of interference with the constitutional "Fundamental Right" to property. The court struck down Sections 7 and 7B(1) which accorded "deemed tenant" status to certain cultivators "honestly believing" themselves to be tenants but lacking documentary evidence. The court held that the provisions may "make a tenant of a trespasser and impose him on the owner of the land."[24] This was precisely the argument used by the opposition in debate on the 1969 act. The provisions in question were designed to protect tenants who accepted tenancies in good faith from landlords who knowingly created illegal tenancies that would be technically null and void.

The critical part of the court's judgment was its reasoning as to why the provisions were not protected as part of an agrarian reform from challenge on the right to property guarantee. The High Court argued that the object of Article 31A in the Constitution

> is not to shield a law doing away with rights in agricultural land as it pleases; its object is to protect laws for the equitable distribution of agricultural lands . . . the touchstone is still the interests of the general public, and it is only a law that passes that test that can be regarded as a measure of agrarian reform—in fact, the very word "reform" implies that. Only orderly and peaceable progress in accordance with law can be in the interests of the general public and be regarded as a measure of reform. [1970 *KLT* 897]

The court decided that the 1969 act was not a "reform," in that it was not a "change for the better," judged by the "general interest," hence could not be protected by the Constitution. The deemed tenant provision in question was struck down for offending Article 19(1)(f), the fundamental right to property.

In dissenting from this extraordinary interpretation of judicial prerogative, Justice K. K. Mathew argued that "to say that such a measure is not a reform, as it is not for something better, is to identify ourselves with that particular school of thought which regards any interference with property by a legislature as a retrograde step" (ibid.).

The chief justice seems to have recognized the strength of Mathew's dissent; his counterreasoning is worth quoting at length:

> Of course not every change is a reform. It must be a change for something better, something calculated to effect an improvement and advance the common good. But this is largely a matter of policy within the province of

23. Narayanan Nair v. State of Kerala, *Kerala Law Times*, 1970 *KLT* 659 ff.
24. Chami Chettiar v. Thirumandham Kunnu Bhagavathi Devaswom, *Kerala Law Times*, 1970 *KLT* 897.

the legislature and not the court unless, of course, the change is something
no reasonable man would regard as a change for the better. [1970 *KLT* 674]

The remarkable presumption, then, was that the elected government of
Kerala did not reflect the judgment of "reasonable men."

The High Court also struck down the provision for discharge of arrears of rent. The legal logic was similar; the measure was not protected
by Article 31A:

> The liquidation of debts due from tenants cannot be said to be necessary
> for implementing the law relating to acquisition. . . . The produce from the
> land is not solely of the tenant's own making. The landlord provides the
> capital asset necessary for the purpose, namely, the land, and it cannot be
> in the interest of the general public to deprive him of his due share of the
> produce. [1970 *KLT* 665]

The legal philosophy expressed in the opinion is that the legislature
is not competent to decide whether or not the landlord has a "due share"
in the produce, nor what that due share should be. In dissenting, Justice
Mathew argued that the other benefits conferred on tenants might prove
illusory if the cultivators were crushed by the burden of debts, that the
legislature should decide whether or not to scale down debts, and that
relief of agricultural indebtedness is an integral part of agrarian reforms.

The court also struck down the provisions for including certain lands
which had been transferred to evade the ceiling in calculation of an owner's
present holdings (1970 *KLT* 663). Section 125(7), which prevented landowners from going to civil courts to have persons evicted while proceedings were in progress, was struck down on the grounds that a land-reform
case was no different from any other case. In both rulings, the majority
opinion refused to recognize the extraordinary demands of agrarian transformation and made effective enforcement of the act more difficult.

A confrontation between diametrically opposed legal philosophies
emerged from the 1970 cases. Justice K. K. Mathew, who was later ele-
vated to the Supreme Court, argued from the minority position that legal
formalism would not do: the times were different from those of Black-
stone and Hugo Grotius. Mathew cited the presence of "mass starvation"
to argue that "fundamental rights" cannot have precedence over peoples'
basic material needs. He added that "the Court cannot profess ignorance
of the change in the concept of property," a change from emphasis on
individual rights to the welfare of the community (1970 *KLT* 708–24).

These legal disputes and outcomes reinforce the CPI(M) argument
that, at least in the short run, radical change within the limitations imposed by the courts was impossible. What seems extraordinary is that the
CPI(M) leadership worried so long over "legal niceties" when the High
Court had the power to throw out sections of the act on the grounds that
"no reasonable man" would consider them in the "public interest" or a
"change for the better."

Popular Protests and Legislative Responses

The adverse court rulings of 1970 and mounting charges of lack of political will in implementing the reform produced changes in the act and its
implementation machinery; the background to these changes was the
demonstrated capacity of the CPI(M) to mobilize rural discontent. For
example, the response to the High Court rulings was the *Kerala Cultivators and Tenants (Temporary Protection) Bill, 1970*. The revenue minister stated that the bill was meant to guarantee rights the "cultivators
had earned after long agitations," agitations which might otherwise "lead
to bloody revolution" (*KLA*, I:10:70). The opposition charged, and the
government admitted, that implementation was tardy: virtually no progress had been made on the ceiling provisions by early 1971.

Partly in response to the failure to show progress in implementation of the ceiling-redistribution provisions and threats by the Marxists
to occupy plantations, the government promulgated an ordinance on
January 20, 1970, taking over without compensation sections of the huge
Kannan Devan tea estate. The area of the estate—137,424 acres—approached the total expected from operation of the ceiling provisions. The
High Court stayed the ordinance; the government appealed the decision
and introduced a bill to the same effect on March 30, 1971.[25] Certainly
the estate made an attractive target—visible, symbolically appropriate (a
colonial legacy), and offering a great deal of land at little administrative
or political cost. The bill was quickly passed, but ran afoul of the courts.

A more dramatic response to the inability to show progress in land
redistribution was the promulgation of an ordinance nationalizing without compensation private forests in Kerala. The rationale for giving no
compensation was that the forests had originally required no investment,
but were appropriated by "a handful of fortunate men." Owners were
allowed to retain 15 acres; the surplus was to be redistributed to dis-
placed laborers and, significantly, the educated unemployed.[26] The debate
on the forest bill opened discussion of proposals for the nationalization
of foreign plantations (which the government had previously advocated)
and a ceiling on plantation land. A Member from the Kerala Congress
astutely observed that the Congress and the CPI(M) seemed to be in competition to bring the most radical proposals to prove themselves the
champions of the masses (*KLA*, III:26:71). The forest bill was eventually

25. *KLA*, II:13:71 (March 30). The final figure for land taken over after the court
battles was 70,522 acres (Land Board records). The Revenue Minister explicitly justified the
bill as a response to the land hunger of the people.

26. The Kerala Private Forests (Vesting and Assignment) Bill; *KLA*, III:14–15:71.
Eventually 197,569 hectares of land became available, though distribution was slowed by
survey problems: answer to an oral question by the finance minister, in Kerala, *Gleanings
from the Question Hour*, 10th sess. (1974: 11); also, 9th sess. (1973: 41). About one-third of
the land was considered cultivable, though serious questions about ecological consequences
have recently been raised.

passed, but the High Court had stayed the ordinance. The proposal for nationalization of foreign-owned plantations was first held up by the Center, then rejected as contrary to national policy.[27]

In response to the sluggish pace of implementation, the government introduced an amendment to streamline certain procedures, in particular to facilitate the distribution of surplus land. However, the problem at that stage was less how to distribute land than how to obtain land to distribute. The amendment also voided certain land transfers and partitions made since 1969. The rate of compensation, originally set at 55 percent of market value, was reduced and fixed according to a scale for different classes of land to avoid the delay, litigation, and corruption inevitable in setting market values (*KLA*, II:23:71).

The debates on the 1971 amendment were uniformly critical of implementation procedures. A. K. Anthony, as leader of the powerful youth wing of the Congress Party, charged that of 200,000 applications of *kudikidappukars*, only 60,000 had been settled. Moreover, the hutment dwellers were being evicted with police assistance. He went on to charge that illegal transactions among landowners had already concealed most of the surplus land originally thought to be available; the only method of recovering the concealed land was to form local popular committees including representatives of all political parties. Both government and opposition benches concurred in the dismal evaluation of implementation (*KLA*, II:23:71). At the end of 1971, after two years of implementation, the record was not impressive. The ceiling remained virtually unimplemented. The only accomplishment in this area was the land theoretically available from the Kannan Devan estate, but that case was still pending in the courts (*KLA*, IV:9:71).

Administrative Failures and Popular Involvement

The governor's address that began the third year of implementation of the reform had much less to say about land reforms than in previous years but did propose the establishment of collective farms (*KLA*, V:2:72). The proposal to nationalize foreign plantations was not reiterated. Opposition attacks on the government's halting implementation of the 1969 act continued; only 230 acres of land had been redistributed. One of the telling criticisms was that the government had not succeeded in having the 1969 act included on the Ninth Schedule; it remained vulnerable to the courts. More evidence of victimization of *kudikidappukars* and administrative tangles in implementation came to light (*KLA*, V:11, 14:72).

The revenue minister defended the government by tabling figures which showed a steady pace of processing cases, including almost 100,000

27. Kerala, *Gleanings*, 5th sess. (1972: 114); 9th sess. (1973: 56). Other than Kannan Devon, foreign-owned plantations were relatively insignificant; eight companies owned an aggregate of 26,510 hectares.

suo moto proceedings by the government, but emphasized the extraordinary difficulties posed by the absence of land records and complicated property laws. The number of land tribunals had been significantly increased and the government was considering an amendment for constituting tribunals at the *panchayat* level. The minister admitted that landowners were not filing declarations of holdings; those who filed had offered to surrender land under water or "otherwise unsuitable for agricultural operations." Compliance by landowners was primarily to obtain compensation for wasteland; otherwise, recalcitrance was typical. Processing these claims was tedious; of 3,620 returned declarations, only 38 had been "disposed of," covering 883 acres of land (*KLA*, V:14:72).

The necessity of popular involvement of some kind to parallel the official administrative apparatus was widely recognized and advocated strongly by the left within the Assembly. The question concerned the nature of involvement and the administrative level. However, that view was not without opponents. The speaker of the Assembly, for example, a Muslim League Member (and former revenue official) opposed popular involvement in implementation, as did the courts (*KLA*, V:25:72).

The pattern of implementation revealed in Assembly debates was corroborated by an authoritative report prepared by a committee composed of legislators from the major parties and based on evidence from both field officers and high officials of the Revenue Department. The committee's report confirmed the frequent charges that *kudikidappu-kars* were being intimidated by "coercive action of the landlords" from exercising their legislated rights. Likewise, the committee was sharply critical of implementation of the ceiling, noting that the government had "no machinery or means of its own for finding out surplus lands" and merely relied on the ceiling returns filed by landowners. Its *Report* expressed distress that "the Government are taking a very lenient view against the landlords who willfully abstain from filing returns." Despite provisions in the law allowing the government to fine those who refused to file, no fines had been imposed. Landowners were not only refusing to surrender surplus lands but were illegally encroaching on government lands as well. To remedy the absence of village-level land records, the committee recommended popular committees at the *taluk* level. But these provisions would be futile, the committee noted, unless the government acted to prevent transfers of land which were dissipating the surplus.[28]

The acute frustration at inability to locate and appropriate surplus land reflects not only the evasive measures of landlords, the leniency of the government toward owners, and technical problems in property law and land records, but also an inevitable weakness in incremental land reform; landowners narrowly escaped a Communist Party reform in 1959

28. Kerala, Fourth Kerala Legislative Assembly, Committee on Estimates (1972–73) *Seventh Report* (Trivandrum: 1972: 11, 13, 14). The committee also supported the formation of cooperative farms for laborers on *kayal* lands in Kuttanad.

and had over a decade of intervening President's Rule, Congress government and coalition instabilities carefully rearranged their property holdings. The debilitating effects of political instability, regime change, and
ineffectual symbolic reform legislation in terms of the redistributive potential of ceiling reform are evident in the estimates of surplus available
for redistribution. M. A. Oommen (1973) has noted that the revenue minister in 1957 estimated a surplus of 1,750,000 acres; by 1967, the estimate
was 150,000 acres, though the ceiling was essentially the same.[29]

Because of the government's failure to implement ceiling provisions, the CPI(M) initiated the "Excess Land Agitation" in 1972. A detailed analysis of that movement in Alleppey district uncovered the familiar malpractices—bribery or influence to conceal holdings, land
transfers and partitions, and so on. A *Samara Samiti* (struggle council)
was formed to investigate land holdings; it publicized results were compared to Revenue Department figures. There were significant differences.
The council then made a list of demands for new legislation. Some of
these demands involved a more radical approach toward abolition of
landlordism (deleting compensation, for example); others recommended
new rights and protection for agricultural laborers. One important demand was that ceiling returns be published for public scrutiny by popular
committees.[30]

At the state level, an Action Council of Peasants and Farm Workers,
led by the CPI(M), demanded that the government remedy lapses in implementation or face a mass agitation. The Youth Congress, too, threatened "an agitational approach" to press for implementation changes and
urged formation of popular committees. The CPI-affiliated peasant association charged at its April convention that official complicity was
thwarting implementation and called for mass action beginning on May
Day. The modus operandi was to be *dharna* (silent picketing) before the
houses of guilty landlords, followed by direct occupation of illegally held
lands. The consensus was that official machinery without mass action
was inadequate.[31]

The chief minister himself had blamed lapses in implementation
on the inadequacy of "administrative mechanisms" and "inadequate mobilization of the people" (*Mainstream*, June 11, 1971). The revenue min-

29. There is some confusion in the exact figures, as the revenue minister was not
referring to surplus land as such, but simply land in holdings of a size above the ceiling;
however, Oommen's point is well taken.

30. T. K. Oommen (1975: 1580–81); E. M. S. Namboodiripad, "Kerala Peasants Implement Programme of Struggle," *Peasant and Labour* 3, no. 6 (August–September 1974).
Krishnaji (1979: 519) rightly notes that the meager yields in terms of land area were less
important than the tremendous mobilization produced by the movement. A. K. Gopalan
(1973: 298), a leader in the movement, claims that 10,000 activists were sentenced for involvement. Cf. Paulini (1978: 310–13).

31. *The Hindu* September 15, 1972; *New Age*, April 16 and 30, 1972; A. K. Gopalan
(1973: 295).

ister stated publicly that because of the need for popular mobilization the government would not interfere in agrarian agitations.[32] But when the government did not move quickly enough on the proposed popular committees, the CPI(M) renewed its agitations, which were sufficiently grave for government leaders to meet with the party's state secretary in August to appeal for a halt. The party agreed to suspend the agitations temporarily, provided the government made serious efforts to establish popular committees (*Economic Times*, Aug. 12, 1972).

Mass agitations had a significant impact on improving implementation; the mechanisms were both direct and indirect. T. K. Oommen has shown that the government responded directly to many of the demands in Alleppey, including the takeover of paddy fields from the largest landlord in the district because he had refused to sow the land to counteract laborer demands (1975: 1582). Mass agitations also affected the bureaucracy; officials with whom I spoke mentioned two kinds of effect. First, the agitations impressed them with the urgency of their task, and acted as a deterrent to lethargy, favoritism, and corruption in implementation. Second, the concrete information uncovered by popular investigations or relayed from local people through political channels aided officials in their search through the maze of evasive maneuvers of landowners,though the militants could not always be precise. An indirect impact was that the government could use the threat of rural violence as a lever for prying rapid consent from the Center on such issues as inclusion of the 1969 act, the 1971 amendment, and the private forest and Kannan Devan confiscatory legislation on the Ninth Schedule of the Constitution. This was accomplished by the Twenty-Ninth Amendment, on May 31, 1972.

The final effect of mass agitations was the formulation and passage of the 1972 amendment. The main features included village-level committees, *taluk*-level land boards with broad powers, new regulations requiring more owners to file declarations, the formation of a cabinet-level Land Reforms Review Board, and miscellaneous minor changes to benefit tenants and *kudikidappukars*.[33]

The organizers of the mass agitations hailed these measures as a response to the militance of the people and vowed to continue agitations whenever necessary. But at the same time the High Court struck down a crucial section of the ceiling provisions; transfers of land made between 1964 and 1970, previously rendered null and void, were revalidated. The government was again faced with amending or appealing (*KLA*, VI:11–13:72).

The 1972 amendment enabled the government to establish village committees consisting of the village officer and six other members nom-

---

32. *The Hindu*, May 6, 1972. This promise was qualified by partisan considerations in practice.

33. *Kerala Land Reforms (Amendment) Act*, no. 17 of 1972, gazetted November 2, 1972; *KLA*, VI:11:72 (October 24).

inated by the government, representing all political parties. The functions of the committees were to be advisory and informational; they had no statutory powers. The provision for Taluk land boards was important in decentralizing the Land Board's functions; nonofficials were to be appointed to these bodies as well, again representing all political parties. The boards were conferred judicial powers, allowing them to summon witnesses, evidence, and documents, and were empowered to try offenses under the amendment, which made failure to file holding declarations, or filing false declarations, criminal offenses with stiff penalties.

The 1972 amendment thus enabled the establishment of important new cybernetic devices. The Taluk Land Boards and village committees promised the institutional mechanism for channeling local demands and information into the implementation process both directly and via political parties. The Land Reforms Review Board chaired by the revenue minister was to perform a coordinating cybernetic function at the highest level; significantly, Ms. K. R. Goury, twice revenue minister and easily the most persistent and perspicacious critic of the government's land-reform policy in the Assembly, was named to the board. Finally, a Task Force on Land Reforms for the Fifth Five Year Plan was formed.

The 1972 amendment was the most significant response in a series of progressive alterations of the reform process to achieve the original objectives of the act. These responses were to criticisms and agitations pressed by political parties and mass organizations, both opponents and supporters of the government. The Marxists and their rural mass base were particularly important in this cybernetic function, though the 1972 amendment was a response to a broader spectrum of political demands. In an important sense, the continual revision of the act and implementation procedures represented the capacity of a highly mobilized and politicized political system to respond to the inevitable and formidable obstacles to agrarian structural transformation. The government had to be goaded, threatened, and shamed into responding; these dynamics characterized the reform process through its conclusion.

The Earthy Problems of Implementation and Evasion

With the ensemble of new institutional arrangements for obtaining information and facilitating administration produced by the 1972 amendment, and the intense political pressure for showing concrete results, one would expect significant improvements in implementation performance. Yet the politics of land reform after 1972 had a curious déjà-vu character. The Marxists and other groups continued to accuse the government of bad faith, particularly in delaying the innovations in the 1972 amendment and going slow on the land ceiling measures to appease its landed supporters. One damaging charge was that, although illegal transfers and noncompliance were common, and stiff penal sanctions existed, landlords were not being prosecuted, despite the strong criticism of the non-partisan Committee on Estimates on this point in 1972. As of March 1973, prosecution had been initiated against only three landlords for not filing declarations.[34] The CPI(M) charged that excess lands identified by the land-grab movement (estimated between 135,000 and 180,000 acres) had not been investigated, and that the militants who occupied the land were being jailed instead of the owners who had broken the law. The left reiterated that only popular action could enforce the land reforms.[35]

The government's position was still that the scrutiny of landholdings in the absence of land records was a tedious task and that the land-grab agitations ignored these legal and technical complexities and retarded rather than aided implementation. The government extended the deadline for filing surplus land forms again and again (finally by an amendment in 1973) and defended the Revenue Department's procedures.

The government's case was seriously weakened by its failure to establish quickly the new institutional devices provided by the 1972 amendment. Whereas delay in constituting the land boards and village committees was understandable, even the Land Reforms Review Board was not constituted until eight months after the amendment and had not begun functioning a year after the amendment. The government attributed the delay to the need for consultation with legal experts.[36]

The Taluk Land Boards began functioning on May 1, 1973. The boards discovered additional surplus land and passed orders for its surrender. High Court stay orders still covered some of the surplus, and almost a fourth of the land taken over was declared unfit for cultivation. More than a fourth of the distributable surplus was *kayal* land, which could be worked only in large units; it was decided to utilize this land for cooperative farming. However, a provision enabling joint alienation of land for the project was struck down by the High Court. The village committees had not been formed.

Although the official position then was that the tenancy provisions could safely be left alone, as tenants were de facto owners, there were problems in this approach. The Task Force argued that the absence of local records and local committees allowed de facto denial of rights to some tenants. As the report noted, "there is no machinery or mechanism

34. Kerala, *Gleanings*, First Session (1973: 77).

35. For example, K. R. Goury, *KLA*, VI:4:72; E. M. S. Namboodiripad, *KLA*, VI:13:72. T. K. Oommen's analysis of Alleppey district (1975) and discussions with revenue officials suggest that the area estimates are high, as local militants had no way of knowing the landowners' particular position vis-à-vis allowed transfers, resumption, etc. But no one in a responsible political or administrative position denied the existence of illegal maneuvers to evade the ceiling.

36. Kerala, *Gleanings*, 9th sess. (1973: 53). Data on implementation from Kerala, Land Board, "Progress Report on the Implementation of the K.L.R. Act for the Period Ended 30–11–1973," mimeograph.

to detect cases of concealed or clandestine tenancies" (Kerala, 1973b: 8). A survey for the Planning Commission in one village selected by the Revenue Department as one in which the reform had gone well found that the great majority of the tenants had no lease documents. About 14 percent of the *kudikidappukars* and tenants had been evicted after the 1964 act took effect. No evictions were reported after the 1969 legislation came into force, but a large minority of the tenants eligible to become owner-cultivators "voluntarily surrendered" their land, either as a compromise or under threats from landlords. Moreover, illegal oral tenancies were still being created (an arguably inevitable phenomenon, given the extreme scarcity of employment opportunities and the desperation of the landless). In addition, some owners had used phony tenants to file joint declarations to evade the ceiling provisions.[37]

The extent of such practices is not known. The village studied was not in an area of militant agrarian organizations; malpractices were more common in the less mobilized, less politicized areas (cf. Paulini, 1978: 450). Moreover, such malpractices were almost certainly less frequent in Kerala's reform that in most contemporary reforms in the region. But irregularities of this kind remind us that even in Kerala the superior resources of the landed count heavily in a context of acute deprivation and insignificant opportunity and security for many of the rural poor, and that the techniques of ordinary administration are not capable of discovering and preventing such abuses.

The earthy problems of administration certainly contributed to delays in implementation and are not given sufficient attention in political controversy. Land records have been mentioned frequently, but the difficulty of land reform through traditional institutions should be emphasized. A major project for survey and recording of land holdings was begun in the late 1960s, but little was accomplished before the land reforms. Thereafter, land survey work became enmeshed in controversy. No record of land could be entered until the land board or land tribunal decided the legal status of rights in the land. Once made, decisions were subject to appeals or review. Thus, in a practical sense, land-record operations had to await the completion of land reforms, yet the task of implementing the land reforms was complicated and slowed by the lack of land records.[38]

This vicious circle was especially critical to implementation of the

37. M. A. Oommen, "Report to the Planning Commission," draft MS (Trivandrum: 1974) and personal communication; M. A. Oommen (1975: 81 and passim).

38. This section is based on extensive interviews with officials from the field level to the top of the Revenue Department in Kerala in 1974 and 1979–80, as well as departmental circulars, progress reports, Proceedings of the Land Board, minutes of the Land Reforms Review Board, individual case-files, and court decisions, in addition to interviews with farmers, laborers, and local leaders of mass organizations (primarily in Palghat district). For more on local-level dynamics and implementation, Paulini (1978: 362–450); Koshy (1976: 310–19).

ceiling. Decentralization of the functions of the land board made sense in terms of moving decisions closer to the land in question, but it then became difficult for any local tribunal to assess the total holdings of a family owning land in scattered plots if some of the land fell within another tribunal's jurisdiction. The only records generally available for determining surplus land were the returns filed by landowners. But for a long time landowners refused to file, or filed inaccurately, or filed only to receive compensation for wasteland. The government complicated the administrative tasks by not prosecuting recalcitrant owners. As of early 1975, not a single person had been punished for violation of any section of the act, though evidence of abuses and irregularities was incontrovertible.

Once filed, declarations had to be investigated. With inadequate land records, this was obviously an extremely difficult task. Moreover, landowners resorted to a number of evasive actions, transfers, partitions, and *benami* registration of the land in the name of a loyal "tenant." Detection of these abuses was possible only through local informants. The politicized and literate population of Kerala offered unique potential; disclosures came through newspapers, local peasant organizations, political workers, and so on, but the process was neither dependable nor institutionalized.

The slow pace of settlement of tenants and *kudikidappukars* reflected not only the absence of land records and continuing problems with adverse court rulings, but also the reluctance of some of these people to apply. Tenants had little incentive, since rent payments ceased January 1, 1970, and purchase installments would begin only after application (cf. Mencher, 1976). Application costs were frequently high. A typical lawyer's fee was Rs 10 per hearing; usually four or five hearings had to be held on each case, unless it was appealed. Lost labor time, travel, and food costs were also incurred. Moreover, the law was extremely complex and intimidated the rural poor to some extent; legislative debates offer clear evidence that not even all legislators understood the fine points, and court interpretations further muddied the situation. Remarkably, it was only after three and a half years of implementation that the government began to translate the administrative rules from English into Malayalam (*KLA*, VIII:6:73). Applications were also hindered in some cases because of intimidation, whether directly by landowners or by local police. Some of the rural poor thus preferred a compromise settlement with owners to the uncertainty of legal proceedings and renounced their rights for some consideration.[39] As in Ceylon's Paddy Lands Act, the data on implementation suggest that reluctance to enter the legal process was

39. In addition to the inferential and interview evidence on this point, T. S. Pillai, in his novel *The Iron Rod* (1974) describes the dilemma of a hutment dweller who finally sells out to the owner, surrenders the *kudikidappu*, signs on illegal document, and, significantly, fears that the local laborer union will discover the transaction.

often experientially rational.[40] For all these reasons, local political activists and organizations were invaluable where they were available—providing legal council, representing claimants, completing forms, and pressuring officials—but the uneven development and spread of such organizations meant that help was not always available.

If a tenant or hutment dweller decided to apply, the case first went to the land tribunal. In the first three years of implementation, many tribunals were block development officers, often young men with little practical experience or legal training, basically unequipped to do land-reform work and simultaneously burdened with other responsibilities.[41] The land tribunal then ordered a revenue inspector to investigate the case. The inspectors are trained only as survey clerks, are poorly paid, and are not immune to intimidation or influence by various means. The inspector made local inquiries about the applicant, using a wide variety of sources to determine bona fides—tax records, housesite and family location, rent receipts, electoral rolls, and so on. The result was a report on local usages and customs and the facts in the case, from which the land tribunal made a decision.

The land tribunals have been severely castigated by the Land Board for malpractices and tardy progress.[42] The tribunals, however, made difficult decisions. Some tenant applications were fraudulent, frequently bogus claims put up by landowners to conceal surplus land. The tribunals, too, were sometimes intimidated and influenced by the local power or political connections of large landowners. In order to play safe, tribunals frequently adhered to the precise letter of the law rather than its spirit, depending, for example, on documentary evidence even when it was recognized that some documents were false or exacted through coercion and that many legitimate tenants had no lease deeds. As one official of long experience said, "for the little man to win, the officer must give special, sympathetic treatment, but often this is not done." The spirit of the legislation demands such treatment, but the letter of the law is less flexible. The administrative means of shifting the burden of proof to create the presumption in favor of the landless that was intended by the legislature remained elusive.

The declaration of a national emergency in July 1975 had ambivalent effects on the implementation process. The positive effect was that

40. *Proceedings of the Land Board* and mimeographed progress reports periodically published data on the reasons for *kudikidappukar* claims being rejected. The cases allowed by the end of 1979 were less than two-thirds of the applications. A reading of the cases reported in the *Kerala Law Times* indicates that an enormous amount of litigation was involved in landowners' attempts to shift *kudikidappukars* from one plot to another. In sum, the obtaining of a *kudikidappu* through official channels was often tedious, costly, and uncertain.

41. The number of land tribunals was increased in late 1974, as was their rank. Cf. M. A. Oommen (1975: chap. 4); Paulini (1978: 330–74).

42. *Proceedings of the Land Board*, Trivandrum, especially for November 25, 1974.

the official machinery, already strengthened numerically in response to militant criticisms of implementation, was pressured to show progress through the issuing of quotas. Dramatic improvement in the pace of implementation as measured by disposal of cases resulted, but the earthy problems of implementation stressed above raise doubts about the *quality* of hasty decisions produced under pressure to fulfill numerical quotas. A negative effect of the Emergency was that mass agitations were effectively quashed, and many radical leaders were forced underground, removing an important constraint on irregularities and abuse. Though a fire was lit underneath the bureaucracy, the reform process was further bureaucratized; results thus became even more dependent on the characteristics of individual officials—their honesty, dedication, skill, and judgment—characteristics in which there was substantial variation (cf. Paulini, 1978: 322–25).

The earthy problems of implementation underline the importance of local-level organization in facilitating proper implementation and preventing victimization during land reform. Kerala State offered unique—though uneven—potential, and this political potential was translated into unique institutional potential through the 1972 amendment's provision for village-level committees. But the committees were never formed. The government claimed that other parties refused to produce lists of potential members. The Marxists claimed that discrimination against their party in nominations to the Taluk Land Boards and the government's mala fides in implementation made cooperation futile and impossible.[43] Revenue Department officials suggested that the government had other concerns: some parties, most pointedly the CPI, have little or no rural mass base, and would be hard-pressed to field representatives in many villages; in contrast, the Marxists would be in a position to dominate many of the committees. There was also a fear that the level and intensity of partisan and class conflict made cooperation among political parties on an issue as explosive as land impossible and would only breed more violence. The impact of partisan competition on land reform was thus ambivalent, both energizing implementation and producing some ironic constraints.

Conclusion: Structural Change and Class Conflict

After a decade in opposition, the CPI(M) returned to office after the January 1980 elections, leading a coalition Left Democratic Front that contained some traditional enemies of land reform, as well as the CPI—an inherently unstable coalition. The CPI(M), by a minuscule margin, received the most votes in the elections but only 18.9 percent of the total. The preceding CPI-led ministry had resigned largely on the issue of di-

43. *Gleanings*, 10th sess. (1974: 258); *KLA*, VII:10:73; XIV:11:76; interview with K. R. Goury, December 1974.

luting the land reforms through the "Gift Deeds Bill" (Herring, 1980). By the time of the new ministry, the reforms had been essentially completed; the impact of the reforms raises new and continuing questions about the strategy and tactics of agrarian mobilization and policy for a self-proclaimed revolutionary party.

As in all land reforms, a summary statement of impact is problematic; the aggregate impact of fraud, evasion, and malpractices cannot be ascertained from isolated studies, as local conditions vary greatly. This problem is compounded by misleading official statements on the number of tenant beneficiaries. However, the best evidence available indicates that implementation of the core of the reforms—the abolition of landlordism—was remarkably successful, despite delays, setbacks, and evasion; corrected data on the number of tenant beneficiaries and the tenanted area transferred indcate very little aggregate slippage between legislation and impact. Interpolating among various sources on implementation, population, and landholding data, I put the number of tenant beneficiaries at almost 1.3 million, or 43.3 percent of the agricultural households in the state in 1971 (Herring, 1980). As importantly, the aggregate area transferred through the abolition of landlordism was almost 2 million acres, or 36.5 percent of the net sown area in the state (42.9 percent of the area excluding plantation crops).

The structural change was thus significant; rentiers as a class were eliminated from agriculture (and many suffered greatly as a consequence) and the rentier mode of appropriation was virtually extinguished. But if rentiers were clearly the losers, it would be imprecise to term tenants the winners. Those who held land on lease were beneficiaries; as emphasized in the first section of this chapter, that category included many relatively privileged farmers as well as socially oppressed poor peasants who owned no land and operated tiny holdings. It is clear from prereform data that though most of the *tenants* were poor smallholders, most of the tenanted *land* was held by the upper echelons of the agrarian hierarchy.

There are no aggregate data on beneficiaries by class, but my calculations from a state-wide sample survey conducted by the Indian School of Social Sciences (Trivandrum) indicate that the primary beneficiaries relative to other classes were indeed the rich peasants (defined as those who do some agricultural work but depend primarily on wage laborers). In that sample, rich peasants were 13.3 percent of the households but received 38.7 percent of the land redistributed via tenancy reforms. Poor and middle peasants gained a far lower percentage of the land than their percentage of the sample. When grouped by size of holding, these differences are equally telling. Households possessing less than five acres constituted 84.2 percent of the sample but received only 36.2 percent of the redistributed area. The smallest peasants (holding less than one acre), though 16.6 percent of the sample (a figure far below that of the landholding census because of the survey's exclusion of smallholders whose primary occupation was agricultural labor), received only 0.9 percent of the land redistributed. In contrast, holders of more than five acres (15.8 percent of the sample) gained 63.8 percent of the redistributed acreage.[44]

The rentiers have thus been replaced by a new tier of proprietors who, as a class, are not unambiguously tillers or even primarily engaged in agriculture. The results reflect both the policy logic—abjuring interference with capitalist farmers via land reform, identifying tenancy with feudalism—and the tactical/electoral imperatives of uniting a broad movement to win power and to abolish landlordism as a social and economic system. The important consequence is that, despite evasions and fraud, the reforms in the end were effectively implemented and produced significant increases in income, security, and opportunity for virtually all strata of the tenantry, a result approached only symbolically by other reforms in the region. But then the Marxists are left in the same tactical and ideological quandary presented at a theoretical level in chapter 6: how can the plight of the laborers—the largest agrarian class—and poor peasantry be alleviated without fracturing the rural social base of the left movement?

Indeed, the most common criticism of the reforms by laborers themselves, and by academics (e.g., Mencher, 1978; Krishnaji, 1979), is that little was done for the laborers. This result stems more from the policy logic than from the admittedly severe administrative problems of ceiling implementation. At the conceptual level, the central attack was on rentiers, and thus the principal beneficiaries were those who leased land, classes one cut above the laborers. Because large owners leased out most of their holdings (63.8 percent of the land for the largest owners [Kerala, 1968/76: tables 8.13, 8.14]), their land was redistributed mostly through the tenancy provisions, not through the ceiling. The exclusion of plantations likewise limited redistributive potential. Because of the political structure, landowners, having narrowly escaped the 1959 reforms because of Delhi's intervention, had sufficient time, reason, and ability to rearrange their holdings to evade the ceiling. Administration of the ceiling was inevitably difficult and further hampered by the absence of village committees: evasion via malpractices was possible.

The aggregate impact of these malpractices is usually exaggerated.

44. Data from Indian School of Social Sciences (no date) draft typescript. For elaboration, Herring (1980). The data in the text are gross figures; net calculations reduce insignificantly the gains of "rich peasants," but the picture remains the same at the bottom of the hierarchy. Even "capitalist landlords" (those who only supervise wage labor and do no fieldwork) were net beneficiaries, having gained possession of more land previously leased in than they lost for having leased it out. These objective indicators are congruent with subjective perceptions of various classes; a majority of every class represented (the pure rentiers were absent) reported the land reforms to have been a "good measure," and the poor peasants reported the lowest percentage of having benefited from the reforms—15.6 percent—the rich peasants, the highest—29.7 percent. Cf. M. A. Oommen (1979: 18–28).

Though the acreage declared surplus was small, it is almost exactly the same as that projected as surplus in the 1966–67 *Survey*. About 150,000 acres were eventually "declared surplus," or only 2.7 percent of net sown area. Distribution has been slowed by adverse court orders; only 47,873 acres had been distributed by the beginning of 1980, after a decade of enforcement, benefiting 75,483 families.[45] The average plot distributed was thus quite small (0.63 acres), often of poor quality, and presented severe problems of financing development for the extremely poor recipients, who consequently often sold or abandoned the land.[46] Laborers who were *kudikidappukars* gained house and garden sites which, though tiny (an average of 0.08 acres), represented considerable security (and often income opportunity), particularly in contrast to their historical condition of slavery and serflike bondage.[47]

The policy logic of land reforms in Kerala, partly of necessity, has not treated the laborers as aspiring would-be peasants, but rather as rural proletarians. As such, their legal gains have been significant. In addition to existing institutions (minimum-wage legislation, arbitration machinery, etc.), the *Kerala Agricultural Workers Act* of 1974 mandated preference for existing workers in employment, regulation of hours and working conditions, overtime pay, other benefits, and even a type of permanency of employment parallel to security of tenure for tenants.[48] Farmers complain bitterly that the act in effect removes control of the labor process from their hands, but the laborers continue to be plagued by severe problems of underemployment and malnutrition (e.g., P. G. K. Panikar, 1979). Moreover, effective enforcement of new gains depends on local mobilization and organization, and here the *indirect* gains of the land-reform process, reflected in increased politicization, awareness, and labor-union activity, are arguably as important as the meager direct benefits. The en-

45. Data from the Land Board. The distributive potential is enhanced by the private forest confiscation, but most of that land is not cultivable.

46. Field investigation, Palghat district, 1979–80. Koshy (1976: 291) found that in his study only 100 of the 349 allottees remained in possession, for the reasons expressed in the text. Cf. Paulini (1978: 450–87, 509); *KLA* VI:2:79. One possible solution—cooperative and collective farms—has been tried on an experimental basis and failed (cf. Jayachandran, 1976) and the left has long recognized the attitudinal and practical barriers to collectivization under existing conditions.

47. Data from Land Board; 265,829 *kudikidappukars* were allowed to purchase their plots, or 77.4 percent of the potential beneficiaries estimated in 1966–67 (Kerala, 1968/76: part 3, table 1). Though some *kudikidappukars* were victimized in the reform, others gained housesites outside official channels and are not reflected in these data (Herring, 1980: A66). *Kudikidappukars* in Trichur district who received tiny plots reported to me monthly incomes from coconut trees that exceeded average wage earnings (though not all plots are so productive and coconut prices were then high).

48. Act No. 18 of 1974; cf. Kerala (1974). For a commentary and critique by an MP and general secretary of the Kerala Karshaka Thozhilali (agricultural laborer) Union, P. K. Kunjachan, *Peasant and Labour* 3, no. 1 (January–February 1974): 12–14.

semble of changes—institutional and political—make the best of an admittedly bad situation for the laborers, particularly in contrast to their
history and to the position of field laborers in other parts of the region.

Whether the social forces which produced the 1969 reforms will
remain united in the struggle for expansion of the rights of the agrarian
underclass, or remain successful in electoral politics if the struggle is
intensified, remains to be seen. But the structural basis for unity among
the agrarian underclasses in demanding redistribution of rights, security,
and opportunity to the tillers of the soil has been further breached by the
reforms. Tenants and laborers in Kerala have always had partially conflicting interests—the laborer's wage is a tenant's cost, and laborers com-
peted with tenants-at-will for tenancies, undermining security and raising rents—but had a common interest in abolishing the rentiers, who
monopolized the land and dominated rural society through the social and
economic oppression of the poor (cf. Krishnaji, 1979). That unity is broken; the tenants are owners, the great landlords are gone. Redistribution
of land or its products is now a threat to a much larger and less vulnerable
section of the agrarian population. The land reforms grew from and
sharpened, and finally resolved, one class conflict; that resolution has
accentuated another; the privileges of the privileged are now smaller and
more difficult to delegitimate within the normative framework of a capitalist society. The rentiers, like the *zamindars* elsewhere, were politically vulnerable and had little legitimacy; the new proprietors are important to every political party.

In an important sense, the CPI(M) is a victim of its own success.
The effects of *embourgeoisement* on electoral politics are difficult to
evaluate, as there are no class-differentiated voting data and electoral alliance strategy profoundly influences party percentages of the vote. But,
as party leaders, local cadres, and peasant association activists recognize,
the political loyalty of the tenants has become problematic since the land
reforms.[49] One peasant leader in Palghat district expressed it to me this
way: "as soon as they got the *patta* (land title), they put on the *khadi*
(handspun cloth symbolic of allegiance to the Congress)." There are two
parallel processes. First, the former tenants quite naturally fear that further land and labor reforms will threaten their new status and privilege,
and thus feel more comfortable with parties of property than with parties

49. Interviews with local leaders of peasant associations and laborer unions and with
local party leaders, primarily in Palghat district, 1980. My village surveys in that district, as
yet unpublished, clearly indicate bitterness on the part of the laborers, who feel that the
tenants benefitted from the land reforms and subsequently refused to share their gains economically or to support the laborers politically. E. M. S. Namboodiripad admits that this
has been one consequence of the reforms but argues that peasants and laborers nevertheless
still have common interests: "Peasants and Agricultural Labourers: Allies in a Common
Struggle," *Peasant and Labour* 3, no. 1 (January–February 1974):5. There is almost certainly
a large–small holding-size distinction in the importance of *embourgeoisement*, and caste/
community considerations influence voting patterns.

of redistribution. This dynamic is reinforced by the Marxists' encouragement of labor radicalism in the early 1970s, which the party admits alienated not only rich peasants but some poor and middle ones as well (cf.
Paulini, 1978: 301).

The second process which undermines the Marxist position vis-à-
vis the poor peasantry is the movement of other parties in the state to
claim the mantle of social justice for the rural poor. For a very long time,
the Communists alone stood consistently for the poor against the wealthy.
Their electoral successes have drawn other parties to champion the cause
of the laborers and small farmers. The land reforms symbolized the process: the bitter irony for the CPI(M) is that, for a decade, credit for land
reform accrued to governments containing or resting upon the Congress,
a party which had blocked radical land reform in Kerala for the previous
two decades. At *pattayemelas* (title-dispensing festivals), the government claimed credit for revolutionizing land relations; the symbolic and
real resources accrued to the Marxists' opponents. There is no doubt that
some farmers who stood aloof from the struggle feel, as one former tenant
said to me: "despite all the flag-holding and trouble-making of the Marxists, it is the party of Mahatma Gandhi which finally gave us the land."
Organizationally, this process is reflected in the proliferation of peasant
and laborer unions sponsored by parties all across the political spectrum,
including those which historically opposed interference with property
privilege (cf. T. K. Oommen, 1976).

At an even more speculative level, it is probable that electoral success has transformed the CPI(M) into a party preoccupied with ordinary
politics. Through the dark years of struggle, party cadres suffered with
the peasants and laborers; a political party in power is a very different
organization. A. K. Gopalan voiced what many of his party colleagues
feared: a new generation of members lacks the experience of struggle and
the conviction forged therein, tasting instead the opportunities and pressures of electoral partisan politics (1973: 263). Regenerating the commitment and enthusiasm while aligning electorally with conservative parties when the burning issues of social justice with obvious solutions have
been removed, presents an extraordinary conundrum.

It is possible, then, that the irony predicted by fears of *embourgeoisement* expressed by Lenin, Gunawardena, and a section of the CPI(M)
has come to pass: has the capitalist revolution in agriculture succeeded,
leaving the Communists to press only reformist agrarian demands? Consider the statement of a former landlord recorded by Joan Mencher (1978:
353–54).

> It is true that the tenants got the land from us. But it is not benefit-
> ting the labourers in any way. Even the good that we were doing for the
> labourers the new landlords are not doing. The old *jenmis* even in the middle
> of the night used to extend help to the labourers . . . , but the new landlords
> are not like that. They will say—do your work and earn your wages. They

will not give loans. And if the labourers refuse to work, then the . . . members of their [the new landlords'] families will enter the fields.

The developing agrarian struggle in Kerala is structurally isomorphic to the historic movement for land to the tiller; those who labor in the fields are organizing to demand greater security of access to the land and a larger share of its product. The organization of laborers qua farm laborers is recent, long antedated by the organization of tenants qua tenants. As the laborers become organized, the conflict assumes different forms. The CPI(M) recognized these contradictions, but a tactical and strategic resolution is not clear; can the party represent laborers against peasants and retain the allegiance of even middle and poor peasants? Can it demand land redistribution for laborers and poor peasants and not alienate rich and middle peasants? The CPI(M) has sought an answer by focusing on expanding the pie—subsidies to the farm sector, credit, better prices, lower taxes, remission of debts, distribution of government lands, and so on—while simultaneously organizing laborers into unions and pressing for enhancement of their rights on the land.[50] These tactics may prove successful but are unlikely to revolutionize Kerala. Moreover, expanding the pie is neither an electoral strategy unique to the Marxists nor one that is viable independent of forces which lie outside the control of the State government. Higher farm prices, subsidies, even the recent granting of pensions to retired laborers, all produce fiscal pressures which underline the dependence of State governments on decisions from Delhi. In a critical sense, state power does not reside at the State level, and thus the strategy for revolution in one State remains elusive.

50. Cf. Krishnaji (1979). For demands of the Kerala Karshaka Sangham and All-India Kisan Sabha connected to the Marxists, *Peasant and Labour* 3, no. 1 (February 1974):5–7; 3, no. 3 (April–May 1974): 16 and passim; 3, no. 7 (November–December 1974):20–23; 4, no. 2 (February–March 1975); Gopalan (1973: 295–98). Although the national CPI(M) has considerably radicalized its agrarian program (CPI(M), 1973), the Kerala party is constrained by its own rural mass base and minority electoral position (necessitating alliances with more conservative parties) from legislating more radical reforms. In theory, a recutting of the pie is advocated; in practice, expanding the pie has been the dominant thrust.

8 The Politics of Land Reform: Class Interests and Regime Interests

It is good to remember that social and economic reforms, intelligently done, are truly conservative in an age of revolution.
—*Professor Kenneth Parsons, Adviser to the Government of India on Land Reforms*

An unweighted political calculus of land-reform policy presents a paradox: there are many more people in rural areas of South Asia who are nonprivileged than privileged by the land-tenure system, suggesting that genuine land reform would be politically expedient; indeed, the radical redistributive rhetoric that has escalated over time throughout the region reflects recognition of the numerical dominance of the disadvantaged. Yet land reforms in most of the region have redistributed very little to those at the bottom of the agrarian hierarchy. Part of the explanation, as usually recognized, is that ruling elites are typically beholden politically to landed classes; the agrarian system fosters the imperfect translation of numbers and interests into political power through the mediation of patron-client relations, "vote banks," dependence, and ideology. There are thus contradictory political imperatives which explain much of the inconsistency in land policy and provide insight into an important question: elite interests and nonredistributive functions of nominally redistributive policy. The importance of the question is underlined by the dominance of elite rather than mass input in the formulation of land reforms. The interests of agrarian underclasses in land reform are straightforward and readily understood: a greater share of the land's product and greater security of access to the land. But sharecroppers and laborers do not sit on Planning Commission panels, land reform commissions, or ministerial drafting committees. What are the interests of those who do?

The first analytical distinction, then, is between regime interests and dominant class interests. Obviously the two may coincide, but a variety of regimes may serve the same class needs, and indeed, a change of regimes may prove useful for placating dissident groups while creating no serious obstacle to pursuit of class-specific ends through public policy. Regime interests are those narrow political concerns of maintaining support, dissipating, suppressing, or coopting opposition, and thus retaining power. Class interests are concerned with the basic economic institutions of society; both class interests and regime interests may thus involve either maintenance or transformation of the agrarian system or aspects thereof, depending on the existing configuration and conjunctural exigencies. Narrow economic interests of dominant classes and regime interests may thus diverge, as regimes must take both a longer and a broader view of societal consequences of economic structure; their understanding of those consequences becomes operative through world-views which often contradict the narrow class ideologies of powerful strata.

The political power of the landed is often, and rightly, given emphasis in the explanation of ineffectual land reforms. But ruling elites have for a long time been more plural than the landlord-dominated caricature allows. Moreover, land reforms of more or less serious intent continue to be promulgated despite objections from landed strata. As is recognized explicitly in Marxian theory, the state is characterized by "relative autonomy" vis-à-vis those classes in the basic interest of which it rules; the notion of relative autonomy recognizes that the preservation of the institutional order, and the long-term interests of dominant classes, may necessitate moves against dominant classes, or fractions thereof (Poulantzas, 1968). Moreover, distinct interests of a governing class of politicians and officials are discernible in the politics of land reforms—interests which often contradict those of economically hegemonic classes in specific conjunctures while not, in most cases, producing policy which negates the fundamental structure of privileges characteristic of capitalist society. The governing class derives a major share of its access to privilege, security, and opportunity from control of the state apparatus, and shares a fundamental interest in preventing cataclysmic change. Typical land reforms extend the control and discretionary power of the state apparatus while simultaneously permitting landed power to assert itself locally, particularly through connections to ruling groups, unless counteracted by local militant mobilization of subordinate classes. Land reforms which operate through radical popular mobilization rather than ordinary administration are a threat to that power and privilege.

The autonomy of the state is "relative" with regard to land reform not only because of the organized political power of the landed, but more fundamentally because regime interests are critically influenced by the centrality of the agricultural system in determining broader economic prospects and political consequences. There is thus a structural dependence of regimes on landed classes independent of the balance of organized political power of the landed and landless. Those who command the agricultural means of production control the surplus, and export earnings or import substitutes, on which the economy depends. So long as their class privileges do not jeopardize economic health or political stability, those privileges have been left largely in place, though whittled at the margin as exigencies arise. In times of crisis, regime interests have prompted more fundamental interference with property.

But not all class privileges are equally acceptable. A dominant world-view of governing classes has held that the "feudal" relations in agriculture are unacceptable—politically, socially, economically. The ideal transformation has posited creation of progressive entrepreneurial capitalism in agriculture, whether of large or small scale. The land reforms in most of the region are consistent with both regime and dominant class interests in facilitating and completing the bourgeois revolution (often from above) in rural areas; the halting and compromised process reflects both the strategic constraints of a partially completed bourgeois revolution and, more proximately decisive, the constraints of ordinary politics and ordinary administration.

Land Reform and the Bourgeois Revolution

Communist theoretician E. M. S. Namboodiripad has advanced the following argument: land reforms have been supported by ruling groups in India because they are necessary for the destruction of feudal production relations, but cannot be carried "too far" because of the interest of the urban and rural bourgeoisie in exploiting the peasantry through ground rent and their positions as sellers, buyers, and usurers in rural areas (1974: 38 and passim). The political function of the reforms is to weaken the (feudal) right and left simultaneously, the latter through coopting peasant demands and left programs (largely symbolically).[1] Namboodiripad argues that the strategy has succeeded, at least partially.

Despite the troublesome complexities of the "bourgeois revolution" as an analytical construct, it is important to consider land reforms in terms of the interests of those groups which explicitly seek to establish dynamic capitalist societies in South Asia.[2] The planning models of Pakistan have directly asserted the need for and legitimacy of progressive entrepreneurial capitalism, in agriculture as in industry. In India, the Congress party has preserved the symbolic commitment to a "socialistic pattern of society," but land-reform policy has not been fundamentally different from that of Pakistan; dissent and ambiguity on the commitment to land redistribution through ceilings exhibited the same concern that the attack on "feudalism" not disrupt the fragile entrepreneurial thrust in modernizing agriculture. It is arguable that the bourgeois revo-

1. For a similar analysis, All India Kisan Sabha (peasant association) (1970: 8 and passim).

2. I concur with Barrington Moore, Jr. (1968: 428–29) that the bourgeois revolution, paradoxically, need not be dominated by the bourgeoisie per se as an organized political force to change the structure of society in the direction of bourgeois forms of property, legal infrastructure, etc. Cf. chapter 4.

lution in Sri Lanka was effected under colonial auspices in the creation of the plantation economy; "feudal" relations remained only in the subsistence sector, and there only partially. The ceiling reform was a response to militant critiques of the inability of the existing, privately controlled, capitalist agricultural economy to provide adequate employment and, to some extent, food. After a brief experiment with various cooperative forms, the system returned to a hierarchial wage-labor system, in which the state replaced private control while providing attractive employment opportunities to bureaucratic and managerial strata and compensation to former owners.

It is worth asking, then, what concrete class interests, other than those of the landless, would be served by an effective attack on feudalism, and why land reform, if it is potentially an effective transformational tool, is wielded so meekly. In the policy logic explored earlier, transformations of agrarian relations have been perceived as necessary to produce rural social stability and economic progress. As long as productivity was low, technique undeveloped, and the underclass brutalized economically and socially, a "contented peasantry" was unlikely. Retarded growth in the agricultural sector forced unemployed rural people into cities, where resources had to be diverted to accommodate them, however marginally, and implied slow development of a rural market for urban products and a constricted flow of raw materials for industrial and agroindustrial development. Food production is especially crucial in an agrarian society. Food shortages not only drive up prices, and thus urban wages, but also create severe dislocations in the national economy. In discussing the need for land reform in 1959, the West Pakistan Land Reforms Commission noted that "the cost of food imports in recent years has thrown the entire economy of the country out of gear."[3] The security, availability, and cost of food supplies are critical political questions.

The attack on "feudalism"[4] has had many prongs. There have been explicitly antifeudal measures, such as the abolition of intermediary property rights—*zamindari, jagirdari,* and so on (*nindagama* in Sri Lanka)—which struck at the formal-legal (and symbolic) basis of feudalism, both economically and in terms of juridical, administrative, and political powers. Likewise, "feudal" means of appropriation of labor—*begar* (labor rent), serfdom, debt bondage—have all been explicitly outlawed. Capitalist farms—plantations, orchards, mechanized farms, "efficient

3. Pakistan (1959b: 73). The *Draft Fourth Five Year Plan* of India discussed land reforms in terms of "tensions" and "disruptions" which endanger "even the national economy" (1974: 27).

4. As explained in chapter 4, the use of "feudalism" in the South Asian context is problematic and usually incorrect, but production, social, and political relations between land and labor in much of the subcontinent retain precapitalist characteristics which may usefully be termed feudal residues, without implying that the social system *as a system* constitutes or constituted feudalism as it is generally understood.

farms," and so on—have been exempted from various confiscatory ceiling laws; standards of land-use efficiency have been legislated. But the attack has been partial, to say the least. The ceiling-redistributive model as an indirect attack contains clear logical gaps in its efficient causation, as explored in chapter 4; it does not seem the most direct or efficient means of either achieving the economic goals posited or destroying feudalism, particularly when we consider the great administrative costs and disruption. Indeed, simple changes in taxation policy could achieve as much as the typical compromised ceiling reform. But indirect methods do not generate the powerful symbolic resources of a land reform, and thus do not serve *regime* needs as effectively.

The ideal type of agrarian change that would result from an effective attack on "feudalism," as posited in the policy logic, would be something like the following. As large holdings were broken up, the vertical dependency ties between lords and tenants would dissolve, economically, socially and politically; former tenants would become independent proprietors. An exploited and bitter agrarian class would become a contented, presumably conservative, class. The breakdown of "feudal" relations would in theory create new ecological niches for employing capital to extract surplus from rural areas on both the input and output sides of the production process; such penetration is more difficult when landlords serve as intermediaries and agriculture is stagnant. The abolition of rental payments improves the cultivators' capacity for technical change, consumption, and investment. The abolition of *begar* and other forms of forced or tied labor creates a competitive, mobile rural proletariat, stripped of protection afforded by traditional patrons. Modern techniques of production introduce new inputs—mechanized implements, agrochemicals, quality seeds (and thus lucrative dealerships). A new fluidity in the land market should result, opening opportunities for businessmen, professionals, bureaucrats, and military officers to purchase or lease land. With a rationalized agriculture, price supports, input subsidies, and minimal taxation combine to create new profitable opportunities for investment by these groups.

It should be emphasized that these transformations would be most effectively served by a land-to-the-tiller reform, since all functionless rentier intermediaries would be eliminated. The resulting mixture of small, dependent proprietors should eventually allow extensive penetration, consolidation, and modernization. Why, then, if a radical ceiling or even land to the tiller would serve important bourgeois interests, do we find such timid policy by regimes openly committed to capitalist modernization?

The position of the bourgeoisie in the politics of land reform is ambiguous. Lenin noted that the political position depends on the stage of historical development. "In the epoch of the bourgeois revolution . . . the objective conditions compel the 'radical bourgeois' to be courageous; for, in solving the historical problem of the given period, they cannot yet, as a class, fear the proletarian revolution. In the epoch of bourgeois revolution the bourgeoisie has not yet territorialized itself; landed property is still too much impregnated with feudalism in such an epoch" (1938: XII, 321). However, as Marx noted of the "radical bourgeois": "In practice he lacks courage, for an attack on one form of property, private property in the conditions of labor, would be very dangerous for another form" (ibid: 330).

The argument is that, of necessity, at some stage in the attack on feudal relations in society a radical land reform will be supported by the bourgeoisie. However, the attack may "lack courage" for two reasons. First, an attack on one form of private property, landed property, raises the spectre of a "socialist attack on all private property" (Lenin, 1938: XII, 330). Second, rural property relations in changing societies are unlikely to be purely "feudal"; the bourgeoisie will typically have begun to "territorialize itself," in Marx's terminology, as capitalism spreads to some geographical areas and some products in the agricultural sector. This situation is particularly characteristic of modern South Asia, as the "feudal" monopoly on land and land relations was seriously eroded by certain colonial policies (land mortgages and foreclosures enforced by courts, heavy land taxes, development of commercial export crops, etc.).

That an attack on landed property can be generalized to an attack on all private property has not been missed by opponents of land reform in South Asia who have argued for delay of ceiling legislation until, in the name of equity, ceilings on urban wealth are legislated. Although there is a genuine concern for equity, politically the attempt is to broaden the base of opposition to attacks on concentrations of wealth in general. Nor is the potential expansion of the attack on property implied by a land reform unrecognized by ruling elites. A senior minister in the United Front government in Sri Lanka publicly chastised a party colleague in 1972 for advocating expropriation of the plantations, arguing that one form of property cannot be expropriated without expropriating all forms. He concluded, decisively: "But the vast majority of us come from electorates where we have got mixed populations. There are property owners in every electorate, whether represented in the Opposition or in the Government. . . ."[5]

The territorialization Marx speaks of is marked in South Asia. Because land has traditionally been the symbol of elite status and social security, aspiring mobile groups have sought to become petty rentiers or gentlemen farmers. Even if not accomplished, the goal of becoming landed remains, perhaps for retirement or for one's children. Sri Lanka illustrates the case dramatically, because the middle class evolved early in response to colonial needs for servicing a plantation export economy. Landed fam-

5. Felix Dias Bandaranaike in Sri Lanka, *National State Assembly Debates, Official Report*, vol. 1, Proceedings of August 3, 1972.

ilies had early access to education and produced middle-class offspring who retained their share in the land if possible. At the same time, the acute credit-capital shortages experienced by the peasantry and the vagaries of monsoon agriculture produced opportunities for anyone in the village with a steady, secure income or surplus capital to buy land or accept mortgages. Salaried teachers, clerks, and bureaucrats, as well as petty traders, lawyers, and businessmen, thus have had special access to village land (chap. 3). Auctions of state land had the same effect (e.g., Herring, 1977b).

The landed middle class and intelligentsia thus cannot be counted on for support of truly radical reforms, though these groups may support ceiling legislation for its presumed contribution to economic growth and political stability, modernization, and social justice. The "shadow" Land Reform Commission of Sri Lanka rejected a land-to-the-tiller reform because as many small rentiers would be alienated as tenants would be benefited, and this explicit calculation was also recognized by politicians;[6] likewise, the ceiling finally adopted reflected a political arithmetic calculation heavily influenced by the holdings of the middle and professional classes.

The extensive and early commercialization and diversification of the rural economy in Sri Lanka thus produced a politically powerful middle class with interests in land which, in the absence of agrarian radicalism on the Malabar model, prevented the abolition of rentiers or an extremely low ceiling, but simultaneously presented no obstacle to a serious ceiling reform in time of crisis. As agriculture is penetrated by modern capitalist forces and technology, scale of operation, not merely size of physical land area, becomes critical for landowners. Moreover, as landowning elites diversify, income from the land is less crucial and compensation can create financial liquidity in place of frozen traditional assets of low productivity. A striking example can be taken from the United Front cabinet which produced the 1972 ceiling.

Felix Dias Bandaranaike argued in Parliament that the new ceiling need not be disastrous to landowners. To buttress his argument, the minister reported that he received more income from his poultry operation (Rs 3,100 per month) on 1 acre than from his coconut estate (Rs 1,700 per month) of nearly 100 acres. In addition, the minister owned a dairy farm. But even with three lucrative agricultural enterprises, most of his income was derived, not from the land, but from professional (legal) fees (National State Assembly Debates, vol. I (1972: August 3).

6. One member of the Assembly in 1972 verbalized what was known to the rest; A. C. S. Hameed stated that there were 240,000 tenants in the country, tilling land which belonged to 290,000 people. Thus a land-to-the-tiller policy "is not going to pay dividends politically." He went on to note that "the owners of these paddy fields do not belong to the 'rich class,' or the 'upper class,' but to the 'lower middle class,' the public servants, school masters, etc." Sri Lanka, *National State Assembly Debates*, vol. 1 (1972: c 2028).

It is important that the 1 acre intensive operation which Banda-ranaike held up as a model to parliamentarians generated more than ten times the income expected from the 2 to 5-acre plots planners recommended distributing through the land reform. The difference, of course, is capital; heavily capitalized agricultural operations make the physical land area ceiling less crucial. Bandaranaike is a scion of a landed aristocratic family, yet his agricultural income from modern capitalist operations far exceeded that of the ancestral lands, and his modern professional skills earned more than the combined agricultural enterprises. This combination of interests in modernized landed elites facilitates serious ceiling-redistributive reforms in time of crisis, but simultaneously blocks a truly radical agrarian reform such as land to the tiller, where "tilling" necessitates work in the fields. Moreover, a superstructural manifestation of a partially completed bourgeois revolution—the legal infrastructure supporting established private property rights in land, backed by an independent judiciary—has often vitiated in practice the more radical strains of legislated land reforms.

The industrial bourgeoisie, small in number but important politically, it is likely to be less "territorialized" and more supportive of pragmatic measures to assure rural progress and stability. But this class, too, may, as Marx argued, "lack courage" in supporting a radical land reform, for reasons outlined by Zulfikar Ali Bhutto in a speech at the Annual Dinner of the Karachi Chamber of Commerce and Industry in 1972:

> Before the land reforms of 1958, the theme of the business community was that land reforms must take place in this country. It was contended that without land reforms there would be no progress. Feudalists are parasites. In those days, all the Zamindars used to get excited and complain that class hatred was being preached against them. Businessmen have been saying for a long time that the Zamindars are parasites. At that time, in this same Beach Luxury Hotel, I used to hear speaches of your Chamber on this theme. You look at your own doings—you talked of land reforms, you criticized the Zamindars, the Vaderas, and rightly so. At that time it suited your interest, but you were preaching class hatred. [Pakistan, 1972b: 219]

President Bhutto, certainly no Marxist-Leninist, continued with an argument that class confrontation, once aroused, is not easily contained in one sector: "Now history has moved a stage further and we have, to some extent, dealt with feudalism. Now we have come to new forces dealing with nascent capitalism. When capitalism comes under pressure, you get worked up and you say that class hatred is being created in the country."

The solution to the political dilemma has been sought in a variety of provisions. First, the "feudal" agriculturalist can be offered various carrots and sticks to modernize and establish capitalist relations on the land; indeed, ceilings are often defended in policy logic as a means of forcing feudalists to modernize and intensify production on the smaller postreform area. The "class hatred" feared by the businessmen whom Bhutto was addressing can be tempered by directing the land reform against a type of production relations, not against property per se, and offering attractive incentives for reformed feudalists to accept the transition. Second, those bourgeois who have become "territorialized" can be protected from the attack on landed property through provisions such as exemption from the ceiling of plantations, "well-managed" or mechanized farms, or bonus ceiling concessions for progressive farmers. These provisions compromise and weaken the attack on "feudalism," but the practical means of attacking landed privilege that is "feudal," while preserving "incentives" (and thus privileges) which are presumed to be conducive to entrepreneurial dynamism, are by no means obvious. These strategic concerns contribute one set of constraints on radical land reform; tactical constraints are more proximate and decisive: unless regimes retain power, strategic considerations become irrelevant.

Regime Interests and Land Reform

The primary regime interest is to retain power, to continue governing. Land reforms provide resources of various kinds, both for generating support (or dissipating opposition) in the day-to-day continuance of ruling and for meeting the demands of crisis. Elias Tuma, in studying land reforms across geographical and historical variations, found that the reforms were usually responses to crisis (1965). Hung-Chao Tai concluded from a study of a broad range of contemporary land reforms that the need to create or maintain regime legitimacy was a common motivating force (1974: chap. 4; 469–79). These observations are confirmed by South Asian experience. Although planning documents frequently included land reforms in transformational strategies, regimes have typically not pressed for implementation until a clear crisis developed. The obvious exception is that parties of the left have tried to implement radical reforms whenever they have come to power, either in their own right (Kerala, 1957) or as part of a coalition (Sri Lanka, 1956, 1970; Kerala, 1967). The political resources created by land reform may be real or symbolic.

Symbolic Resources

By "symbolic" I mean simply that the reform stands for, is a symbol of, something which it does not really do. One important mode of interaction between governing elites and governed masses involves the manipulation of symbols (cf. Edelman, 1962; 1977). Mild initiatives, such as tenure reform, can serve symbolic functions, but the potential is limited because the reform is limited, even de jure. The land reforms of contemporary South Asia generate powerful political symbolism, announced as an attack on the traditional rulers of society, an almost awesome class. The great *zamindars* were not merely landlords but held juridical and administrative powers over the peasantry. In attacking such potentates, the government presents a dramatic confrontation, taking the role of defender of the weak and powerless, the exploited and oppressed, against the most powerful class the peasantry experiences.

Both the rhetoric and the process of ceiling reform lend themselves to dramaturgical treatment. The government portrays itself as powerful, though opposed by powerful interests; redistribution is to show the regime's commitment to powerless people at the expense of alienating the powerful. Land reforms are perhaps the most common evidence advanced by government leaders that their regimes are "socialist," or "dedicated to the little man." The 1975 reform of Sri Lanka symbolized an anti-imperialist stance as well. Reforms stand as symbols of commitment and sincerity. Ghulam Mustafa Jatoi, as Bhutto's minister for political affairs, stated publicly: "Many people had cast doubts on our sincerity and insinuated that, as the President is a landowner himself, he would not introduce land reforms."[7] It is precisely because ruling elites come from privileged groups that dramatic illustration of good faith and dedication to the masses is necessary to establish their legitimacy.

Distribution ceremonies highlight the benevolence of the government, further dramatizing its commitment to the dispossessed. Huge crowds are gathered and deeds distributed, accompanied by speeches from important religious functionaries and government leaders. Leaders arrive dramatically, sometimes dropping from the sky via helicopter.

Although these symbolic functions may be important for identifying isolated rural areas with the regime and generating legitimacy for the daily functioning of an existing government, they are particularly crucial when a new regime assumes power after a crisis. Ayub Khan's land reforms directly followed a political crisis and military coup. Zulfikar Ali Bhutto's reforms followed the traumatic civil war and dismemberment of the country. Following a crisis, promulgation of a land reform serves the general symbolic function of assuring all groups in society that the government is capable of acting forcefully and with certainty, that it knows what to do and is capable of doing something both difficult and fundamental. By acting authoritatively, the regime seeks to establish its authority. In Pakistan, governing has required a clear message to landed satraps: this government is not to be ignored or disobeyed.

Specific groups are to be impressed by different aspects of the reform. For journalists and intellectuals, the reforms stand for modernity,

7. Press Conference explaining the land reforms, March 2, 1972. Denzil Pieris reports that Bhutto told a Lahore journalist who asked why he did not push more on land reforms: "The first land reforms made my hair grey. I do not want to go bald" *Mainstream* 16:8 (Oct. 22, 1977): 2. As discussed in chapter 4, Shaikh Rashid also portrayed the land reform as a ferocious battle with feudal forces.

the abolition of grotesque feudal exploitation and backwardness. Groups such as students who mobilize support for populist regimes need to be reassured of the regime's bona fides as a leftist force. For the middle class, reforms are symbols of rural stability, democracy, agricultural growth, and national respectability; for businessmen, modern progressive production relations in agriculture and a commitment to abolishing parasitic and backward relations in the economy.[8] The symbolism in Pakistan even attempted to allay the fears of religious leaders who distrusted Bhutto; the first sentence of the 1972 land reforms reads: "Whereas Islam enjoins equitable distribution of wealth and economic powers and abhors their concentration in a few hands. . . ." The land reform was thus offered as concrete evidence of Bhutto's commitment to "Islamic socialism," a precarious legitimating theme of the regime.

All government policy serves symbolic functions, but a land reform is special because land is itself a symbol of prestige and power in an agrarian society, the symbol of existing patterns of privilege and authority.

Land Reform as a Real Resource in Ordinary Politics

Ordinary political resources are the means by which regimes carry on tactical politics, rewarding supporters, or potential supporters, and punishing opponents or threatening potential opponents. As the relationship between rulers and ruled is overlaid with paternalism, part of this process is the dispensing of boons, favors, and gifts. It is striking how frequently terminology in the land-reform process refers to the concept of "a gift to the masses." When Prime Minister Sirimavo surrendered 1,300 acres to the Land Reform Commission, one SLFP parliamentarian stated that the people should "worship" her for the act, terming it a great "sacrifice" and lauding her "willingness" to surrender the land (CDM, August 3, 1972). The minister of agriculture and lands added that "the whole world should be proud of Mrs. Sirima Bandaranaike for offering 1,300 acres of land to the poor" (CDN, August 12, 1972). What the prime minister had

8. Land reforms in Pakistan received enthusiastic support in the popular press. Selections from editorials presented in *Economic Digest* 2:3–4 (March–April 1959) stressed the value of the reform in abolishing the anachronistic feudal system, ushering in new possibilities for democracy and modernity, political freedom and production. Even the periodical *Zamindar* (Lahore) hailed the reforms for increasing productive potential. Similar press response met Bhutto's reforms. The *Business Recorder* (March 3, 1972) editorialized that the reforms were necessary for democracy, rural progress, the end of feudalism, and the health of the national economy, and would serve as "a spur or a challenge to the remnants of landed aristocracy, who will have to redouble their efforts to maintain their supremacy." Editorials in *Dawn, Pakistan Times, Morning News, Jang, Mashriq,* and *Hurriyet* echoed these opinions. A voice of Indian industry, *Commerce,* editorialized in its review of agriculture for 1973 that land reforms were necessary to rehabilitate the rural poor, "destroy the dominance of an unproductive elite," and "fight 'traditionalistic fatalism'" (*Bulletin of Concerned Asian Scholars* [October–December, 1975], p. 6).

done was simply to comply with the law (and only partially at that, later investigations showed).[9]

The distribution of state lands has always been a patronage resource for relieving landlessness and rewarding supporters. Ceiling-redistributive reforms augment these resources and add an important element. Because of the numerous discretionary provisions in most laws, political enemies can be easily victimized, friends rewarded. Reforms with severe penalties, such as Bhutto's 1972 law (seven years' rigorous imprisonment and confiscation of property) can be powerful tools for rewarding friends and punishing enemies and convincing fence-straddlers to commit themselves. This threat was enhanced by the commonly acknowledged evasion of the law by landowners; there was a skeleton in most large closets.

Few people in Pakistan doubt that the land reforms were used politically, as were all discretionary measures.[10] On April 30, 1974, it was announced in several Urdu-language newspapers and the semiofficial *Pakistan Times* that two Baluchi rebel tribal leaders, held in custody for months prior to the announcement, would be prosecuted for violation of the ceiling law. Each was said to possess more than 4,000 acres. The former governor of Baluchistan, Akbar Bugti, had also allegedly violated the law. The three, one dissident member of the National Assembly and two former governors of the rebellious province, were bitter enemies of Bhutto's regime. They were charged with failing to file land ownership declarations. The penalty was potentially harsh, though the offense was common and no one had up to then been prosecuted. The three had been imprisoned for some time without formal charges, stirring civil libertarian demands that cause be shown for their detainment. When the charges came, they related to a common, and little pursued, violation of the land reform.

Moreover, reform laws frequently contain provision that transfers made with the *intent* of evading the ceiling are illegal; providing mala fides in "intent" is slippery legal ground and allows great scope for discretionary judgment by authorities. The 1972 law in Pakistan made one provision that seems to serve no function other than increasing its utility in ordinary politics. Though it was acknowledged that vast amounts of resumable land were being illegally concealed or transferred, and that

9. Sri Lanka (1980), *Special Presidential Commission of Inquiry.* Mrs. Bandaranaike was found guilty of violating the Land Reform Act; Felix Dias Bandaranaike was found to have sold land to evade the law, but was not held criminally culpable. The commission charged that the Land Reform Commission failed to investigate the land dealings of ministers in order to "play for safety" politically (p. 26).

10. Though difficult to verify rigorously, the belief that land reform is used to reward friends and punish enemies is widely shared. For example, one provincial opposition leader in Pakistan argued against centralization of the land reform apparatus in Rawalpindi, claiming that the "Government wanted to snatch away land given certain people by the Provincial Land Commission and offer it to persons favorably disposed towards it politically" *Business Recorder* (April 12, 1974). The belief alone, even if ill founded, serves political functions.

only local information could reveal the true situation, the reform provisions state: "No court shall take cognizance of an offence under this regulation except on a complaint in writing made by order of, or under authority from, the Commission" (Pakistan, 1972c: IX, 31). The commission consisted of a cabinet minister (the chairman) and two very senior civil servants, appointed by Prime Minister Bhutto. It was this body, rather than local institutions or officers, which decided whether or not a case would be prosecuted and what appeals would be heard.

Boon distribution is probably a more important political resource than the punitive possibilities; few people have been prosecuted under any of the laws discussed, and even fewer penalties assessed. Yet everyone knows that discretionary powers lie with the government and can dramatically affect the fortunes of individuals during the reform. The distribution of boons, on the other hand, gives recipients a concrete stake in the regime and has great symbolic value as well. This partisan use of land reforms appears repeatedly in the case studies in previous chapters.

The Political Arithmetic of Ceilings: Real Resources and Real Costs

If the ceiling is primarily a political, not an economic, tool, it raises a sensitive political question—where should the ceiling be set? The arithmetic ceiling has symbolic importance; loopholes and discretionary implementation determine net redistributive impact and allow differentiation among victims. One could reasonably hypothesize that a delicate political balance is sought: the maximum number of landless must be benefited at the minimum cost in terms of alienating powerful large holders.

There is little doubt that the political minimax strategy plays a crucial role in determining ceilings, though it is obviously seldom discussed publicly. One supporting indication is that the ceilings seldom correspond to any reasonable economic criteria (though it would admittedly be difficult to establish exact criteria with available data and economic theory). Occasionally hard evidence surfaces. Ayub Khan ordered information collected on the family holdings of leading officers in the armed forces in Pakistan and decided on a ceiling only after he was convinced it would not adversely affect the military, on whom his power depended.[11] With similar concern, Mr. Bhutto ordered data collected on distribution of land holdings by size and region before setting the 1977 ceiling.

The 1972 ceiling in Sri Lanka was extensively discussed in terms of political arithmetic. The unpublished draft report of the shadow Land Reform Commission went to great lengths to make such calculations, in

11. Sanderatne and Zaman (1973: 15). I corroborated this account through an interview with an influential landowner who consulted with Ayub Khan about the ceiling (Lahore, January 13, 1975).

the shadow of the controversial ILO team's explicit political calculations in recommending a ceiling-redistributive land reform. The ILO report had suggested a possible range of ratios between ceiling and floor of between 5:1 and 2.5:1, depending on what is "politically practicable," explicitly warning: "Ceilings so high as to lead to explosive political frustration (a reform based on ceilings above 10 typical acres of paddy, or 25 of coconut) would hardly be worth the inevitable administrative and political cost, effort and disruption" (ILO, 1971:94).

On economic grounds, the report concluded that a low ceiling (5–10 acres of paddy, 25 of cocnut) was desirable and would increase productivity and employment. Tea and rubber lands *below* fifty acres could be redistributed as well, as these holdings were economically inefficient. But tea and rubber holdings *above* 50 acres allegedly exhibited economies of scale, higher yields, better management, and greater labor intensity than smaller holdings, and thus should not be subjected to a ceiling (ibid.: 96). The 1972 reform was the obverse of these recommendations.

The shadow Land Reform Commission stated flatly in its unpublished draft report that "there is no case at all for allowing a ceiling larger than an economic holding." An "economic holding" for the commission meant between 1.5 and 3 acres of irrigated paddy and 2–5 acres of fruit, rubber, tea, or coconut lands. The officials admitted, however: "It is unlikely such a low ceiling could be imposed under a democratic government in Ceylon. . . . As a practical compromise, the Government may decide to impose a ceiling as low as 25 acres with a maximum of 5 acres in paddy" (Ceylon, 1971c: 18).

The actual ceiling legislated was 50 acres, of which 25 acres could be paddy. In the light of the ILO team's study and that of the government's own commission, and the stance of the left parties in the United Front, the arithmetic ceiling was extremely surprising. The 25-acre ceiling on paddy is especially hard to understand, as virtually no paddy land was held in such large pieces in the Kandyan and coastal areas, where the pressure for redistribution is greatest. Only 8.7 percent of the nation's paddy land was in holdings larger then 25 acres; moreover, the bulk of this land was located in the dry zone, and much of it unreliable *mana-wari* land (rain-fed) (Ceylon, 1962: vol. 2, table 13).

How, then, did the ceiling come to be so high? A candid view of the political considerations was expressed by a senior minister in Parliament, who asked rhetorically: why was the ceiling set at 50 acres instead of 25 or 10 as urged by the coalition partner LSSP? He answered his own question: "if you set the limit at . . . 100 acres, . . . a small number of persons are affected." If it is set at 50 acres, a larger number; if 25, a larger number still. "If you set it at 10 acres, even a much wider set of people are affected. If you set it at five acres, practically the whole country is affected." (National State Assembly Debates, vol. 1 [1972: August 3]). Actually, the "whole country" would not be affected by a 5-acre ceiling:

only 15.7 percent of all cultivators had holdings larger than 5 acres, and 4.4 percent, larger than 10 acres (Ceylon, 1962: vol. 2, 25). What the minister evidently meant was not that the whole country would be affected, but rather a large percentage of the people who counted politically. As decisively, the minister concluded: "In every electorate you will find 5-acre holders."[12]

Preemptive or Cooptive Resources.

Land reform offers the potential of both symbolic and real resources for meeting the threats of rural unrest. The fear is that rural dissatisfaction will result either in violent confrontation with the regime (as in the 1971 Insurrection in Sri Lanka) or in the mobilization of the disaffected by counterelites (the explicit warning of the Home Ministry's 1969 report on "agrarian tension" in India). Both outcomes constitute threats to the continuance of existing regimes and potentially to the governing class in general. Indira Gandhi argued forcefully the case for land reform averting a rural crisis in her speech to the State chief ministers in 1970: "Land reform is the most crucial test which our political system must meet in order to survive" (Joshi, 1975: 90; India, 1972: appendices 2, 3). Reforms are frequently defended by the promulgating regime, almost as an apology to landed groups, as the only alternative to bloodshed and revolution. That logic has received important international support as the only alternative to Communist mobilization.[13] In this sense, the fears of elites are expressed in a policy logic which is more Maoist than Marxist: we hear promises of land to the tiller but not capital to the worker.

Preemptive and cooptive strategies typically depend heavily on symbolic functions rather than genuine reform; though there is little actual redistribution, limited reforms may also divide the peasant movement by differentiating classes (superior tenants vs. sharecroppers vs. laborers) and demonstrating that mobility within the system is possible by benefiting some peasants. The symbolic commitment to land reform has escalated over time in India, each time citing the threat of violence; but on a national level, the threshold of distributing land, power, and privilege rather than symbols has not yet been reached. In phrases that rever-

12. The truly surprising 25-acre ceiling on paddy land may have resulted from such political calculations or from a less complicated political calculation: a member of the Land Reform Commission told me that the ceiling was 25 acres simply because one minister happened to own 25 acres of paddy (September 20, 1973).

13. A powerful expression is the career and writings of Wolf Ladejinsky who, as consultant to the United States government, the Ford Foundation, and the World Bank, promoted land reform throughout Asia, particularly in Japan and Taiwan. For a flavor of the position, "The Plow Outbids the Sword in Asia: How General MacArthur Stole Communist Thunder in Japan with Democratic Land Reforms, Our Most Potent Weapon for Peace," *Country Gentleman* (now *Farm Journal*), June 1951 pp. 65–68). Ladejinsky ended his influential career in India. Cf. McCoy (1971).

berated in the early 1970s, the Congress Agrarian Reforms Committee warned the new republic in 1949:

> Failure any longer on our part to make the mother earth yield adequate nutrition and clothing for the people and to evolve a system for sharing the fruits of labor among the classes clustering around the agrarian economy will take the country to the verge of a revolution and the revolutionary situation can be met by nothing short of a revolutionary approach to the problem. [AICC, 1949: 80].

The Task Force on Agrarian Relations echoed the fear in 1973 and made similar "revolutionary" proposals, but it was still not clear that the necessary political will or administrative capacity could be mobilized.

In contrast, the United Front government of Sri Lanka enacted and implemented a serious land reform following the traumatic 1971 Insurrection without symbolic prelude or elaborate strategic planning. It seems likely that symbolic resources, though less costly in political terms than real resources, are unlikely to serve cooptive and preemptive functions effectively in the long run but eventually contribute to rural bitterness and cynicism (the product of which may be quiescence rather than mobilization, for reasons explored in chapters 2 and 3).

Statist Imperatives and Political Integration

Land reforms offer resources for connecting large numbers of people to the political system in new ways, consolidating regime and state power. The attack on "feudal" dependency ties creates new needs on the part of former dependents. New links are possible because large numbers of farmers need state services to replace those formerly supplied by landlords—credit, marketing, working capital, and so on. Just as former tenants come into direct contact with state bureaucracies—taxation, finance, agricultural, developmental—they are also more open to direct political links with ruling parties that can serve as brokers vis-à-vis the bureaucracy. Moreover, the power at the center assumes new importance for the peasantry because of the new relevance of public policy—taxation, prices, subsidies, credit—for small proprietors. This political function was a more serious possibility in the abolition of intermediaries in India than in the formal ceiling legislation in India and Pakistan which allowed so little land to be redistributed. The Planning Commission of India estimates that 20 million tenants were brought into "direct contact with the State" during the early reforms (India, 1974: 42).

The Insurrection in Sri Lanka prompted serious infringement on private property in 1972 and experimentation with cooperative farms to relieve rural unemployment. The nationalization of estates in 1975, thought virtually impossible by some observers (Paige, 1975: 54), had multiple causes, as explained in chapter 5, but included a statist imperative to protect and invigorate the export-crop sector, which is the center of the national economy, in the context of extreme international economic vulnerability. Moreover, nationalization put important patronage resources under state control. The otherwise free-market ideology of the UNP regime has not prompted reversal of the nationalization, despite attacks on other public-sector enterprises and cooperative farming.

Partly through real changes, partly through manipulation of symbols, land reforms enable regimes to comply with internationally sanctioned notions of what a modern state should do. One incentive is concrete, as international agencies have material resources to be dispensed to governments which seem progressive and cooperative. The international paradigm has long stressed land reform as necessary for gains in productivity and selectively stresses the consideration of equity. Creating an ambience of self-help and showing a determination to "make the tough political choices" may improve a regime's prospects of international recognition and aid. This imperative has been more evident in Latin America (under the Alliance for Progress) than in South Asia, but planning documents in the region show marked concern for international models and opinion. Ironically, concessional food aid simultaneously reduces two of the pressures for land reform identified in policy logic—production and deprivation-induced discontent—for favored regimes.

More than material consequence is involved. The poverty, misery, backwardness, and exploitation associated with rural areas of South Asia genuinely embarrass and distress political elites. The degradation of rural areas offends their sense of national pride and modernization; in nationalist ideology, these conditions resulted from colonial rule and thus are an embarrassment to independence. There is a special shame in not being able to feed one's population, the shame of, as Prime Minister Sirimavo Bandaranaike put it, traveling the face of the earth with a begging bowl. And even though political leaders may be skeptical of the economic arguments, land reform serves as a symbol of regime commitment and national determination on the economic front, providing political cues to landed classes even when little change takes place.

In conclusion, the interests of ruling elites with regard to land reform are complex and contradictory. The interest in rural stability is at odds with the necessity of rural transformation. The interest in political stability is at odds with the class confrontation inevitable in any fundamental change in the agrarian structure. The need to attack and rationalize parasitic backward modes of appropriation of agricultural surplus is at odds with the adoption and utilization of those modes by various sections of the bourgeoisie or their rural kin or immediate political allies. The need to attack rural power and property relations is at odds with the structural imperative to coax existing propertied classes to invest and produce, and to ignore the official attacks on privilege and inequality. The gap between radical rhetoric and compromised reform programs is thus in part a reflection of the complex and contradictory nature of the objective interests of ruling groups. It is also the result of the imperative that land reform serve the needs of specific regimes that are forced to act with more concern for the immediate imperatives of ordinary politics and regime crises than for the long-term objectives of rational agrarian transformation.

Theories of Land Reform and Politics

What do the variations in the extent of reform in the region tell us about theories of land reform? The conventional-wisdom arguments that "the competitive system is less efficacious than the noncompetitive in bringing about reform" (Hung-Chao Tai, 1974: 469), or that "concentrated power" is necessary for reform (Huntington, 1968: 381–96), are not supported by this study. In the intensely competitive political system of Kerala, landlordism has been attacked, and abolished, in a way practiced only in rhetoric in the rest of the subcontinent. Huntington (388–89) explicitly cites the martial-law regime of Ayub Khan as an example of concentrated authority succeeding in land reforms where parliaments fail; yet competitive politics in Sri Lanka produced a United Front coalition which, goaded by a rural insurrection, seized the land of very powerful individuals and corporations in a way approached only symbolically by the concentrated power of noncompetitive regimes of Pakistan. It is not concentration of power in noncompetitive systems which has redistributed rights in land in South Asia, but the mobilization of rural people, electorally and otherwise, to demand redistribution.

The emphasis on regime type is totally inadequate without an analysis of specific regime interests and the effective balance of class forces represented within or outside parliament. The legislative bodies that proved incapable of land reform prior to Ayub's coup were incapable because they were dominated by the landlord class, not because they were parliamentary in form. Bhutto's significant reductions of Ayub's ceiling in 1972 and 1977 were produced by the imperatives of competitive politics; it was the return of concentrated power and the abolition of democracy through military coup that made the 1977 ceiling a dead letter. As important, emphasis on regime type obscures the critical question of village-level dynamics by which the actual impact of reform is profoundly influenced.

Huntington argued that "a basic incompatibility exists between parliaments and land reform" (1968: 388). The South Asian experience demonstrates specific constraints of parliamentary systems but does not support the implication that political structure primarily determines outcome. Ceylon's experience with the Paddy Lands Act concretely demonstrates how seemingly minor political compromises can have devastating consequences in the reform process. Parliamentary systems also institutionalize the "change of sky"[14] phenomenon: the possibility that the party of privilege will return to power. Chapters 2 and 3 argued that the tenant initiative upon which tenure reform depends is weakened by such expectations; the rational response to a reform by individual tenants is to avoid alienating powerful people, as reformist regimes and initiatives often prove ephemeral. While entirely rational from the individual perspective, quiescence and accommodation in the underclass vitiate the reforms' potential. The "change of sky" phenomenon also conditions the actions of bureaucrats and landowners, weakening the potential impact of the reform and discouraging investment on the land. Parliamentary systems are characteristically unable to act quickly, decisively, and consistently. Ceiling legislation is introduced, landlords begin concealing land, the final legislation is years in coming, compromised by loopholes, and stayed by court orders; over time the surplus land disappears. Yet the same disappearance of surplus appears in a nonparliamentary reform behind which there is little political will or local mobilization.

Parliaments produce compromises and delays that blunt the potential impact of reform, yet the more serious obstacle to restructuring rural South Asia has been dynamics of implementation that deny even the compromised benefits of legislation to the agrarian underclass. Here a second aspect of political structure has been important: autonomous courts and their operative methodology and legal philosophy, in conjunction with the working rules, interests, and social character of the bureaucracy. These structural factors become operative through the mediation of and articulation with local structures of power—the balance of dependence, consciousness, and organization in the villages. Sharecroppers were treated far better by Kerala's Assembly, for example, than by Ayub Khan's martial law (one of Huntington's examples of effective reform), but the innovative Kerala legislation was thwarted at times by the Center, the courts, the dynamics of administration in rural areas, and the local power of the landed—power which varied from field to field, village to village.

Moreover, the competition allowed by parliamentary systems provides the mechanism for the political expression of agrarian inequality. That there is no automatic, effective political expression of the objective interests of the agrarian underclasses is obvious from the case studies; yet the structure may be translated into political forces for change under certain conditions. Competition in a system that is numerically dominated by the very poor and insecure produces a kind of ratchet effect; each new set of rights won by the underclasses is embedded in collective expectations: it is difficult to raise ceilings or rents after years of electoral

14. Tenants and laborers in the Chinese land reforms hesitated to step forward to take the property of landlords, fearing a "change of sky" in which the landlords' power would be reestablished; Hinton (1966: 166 and passim); Belden (1970: 261, 267 and passim).

competition to lower them. Defects in reform laws, perhaps an inevitable consequence of parliamentary compromises, can be remedied both on the ground and through the parliament, provided the forces for change are mobilized and militant. The same defects, incorporated in authoritarian fiat, prove difficult to remedy. This is not to argue that parliamentary systems are optimal for effecting agrarian transformation—the case studies highlight serious obstacles—but that such systems in the region have accomplished more than authoritarian alternatives.

Whether the limits imposed on agrarian transformation by parliamentary systems can be surpassed within those systems remains an open question, and one of great importance. The federal structure of power in India poses a special conundrum. Though the initiative of the Center in forcing land reforms on conservative States is often stressed, Delhi seriously *undermined* the potential for radical reform in Kerala—dismissing the first Communist ministry, rejecting popular committees, preventing nationalization of plantations, requiring special treatment of religious holdings, mandating compensation, delaying approval of measures, and, perhaps most important, requiring that the State government work within constraints set by the courts, existing law, and ordinary administration. The uneven development of political forces in India makes it more likely that radical programs will emerge at the State level rather than at the Center. Because land reforms are a State subject, regional forces for redistribution can be translated into legislation. Yet, ironically, it remains likely that Delhi would hamper or even dismiss any State government which encouraged or facilitated the radical mobilization of the rural poor to overturn the agrarian system as recommended by Central task forces and Planning Commission committees; the federal political structure provides the power to do so. The critical question is the configuration of power and interests which rules at the Center.

One theme of the conventional wisdom stands confirmed: agrarian reforms are taken most seriously and implemented most effectively when landowners and governing elites alike realize that the alternative is rural violence. Both Tai (1974: 280) and Huntington (1968: 394) conclude from their comparative analyses that land reforms are most likely when elites perceive, as landlords in Iran were told, that the alternative to reform is "revolution or death." Imperatives of rural "harmony" and "stability" join the dyad of justice and productivity in justifying reforms and are linked concretely to both through elite perceptions and policy logic.

Land reforms in the region have been framed against a background of peasant militance and violence, often more feared than observed. Interest in land reform not only peaks during periods of rural unrest, but the content of the reform and its implementation are influenced by perceptions of the causes and likely consequences of agrarian "tensions"— the markedly expeditious and effective ceiling reform of Sri Lanka focused on rural unemployment after the 1971 Insurrection, for example.

For fear of violence to become a source of serious reform, however, certain elements of the traditional cognitive paradigm had to go: the agrarian underclass could no longer be viewed as infinitely malleable, cowering, ignorant, and incapable of collective action. Social mythologies die hard, but this one is under special strain because the consequences of inaccuracy are demonstrably severe. Ruling elites in South Asia seem increasingly sensitive to two major contentions of social scientists: share tenancy is among the most unstable and conflictual organizations of production, and extreme inequalities of land ownership threaten rural violence.[15] When the laborers demonstrate more broadly a capacity to organize militantly, they will take the historic place of tenants as a source of official worry about stability and production, and perhaps will consequently be considered more seriously as tillers.

Why are there land reforms in some situations and not others, some genuine and some token? My analysis strongly suggests that reductionist or determinist answers do not take us very far. Agrarian structure is critical, but there is no simple or automatic translation from structure to outcome.[16] Obviously there will be no strong tenant movements in areas where small owner-cultivators dominate the system, but there is no deterministic causality running from high population–land ratios, skewedness of holdings, and percentage of population landless to either agrarian radicalism or land reform. The rack-rented and eviction-prone tenurial system of Malabar spawned tenant agitations and eventual peasant alliance with the Communist Party; similar conditions elsewhere (Bangladesh, Sind) have spawned only widespread misery. Kerala does rank high on the dimensions usually associated with "agrarian radicalism" (Zagoria, 1971), and the agrarian and economic structures are crucial to determining conjunctural possibilities, but the translation of these structural facts into effective reform raises the decisive analytical questions of differential dynamics of mobilization: development of consciousness, leadership, electoral tactics, and ideology.

The case studies illustrate the importance of structure—agrarian and political—but demonstrate that an adequate understanding of land reform depends on analysis of concrete historical conditions: Sri Lanka's insurrection in 1971; the simple fact that Gunawardena became minister of agriculture, not finance; the dismissal of the first communist ministry in Kerala by the Center after long vacillation. Structure affects outcomes only through specific processes and dynamics, including the perception

15. For an insightful discussion of the political instability of share-tenancy systems, Stinchcombe (1961). An elaboration and formalization with case studies and (problematic) comparative data is Paige (1975). Also, Russett (1964); Tanter and Midlarsky (1967).

16. Paige, in *Agrarian Revolution* (1975), approaches a totally deterministic view of the effect of agrarian structure on political outcomes; an equally hard determinism, treating land reform more narrowly, is Gutelman, *Sturctures et réformes agraires: Instruments pour l'analyse* (1974).

of structure and its dynamics by those with political power. To analyze either in isolation, or to expect ahistorical grand theory, is to court disappointment and misunderstanding.

In preference to the emphasis of Huntington and Tai on regime type, I return to the simple conclusion of Doreen Warriner: the balance of political power determines the extent of reform (1962: 3). This balance requires specification in terms of local power configurations (which vary significantly with demography, tenure system, caste composition, political organization, etc.), national power configurations (the class composition of the regime and the interests and ideology of ruling groups) and the social composition, relative power and interests of the state apparatus: the courts, bureaucracies, and police. The balance of political power then enters the analysis at various levels: the content of reform measures, the dynamics of implementation, cybernetic responsiveness to implementation failures. A critical mediating variable is the conjunctural factor of specific imperatives of retaining power faced by regimes in specific historical situations (the Insurrection in Sri Lanka, Ayub Khan's effort to establish centralized authority and agricultural dynamism, Indira Gandhi's bid for a populist support base, and so on). These regime-specific and historically unique pressures become operative through the policy logic of ruling groups—their views of the rural world and its dynamics, notions of economic causation, and theories of practical politics. Concentration of political power per se is less important than the class interests, regime needs, and world-views of those groups or individuals who hold power, in interaction with the historical conditions under which they rule, just as competition per se is less important than the balance of political forces competing—their degree of consciousness, mobilization, economic strength, and tactics—in conjunction with specific historical circumstances that offer unique opportunities and constraints.[17]

17. For a comparative analysis which seeks to integrate the effects of agrarian structure, political structure, unique historical conjunctures, and broader political dynamics in explaining differential land-reform outcomes in two States of India, Hart and Herring (1977).

9 The Economic Logic of Land Reform

Holdings are either too large or too small. The small holder can barely live, and the large barely work.
—*Sir Malcolm Lyall Darling (1928)*

In the views of the rural world that have dominated planning documents and political manifestos supporting land reform, economic arguments figure prominently. The divergence between the economic analysis and the policy response, as emphasized in previous chapters, tells us a great deal about the effective political power distribution and the operative (as opposed to professed) political values of the regime. The purpose of this chapter is to examine the economic arguments themselves, and their empirical base. There are considerable discrepancies, inconsistencies, and leaps of faith; the economic logic embedded in policy models is as ideological as scientific.

Without any evidence at all or with conflicting, ambiguous evidence or even in the face of flatly contradictory evidence, political and administrative elites have taken stands on the economics of land reform consistent with their ideological positions. The political right inevitably argues that land reforms will destroy agriculture; the left consistently argues that land reforms are necessary to "unleash the productive forces in society." The reformist center worries about incentives and moderation but argues that changes are essential for the rationalization of agriculture.[1] The congruence between the economic logic and the conceptualization of social justice is striking: the right argues that the inequalities which constitute privilege are essential to provide incentives and dynamism, and, partly in consequence, are socially just; the left sees the same inequalities as sources of disincentive for the disadvantaged and irratio-

---

1. It should be emphasized that "left" and "right" have meaning only in a concrete historical situation, just as the same body of ideas may be in one period "utopian" and in another "ideological" (in Mannheim's (1936) formulation). I have already discussed the potential use of land reforms by the bourgeoisie when it is the political left in the attack on "feudalism."

nalities in the organization of production and utilization of the economic surplus.

Farm Size and Productivity: The Prevailing Paradigm

The critique of large holdings in the economic logic of land reform combines two strands. First, the social organization of production on the large estates has typically been landlord–tenant, largely for historical and technological reasons. Thus, all the critiques of the bad landlord—parasitism, backwardness, oppression—and the associated critiques of share tenancy condemn the large holdings. Second, the large holdings are condemned on more narrowly technical economic grounds: small farms tend to be organized in ways that are economically preferable. The case would appear to be quite simple: empirically, studies from all over the world show that yields (output per acre) are higher on small farms than on large.[2] Gross output per acre seems to be a decreasing function of farm size; every acre redistributed from large farms to small should increase aggregate production. The Congress Agrarian Reforms Committee (1949), for example, cited just such evidence to justify a very low ceiling and extensive land redistribution.

This argument received substantial support in the early 1960s in India from the *Studies in the Economics of Farm Management* conducted in various states for the ministry of agriculture.[3] The data indicated, in virtually every case, that gross output per acre was higher on small farms than on large, suggesting strongly that in a land-scarce economy small farms were to be preferred on the grounds of efficiency in order to maximize returns to the scarce factor.

The seemingly overwhelming evidence that small farms were more productive than large farms added respectability to the ceiling model as a development tool but simultaneously weakened the cooperative farming model that had been important in the 1950s in India. The cooperative model had assumed that smallholders could be optimally productive only through aggregation of holdings in cooperatives to achieve economies of scale in production.[4]

The conclusions of the farm-management studies were not universally accepted, however; the issue has stirred persistent controversy among Indian agricultural economists. Over the years, challenges to the domi-

2. An exposition of the dominant paradigm is Dorner (1972: esp. 119 ff.); also, Dorner and Kanel (1971); Berry and Cline (1979); UNFAO (1979: 36 and passim); in more popular treatments, Lappé and Collins (1977); Eckholm (1979).

3. India (1966a). The proceedings of landmark conference of the Indian Society of Agricultural Economists were published as "Input-Output Relations in Indian Agriculture," *Indian Journal of Agricultural Economics* 13, no. 1 (January–March 1958).

4. An important statement of this paradigm, which received official support but little political expression, was the *Report of the Indian Delegation to China on Agrarian Co-operatives* (India, 1957); (cf. AICC (1949).

nant model appeared (e.g., Rao, 1967, 1968). Ashok Rudra, for example, supported the skeptical case with two articles challenging the statistical methodology of the earlier studies. Rudra argued that linear regression analysis was a Procrustean bed for the data; using nonparametric tests, he concluded that there was no statistically significant relationship between size and yield (1968a). In a second article, Rudra argued forcefully that there is no reason to believe that the same relationship between size and yields should hold across the extremely diverse agronomic regions of India (1968b). Using rank-order correlations, he found that the correlations were primarily negative, as the dominant logic would predict, but statistically significant in only a few cases.

Rudra concluded that for most districts for which farm-management data existed, there was indeed an inverse relationship between size and yield, but that the case was very weak statistically. Moreover, in some districts, the *obverse* relationship held strongly and significantly. Rudra did not make much of a point which seems important: this obverse relationship appeared in the farm-management districts of the Punjab— Amritsar and Ferozepur—where per-acre output increased with size of farm. As the Punjab is the most technologically advanced agronomic area, these results could have serious implications for the prevailing paradigm.

Though there has been a great deal of controversy, professional economists in India have generally concluded that yields were typically, though perhaps weakly, inversely proportional to size of holding, but with important qualifications. Utilizing similar data from farm-management studies in Pakistan for the mid-1960s, Herring and Chaudhry concluded that gross income per acre declined sharply as size of holding increased but were skeptical of the quality of the data. Computations from better data from a small pilot project again showed smaller farms to be more productive, but the differences among size groups were small. The pilot project was located in an area of heavily capitalized farms characterized by modern production technologies and relations (1974: 263–64).

Reviewing the best available data for Sri Lanka, Hiran Dias (1973) concluded that the relationship between size of (paddy) holding and productivity was not systematic. Although Dias noted some tendency for small farms to have higher yields, he argued that the data will not permit a conclusion that size of holding is the critical variable. Detailed micro-level studies support these conclusions (ARTI, 1975: Part 6, 23), as does a broader survey of studies by Gerald Peiris (1975).

The presentation of a representative range of studies from South Asia illustrates that the international paradigm claiming that yields are inversely proportional to farm size is only ambiguously supported in recent South Asian studies, and that the *reasons* for the relationships are by no means clear. The most serious nagging doubt has been that the high productivity on small farms may be an artifact of land quality: there are good reasons to believe that, over time, the best land attracts and sustains the largest population, resulting in small holdings, whereas in marginal areas large holdings are necessary and common.[5]

The dominant explanation for higher yields on smaller farms has been the greater intensity of cultivation on small farms, reflected in higher labor inputs per unit of land. Herring and Chaudhry (1974: 260–61) found that this is unambigiously the case for Pakistan, where cropping intensities (the ratio of cropped area to cultivated area), land-use intensity (the ration of cultivated to owned area), and labor inputs per acre are consistently inversely proportional to size of holding. It is critical to note that this greater intensity of labor inputs would produce higher yields on small holdings even if there were no differences in land quality by size of holding, *given traditional technology*. This last point is extremely important, as will become evident.

The same relationships seem to hold generally for India. G. R. Saini (1969) attributed the higher yields on small farms to intensive labor inputs and made a crucial conceptual clarification. In his analysis, physical land area was considered an inadequate measure of scale in the economic sense. Thus, the observed differences in yields did not indicate economies or diseconomies of scale, but rather differences in the proportions of various factors used in the production process. The higher return to the land factor on small farms was then simply the result of combining each unit of land with more labor (and other divisible inputs) than on larger farms.

The dominant economic explanation for this factor mix is that small farmers maximize returns to their relatively scarce factor of production (land) by intensifying inputs of their relatively abundant factors (labor and managerial time). The small peasant farm has unique economic characteristics which differentiate it from the large peasant farm or capitalist

5. The simple answer would seem to be: control for land quality statistically to see if yield differences disappear. The problem is that there is *no independent measure* of land quality; yields obviously will not do. Proxies have been tried—irrigation, land revenue, market price—but all have serious problems. A systematic attempt is A. M. Khusro (1973), where the land-revenue tax is used to deflate yields on small farms, producing no consistent size effect on yields. But the revenue ratings are archaic, haphazard, corruptible, not comparable, and too gross to reflect important differences. For a critique, S. C. Jha (1971: 22). Moreover, the static argument ignores the dynamics of land quality: small farmers, through labor-intensive means and careful management, presumably over time systematically improve the quality of their holdings in ways that large holders do not (in traditional systems, before the advent of mechanical land-leveling and tubewells). For the plausibility of the argument that historical forces concentrate the best land in small holdings, see Malcolm Darling (1932), especially chapters 2–8. My own conclusion, drawn from studies by agricultural economists, historical accounts, and anthropological sources, is that land in smaller holdings is indeed superior, but (a) it is so partly because of the labor invested in it by small farmers and (b) land quality will not explain all of the variance in yield, since the traditional greater labor intensity on small farms is well established. Modernization of agriculture produces new dynamics. Cf. Sanyal (1969); Raini (1971).

farm, as A. V. Chayanov (1966) systematically argued. Empirically, the small peasant continues to add labor to the production process even if the marginal return to a unit of labor is very low. In contrast, a farmer hiring labor will presumably conform to neoclassical rationality: at the point at which marginal returns from a unit of labor equal the marginal cost of that unit, the farmer will apply no more labor, as each additional unit would cost more than its return.

The small peasant farmer does not confront the same economic calculus. The costs of family labor are to a large extent fixed; the family (and bullocks) must be maintained whether they contribute five, ten, or zero hours of labor per day. Alternative economic opportunities, particularly for children and women, are typically limited, and thus family labor has little, if any, opportunity cost. Since any increment to family income is important, the small farmer employs labor-intensive techniques, even if the return to additional labor hours is very low. Because of this labor market dualism, the same intensification would prove economically irrational for a farmer who had to hire labor at the market rate for the same purpose (cf. Banaji, 1976a). On large farms, a much higher percentage of total labor is hired. Intensification on small holdings may be manifest in such yield-increasing techniques as meticulous seed bed and ground preparation, weeding, care of the field channels, and pest prevention. More significantly, intensity of land use may be increased by multiple cropping, taking catch crops, intercultivation, and so on, wherever agronomically feasible (cf. Sanyal, 1969; Raini, 1971).

The dominant policy logic finds problems at both ends of the size spectrum: not only are large farms managed in socially irrational ways, providing less employment and produce per acre than small farms, but the smallest farms are *too* small to be efficient. There would also be aggregate gains in efficiency by upgrading the smallest farms by redistributing land. Thus the logic implies a floor as well as a ceiling. A. M. Khusro (1973) has argued that this floor in India was five acres at the time of his study; below five acres, yields per acre were lower because small farms suffer various disabilities, the most serious of which is inability to generate sufficient income to allow investment in fixed and working capital.

Similar conclusions follow from Don Kanel's (1967) analysis of Indian farm-management data and the recent fieldwork of John Harriss (1979). The problem of extremely small farms, in this view, is that the farmer's labor and indivisible capital inputs are combined with so little land that inefficiencies result. A classic example is the bullock team, the largest capital expense of a small farmer other than land. When used on a farm of between ten and fifteen acres (or more or less, depending on the agronomic situation), the fixed costs of buying, maintaining, and depreciating bullocks are spread over a large output, reducing the per-unit cost of draft power. A farmer with much less land, but facing the same fixed and variable costs of bullocks, will obviously have a higher per-unit cost of production, as the costs are spread over fewer units of output.[6] Likewise, data from the farm-management studies in Kerala show that interest on fixed capital, upkeep of farm buildings, and upkeep of implements per unit of land all tended to be higher on small farms, though gross yields were no higher. As a consequence, return to invested capital per hectare was directly proportional to farm size, and extremely low on the smallest farms, indeed negative in 1962–63. If an imputed value was given to land rent and family labor, returns on holdings below five acres were generally negative.[7]

The paradigmatic response has been to the define floors as well as ceilings on holdings—the various notions of an "economic holding," a "family holding," a "basic holding." To eliminate diseconomies of small scale, the minimum size farm should provide full employment for a bullock team and family, as well as a decent standard of living (cf. Khusro, 1973: 42).

A summary of the issues to this point seems appropriate here. Early analysis of the farm-management data in India concluded that small farms were more productive than large, suggesting that a ceiling reform would lead to more efficient use of scarce land resources. Though the relationship does seem to hold generally, there are important counterexamples, and the relationship is not universally strong or statistically significant. Moreover, there are changes over time (Bhattacharya and Saini, 1972: A63).

The dominant explanation for the phenomenon has been that smaller holdings are farmed more intensively, with more labor inputs per acre. This phenomenon is clearly established, the occasional exception being those tiny plots which offer no real opportunity for economic viability as a farm enterprise. These characteristics of small farms seemed to make a solid case for a fairly low ceiling: each acre redistributed would result in greater output, and also in greater employment. Evidently the critical problems of unemployment, inadequate production, and rural poverty could be addressed through a ceiling reform.

Unfortunately the situation is more complex. The criterion for efficiency in this argument is output per unit of land; because land is critically scarce and labor abundant, returns to labor are considered largely irrelevant (cf. Dorner, 1972: 101–02). But in traditional agrarian economies a great deal of agricultural capital is simply and directly the accumulated physical labor of men and women. Though from the individual's private point of view the opportunity costs of labor may be negligible, from a social perspective the costs are quite high.

6. Bullock rental markets would be the expected response, but small farmers resist being dependent on others for anything so crucial as draft power when any delay may threaten the crop.

7. India (1971/72), *Studies in the Economics of Farm Management in Kerala*, 1962–63 (published 1971: 193, 168); 1963–64 (1971: 138, 110); 1964–65 (1972: 145–147, 120).

The most common economic notion of efficiency is maximization of output per unit of inputs. Seemingly this criterion would be easy to operationalize: what size farm produces the most at the least cost? But the choice of accounting procedures depends on a prior decision about developmental priorities: what counts as a cost?

For example, the Indian Farm Management Studies employ four distinct measures of cost. Cost A_1 measures only paid-out costs actually incurred by the farmer. Imputed costs are added for costs A_2 and B, and cost C includes an imputed value for land and labor, based on presumed opportunity costs. Each of these measures has problems. The most comprehensive cost (C) is objectionable because family labor is imputed a wage at the market level, although for the farmer the market-wage rate is largely irrelevant since the real cost of family labor is typically negligible. Thus, the small farmer is made to look artificially inefficient by inflating his costs through imputation of the market wage to family labor. The alternative, using only costs incurred via transfer of resources, is open to serious objection because large farmers pay for such inputs as labor and manure which the small farmers use but do not buy in the market; the large farmer then appears to be less efficient simply because more of his costs are counted.

When cost C is used, imputing the market wage to family labor, a very large percentage of the farms in India show a negative farm business income (cf. Khusro, 1973: 108–09 ff.). Economists react by arguing that cost C obviously is not appropriate since, by microeconomic logic, the farms would cease to produce if business income were really negative. But the more important conclusion is seldom drawn. If small-farm families cannot pay themselves the market rate for labor and make a profit, or break even, it would seem that creation of more tiny holdings aggravates the "self-exploitation" of the poor peasantry. In an agrarian society dominated by tiny farms, most families are forced to combine their labor with so little capital (primarily land) that returns to labor are minimal. From a social point of view, this is serious underutilization of labor resources; from a private point of view, it means poverty.

One major conceptual problem in the prevailing paradigm is thus that the notion of efficiency implied—maximizing gross production per unit of land—is by no means unexceptionable; the simple fact that an economy is short of land does not mean that returns to land must be maximized at the expense of returns to labor. Indeed, the shortage and poor quality of the agricultural capital stock is in part a consequence of inadequate mobilization of labor.

A second conceptual problem in the prevailing paradigm is that physical land area and scale of production are used interchangeably. But there is no reason to expect the economic characterisitcs of a five-acre rain-fed plot growing one crop per year with traditional technology to be the same as those of a five-acre irrigated vegetable farm near an urban

market. The size of the two farms is the same, but the scale of production, by any measure, is quite different. As Lenin argued, as modern techniques and production relations become established in agriculture, more
differentiation among farms of the same size group is possible (1938: vol.
12, 280–82, 235–41, passim). Land is only one factor of production; as
other capital becomes more important, the size of physical land area becomes relatively less determinate. Unfortunately, in surveys of farm economics in South Asia, as in the dominant international paradigm, size,
not scale, is the organizing category. It therefore seems quite likely that
the confusing and contradictory evidence on the relationship between
economic characteristics and farm size is partly due to a failure to analyze farms according to scale.

An important attempt to remedy this problem is the work of Utsa
Patnaik (1972). Drawing on data collected from throughout India on sixty-
six large farms, Patnaik found that analysis in terms of scale (measured
by gross value of production) rather than size alone, made a great deal of
difference. Although output per acre was in general inversely proportional to size of holding, it was *directly* proportional to scale of operation.
By any measure of efficiency, the large-scale farms studied were more
efficient than small-scale farms. Most significantly, though gross value of
output per rupee of total cost showed no consistent relationship to size
of holding, this measure of efficiency was directly proportional to scale
of operation; the larger the farm's scale, the greater the output per rupee
of cost incurred. Farm business income per acre declined as size of farm
increased, but increased with scale. Investible surplus per acre showed
no trend when farms were grouped by size, but increased sharply with
increases in scale. Other studies find that when heavy working capital
expenses characterize production, large farmers obtain higher yields than
capital-starved smallholders (Singh, 1972; Harris, 1979).

The thrust of Patnaik's work is to reinforce doubts about what Lenin
termed the "erroneous notion of the 'superiority' of small-scale agriculture." Large-scale production (under capitalist auspices in Patnaik's data)
seems to be characterized by increased output per unit of land *and* per
unit of labor, as well as by reduction of per-unit cost of production and
an increase in investible surplus per worker and per acre. The data are by
no means conclusive but suggest that glorification of the existing characteristics of small-scale agriculture may be a disservice both to small
farmers and to agriculture. The traditional paradigm applies fairly well
to traditional systems, where land and labor are the dominant inputs and
technology constant. But where modern production relations have taken
hold, we should expect to find the efficiency advantages of large size to
appear—lower unit costs for indivisible investments, larger on-farm surplus, access to advantageous credit and marketing terms, and so on—as
suggested by the Punjab exceptionalism in the Farm Management data
and later findings that the small-farm yield advantage has weakened over

time, presumably because of technological changes of the "green revolution" (Berry and Cline, 1979: 108–09, 114; ICSSR, 1980: 14, 46).

This phenomenon appears to hold in Pakistan as well. Studies by M. H. Khan (1975, 1977) have found that the traditional yield advantage of small farmers identified by Herring and Chaudhry (1974) does hold when all crops are considered, but does not hold in the agronomically most progressive regions nor for those crops which have been the major beneficiaries of the "green revolution"—wheat and rice. The data in table 9.1 reinforce Khan's arguments, as well as the more recent findings in India. The data represent almost a decade of technical change and further commercialization of agriculture since the farm-management studies used by Herring and Chaudhry; the output differences across farm-size categories are not so great, and for some crops the traditional direction is reversed. There is little difference by size of holding in wheat yields, whereas large farms exhibit higher yields of rice and cotton (a commercial crop). The small-farm-yield advantage still appears in maize (largely a subsistence crop), sugarcane, and tobacco (in which yields are extremely sensitive to careful cultural practices).

The yield advantage of small farms seems to be most marked when intensity of labor use explains a relatively large percentage of the variance in yields and when small farms exhibit more classically "peasantist" economic characteristics. Technical change which puts a premium on access to financial resources, risk-taking ability, and extension information weakens or reverses that advantage; scale neutrality of inputs in the narrow technical sense is often contradicted by the social reality of superior ability of larger farmers to adopt technical changes effectively. Moreover, the supporting infrastructure of technical change (tubewells and pumping sets, for example) is not always scale-neutral. Small farmers may be able to compete, primarily through intensification of labor, but with important economic costs both individually and socially, as a more detailed analysis of the situation in Kerala illustrates.

Table 9.1: Yields by Size of Holding in Pakistan, 1972

Farm Size (Acres)	Yields (Maunds Per Acre)					
	Wheat	Rice	Cotton	Sugarcane	Tobacco	Maize
Less than 5	13.74	12.57	8.47	341.31	27.00	14.32
5–15	13.00	10.94	8.56	305.19	21.61	10.87
15–25	12.84	11.49	9.11	302.51	33.23	10.77
25–50	11.98	12.62	8.83	300.40	18.67	9.04
Greater than 50	12.98	15.03	10.37	304.11	12.03	10.42
All farms	12.83	12.02	9.15	307.42	23.60	11.44

SOURCE: Calculations from unpublished data collected by the Agricultural Census Organization, Lahore, for 57,000 farm families. One maund equals approximately 82.3 lbs.

Farm Size and Productivity in Kerala

Kerala represents the agrarian crisis in extremis, but demographic pressures throughout the subcontinent are generating comparable situations.
The farm-management survey covered holdings in Alleppey and Quilon
districts for the three crop years 1962–63, 1963–64, and 1964–65 (India,
1971/72). Table 9.2 illustrates the pattern of inputs and outputs in rupee
value for all crops. The value of inputs per hectare, measured by the comprehensive cost C, decreases as size of holding increases. Output per hectare shows no tendency to vary with size of holding when the three years
are averaged together, except that yields on the largest farms were markedly lower than on smaller farms.

The input-output ratios suggest that for farms less than five acres
(more than 92 percent of all holdings), and especially for farms of less
than one acre (two-thirds of all holdings), returns from cultivation did
not cover costs when costs included imputed values for land and labor.
For landowners this situation does not necessarily mean severe self-
exploitation, as the full return to land (imputed rent) accrued to the owner,
though the return to labor was below the market rate. But for tenants the
exploitation seems clear, since the rent accrued to a landlord, not to the
cultivator, leaving only the pitiful return to labor. On holdings below five
acres, family labor income per working day did not exceed a small fraction of the wage rate paid to hired labor. For holdings of less than one
acre, the return to labor on the farm was only Rs 0.23 in 1964–65, about
one-tenth the market wage. Between five and ten acres, the figure was
Rs 2.16, and for holdings larger than 25 acres, Rs 14.10. These differences
of course reflect the differing amounts of capital (primarily land) with
which labor is combined on different size holdings.

To address one of the nagging problems in the ceiling-redistributive
economic logic, we need to know if there are systematic differences in
land quality by size of farm. Though farm-management data provide no

Table 9.2: Input-Output Ratios in Kerala Agriculture

Farm Size (Acres)	Total Inputs (Rs/Hectare)	Total Output (Rs/Hectare)	Input-Output Ratio
0–1	1,286	1,018	1.26
1–2.5	1,245	1,078	1.15
2.5–5	1,100	977	1.16
5–10	1,057	1,095	0.97
10–15	1,057	1,070	0.99
15–25	971	1,078	0.90
25 and above	754	767	0.98

Figures represent a three-year average. Input value is Cost C.
Source: *Studies in the Economics of Farm Management in Kerala* for 1962–63, 1963–64,
1964–75.

measure of land quality independent of yields (which obviously will not do), land and rental prices are estimated. Land prices reflect more than the inherent productive capacity of the land, as there are scarcity and security effects as well. But land and rental prices may be taken as a better proxy for inherent land quality than the revenue rates used in some studies. Table 9.3 presents land and rental values by size of holding, averaged over the three-year period.

Obviously, if the land values reported reflect inherent land quality even approximately, the yield data would have to be modified considerably, as the best land appears to be in the smallest holdings. The result is a direct linear relationship between standardized size of holding and gross output, the obverse of the conclusions of the dominant paradigm. The results seem too dubious to report in detail, because it is uncertain to what extent undervaluation of assets was systematically related to holding size; larger holders would arguably be somewhat more likely to undervalue their land. Land values also fluctuate with the prices of the crops for which they are suited and the cropping mix may vary systematically by size of holding. It would thus be unwise to inflate yields mechanically to compensate for land quality. Similar caveats apply to rent. But, again, if the yield data were "corrected" for land quality with rental value employed as a proxy for that variable, the result would contradict the general assumption of the ceiling-redistributive model; output per standard acre would increase with holding size.

A more meaningful comparison of yields among size groups can be made when all producers are growing the same crop. Table 9.4 presents data for production of paddy, the major crop in both districts surveyed. Unfortunately, there are no separate data on paddy rents or land values.

The data in table 9.4 present an interesting variation on the dominant theme. Grain yields show no consistent trend by size of holding, but value of total paddy production per acre declines as size of holding

Table 9.3: Land and Rental Values by Size of Holding in Kerala

Holding Size (Acres)	Average Rental Value (Rs/Hectare)	Index	Average Value of Land (Rs/Hectare)	Index
0–1	446	1.00	10,446	1.00
1–2.5	450	1.01	10,018	.96
2.5–5	413	.93	9,014	.86
5–10	377	.85	9,029	.86
10–15	356	.80	8,173	.78
15–25	339	.76	7,195	.69
25 and above	290	.65	3,695	.35

SOURCE: *Studies in the Economics of Farm Management in Kerala*. Calculated as an average for the years 1962–63, 1963–64, 1964–65.

Table 9.4: Paddy Production and Costs by Size of Holding in Kerala

Holding Size (Acres)	Grain Yield (Quintals/Hectare)	Total Value (Rs/Hectare)	Value of Straw (Rs/Hectare)	Cost (Rs/Quintal)	Index of Labor Input per Unit of Land
0–1	17.26	1340	271	85.51	1.00
1–2.5	21.37	1326	166	57.56	.97
1.5–5	19.70	1250	159	60.92	.79
5–10	20.14	1220	122	50.69	.69
10–15	22.81	1201	116	45.48	.71
15–25	23.84	1184	99	39.87	.64
25 and above	17.60	843	49	46.32	.48

Three-year average for 1962–63, 63–64, and 64–65. Cost includes imputed values for owned land and labor. Figures were rounded in calculation. Index of labor inputs was constructed to render data from different years comparable.
SOURCE: *Studies in the Economics of Farm Management in Kerala.*

increases. The difference is in the value of straw produced; smallholders collect every spare bit of straw and sell or utilize the product; larger owners leave more straw in the fields or on the threshing floor, considering the labor of collecting it more costly than the return. The smallest holdings and the largest holdings stand out distinctly in terms of low grain yields.

The cost of producing a bushel of paddy declines as holding size increases, though the very largest holdings are not as efficient by this measure as are other large holdings. The high cost of production on small farms is a function of heavy labor costs; labor input per acre is inversely proportional to holding size. Even for full-time agriculturalists, the number of days worked on the farm was quite small. An adult in the 1964–65 farm management survey worked an average of 157.2 standard (eight-hour) days; only 63 of these days were on the farm. For the smallest farmers, only 23.8 days were on the farm; the remaining days were worked primarily as hired labor (India, 1971/72: 130–31).

When all inputs are valued at market rates, the small farms of Kerala are thus not the most efficient but rather the least efficient, especially when we consider that the best land seems to be in the smaller holdings. Paddy production on tiny holdings in Kerala does "absorb" more labor, or "generate employment," but this is simply another way of saying that production of each bushel of paddy on tiny farms requires more labor. Moreover, the return to small farmers for that labor is abysmally low, far below the pitiful market wage. The farm-management surveys indicate that smallholders operate on a very thin margin, with little chance to accumulate capital. Moreover, when holdings are extremely small, the farm family searches for alternative employment, often neglecting the fields at critical times. The low productivity of labor on technologically constrained dwarf farms must be a serious concern in planning for development, not a cause for celebration of the superiority of smallholdings.

There is, however, an efficiency argument which should receive more attention, given present constraints on development in poor nations. Small farms are relatively efficient if one adopts a criterion such as return per unit of foreign exchange expended. It is the large farm that typically exhibits methods of production which contain some element of foreign-exchange expenditure—chemical fertilizers, pesticides, herbicides, mechanized equipment. Small farmers in Kerala, largely from necessity, have employed more traditional techniques and inputs, substituting labor for cash outlays—hand weeding, manuring, and so on. (Kerala, 1973b: 251).

In the Kerala context, what would a ceiling-redistributive reform accomplish in economic terms? There would evidently be no net increase in value of production per acre no matter where the ceiling was set. If only paddy lands were affected, there would be some increase in total value of production per acre wherever the ceiling was set, though no significant increase in grain production if the ceiling were below 25 acres. More labor hours would be absorbed per unit of land and each bushel of paddy would require more labor hours for its production. The increase in labor hours of employment would not, however, have unambiguously positive net social consequences. For families who received land via redistribution, family labor opportunities, security of employment, and income would be increased, but at the expense of other families of laborers who had previously worked on the larger holdings at the market wage rate (cf. Berry, 1971).

The Kerala farm-management surveys thus reinforce doubts about the economic logic of the ceiling-redistributive model. The smallest farmers in Kerala, and in South Asia generally, struggle against tremendous odds to patch together a livelihood; their seeming superiority is a reflection of labor intensification with meager returns. Their unit costs of production are high because of the paucity of capital, primarily land, they control and their well-known disabilities vis-à-vis sources of working capital. Their capacity to save and invest is minimal. Do these points buttress the argument that land should not be distributed, since distribution of plots of an "economic" size to all claimants is demonstrably impossible? The answer is no, but these considerations do alter the prescriptive logic of land reform.

The Economic Evils of Share Tenancy

The various arguments against share tenancy on economic grounds have a long history, dating at least to Adam Smith.[8] One category of objections relates to how the microeconomic situation—cost of and returns to working capital and labor—of a share tenant as manager of a farm enterprise differs from the situation of an owner-cultivator (or fixed-lease tenant). Briefly, it is argued that the share tenant does not have the economic *incentive* to apply sufficient working capital and labor to achieve maximum output, or to make permanent improvements on the land. If the tenant bears the full cost of investments but receives only half of the increment to output, he will rationally resist heavy expenditures on working capital (whether in cash, kind, or labor power) and long-term capital formation. The result is lower output per unit of land (yields) compared to owner-operated farms and technological stagnation. The

---

8. For representative modern treatments, Schultz (1940); Heady (1947); Ruttan (1966); Bardhan and Srinivasan (1971). The dominant policy logic on the inefficiencies of share tenancy has been attacked from within the neoclassical tradition by Cheung (1966; 1969); Reid (1976). A sophisticated treatment of differences between the "Marshallian" and revisionist neoclassical approaches is Bell (1977). Despite disputes among economic theorists, the dominant critique of share tenancy on economic grounds remains ensconced in policy logic; e.g., World Bank (1974: 16 and passim). For influential presentations of the dominant critique in the South Asian context, Thorner (1956); Myrdal (1968: vol. 2, pt. 5, chap. 22). The text draws heavily on Herring (1978). See also chapter 2.

second objection is that whatever the disincentives in sharecropping, the usual economic situation of the share tenant is such that there is little *capacity* to invest. Failure to distinguish between these issues has led to confusion in the empirical question of the economic efficiency of share tenancy.

If landlords and tenants share costs in the same proportion as output is shared, no disincentive arises as far as purchased inputs are concerned. But labor is a major input in peasant agriculture, often half the variable costs. Moreover, labor is crucial to such yield-increasing techniques as transplanting rice, weeding, field channel upkeep, and so on. The tenant receives only half of the marginal return from his own labor and thus should apply less labor, ceteris paribus, than an owner who received the full return from his labor.

The ill effects of share tenancy in the policy logic extend beyond the input mix of each production season. An insecure tenant has little incentive to invest in land improvement, soil conservation, or biological capital such as timber or fruit trees. If his tenure is terminated, the benefits of these large investments would not accrue to him.[9] These disincentives extend to technological change as well. If the rate of return on any output-augmenting investment is halved by the landlord's share, any new investment must be twice as profitable to be adopted by a rational tenant compared to a rational owner-cultivator.[10]

Besides the theoretical disincentives to maximum productivity and technical change imposed by the microeconomic situation of the sharecropper, there is his or her poverty. Subsistence agriculture can be transformed only if sufficient capital is put into the production process to raise yields per worker and per acre. Low yields and the heavy burden of family consumption that results from a high worker–land ratio leave little surplus. Share tenancy aggravates the situation by depriving cultivators of a large share of the gross produce, leaving so little that even meager requirements such as seed for the next crop often must be borrowed; there is little opportunity for technological change, expensive new inputs, or permanent capital works on the land. Thus, the poverty of the cultivator is itself a drag on production, and the extraction of ground rent aggravates the poverty of the tenant class.

If the tenant lacks both incentive and capability for productive in-

9. If there is some security of tenure, but for an uncertain period, the tenant must discount potential returns, discouraging investment, a point stressed, and formally treated, in Sanderatne (1974b: 82–86).

10. Subject to Ruttan's (1966: 49–53) important qualification that share tenants may *prematurely* adopt labor-saving technical changes (e.g., herbicides) because the tenure arrangement reduces returns to their labor. Yield-increasing technological change which augments costs and labor input (e.g., transplanting paddy) will be resisted by the rational share tenant in theory. In either case, the tenurial situation is objectionable with regard to desirable technological change (given the factor endowments of most agrarian societies). Cf. Cline (n.d.: 29–32).

vestment, what of the landlord? The rental income should give landowners the ability to make the investments that tenants are too poor to make. But unless input costs are shared in the same ratio as outputs, the landlord in theory faces the same problem of decreased marginal returns imposed by the sharing of output, assuming that the rent cannot be easily increased to compensate for increased investment. Moreover, the rate of return in peasant agriculture is unlikely to equal the return of alternative opportunities open to landlords, such as commodity speculation, moneylending, residential properties, or even foreign education.[11] In theory, the combined investments of landlord and tenant will fall short of those of the owner-cultivator facing a comparable agroeconomic situation.

Share Tenancy and Productivity: The Empirical Case

The evils-of-sharecropping model derived from the conceptual framework of neoclassical economics has a certain plausibility in commonsense terms and is firmly ensconced in the policy logic of agrarian reform. But how closely does the theory describe the real world of peasant production?

A number of studies in South Asia have concluded that the data do not consistently support the theoretical conclusions on the short-term ill effects of share tenancy.[12] Indeed, it is difficult to find studies which confirm the prevalent argument that tenants are consistently less efficient than owners of a smiliar size of holding.[13]

In Ceylon, as the first serious land reform to address the economic problems of share tenancy was being drafted, a study from Kandy district found that tenants produced higher, not lower, yields than comparable owner-cultivators (Sarkar and Tambiah, 1957: 20). Analysis of more recent data from Sri Lanka shows that tenants received higher yields than owners in three of the five surveyed districts (Dias, 1973: 12–13). The data for two of the five districts are presented in Table 9.5. These districts present an especially appropriate comparison, as the tenurial configurations and agronomic characteristics vary greatly and represent both ends of the agrarian spectrum in Sri Lanka.

11. Bhaduri (1973) has argued that conditions of "semifeudalism," discernible in parts of India, prevent innovation because the landlord would lose opportunities to exploit share tenants via usury if dramatic productivity increases were allowed to increase tenant income (and thus reduce the need for usurious credit). Bhaduri's static equilibrium model makes problematic assumptions and underemphasizes the dynamic potential for rearranging modes of surplus extraction at a higher production level. Cf. Newberg (1975).

12. Jha (197180 ff.); Sanderatne (1974b: 57); Harriss (1979); Chadha (1978); Rudra and Chakravarty (1973); Peiris (1976); Berry and Cline (1979: 115, 175). Ruttan (1966) finds comparable disconfirming evidence for the Philippines.

13. A notable exception is Bell (1977), whose sophisticated analysis of a very restricted sample finds support for the "Marshallian position" on the tenanted portion of farms containing *both* tenanted and owned land, but not on the farms of pure tenants.

Table 9.5: Paddy Yields by Tenurial Status in Hambantota and Kandy
Districts (Ceylon), 1971–1972

| | Yield (Bushels per Acre) | |
	Maha Season	Yala Season
Kandy District		
Owners	46.4	36.9
Tenants	50.0	44.3
Owner-tenants	53.6	47.8
Tenant-owners	57.4	46.3
Hambantota District		
Owners	44.5	43.4
Tenants	34.7	22.0
Owner-tenants	24.1	15.9
Tenant-owners	31.2	15.6

SOURCE: ARTI (1974: pts. 1, 2). The Yala season is that of the southwest monsoon; Maha,
of the northeast monsoon. Tenant-owners lease more land than they own; owner-tenants,
vice versa.

In Hambantota, pure tenants produced lower yields than pure owner-
cultivators for the year studied, confirming earlier official reports of tenurial disincentives to production in the district. In Kandy, the position
was exactly the reverse; tenants, as in the 1957 study in the district,
produced higher yields than owners within the same size category.

In Pakistan, there is evidence that tenants receive higher yields on
some crops and in some areas compared to owners. Table 9.6 presents
data for the entire country based on a 1972 sample survey of more than
57,000 farm families. The best aggregate data available indicate higher
tenant yields of maize (a subsistence crop) and of the commercial crops
tobacco and sugarcane. Rice is the only crop for which tenant yields fall
below those of owner-cultivators in the aggregate data; more reliable disaggregated district-level data show similar, inconsistent patterns. In his
review of Indian studies, S. C. Jha notes the same phenomenon (1971:
chap. 5).

To understanding this confusing pattern the variable of land quality
is again central. One can construct a good logical case that the more
certain and higher yields of fertile irrigated plains and deltas have, over
time, attracted the capital of noncultivators and facilitated the emergence of a rentier class, thus concentrating tenancy where yields are high
and predictable. Marginal agronomic areas produce too little social surplus to attract, produce, or maintain a rentier class. Malcolm Darling
documented a similar phenomenon in the Punjab: as new areas were
irrigated, land values rose, leading to an expansion of credit and agricultural debt, and eventually foreclosure and the disintegration of the owner-
cultivator system, producing a landlord-tenant organization of production (1932: 188–239). The sharp-eyed moneylender or local landlord is

Table 9.6: Yields of Major Crops in Pakistan by Tenurial Status
(Maunds per Acre)

Crop	All Farms	Owner-Operators	Owner-Cum-Tenants	Tenants
Wheat	12.83	12.85	12.53	13.11
Rice	12.02	12.94	12.31	11.12
Cotton	9.15	9.17	9.10	9.17
Maize	11.44	9.61	13.04	15.11
Tobacco	23.40	23.60	20.22	25.73
Sugarcane	307.41	299.02	303.86	326.30

SOURCE: Calculations from unpublished data collected by the Agricultural Census Organization, Lahore, 1972.

likely to covet and obtain the best patches of land locally available, so that over time sharecropping tends to appear on the land with the highest agronomic potential. S. C. Jha argues that in India tenanted land is indeed superior, on the average (1973: 80). In the Hambantota district of Sri Lanka, the best lands are in areas of extremely high rates of tenancy, whereas the owner-cultivator regions are in general agronomically inferior. While the richest land breeds tenurial discontinuities, the poorest land often simply will not support both cultivator and rentier. The colonial system of auctioning newly irrigated prime tracts accentuated this phenomenon (Herring, 1977b).

Irrigation is not a perfect proxy for agronomic potential, but tenancy does seem to be concentrated in irrigated areas, confounding aggregate comparisons which do not (often cannot) control for irrigation. Moreover, classification of two fields as "irrigated" may not insure comparability even on the dimension of access to water. Placement on the canal, political connections, bribes, and brute force influence which fields receive adequate and timely water. Thus, gross-yield data showing either higher or lower productivity on tenanted farms will not settle the microeconomic disincentive question without an independent measure of agronomic potential.

A second method of addressing the question has been to ask whether farm-management practices differ significantly between owner and tenant farms. In terms of adoption of high-yielding varieties, transplanting, and fertilizing in paddy production, the data for Hambantota and Kandy districts show no differences by tenure in the direction predicted by the policy logic. Indeed, in Kandy district owners appeared to be less progressive agronomically than were tenants (ARTI, 1974: pt. 1, 96; pt. 2, 89–91). K. M. Azam (1973) has shown that tenants in Pakistan do not lag far, if at all, behind owners in participating in the "green revolution"; the major constraint facing small cultivators in adopting new varieties has been inaccessibility of irrigation water and credit. The latest Census of

Agriculture for Pakistan indicates use of fertilizer on a greater percentage of tenant farms *and* a greater percentage of tenant farms' cropped area, compared to owner-operators.[14]

In summary, though all share tenants face the same tenurial disincentives indicated in the policy logic, they behave in quite different ways economically, often producing higher yields and utilizing more labor and other inputs per acre than owner-cultivators of a comparable size. It would seem that the Marshallian logic of marginal costs and returns is incomplete at best, perhaps even inappropriate, and that a broader conceptualization of the peasant farm is in order. One important qualification is suggested by the intensification and high yields on extremely small farms generally. The emphasis of A. V. Chayanov on a homey dynamic of intensification depending on how many mouths have to be fed by how many on how much land seems especially appropriate when the family is so poor that every additional unit of income is crucial, whatever its "cost." Indeed, for the extremely poor share tenant operating with primitive techniques on a small farm and losing half or more of the gross produce to a landlord every harvest, the "whip of hunger" may be so strong a driving force that a different economic calculus—one of ensuring survival—comes into play.

To illustrate this point, we may consider the two districts in Sri Lanka from table 9.5. In Kandy district, tenants produced higher yields than owners; in Hambantota, tenants conformed to the dominant policy logic, producing lower yields though situated on decidedly superior land. Although tenants in both districts were extremely poor, tenants in Hambantota did not employ yield-increasing techniques such as transplanting. Why? If family labor is not available, labor must be hired, and here the resource constraints of poor peasants are important. In Hambantota, there were only 0.81 adult labor units available per operated acre on tenant farms, compared to 1.36 per acre on owner-cultivated farms. In Kandy, where tenants produced higher yields, the situation was exactly reversed; tenants averaged 2.2 adult labor units per acre, owners 1.5 (ARTI, 1974: pt. 1, 109–15; pt. 2, 104–06). When farmers in Hambantota who did not transplant paddy were asked why, the largest number of responses indicated lack of funds; shortage of labor and undependable water supply also figured prominently, but the classically predicted reply—"has to share benefits with the landlord"—was mentioned least frequently, in about 3 percent of the total responses (ARTI, 1974: pt. 1, 86).

A second major qualification to the policy logic is the character of production relations—the distinction between the "good landlords" and "bad landlords" of political rhetoric. Sarkar and Tambiah's (1957: 20) study attributed higher yields on tenanted farms in Kandy district to the fact

---

14. Pakistan (1975a: vol. 1, tables 55–57). There are variations by district, and tenanted farms are somewhat more likely to be irrigated (84 percent of cropped area compared to 74 percent in the aggregate).

that tenant cultivators received some aid from landlords whereas owner-cultivators were so poor that even minimal levels of working capital were often beyond their means. The inability of poor peasants to afford even seed for the next crop has historically obtained in Hambantota district (Herring, 1977b). More recent data support the 1957 study's conclusion; most landlords in Kandy—unlike Hambantota—are residents, not absentees. In Kandy one-third of the pure tenants received "collateral help" from landlords, as did 54 percent of the owner-tenants and 69 percent of the tenant-owners. The modal form of such aid was provision of seed and fertilizers. In Hambantota, only 9 percent of all tenants received any contribution from landlords (ARTI, 1974: pt. 1, 33; pt. 2, table 2–14).

Contributions to working capital by landowners were not without significant costs, however. In Hambantota, tenants who received such aid paid higher rents, up to two-thirds of the crop. Rents in Kandy district were less variable; 83 percent of the tenants paid the traditional half share (more than double the statutory maximum sanctioned by the Paddy Lands Act); half of these tenants received no aid from owners.[15] Interest rates on production loans generally in the two districts ranged between 40 and 60 percent, though rates as high as 150 percent were recorded.[16] In situations of acute scarcity, landlords may provide working capital to tenants that is unavailable to poor peasants without influential and wealthy patrons,[17] though by no means all landlords perform such functions, and those who do frequently use the working capital nexus to extract a larger share of the product from tenants.

Landlords figure prominantly in tenant cultivation practices in other ways. When competition for land is extreme, landlords are frequently able to insist that tenants follow certain practices and show high yields as a condition for security of tenure. Herbert Albrecht's study of Daudzai district in the Northwest Frontier Province of Pakistan attributed the higher yields and more intensive cultivation on tenant farms partly to the superior bargaining position of landlords; only tenants of "good character"—diligent, honest, and loyal—could expect to obtain and retain tenancies (1974: 86–88). Under conditions inducing competition for tenancies, a selection pressure may thus operate to assure that inefficient

15. ARTI (1974: pt. 2, 37–38). These data should remind us to look skeptically upon the idealized patron–client model of landlord–tenant relations, in which a wide range of services is provided by the landlord in exchange for the lion's share of the social surplus. The reality on the ground is often quite different.

16. ARTI (1974: pt. 1, 44; pt. 2, 53). My own field investigations in 1973 corroborate the figures at the high end of the spectrum.

17. For example, in data collected by K. M. Azam (1973: 414–18) of small farmers in Pakistan who did not use the optimal level of fertilizer on high-yielding wheat varieties, 94 percent cited lack of credit as a problem. My calculations from the unpublished Rural Credit Survey aggregate data (1972) collected by the Agricultural Census Organization indicate that landlords were overwhelmingly the main source of credit for Pakistani tenants.

cultivators do not become or remain tenants; comparable selection pressure does not operate on subsistence owners, at least in the short run.

Just as the landlord can serve as a hinge in obtaining scarce working capital, the "good landlord" can perform managerial and technical intermediary functions as well. Sir Malcolm Darling, reflecting an important colonial policy model, referred to the landlord estates of the Punjab as potential, though less frequently actual, "centres of education and progress" (1932: 128). In Albrecht's (1974) study, a subset of "modern" landlords decided cropping patterns, provided and determined the level of use of chemical fertilizer and manure, and also provided credit, and often a full-time manager (salidar), who transmitted agronomic and marketing information (which was in scarce supply locally).

The function of landlords in facilitating tenant adoption of yield-increasing technologies may extend beyond provision of capital and scarce inputs and knowledge. A major constraint on technical change in a poor economy is that few can afford to take risks. By sharing the risk, and perhaps providing "subsistence insurance" (cf. Scott, 1976: 44–55) in case of failure, the "good landlord" may increase the likelihood and rate of tenant adoption relative to that of poor owner-operators.

The most serious objection to the landlord–tenant social organization of production has been that permanent improvements on the land, or even conservation, are discouraged, leading to stagnation or deterioration of the capital stock. In Calvert's *The Wealth and Welfare of Punjab*, we find: "Tenants generally take less care in preparing the land for crops, plough it less often, manure it less and use fewer implements upon it than owners. They grow less valuable crops, especially avoiding those requiring the sinking of capital in the land; they make little or no effect at improving their fields; they often keep a lower type of cattle; they avoid perennials and bestow no care on trees" (Punjab, 1938: 36).

To judge this matter empirically is extraordinarily difficult, however. Not only are proper data lacking, but existing data almost invariably allow only static comparisons. The World Bank's report on land reforms concludes that settling the issue in practice is not possible (but recommends land reform anyway; 1974: 21). To give some empirical dimension to this question, table 9.7 presents recent data from a sample survey of 66,000 farm families in Pakistan, conducted in 1972. The data show that even if tenant investment is added to rentier investment, the total expenditure per acre on land improvement is well below that of owner-operators. Rentiers allocated a smaller percentage of their total expenditures to land improvement than did owner-operators. Tenants allocated the lowest percentage of expenditure of all groups to land improvement. Land purchase is not a productive investment but merely a transfer of proprietary rights. Rentiers allocated as large a percentage of their expenditures to new land purchases as to land development. Tenants de-

voted more of their resources to land improvement than to land purchase, but fell far below other tenurial groups on both measures.

Although these data present a static view, the implication is that
tenants in Pakistan do not invest in land development on the same scale
as those who own all or some of the land they operate; this is true whether
we measure investment in rupees per operated acre or as a percentage of
total expenditure. Moreover, this difference is not compensated by the
investments of rentiers who own the tenanted land. It is not clear whether
the differences in investment relate to differences in incentives (including insecurity of tenure) or ability (when ability includes both surplus
resources and access to long-term credit on reasonable terms). There is
no need to document the extreme poverty of most share tenants in South
Asia, nor their lack of access to institutional credit (cf. Herring, 1977a).

In summary, there is strong evidence that a large part of the economic
evils of share-tenancy policy logic is inaccurate, assuming, as I think both
reasonable and demonstrable, that not all results are contaminated by
land-quality differentials; explanations are necessary. A major explanation for discrepancies must be the economic character of the poor peasant
farm. Having few alternative economic opportunities and facing severe
deprivation if the harvest is poor, the tenant farmer of South Asia arguably operates according to an economic logic somewhat different from
that of Alfred Marshall. The neoclassical calculation of marginal returns
is less important than the classical "whip of hunger." This argument is
consistent with the findings of Bell (1977) that tenants who also owned
land, and thus had alternative opportunities, conformed more to Marshallian logic on their tenanted parcels, in contrast to totally landless
tenants with few alternatives.

Second, the patron-client nature of the social organization of share-

Table 9.7: Investment on the Land by Tenurial Classes in Pakistan,
            1972

| Investment | Rupees per Acre | | | |
	Rentiers	Tenants	Owner-Cum- Tenants	Owner- Operators
1. Land clearing, grading, etc.	3.13	1.95	4.81	6.72
2. Traditional wells	0.15	0.12	0.66	0.82
3. Tubewells, pumps	1.30	0.87	6.55	5.36
Total land improvement	4.58	2.94	12.02	12.90
	Percentage of Total Expenditures			
4. Land purchase	2.6	0.5	5.5	4.0
5. Land improvement	2.4	1.3	4.8	5.3

SOURCE: Calculations from survey data from the Agricultural Census Organization, Lahore,
unpublished.

tenancy production is important; landlord behavior as intermediary, or broker vis-à-vis the larger society is an important determinant of tenant economic potential and behavior. In highly stratified societies with vast differentials of access to knowledge, extension personnel, agricultural inputs, local political influence, and credit, the tenant with a "good landlord" as patron is operating in a different realm of production possibilities than is the marginal, isolated owner-cultivator. So long as powerful intermediaries remain necessary for assured access to production requisites, tenants as a group, because of their place in the production system, are potentially plugged into channels which may counteract the microeconomic "depressant" effects *even when* (or if) such considerations influence farm-management behavior. Moreover, where competition for tenancies is extreme, the landlord who is interested in agriculture can demand advanced cultural practices, sound management (and hard work) from his sharecroppers as conditions for security of tenure.

Just as there are different kinds of landlords, so there are different kinds of tenants, though available aggregate data typically do not allow controls for differences that social theory indicates will be crucial. For example, we would, at a minimum, need to separate share tenants from lease tenants, insecure marginal tenants-at-will from secure tenant cultivators, and probably cultivator caste tenants from outcaste tenants. In aggregate data, "tenant" refers both to the socially oppressed *bataidars* and to capitalist farmer-entrepreneurs who lease land for commercial production (cf. ICSSR, 1980: 22).

The policy logic of long-term investment deficiencies in share-tenancy systems is more supportable, logically and empirically.[18] There are good landlords and bad landlords, but there is little reason to expect the landlord–tenant social organization of production to maximize the probability that the economic surplus in agriculture will be reinvested on the land. The surplus extracted by landlords may be large, but the *utilization* of the surplus is as important as its size (cf. Baran, 1957: 22–43). Thus tenancy may paradoxically be an efficient system in terms of producing and extracting surplus, and simultaneously exhibit severe deficiencies in terms of rational utilization and investment of that surplus.

The real indictment of share tenancy is that the terms of exchange between the landed and the landless are such that share tenants live in poverty with no guarantee that the surplus squeezed from their labor will be reinvested on the land they work, or even in agriculture generally. Indeed, there is no guarantee that the agricultural surplus garnered by rentiers will not be dissipated in luxury consumption, or invested in labor-displacing machinery (tractors, threshers) that threatens the livelihood of the agrarian underclass. The poverty of the sharecropper, a direct conse-

18. In addition to the data in table 9.7, see Jha (1971: appendix 3, table 1); Khusro (1958: 151–76); Chenery et al. (1974: 131).

quence of the tenancy system, may serve as a "whip" to induce extra labor in the fields, but it is labor with extremely low real returns and quite high social (if not private) opportunity costs. And the poverty of the cultivator, and his consequent state of ill-health and malnourishment, not only exact unacceptable human costs, but almost certainly decrease the prospects for a dynamic agricultural sector in the long run.

The empirical ambiguity of the neoclassical indictment of share tenancy should thus in no sense be seen as a justification for share tenancy nor as having laissez-faire policy implications. Tenancy systems are compared to owner–cultivator systems; that one is marginally superior to the other in productivity is of little consequence because *both* systems fall pathetically short of the potential in terms of both labor and land productivity. That tenants may on occasion have easier access to production credit than do owner-cultivators argues not for the superiority of share tenancy as an organization of production but rather against the existing distribution of production credit, which severely handicaps poor and powerless farmers. There is one clear policy implication, however: if land reforms and other redistributive measures deprive share tenants of certain landlords' services, vigorous compensatory policy must be implemented to prevent a net deterioration in both productivity and tenant welfare.

Conclusions: Land Reform and Development Strategy

There is no simple answer to the question of productivity; the first conclusion is that the comparisons which have dominated the field of inquiry are demonstrably inadequate. Unfortunately, the available data do not always allow more refined analysis. There is no dispute, however, about one point: both land and labor remain underutilized, with serious social and economic consequences. It is also clear that land reforms must be formulated with considerations of raising the productivity per unit of land and labor through simultaneous intensification, crop diversification, land development, capital formation, and technological change.

The conventional wisdom displays an inappropriate disregard of potentiality. When researchers show that smallholders produce more per acre, the conclusion is that small farms are superior to large and should be promoted. This perspective ignores the serious constraints under which small producers labor—constraints which relate in part to the small scale of operation. If these constraints—diseconomies of small scale, low investible surplus, inadequate credit and capital—could be removed, the growth potential seems enormous. Yet the conventional wisdom takes the best existing situation to be the best possible—small proprietors producing at levels which offer an extremely low return to labor and little opportunity for capital formation. The obsession with "creating employment" neglects the critical issues—at what level of productivity, with what return to the laborer—and thus implicitly denies the potentiality of rational labor utilization to increase the rate of capital formation and return to farm labor.

Utsa Patnaik's work, as discussed earlier, demonstrates the potential of large-scale operations for increasing output per acre, output per worker, investible surplus per acre and per worker, employment per acre, and for reducing cost per unit of output. In contrast, continuing subdivision and fragmentation of small operational units which already do not elicit the full-time managerial or cultivating involvement of the proprietor seem to be an agroeconomic cul-de-sac; Kerala's involuted agrarian system is archetypal.

There are three broad strategies for increasing the scale of production to raise land and labor productivity. One is the rapid development of the capitalist farming sector to absorb most of the peasant sector; the second is state initiatives to provide large-scale cooperative or collective farms. Finally, there is the Japanese or Taiwanese model of capital intensive farming on small holdings.

The economic arguments for production cooperatives or collectives are well known:

1. Economies of scale, both internal (reducing unit costs by spreading fixed-capital costs over a greater output) and external (marketing, credit, etc.). There are also social or administrative economies of scale, as in taxing, extension, and credit, when the state deals with one large unit rather than hundreds of small units.

2. Greater investment potential generated from (a) a larger investible surplus per unit of land resulting from scale efficiency, and (b) the pooling of resources to purchase lumpy capital items (tubewells, for example) and subsidiary investment to generate additional sources of income (such as livestock, processing equipment, etc.)

3. Improved efficiency in utilization of labor, resulting in a greater potential for nonmonetized capital creation and improvements in management through specialization and increasing the talent pool (assuming that of any group of proprietors, not all are equally qualified for managerial roles, yet under present conditions all are, perforce, managers).

However, a theoretical argument for some form of communalization of agricultural production is not sufficient; the practical difficulties are severe and well known (cf. Raj Krishna, 1961: 235 ff.). The process would require creative administrative efforts, presupposing a corps of committed cadres. The existing bureaucracies of South Asia can hardly be expected to provide innovative energies for societal transformation. The pervasive elitism of development bureaucracies and the social, cultural, class, and even linguistic barriers between officers and the poorest agriculturalists hinder collaboration. Political parties have not offered an effective alternative; left parties are often urban-oriented and generally lack extensive, effective rural cadre systems. Where cadres operate, they are more attuned to winning elections and extracting boons through the patronage network than to mobilizing farmers for development. Even in Kerala, where the agroeconomic situation strongly suggests collectivization and the strongest leftist party has extensive rural cadre networks and has shared state power, it has not proved possible to make progress in this direction (Jayachandran, 1976).

In addition to these serious organizational difficulties, the presumed adamant individualism of the peasant and consequent attachment to private plots are cited as cause for dimissing collectivization in South Asia. It is not clear to what extent observed individualism is a product of the existing economic and social framework; nor do we know how amenable to change present attitudes would be once fundamental structural changes were made. But it is important to remember Namboodiripad's cardinal rule of land reform: any reform scheme that does not grow from and build upon the experience and needs of the peasantry is impracticable.

The range of creative alternatives in organizing large-scale agriculture has not been given a real test in South Asia, though analysis of recent experiments in Sri Lanka should add to our understanding. Moreover, agrarian and tenurial structures must be sensitively disaggregated in determining potential. But it should be emphasized that the difficulties of innovating in communal directions are exacerbated by the isolation of such experiments as "collective islands in a sea of individualism." Moreover, collective or cooperative farmers can hardly be expected to be committed to their enterprise when conservative regimes are waiting in the wings to dismantle social experiments.

Though the problems of innovation in the direction of collective control of the means of production are frequently presented in detail, the problems of the alternative large-scale agricultural model are less frequently analyzed. First, though it is pure ideology to deny the energy and productivity of the "kulaks" and capitalist farmers, bad landlords are still with us. Not all large farmers are progressive or knowledgeable; many are content to live as traditional, often absentee, rentiers. Others have nonagricultural involvements and ambitions, draining surplus from the land into politics, speculation, moneylending, residential properties, luxury consumption, and black-market operations. Moreover, even if agricultural entrepreneurs arise in sufficient numbers with sufficient resources, small farmers will resist amalgamation. As long as the land offers the only real social security, tiny proprietors will cling to it, limiting the potential expansion of the large-scale sector.

The historic role of the agricultural entrepreneurs is also complicated by the state of political consciousness and increasing organization of the laborers. In parts of Kerala, particularly Kuttanad and Palghat district, production has been seriously disrupted by strikes, lockouts, and violence. Indeed, in parts of Kerala, landowners are increasingly unable to control the production process. Because of the difficulties of managing organized wage labor, and its (perceived) high cost, rural capitalists seek to mechanize operations, vitiating the potential for labor-intensive capital formation (cf. Hewavitharana, 1974) and cultivation. Considerations of private returns not only promote patterns of technical change of dubious value in social terms (ICSSR, 1980: 20), but also evoke production-disrupting struggles between labor and capital.

Moreover, further concentration of agricultural capital constrains the potential for new policy. Increased concentration of economic power in rural areas undermines the potential for redistributive or developmental policies opposed by large farmers. Without extensive redistribution of purchasing power, the structure of demand in the society as a whole remains unchanged; elite consumption patterns threaten to perpetuate a pattern of investment (or importation) which generates too few jobs and a level of investment constricted by an artificially small market. Moreover, the capitalist amalgamation model implies heavy costs imposed on the most deprived sections of society, an imposition that seems impossible to justify.

Both large-scale patterns thus hold potential for agricultural dynamism, and both introduce serious practical problems. But what of the smallholder pattern which is dominant in the region? Given the economic attractiveness of large-scale production, and the serious problems of very small-scale producers presented above, is there an economic case for a society dominated by small farms?

The answer is affirmative, but the analysis of this chapter establishes important caveats. Innovative efforts must be made to (a) provide smallholders with opportunities to increase the scale of production (diversified cropping patterns, dairying, working capital for high-value crops, etc.) on a limited land area; (b) provide alternative economic opportunities, particularly those which mobilize underemployed labor to improve the stock of agricultural capital (irrigation projects, reclamation, land leveling, etc.) but including agroindustrial development and decentralized manufacturing; (c) alleviate the "self-exploitation"[19] of the small farmer through input subsidies, price supports, marketing credit, and rural service developments; (d) promote and assist cooperative and collective activities by small farmers to alleviate diseconomies of small scale and to allow technical change which requires indivisible capital (tubewells, etc.). These policies are admittedly expensive and difficult to administer, but the alternatives are less attractive.

Agrarian reform thus requires attention to the spheres of circula-

19. "Self-exploitation," as used by Chayanov and others, is descriptively accurate but implies more volition than is warranted. The returns to a peasant's labor are structured by the size of holding, prices of inputs and products, alternative employment opportunities, the rural-urban terms of trade, and other factors which the peasantry does not create or choose, either individually or collectively.

tion and exchange as well as production; with fair prices and nonusurious credit, improved cropping patterns and varieties, even tiny holders can be viable, if not wealthy (cf. K. N. Raj, 1975). Nor does the predominance of such farms preclude collectivist options. A society of smallholders will by no means move automatically toward consolidation of services and production, but the economic logic for eventual amalgamation of functions and even assets is powerful. A major reason for the failure of cooperatives has been, as Myrdal noted, "long-standing cleavages in status and power that divide the agricultural community" (1968: vol. 2, 1355). With a radical appropriation of land, the obstacles to genuine cooperative efforts would be weakened as the potential for innovation is simultaneously improved. But before such forces can develop, there must be a political and ideological consensus on the normative principles of the political economy so that farmers know, shape, and share the rules of the game.

This raises a final crucial point: the reform process itself has economic implications. Promulgation of even insincere land reforms is certain to have a negative impact on landowners' propensity to invest; deterioration of the land can hardly be afforded. The Central Bank of Ceylon argued the case forcefully (*Annual Report*, 1974: 16–17):

> The decline in output in the plantation sector . . . could have very serious long term implications for the availability of foreign exchange in particular and for economic growth. . . . The overall decline in the plantation crop sector could . . . be attributed to the sharp curtailment in expenditure and the climate of uncertainty that has prevailed in the last three years since the implementation of the Land Reforms Scheme. All this resulted in a sharp cutback in expenditure on replanting, manuring and maintaining properties in the best possible condition.

The negative effects of a hesitant and indecisive reform process extend beyond the curtailment of investment and maintenance. A major effect of land reforms has been, ironically, to change "good" landlords into "bad" landlords. Production suffers as tenants are evicted or continuously shifted, loans are withdrawn, tenant-owner cooperation deteriorates, and owners expend their energies in concealing their control of land. In the uncertain field of the economic effects of land reform, the only certainty is that uncertainty itself is economically deleterious (cf. Bell, in Lehmann, ed., 1974: 212).

The net economic effects of land reforms probably are, as the World Bank concluded upon recommending land reform, unknowable—certainly in practical terms, perhaps in principle. Too many other policies and variables shape agricultural decisions and affect outcomes. The size distribution of holdings and tenure structure are unlikely to be the major determinants of growth rates, though both profoundly influence employment levels, technology choice, income distribution, and thus the structure of effective demand. The strongest economic case for land reforms is in terms of development; if development means anything at all, it means the alleviation of poverty, unemployment, hunger, and backwardness. These conditions characterize the agrarian underclass; a radical land reform addresses these issues directly and is thus preferable, ceteris paribus, to a strategy that addresses them only indirectly and offers only plausible scenarios, not evidence, that eventually everyone will be better off.

It is here that the "trickle-down" and "create-the-surplus-and-then-tax-it" rationales for postponing land reform in favor of entrepreneurial dynamism break down. As likely as trickle-down are trickle-up and marginalization.[20] Moreover, the concentration of economic power now hardly augers well for redistribution in the near future. In economic terms, all three strategies discussed above are demonstrably capable of generating growth and raising productivity. The entrepreneurial amalgamation model is inferior in terms of income distribution and tends to encourage a pattern of resource use and technical change less conducive to nondependent development and less in line with existing factor endowments and employment imperatives (in the long term) than the alternatives. But the uncertainty and the contingent character of narrowly economic arguments on both sides underlines the fact that the issue of land reform must be addressed primarily in terms of its effects on broader social and political development and the imperatives of social justice, which are the subjects of the concluding chapter.

20. For development of the argument, and evidence, Griffin (1974; 1976; 1979); for illustrative case studies, UNRISD (1974); Rajaraman (1975); Kurien (1980).

10 The Argument for Land to the Tiller

The frontier that divides the morally possible from the morally impossible is less constricting than we take it to be; and the things that hem the former in are our own weaknesses, our own vices, our own prejudices.
—Jean-Jacques Rousseau

Concluding a book on land reform presents a special dilemma; one can conclude with what has been done, but readers justifiably ask what should be done. Our peculiar social-science weltanschauung makes this an uncomfortable question. More than uncomfortable, the question poses a severe problem of standing: should be done by whom? Land reforms that genuinely overturn the rural society and economy are frequently the product of cataclysmic historical events, often revolutions, which are neither policy options nor common occurrences. Moreover, the question contains an exquisite tension between structural constraints and optimal policy; landlordism can be abolished in Kerala because of the historically rooted left mobilization of the agrarian underclasses and their numerous urban allies, and because tenants and laborers outnumber cultivators and landlords; but the same structural and historical conditions do not obtain in the Punjab or Sind. That structural conditions vary does not make rural inequality more acceptable in normative terms, just as the difficulty of abolishing crime does not justify criminal activity. The objective of this chapter is to assess land reforms in terms of social justice; that particular regimes and policymakers may have little interest in pursuing social justice goes without saying, but does not diminish the importance of clarifying the issues.

Any prescription, to be complete, entails levels of argument, from the most basic normative principles to prudential and practical questions. First principles of social justice are, of course, widely disputed, yet any case for land reform must argue that some systems are more just than others. To argue for radical land reform presupposes an argument that the inequalities represented by rent and concentration of holdings are not justified. Is it possible, then, to escape the infinite regress of ideological disputes over the meaning of social justice? In any decisive way, no; but a position must be taken. To argue complete relativism of values or reject the inquiry as fruitless is either (a) to retreat to the level of offering emotive responses, each of which has no more validity than its opposite; or (b) to accept without grounds the critical values embedded in existing reform legislation; or (c) to deny the very possibility of normative analysis, and thus of critical social theory, and thus to validate implicitly, by default, justifications of existing patterns of power and privilege. This final option is characteristic of positivist social science but is, ironically, itself a normative position functionally, and an undefended one at that.

Land Reform and Structural Change

Much of the literature on land reform in the subcontinent dismisses the reforms as mere charades manipulated by ruling elites to pacify the peasantry, coopt leftist critics, and satisfy modernist elite sectors while effecting little structural change in rural areas. Such a view, while certainly accurate in part, as documented in preceding chapters, requires considerable modification. The case studies clearly indicate change induced by land reforms, though not always in directions indicated by reform rhetoric. This structural change is of two kinds—apparent and real. Though it seems contradictory to write of "apparent" structural change, the usage is meaningful. Land reforms produce important alterations in the *observable* structure of the agrarian system—land records are altered, census data collected, reports are made—all presenting a picture of the rural world that is more congruent with the needs of landed elites, administrators, and ruling politicians than with reality on the ground. Landowners have strong incentives to show that they own very little land and that there are no tenants on it; reform administrators are pressured to show progress in implementation.

The apparent change is important because it is this data-built façade which goes into planning documents, policy debates, reports of international agencies, and all too many scholarly treatments. The distortions become social facts, the primary resources for understanding the rural world for nonrural groups who are, after all, the primary movers of rural policy. For example, it is now widely recognized that the apparent decline in tenancy in India is partly real (attributable in part to tenancy legislation and in part to other dynamics sketched in earlier chapters), but partly bogus, a reflection of widespread concealment (cf. Sanyal, 1972). It is, however, widely believed in India that the concentration of land ownership has marginally declined (e.g., ICSSR, 1980: 37–41); the dynamics analyzed in preceding chapters offer strong reason to question the reality and meaning of that phenomenon.

What changes have land reforms made? First, the common metaphor of the South Asian agrarian system as a pyramid is useful. The pyramid itself is relatively squat, certainly compared to Latin America (or California), but those at the base are both numerous and acutely deprived. Land reforms in the region have typically lopped pieces from the apex, not shifting the entire pyramid upward, but granting the privileges of apex classes to strata further down but not at the base of the pyramid. *Zamindari* abolition was archetypal: the "superior" tenants with stronger traditional proprietary claims and standing moved up the pyramid; share-croppers, tenants-at-will, and laborers moved hardly at all, though in some cases they faced increased eviction pressure. Tenure reforms likewise worked best for relatively privileged tenants. Ceiling reforms in Sri Lanka had a significant impact at the top—a large percentage of the best land was seized, in marked contrast to India and Pakistan. But the major beneficiaries were not those at the productive base—the noncitizen Tamil laborers, or even the landless Sinhalese laborers, but primarily the state, through its increased control of both patronage resources and the national economy. Indeed, the state, and therefore the governing class, has been a major beneficiary of reforms in the region, but the state is certainly not controlled by the sharecroppers, laborers, and poor peasants.

The Kerala reforms were qualitatively different, but the upwardly mobile pyramid metaphor still applies. As the evidence of chapters 6 and 7 indicated, about half of the tenants belonged to relatively privileged agrarian strata; land to the tiller has made many of them "new landlords," though employers of wage labor, not sharecroppers. The landless laborers remained at the bottom of the pyramid, and the whole productive pyramid rests on their shoulders. A section of the laborers received tiny plots of land of both economic and social importance. The laborers' unions are making some headway, and innovative, though inadequate, legislation grants the legitimacy of their normative claim to security and a decent living from the land. The tenants won land through decades of struggle; the laborers have struggled as well, but their claims are not yet normatively recognized in full. Even in Kerala, it is possible to claim land as a "tiller" without laboring on the land.

Second, though the outcomes of a land reform demonstrably depend more on operative social and political forces than on legal specifications, the law itself is not unimportant. Reform law defines classes and focuses class conflict. Land reforms prompt the organization of landed interests where none had previously existed; the landless are mobilized and organized with demands to enforce tenancy legislation or redistribute land. Lax enforcement of primarily symbolic ceiling measures in India provided the focal point of "land grab" mass mobilizations. Whatever the existential character of the landlord–tenant nexus—and it is often experientially neither class nor conflictual—reform legislation defines rights, duties, and deprivations in class-specific terms. Rentier landlords are explicitly separated from cultivating farmers, secure tenants from tenants-at-will, sharecroppers from field laborers. These provisions then provide frames of interest and action for those groups.

The structural change which is seldom analyzed by scholars of land

reform is at the ideational level. Land reforms in the region have established legal norms which collectively and cumulatively establish new
constraints on property, new rights for propertyless classes, and new principles of distributive justice. That the movement at the ideological level
has far surpassed structural change on the ground has been demonstrated, as has the ambiguity of seeming consensus on principles of land
reform. It thus seems important to turn to an analysis of those principles
and their possible justification.

Ideology and Justice

An important recent contribution to the question at hand is John Rawls's
A Theory of Justice (1971). Though his work has been subjected to
trenchant and telling criticism (e.g., Wolff, 1977), Rawls still provides a
useful methodology for analyzing social justice. He poses the issue as
follows: "Justice is the first virtue of social institutions as truth is of
systems of thought. A theory however elegant and economical must be
rejected or revised if it is untrue; likewise, laws and institutions no matter how efficient and well-arranged must be reformed or abolished if they
are unjust" (p. 3). The position is not perfectionist or absolutist, but justice constitutes an imperative claim: "The only thing that permits us to
acquiesce in an erroneous theory is the lack of a better one; analogously,
an injustice is tolerable only when it is necessary to avoid an even greater
injustice" (p. 4).

The Rawlsian methodology is an intriguing blend of the tradition
of social contract theory and Kantian metatheory. Rawls argues that social institutions are just only if those institutions would have been agreed
upon ("contracted into") by individuals in an "original position" behind
a "veil of ignorance"—that is, not knowing what position they would
ultimately occupy in the system of roles, rights, duties, and privileges
which are the subject of the contract.

The strength of the method is masked by its formal, almost game-
like, analytical procedure. The argument is essentially that social institutions are unjust if individuals would not have agreed to them independently of their existing self-interest, in other words, if they had not known
where they would be, their privileges and disabilities, in the resulting
society. Distributive norms that would not have been agreed to by members of society is an original position—norms that are not (analytically)
self-imposed—are not acceptable. The "justice as fairness" doctrine which
results resembles a sophisticated form of a common empathetic folk concept of justice: "put yourself in the other fellow's shoes." Analytically,
the argument is: if you were not in the position you are in (but were
instead in the other fellow's shoes), would you think the situation fair?
Rawls simply takes the proposition back one step and generalizes it—no
concept of justice is adequate unless any representative person would

view it as just not knowing which pair of shoes he or she is to fill. The original-position participants would establish no inequalities that would result in roles they themselves would be unwilling to accept in the resultant society.

Rawls's methodology permits an approach to the most tangled problem in discussions of social justice: the radical critique of Marx, Mannheim, et al., that ideology reflects position in the social structure and that the dominant ideas of any historical period reflect the ideology of the dominant class. The methodology also offers a partial response to Rousseau's critique: notions of the good in an existing corrupt society are inevitably corrupt. The "veil of ignorance" shields moral deliberations from ideological conceptions of justice that are mere rationalizations of the personal interests of individuals in any existing society. In the original position, representative rational beings do not know whether they are to be landlords or serfs, tenants or laborers, or whether such roles should exist, but must choose institutions that provide a just share of the social product to every occupant of the various roles in society.

Landlords in an existing agrarian system, for example, would be unlikely, perhaps unable, to conceptualize a model of justice which discredited a return to land ownership independent of cultivation responsibilities. There is also the possibility that the serf or tenant, no matter how objectively deprived by existing social institutions, may perceive them as just. This phenomenon, while often used by elites (and even social scientists) as evidence that a system of institutions is just, hence legitimate, is obviously inadequate. Simply on grounds of cognitive consonance, we would expect some of the most deprived members of society to accept rationalizations of their deprivation. If opposition is irrational or impossible, there is real comfort in an ideology that explains an inferior position as just, dutiful, meritorious, perhaps conducive to extraterrestrial benefits, and real pain in the continued dissonance implied by the belief that one's lot is unfair but immutable (cf. Moore, 1978: pt. 1). Likewise, the consonance model would suggest that it is difficult for the landlord to live on the fruits of the labor of others unless he accepts a normative position which justifies such appropriation as legitimate, merited, inevitable, or ordained.

Mutually exclusive conceptualizations of justice are not merely theoretical possibilities but exist on the ground. Moreover, there is evidence of tension between acceptance and rejection of legitimating ideologies by the rural poor. Consider the case of the Kuttanad region in Kerala, where farmer-labor conflict has been intense and bitter. A study by K. C. Alexander confirms anthropological and literary accounts of the tension between ideology and consciousness among Kerala's poor. Laborers rejected in part the traditional justifications for inequality; 83 percent of the laborers (and 16 percent of the farmers) agreed that "the rich became rich by exploiting the poor," whereas 92 percent of the farmers, not surprisingly, but also more than half of the laborers agreed that "people became rich through hard work and frugal expenditure." Over half of the laborers, but only 4 percent of the farmers, agreed that "there should be a revolution in this country to bring about equality." However, almost a fifth of the laborers (and a third of the farmers) agreed that "the status of a person in the society is the result of his *karmas* in the previous incarnations."[1]

The problem is thus set: on the ground there will be a mixture of acceptance and rejection of traditional legitimating ideologies even by those degraded and exploited by them. It is not surprising that slaves in a slave society should adopt at least some of the dominant legitimating ideology, but such acceptance did not legitimate slavery. It would be elitist to ignore the acceptance of dominant ideologies by some deprived members of agrarian societies, but rigidly ideological and ahistorical to refuse to subject such world-views to rational criticism.

The outcome of Rawls's methodology is the following proposition: "All social primary goods—liberty and opportunity, income and wealth, and the bases of self-respect—are to be distributed equally unless unequal distribution of any or all of these goods is to the advantage of the least favored. . . . Injustice, then, is simply inequalities that are not to the benefit of all."[2]

For Rawls, this outcome is inevitable because no rational individuals would be parties to a contract if, considering they might be the least advantaged, inequalities were sanctioned that did not benefit the least advantaged. A stronger case can be made by relaxing Rawls's assumption that human nature necessarily involves self-centered utility maximization; it is arguable that from an original position few would *choose* to live in a society that was systematically unfair and exploitative, realizing that even if they benefit from the inequalities, the good life built on others' unjustifiable suffering is unlikely to be satisfying or (perhaps more importantly) peaceful. The formulation of Rawls is important for two reasons. First, the burden of proof is shifted to the defense of inequality. Because inequalities are profoundly embedded in our social experience, even in our cognitive models of the way the world works (though a pervasive functionalist world-view), it is often difficult to imagine how matters could go on without existing inequalities. The burden of proof is usually on advocates of equality. Rawls rightly asks: what is the justification for existing inequalities? Would the institutions which create or

1. K. C. Alexander (1975: 173). For a literary account of changes in consciousness in the same area, Pillai, *Two Measures of Rice* (1967). An anthropological account of ideology and consciousness among the "serf castes" of Kerala is A. Aiyappan (1965). Cf. Harriss (1979) on Tamilnadu.

2. Rawls (1971: 303, 62). The analysis in the text centers on Rawls's "difference principle." The conclusions would hold if considered in light of the "fair equal opportunity principle" applied to an agrarian society faced with extreme scarcity.

reproduce the inequality in question be chosen by disinterested (actually, *pre*interested) parties contracting together for a just society? Second, the formulation allows, in fact demands, an empirical response. Is the inequality in question necessary for increasing the well-being of the least advantaged?

Weather Prophets and Landlords: Is Rent Justifiable?

The weather prophet, or *beruvaga*, was historically accorded a share of the agricultural product under one institutional arrangement in the Hambantota district of Ceylon.[3] If we express the institutional framework in neoclassical economic terms, the share of the weather prophet is a return to weather as a factor of production, appropriated by the individual who contributed the factor. We would dismiss this analysis because control of weather as a factor of production makes sense only in terms of a prescientific perception of the world (i.e., it cannot be, or at least has not been, empirically demonstrated that anyone controls the weather, or that production outcomes would be different if the contribution of that factor of production were curtailed).

This example underlines the ideological character of normative institutions that govern distributions of product from the land. Rent as an institution allocates a share of the product to an owner who "provides the land factor." The cultivator likewise receives a share for providing the labor factor. It is clear why labor is a factor of production—without the physical operations of plowing, sowing, cultivating, harvesting, threshing, and so on, there would be no crop production. Is "land" a factor of production in the same sense? For it to be so, we would have to establish that removal of the factor from the production process would produce different outcomes. Of course, land as physical soil area can no more be eliminated from agricultural production than can the weather. But what is meant by contribution of the land factor is not provision of a physical patch of soil, which exists with or without owners, but rather a transfer of *rights* to land as defined in a concrete institutional framework. In this simple two-factor model, there is no need for a cognitivist positing of a labor theory of value; the physical surface of the earth becomes agricultural land, capital, through the application of human labor and continues to produce only so long as labor is expended.

When land is conceptualized as a factor of production, what is meant is not physical soil but rights to land as socially defined. Land is controlled in the same sense that weather is controlled; it is only because of

3. Robert Chelvathurai Proctor, "The Ceylon Peasantry," *Tropical Agriculture*, issues of August, September, and December 1914, January 1915. Cf. Herring (1977b). The allocation of a share of the agriculture product to village functionaries was common under traditional institutional arrangements of the *jajmani* type throughout the region.

particular social arrangements that either becomes the proprietary interest of one individual as opposed to another. "Return to the land factor"
is as much as ideological expression as "return to the weather factor," yet
because the former is sanctioned by an elaborate theoretical structure of
neoclassical economics whereas the latter was sanctioned only by village
superstitions, the former is frequently accepted as reasonable and right,
the latter as quaint curiosity. The point is that the neoclassical framework, like the village world-view, is an organization of mental concepts,
not of physical production relations.

The above is not meant to deny the validity of production function
analysis; it is demonstrably true that adding one unit of physical land
area to the farming operation will have concrete, measurable consequences for the productivity of labor, gross output, and microeconomic
decisions. Land clearly has a return in this sense, and the questions raised
by production function analysis are important. But to carry the physical
input analysis a step further in a functionalist manner, and assign as inevitable and necessary a share of the product to the party controlling a
particular institutional right in land independent of cultivation responsibilities, is purely ideological.

This is not to say that *landowners* perform no economic function;
they may or may not. The pure rentier performs no function at all; the
range of functions performed by noncultivating owners other than rentiers is a broad one. But even when such owners provide other services,
such as management, supply of inputs, marketing, and so on, their total
return includes a functional equivalent of that of rentiers, namely, return
to landownership. The distinction between landlords and capitalist farmers thus begins to blur, with the justice claims of the latter resting largely
on acceptance of the risks of cultivation (which in turn requires justification in terms of differential opportunity to bear such risks—that is, the
original distribution of assets).

In modified Rawlsian terms, justification for absolute rent would
require an argument that the cultivator receives some advantage from
the allocation of a share of the product to a nonlaboring rentier as rent.
No such argument can be produced, as the rental payment serves no economic function once land is in production. Whatever the owner takes
from the pile of grain at harvest is lost to the tenant, with no commensurate gain. The arguments supporting landlordism thus focus on (a) the
provision of services to the tenant, and (b) the potential for productivity-
increasing investment on the part of owners (who are presumably wealthy
compared to tenants). Neither argument supports the justice claim of
land rent as an institution, but both must be considered.

As to the provision of services, there are caveats. First, the services
themselves often require additional payments, and often at exhorbitant
rates. Rather than being an advantage to the tenant, the extra services

(marketing, credit, etc.) have historically proved to be means of extracting a surplus *in addition to* rent.

Real services are provided in many cases—interest-free loans, technical knowledge—but our line of inquiry suggests a critical question: would a rational individual contract for the social institution of rent, with its resultant inequalities, in return for the uncertain provision of some services which could be otherwise obtained or collectively organized? How many of the "services" would be necessary in a different organization of production-distribution relations? For example, in a society without existing concentrations of privilege, would all farmers not have the same access to education and government extension officers, to credit and subsidized capital, now enjoyed by landlords, thus dispensing with the need for mediation in technique improvement? Would subsistence loans, interest-free or usurious, be as necessary if cultivators were allowed to retain their entire product? Or could such aid not be obtained more cheaply through crop insurance programs or other arrangements?

The defense of landlordism thus reduces to a demonstration that (a) the rental exaction is *necessary* for improving the well-being of cultivators and that (b) the rental exaction is in fact so utilized. The second argument is by far the less demanding, but as the aggregate data for Pakistan in the preceding chapter demonstrate, even this minimal defense would be very hard to mount. In sum, the exaction of ground rent will not stand the test of justification.

The second major inequality attacked by existing land reforms in the region is the skewed distribution of holdings. The Kerala data in the previous chapter illustrate the point: not only do inequalities in land wealth produce inequalities in aggregate income and investible surplus, and thus in fundamental life chances, but also introduce significant inequalities in labor opportunities and returns to labor. Return to a day's labor on the farms of Kerala varies dramatically by size of holding; most farmers combine their labor with so little land that the return is minimal. Other farmers hold enough land so that labor in the fields produces a decent wage. Others control sufficient land to retire from cultivation and hire wage labor to till their holdings. This last category merges with that of landlord, since the return to land ownership is the dominant portion of total income from the land; the supervisory function (often quite perfunctory) is by no calculation valuable enough in production terms to merit the full return reaped by the owner, as illustrated by the phenomenon of some owners' hiring supervisors and still living on the land's income.

Thus inequalities in land distribution require justification both in and of themselves and in terms of the resulting differential opportunity, security, and returns to labor that result. In both policy and academic discourse, the strongest argument in defense of inequality has been that large farms are necessary to generate surpluses which are reinvested to create a dynamic agriculture: in Rawlsian terms, there is an "inequality bonus" for the least advantaged.[4] That argument is flawed both empirically and conceptually.

Empirically, it has never been demonstrated (a) that large inequalities are either necessary or sufficient to produce dynamism (cf. Berry and Cline, 1979: 43, 134–35); indeed, skewed distributions may produce absenteeism and extravagant consumption instead; or, more importantly, (b) that dynamism itself, however produced, is sufficient to guarantee amelioration of the position of the least advantaged. There are specifiable mechanisms whereby dynamism may produce marginalization and insecurity rather than a trickling down. Keith Griffin's conclusion from careful analysis of empirical studies from rural Asia is that "the view that the benefits of overall growth automatically will 'trickle down' to the lowest income groups within a reasonable period of time no longer is tenable by informed observers" (1979: 379). Griffin relies heavily on South Asian data to make this case, and his argument is correct. But the defense of inequality in land ownership would have to make a case even stronger than the one Griffin destroys: it would have to be shown not only that dynamism benefits the poor but also the inequalities are necessary to produce dynamism. Otherwise there is no justification for imposing the suffering experienced by those at the bottom of the pyramid.

Rapid growth in agriculture imposes class-differentiated costs and benefits. That the poor frequently benefit is denied by no sensible analyst, but the poor also bear the brunt of the dislocations—the evicted sharecroppers, the laborers replaced by machinery—and the benefits disproportionately go to those already advantaged by control of land and capital. The partial exceptions are typically those areas where the rural poor are conscious and mobilized and the state is responsive to underclass demands.[5]

Whatever the empirical case—and there is much dispute—the con-

4. Mellor (1976: 267 and passim) specifically invokes Rawls and implicitly accepts the notion of an inequality bonus to justify existing and increased disparities; cf. Lipton (1977: 268).

5. The issue is empirically very complex; real daily-wage increases for laborers may be accompanied by fewer days of work per season, and different trends appear when different endpoints for time series are chosen (cf. Jose, 1973). A collection of empirical studies which supports the text is "Wages and Incomes of the Weaker Sector in Rural India," *Indian Journal of Agricultural Economics* (1974). See, especially, pp. 83 ff. The studies found increases in *money* wages in dynamic areas, as expected, but a general stagnation or decline in real wages, the exceptions being politicized Kerala and Bengal, not dynamic Punjab. The statistical relationship between wages and productivity was weak and insignificant, and there was more evidence of the familiar phenomenon of the eviction of sharecroppers in order to take full advantage of productivity increases. For confirmation of the Kerala/Punjab findings, Bardhan (1973). The Kerala exceptionalism should not be exaggerated, however; Panikar (1979) demonstrates extensive malnutrition and unemployment among laborers in one of Kerala's most dynamic areas. Cf. Mencher (1980).

ceptualization of the justice-from-dynamism model is demonstrably weak.[6] It would have to be shown that technological change and investment require wide inequalities in income and access to opportunity, and this case is difficult to make. Indeed, it can be argued forcefully that inequalities in very poor agrarian systems inhibit technological change and dynamism by leaving some cultivators so poor that there is little margin for investment or risk-taking. More fundamentally, the inequalities do not guarantee either security or improvement for the least favored and certainly present the possibility of net deterioration, whatever the aggregate gains generated (cf. Byres, 1972). Given a full range of possible institutions and free choice, the preinterested individual would not choose the existing inequalities in distribution of assets as a means of guaranteeing dynamism, nor, therefore, as just.

To this point, the argument has rested heavily on economic inequalities and consequences. Rawls considers the distribution of "all primary social goods," including "liberty and opportunity" and "the bases of self-respect" (1971: 303). That "equal basic liberty" is denied in practice by extreme economic dependence among the landless is undeniable. Political democracy and the possibilities for the disadvantages to increase their well-being through concerted efforts thus require alleviation of dependence, whatever one may think of the economic arguments. The analysis of chapters 2 and 3 suggests that such alleviation would simultaneously increase the potential for meaningful local participatory democracy and thus generate greater political potential for protecting and energizing redistribution.

The conclusion of this analysis is not surprising, and may well be considered tedious and irrelevant by agrarian reformers: that is, the types and levels of inequalities addressed by land reforms are not justifiable, but rather represent considerable social injustice. For land reforms to be normatively acceptable, a convincing argument must be made that real injustices, and not windmills, are being attacked. Indeed, the absence of normative consensus on first principles of justice in agrarian systems has contributed to the vacillation, compromise, and backsliding on land reforms documented in the preceding case studies. My conclusion is that, at the level of first principles, in the absence of empirical verification of an "inequality bonus," existing inequalities in land control cannot be justified, and that unjustified inequalities should be abolished through

6. Ahluwalia's (1978) treatment is frequently used to support the trickle-down view. Though effectively refuted by Griffin (1979), the article is still interpreted too strongly. What Ahluwalia shows is simply that in good-crop years the incidence of rural poverty declines, though the absolute number of impoverished rural people continues to increase. Moreover, Ahluwalia finds no evidence of a trend decline in incidence of poverty in the more dynamic states (p. 312), and the "most disquieting" result is that "evidence from Punjab and Haryana does not support the hypothesis that improved agricultural performance will help reduce the incidence of poverty" (p. 315). For a discussion of the range of empirical evidence, ICSSR (1980: 12–41).

appropriate reforms. At the level of first principles, a very egalitarian distribution of produce from the land seems justified. The translation of these principles into normatively acceptable social programs requires a second level of argumentation in which the real world counts.

What Should Be Done?

The conclusion of the previous chapter was that an economic case can be made for a variety of agrarian structures, though considerations of scale *are* critical for raising productivity of land and labor. The usual bromide that nonagricultural employment must absorb large sections of the agrarian underemployed and unemployed is now widely recognized as unrealistic; a solution to the agrarian crisis must be sought largely on the land. The three strategies of chapter 9 for increasing land and labor productivity differ not so much in economic rationality as in their implications for the critical questions of any development strategy: at whose cost, to whose benefit? These are political and normative questions, and cannot be settled by any appeal to economic rationality. But one clear economic imperative is that uncertainty and backtracking on land reforms is economically deleterious and contributes to the failure of land reforms.

The implication is that an agreement must be forged on the normative principles which govern the rural political economy, an agreement comparable to the historical rejection of slave labor and serfdom. Here the *process* of land reforms is critical—the issues are hammered out on a very hot forge. Justification of privilege becomes hard to sustain when subjected to rational inquiry and public scrutiny and when the underprivileged are both demonstrably dehumanized by deprivation and are increasingly unwilling to accept existing legitimations of their suffering. It therefore seems critical to base land-reform policy on principles which do not include unjustifiable privilege, despite the fact that the poor at any given time may be willing to grant more privilege to the advantaged than is justified.

As beginning principles for formulating agrarian reforms aimed at reducing social injustice, I suggest that: (1) there should be no return from the land independent of labor on the land, with exceptions being made for those unable to work; (2) return to labor on the land should be commensurate with effort, not determined by the morally arbitrary criterion of accident of birth, and conditioned by consideration of a "floor income"; this implies a land ceiling near the mean size of holding,[7] with adjustments for family size and land quality.

These principles resemble in part the 1969 Kerala legislation, though the Kerala reforms allow a greater concentration of wealth than seems

---

7. Any higher ceiling would be arbitrary from the standpoint of justice, unless it can be demonstrated that specifiable agroeconomic imperatives are violated by so low a ceiling in specific cropping configurations.

justifiable when so many are landless. Moreover, those reforms draw the line between rentiers and capitalist farmers, eliminating the former, legitimating the latter. But the "capitalist farmers" of South Asia appropriate a return which is functionally equivalent to rent, though paying wages rather than crop shares. Here the Congress Agrarian Reforms Committee recommendations seem, as now explicitly recognized by the CPI(M) (1973), superior—land ought to be for the use of tillers, where tilling means plowing, sowing, weeding, harvesting. Too many of the landowners in South Asia—the data from Kerala in chapter 7 are especially revealing—do not derive their income primarily from, nor invest their energies primarily in, agriculture. That situation is difficult to justify when there are so many who are desperate for an agricultural livelihood and have no other options.[8] The operative rule should exclude income from the land to anyone who is able to work the land and chooses not to.

An important objection to these proposals is that those disadvantaged by redistribution are treated unjustly. The "entitlement" argument against redistribution makes one valid claim: the privileged often obtained their privilege by acting in accordance with existing social and legal norms (Nozick, 1974). Is it fair, then, to change the rules of the game and victimize the advantaged? It seems reasonable that deliberations from .an original position behind a veil of ignorance would assert the prior claim of reforming unjust institutions while simultaneously establishing criteria for compensation of the victims of social change. Such criteria would arguably include: the contributions of the owner to creating and improving the asset in question, the mode of acquisition, the advantages already received through unjust appropriation, and the remaining wealth and economic opportunities of the owner.

The operation of these principles would make available a great deal of land; the question of distribution raises difficult questions of justice and efficiency. In discussion of these issues, too often the distinction between physical land and the "bundle of rights" we call ownership is neglected. Redistribution of security, income, and authority in production relations may be conceptually and practically separated from redistribution of physical land area (though in a society in which the legal infrastructure is based on private ownership of the means of production, admittedly the surest way to redistribute rights is to redistribute proprietary claims). In pure tenancy, abolition of rent entails no change in size of operational holding but provides more income for investment by the new owner. The laborers present the most difficult problem, and in many parts of the region distribution of land in plots which are not "palpably uneconomic" to all claimants is impossible (though the problematic notion of

8. The State government of Uttar Pradesh recently circulated a proposal to acquire the agricultural lands of any individual earning Rs 10,000 annually from other occupations (*Sunday Standard*, December 7, 1980).

"uneconomic" necessitates a hard look at potential in specific agroeconomic situations). The economically optimal solution is, then, joint alienation to groups of laborers or joint management by the "village community" as recommended by the Congress Agrarian Reforms Committee, assuming workable arrangements can be established.[9]

Where such arrangements are impracticable, the surplus land could be distributed in locally defined minimum holdings; the laborers who receive no farms should be provided house and garden sites, both because such plots are intensively used (thus improving aggregate production and nutrition), and because of the increased standing and independence gained thereby. The justice claims of the laborers can then be met through legislation similar to that of the Kerala Agricultural Workers Act (chap. 6, 7), recognizing the claim of the workers to guaranteed access to the means of production and a share of the product, adjusted continuously with changes in technology and prices. Simultaneously, local public works that improve productivity should provide additional employment, and taxation policy should discourage underutilization of land.

There are four major objections to radical redistribution. First, will redistribution not exacerbate the problem of inefficient small farms and Chayanovian "self-exploitation"? Second, the possible answer to the first objection—various cooperative arrangements—seems impractical in light of previous failures. Third, would redistribution not have a detrimental effect on aggregate savings and investment and on marketed surplus? Finally, whatever the desirability of redistribution, it seems politically unrealistic. No one should doubt the seriousness of these objections; what most observers slight is the serious objections to the alternatives. A final caveat is that of Namboodiripad, expressed in chapter 6: reform schemes cannot be detailed from above, but must build on peasant demands and consciousness. Yet consciousness and demands exhibit marked unevenness in development. There is thus a delicate tension between policy as a potentiating force and policy as impracticable utopianism, between underestimating and overestimating potential for change. There is a further tension in the line between "commandism" and leadership. These tensions can be resolved only as the reform process generates its own corrective measures and innovations once the obstacles to change are weakened and new institutions are in place. But the tensions will remain.

---

9. The CARC proposal would work better in some areas than others, since the existence of villages as operative social entities varies greatly across regions. A similar perspective is what the ICSSR working group (1980: 56) proposes as the "village community agrarian perspective." Both perspectives imply the strong assumption that local democratic institutions can become instruments of the entire village community, an assumption more tenable with decreases in economic inequalities and dependence but still problematic for much of the region. The tension between statist initiatives and local democracy, analyzed throughout, cannot be easily resolved.

The second objection, since it is a response to the first, takes prior-ity. The advantages and problems of cooperative or collective organiza-tion of services, lumpy investment items, and (perhaps) production are analyzed in chapter 9. Officials and politicians say the farmers are op-posed, and this seems to be true. But it is difficult for farmers to imagine institutions that do not exist. It is difficult for leaders and administrators with no faith in cooperative forms to build confidence and encourage innovation. The agroeconomic logic is powerful and can be reinforced by public incentives. Previous attempts, as emphasized in the analysis of Sri Lanka, suffered from isolation and the vicissitudes of partisan politics. Though it seems too early to dismiss the potential, it must be recognized that so radical an institutional change would necessitate major reforms in the official apparatus and sensitivity to local variations in peasant needs, attitudes, and receptivity to incentives.

Should cooperatives prove genuinely impracticable, is the implica-tion of redistribution economic inefficiency and worsening Chayanovian "self-exploitation"? The answer is no, primarily because of the distinc-tion between physical size of holding and economic scale. Scale can be dramatically increased on very small farms given present technological capabilities and public investment in indivisible capital. It has been a theme of this book that land-reform logic and legislation have been land-centered, but agricultural production and distributive patterns are criti-cally dependent on terms of access to non-land capital as well. With the technical modernization of agriculture, reform must consider production relations in broader terms—working capital, investment capital, market-ing relations, technical knowledge, and so on. This recognition fre-quently leads to the call for agrarian reform rather than land reform, for a broader focus on agricultural development. That focus is appropriate, but a fundamental insight of agrarian political economy is lacking. In agrarian societies, the flow of credit, irrigation water, extension services, electric connections, and so on—all the infrastructure of agriculture—are profoundly influenced by the structure of local power—social, politi-cal, and economic—which in turn reflects (but does not mirror) the struc-ture of land control.[10] Effective agrarian reform arguably does not include, supplement, or replace land reform, but rather *presupposes* land reform. Otherwise, programs designed for the disadvantaged are coopted and dis-torted by locally dominant elites.

What of the third objection—that redistribution will allow the poor

10. This phenomenon is by now so well established that extensive documentation is redundant. Raj Krishna (1979: 15–16) argues that misappropriation of the huge sums of money channeled into rural development "may aggravate rural inequality instead of alle-viating it." The ICSSR study group (1980: 51) noted that, too often, rural development proj-ects become "subsidy schemes for the rich." On dynamics, interesting studies include Hale (1978) on India, Gotsch (1971) on Pakistan.

to consume the currently available surplus? There is no doubt that consumption by the poor would increase, and there are grounds for being
concerned about intergenerational justice if the investment rate and economic growth were to suffer thereby. But the objection rests on the curious assumption that present patterns of elite expenditures are superior
in terms of the development of agriculture, though such patterns include
a great deal of unnecessary consumption, nonproductive "investment,"
and labor-displacing technical change, while a great deal of land is neglected or underutilized (cf. India, 1976: II, 38 and passim). Moreover,
improved nutrition and health for the poorest would almost certainly
remove one obstacle to increasing labor productivity (Myrdal, 1968; Ram
and Schultz, 1979), just as a more egalitarian distribution of assets should
remove one motivational obstacle to mobilizing underemployed labor for
rural capital works—namely, the widespread feeling that such works
presently benefit only the minority who own most of the land. The Indian National Commission on Agriculture (1976: II, 40) argued that aggregate savings might actually increase and be accompanied by nonmonetized capital formation by land recipients following redistribution, adding
that "the rate of savings in countries with low distributive equity has not
been particularly high." Finally, the state is not incapable of investing in
agricultural dynamism, and does so heavily at present.

The obsession with marketed surplus reflects in part a genuine concern, and requires thoughtful policy responses, but seems to imply that
the rural poor are to increase production but not eat adequately. The large
grain surpluses of the late 1970s in India reflected the irony of success in
marketing "surplus" coexisting with inadequate consumption by a large
percentage of the rural *and* urban poor. Beyond the issue of "human capital formation," surely any justifiable development strategy must place a
high priority on improving the standard of living of those who suffer from
underdevelopment.

The most curious objection to redistribution is that there is not
enough to go around. B. S. Minhas (1970) has questioned redistribution
because, by his assumptions (which are far more conservative than the
proposals above), the percentage of rural people below the poverty line
would be reduced only from two-fifths to one-third of the population (cf.
Dandekar and Rath, 1971). That poverty cannot be abolished at one go
does not weaken the case for reducing the incidence of poverty *unless*
such a reduction results in serious reductions in economic prospects for
society as a whole. Such an argument seems untenable in the light of
evidence of small-farm productive potential when access to inputs and
infrastructure is guaranteed. When opponents of land redistribution argue the "economic viability" position, they fail to recognize that (*a*) a
large percentage of the rural poor are already "nonviable" but survive in
spite of that, and (*b*) redistribution of rights to the agricultural product

need not entail irrational use of the land, and (c) that land area is only one of the determinants of scale of operations; redistribution must address non-land capital simultaneously.

The final objection to radical redistribution is its apparent political impossibility, at least within a liberal and democratic framework. There are three responses. First, to do only what is "politically possible" frequently means to reproduce the status quo. Second, political possibilities are difficult to judge. The Government of Sri Lanka was able to appropriate a large share of the finest agricultural assets, despite earlier doubts about the possibility of same. Both social scientists and elites too frequently view the present distribution of power as given, ignoring the potential for mobilizing new bases of political support. The failures of land reforms in the region, and the contributing bureaucratic inertia and popular quiescence, must be analyzed in the context of the contradictory and ambivalent leadership and cynical compromise typical of politics as usual. A radical land reform is part of a revolutionary process and thus encounters extraordinary difficulties, but for the same reason releases extraordinary potential and energy. Finally, the political realists seem to assume, rather curiously, that it is politically realistic to leave the status quo in place.

That regimes may choose not to unleash forces for fundamental change is undeniable; policy, to be desirable, need not be optimal but must be superior to the alternatives. The alternatives to continuing pressure to establish dignity, security, opportunity, and standing for those who till the land are unacceptable.

One alternative is to do nothing. But the burden of justifying the human misery which is potentially amenable to alleviation does not seem supportable. Moreover, the historical development of political and ideological forces for change has gone too far for the do-nothing option to be realistic. A second strategy prominently discussed in India is that of "regulated capitalism" (cf. Dandekar and Rath, 1971; ICSSR, 1980: 46–47; Joshi, 1978b). While recognizing the attractiveness of this alternative because of the undeniable vigor of the rich peasants and capitalist farmers of South Asia, I think it has three major flaws. First, the historical attractiveness of capitalism is its brute force; strict regulation makes it anemic and vacillating. Second, extensive regulation is quite costly in social terms, as are the subsidies which have made agrarian capitalism dynamic; the resources are desperately needed elsewhere. Third, despite its great cost, regulation of agrarian capitalism is no more likely to succeed then regulation of landlordism, and for similar reasons. If tenure reform in the subcontinent proved anything, it was that regulatory fiats contrary to prevailing economic forces and local power structures are ineffectual, often counterproductive.

A variant on the regulated capitalism theme is public redistribution of the surplus. But rich farmers with rural power are unlikely to allow erosion of their privilege, and subsidized programs for the poor tend to fall under the control of and work for the benefit of local power elites; the case of subsidized agricultural credit is classic. Moreover, the regulatory and redistributive systems leak resources badly and approach the problem indirectly.[11] Developmental strategy that is justifiable in terms of alleviating human misery must thus address those conditions directly or demonstrate convincingly that indirect solutions are possible and will follow from nonredistributive policies. Such evidence is difficult to discern in contemporary South Asia. Despite the extensive redistributive and compensatory legislation in India aimed at the rural poor, there has been no reduction in the incidence of poverty over time, and the absolute number of rural poor continues to increase (by about five million a year) (Ahluwalia, 1978). Moreover, the concentration of rural assets actually increased between 1960–61 and 1970–71 (Pathak, et al., 1977).

But if regimes with genuine political will[12] are unlikely to emerge in much of the subcontinent, are efforts to press for reform legislation desirable? Land reforms, even when legislated with little redistributive intent, have produced observable negative results for some sections of the rural poor as rural elites take countermeasures. As critically, the climate of apprehension surrounding even rhetorical attacks on private property and privilege is hardly conducive to investment on the land. This conclusion is written under the dark cloud of Daniel Thorner's argument that "if India's recent agrarian history demonstrates anything, it is that doing and saying nothing is preferable to taking small steps slowly and timidly" (Thorner, 1973: 75).

Thorner's argument must be taken seriously but requires qualification. Poorly implemented reforms may be historically progressive even while imposing deprivation on individuals who deserve no deprivation. Land reforms have produced evictions, but evictions have fed peasant movements which have demanded further reforms. Historical change on a grand scale inevitably creates dislocations, usually for the least advantaged; with redistributive land reforms there is at least movement on some levels toward a society that is more just. But the stronger argument is that there is no way to protect the agrarian underclass from deprivation without agrarian reforms; tenants in Pakistan escaped the "waves of

11. An exposition of these well-established points in the context of land reform is Griffin (1979); on credit, Herring (1977a); a useful overview is Guhan (1980). Cf. the position of the Indian National Commission on Agriculture (India, 1976: vol. 2, 32; vol. 15, 85).

12. "Political will" has been used throughout. The concept is a vector sum of forces for and against reform, weighted by power resources. Though of dubious theoretical status, the concept is useful and could even be measured (lending an unwarranted but fashionable positivist concreteness) in terms of financial commitments to reform, administrative allocations, speed of reaction to judicial attacks or implementation snares, and so on. It is useful shorthand to say that, for example, there was virtually no political will behind the 1964 Kerala Land Reforms Act and a compromised but positive political will behind enforcement of the 1969 reforms.

eviction" produced by tenure reforms in India only to face eviction from waves of tractors.

Thorner's comment does challenge the compromise position of most development experts concerned with India's land problem—I previously used Mellor, Myrdal, and Ladejinksy as examples—that since radical reforms are unrealistic, one should recommend minimal tenure reforms. Minimal reforms alienate rural elites and help to coalesce opposition to genuine reform, incur heavy administrative costs, but accomplish little, create uncertainty in agriculture, distort land records, and expose the rural poor to countermeasures, including the dissolution of patron–client networks which provide some security in a very insecure world.[13] The importance of a *radical* land reform is underlined by the ephemeral character of reforms that do not change the balance of class forces in the countryside. To alienate powerful people and yet leave power in their hands is to open the possibility of retaliation and retrogression when reformist regimes fall or the land-reform team moves on to the next block; the post-Emergency violence against outcaste beneficiaries of redistributive measures in India is one tragic example.

Thorner's argument also has implications for the implementation process. The police, courts, and bureaucracy must be simultaneously reformed. The ordinary administrative mechanisms should be paralleled, monitored, and energized by new organizational forms and popular committees. The Department of Agrarian Services in Ceylon is a model, of sorts; a reform authority staffed by officers whose sole function and professional responsibility is land reform could parallel and override the land-revenue bureaucracy, which is compromised deeply with landed interests but contains officers of long experience and intimate knowledge about land systems and land control. Public scrutiny of declarations, records, and testimony is crucial, as are harsh penalties for fraud.

The student of development in the region is likely to sigh that this has all been tried and has largely failed. There are two answers. First, reorganization of the village and the local administration has been tried in the absence of genuine land reform; it is not surprising that such efforts have faced special difficulties. The analysis of chapters 2 and 3 suggest that an "embedded bureaucracy" responds to the existing and probable future distribution of rural power, just as a rational peasantry refrains from activism when there is little likelihood that reform will fundamentally change the rural world. Reforms which proceed simultaneously with a comprehensive restructuring of the base of rural power should stand a better chance (cf. Bell, in Chenery et al., 1974: 68). Second, commitment of regimes to land reforms in much of the region has been so minimal

---

13. Jan Breman, in *Patronage and Exploitation* (1974: 236 and passim), concludes from his field study that, though the patron–client relationship is exploitative, its breakdown often subjects the former client to a net deterioration in security and standard of living.

that widespread ignorance of reform provisions is a common theme of implementation studies, conditioning the actions of both officials and peasants. Bureaucratic performance in Sri Lanka's ceiling reforms and Kerala's abolition of landlordism contrast markedly with the more common pattern.

If pressure for radical reform does not succeed, the social process set in motion is nevertheless important. The process heightens class conflicts in the countryside and simultaneously responds to them and thus raises new social forces. Land reforms also have considerable potential for opening public debate about normative principles and, over time, delegitimizing unjustifiable privilege. Even limited tenure reform invokes constraints on the prerogatives of property, explicitly recognizing the right of labor to guaranteed access to the means of production and a specified share of the product, regardless of what the market will bear. The ceiling model introduces a more radical principle: there is a socially definable limit to legitimate accumulation. Beyond a specifiable level, an individual has no right to property when others are propertyless; there is a notion of "surplus," of having enough, and of social claims on the surplus. A land-to-the-tiller reform delegitimizes rents, and thus rights to unearned property income and to the property itself.

The normative principles of agrarian reform are thus more radical, and important, than is realized in critiques from the left, which dismiss land to the tiller as reformist and conservatizing. Conservative theorists have also seen a contented peasantry as a bulwark of the status quo.[14] But the relation between a poor peasantry and market capitalism has shown signs of stress, to say the least, in the twentieth century. It is not certain that the *embourgeoisement* feared by the left and promoted by the right would function in contemporary South Asia as it did in Japan.[15]

The incongruity between curtailment of rural privilege and encouragement of urban accumulation has not gone unnoticed by agrarian elites. In his dissent opposing ceilings on the Planning Commission's Panel on Land Reforms, progressive farmer and parliamentarian Sardar Lal Singh argued:

> I am also as keen as anybody else to *level down the differences between "haves and have-nots"* to remove economic disparities—some people owning crores and earning lakhs and others dying for a loaf of bread, *provided that a uniform principle is applied to all classes of people and all kinds of property.* There is nothing to prevent a man in the urban area owning prop-

14. Hung-Chao Tai (1974: 433–37) effectively presents the variety of conservative arguments for land reform (pp. 433–37), including the possibility of using a stable, conservative rural populace as a base for crushing radical urban upheavals. Wolf Ladejinsky often spoke of land reforms in terms of "strengthening the property system where it is weakest, at its base."

15. On the conservatizing effect in Japan, Huntington (1968: 396). On the tension between capitalism and the peasantry, Wolf (1969); cf. Scott (1976).

erty worth crores and earning lakhs. *What a strange sense of justice—for urban people a capitalistic pattern of no mean type and for rural people a socialistic and communistic pattern with a vengeance.*[16]

Sardar Singh was correct, of course. As discussed previously, Lenin noted long ago the ambivalence of the bourgeois land reformer: attacks on one form of private property are difficult to isolate from attacks on property in general. If landed privilege and inequalities are difficult to justify, how can urban-rural inequalities or urban elite privileges be defended? If a rentier's rent is unearned, what of a stockholder's dividend? If land to the tiller is the "logic of development" in land reforms, is capital to the workers the logic of development in industrial relations? The importance of land reform extends beyond rural South Asia and energizes a broader social debate on inequality and privilege, security and opportunity, and the principles of social justice embedded in social relations generally.

16. India (1959: 113, 121). A *lakh* is 100,000; a *crore*, 10,000,000. Emphasis in original.

References

(Works not fully cited in footnotes)

Abbreviations

AICC	All India Congress Committee (New Delhi)
ARTI	Agrarian Research and Training Institute (Colombo)
CAR	Ceylon Administration Reports (Colombo)
CDM	*Ceylon Daily Mirror* (Colombo)
CDN	*Ceylon Daily News* (Colombo)
DAS	Department of Agrarian Services (Ceylon)
EPW	*Economic and Political Weekly* (Bombay)
Gleanings	Kerala Assembly, Gleanings from the Question Hour
KLA	Synopsis of the Proceedings of the Kerala Legislative Assembly (Trivandrum)
KLT	*Kerala Law Times* (Ernakulam)
ICSSR	Indian Council of Social Science Research
ILO	International Labour Office (Geneva)
PD	Parliamentary Debates, Official Report (Hansard) (Ceylon, House of Representatives, unless noted)
RCAS	Report for the Commissioner of Agrarian Services (Ceylon)
RGA	Report of the [District] Government Agent (Ceylon)
TC	*Times of Ceylon* (Colombo)
UNFAO	United Nations Food and Agriculture Organization (Rome)
UNRISD	United Nations Research Institute for Social Development (Geneva)

Abeysinghe, Ariya. 1979. *Ancient Land Tenure to Modern Land Reform*. Vol. 2. Colombo: The Center for Religion and Society.

Agrarian Research and Training Institute. 1973. "Synopsis of a Two Day Course on Land Reform." Mimeographed. Colombo.

———. 1974. *The Agrarian Situation Relating to Paddy Cultivation in Five Selected Districts of Sri Lanka*. Part 1, Hambantota District; Part 2, Kandy District. Colombo.

———. 1975. *The Agrarian Situation Relating to Paddy Cultivation in Five Selected Districts of Sri Lanka*. Part 6, Comparative Analysis, Colombo.

———. 1977. *Land Reform and the Development of Coconut Lands*. Colombo.

———. 1979. *Policies and Implementation of Land Reform in Selected Villages of Sri Lanka*, by R. D. Wanigaratne, W. Gooneratne, N. Shanmugaratnam. Colombo.

———. 1980. *Land Alienation under Recent Land Reforms*, by R. D. Wanigaratne, M. Samad. Colombo.

Ahluwalia, Montek S. 1978. "Rural Poverty and Agricultural Performance in India." *The Journal of Development Studies* 14:3 (April).

Ahmad, Aijaz. 1973. "Baluchistan's Agrarian Question." *Pakistan Forum IV* (May–June).

Ahmad, Saghir. 1977. *Class and Power in a Punjabi Village*. New York: Monthly Review Press.

Ahmed, Feroze. 1972. "Supplementary Remarks." *Pakistan Forum* 3: 3 (December).

Alam, M. Shahid. 1973. "Economics of the Landed Interests." *Pakistan Economist* (August 25).

Ahmed, Mushtaq. 1970. *Government and Politics in Pakistan*. Karachi: Space.

Aiyappan, A. 1965. *Social Revolution in a Kerala Village*. Bombay: Asia Publishing.

Akram, Muhammad. 1973. *Manal of Land Reforms*. Lahore: National Law Publications.

Alavi, Hamza. 1971. "The Politics of Dependence: A Village in West Punjab." *South Asian Review* 2 (January).

———. 1973. "The State in Postcolonial Societies." In Kathleen Gough and Hari P. Sharma, eds., *Imperialism and Revolution in South Asia*. New York: Monthly Review Press.

———. 1976. "The Rural Elite and Agricultural Development in Pakistan." In Stevens, et al., eds., *Rural Development in Bangladesh and Pakistan*.

Albrecht, Herbert. 1974. *Living Conditions of Rural Families in Pakistan*, trans. from the German by June Hager. Islamabad: Embassy of the Federal Republic of Germany.

Alexander, K. C. 1975. "Nature and Background of the Agrarian Unrest in Kuttanad." *Journal of Kerala Studies* 11, pt. 2 (June).

All India Congress Committee. 1949. *Report of the Congress Agrarian Reform Committee* New Delhi.

All India Kisan Sabha (Peasant Association). 1970. *Report of the General Secretary, Twentieth Session* (Barasat). New Delhi.

Alles, A. C. 1979. *Insurrection 1971*. 3d ed. Colombo: Colombo Apothecaries.

Ambirajan, S. 1978. *Classical Political Economy and British Policy in India*. London: Cambridge University Press.

Anderson, Perry. 1974. *Lineages of the Absolutist State*. London: New Left Books.

———. 1978. *Passages from Antiquity to Feudalism*. London: Verso.

Ayyar, K. V. Krishna. 1966. *A Short History of Kerala* Ernakulam, Kerala: Pai.

Azam, K. M. 1973. "The Future of the Green Revolution in West Pakistan: A Choice of Strategy." *International Journal of Agrarian Affairs* 5 (March).

Baden-Powell, B. H. 1892. *The Land Systems of British India* 3 vols. Oxford: The Clarendon Press.

Balaram, N. E. 1973. *Kerala: Three Years of UF Government Headed by C. Achutha Menon*. New Delhi: People's Publishing House.

Banaji, Jairus. 1976a. "Chayanov, Kautsky, Lenin: Considerations toward a Synthesis." *EPW* 11:40 (October 2).

———. 1976b. "The Peasantry in the Feudal Mode of Production: Towards an Economic Model." *Journal of Peasant Studies* 3:3 (April).

Baran, Paul. 1957. *The Political Economy of Growth*. New York: Monthly Review Press.

Bardhan, P. K. 1973. "Variations in Agricultural Wages." *EPW* 8 (May 26).

———, and Srinivasan, T. N. 1971. "Cropsharing Tenancy in Agriculture: A Theoretical and Empirical Analysis." *American Economic Review* 61:1 (March).

Bardhan, Pranab, and Rudra, Ashok. 1978. "Interlinkage of Land, Labour, and Credit Relations." *EPW* 12: Annual Number (February).

Barth, Frederick. 1959. *Political Leadership among Swat Pathans*. London: University of London Athlone Press.

Belden, Jack. 1970. *China Shakes the World*. New York: Monthly Review Press.

Bell, Clive. 1974. "The Political Framework." In Hollis Chenery et al., eds., *Redistribution with Growth*.

———. 1977. "Alternative Theories of Sharecropping: Some Tests Using Evidence from Northeast India." *The Journal of Development Studies* 13:4 (July).

Berry, R. A. 1971. "Land Reform and Agricultural Income Distribution." *Pakistan Development Review* 11:1 (Spring).

Berry, R. Albert, and Cline, William R. 1979. *Agrarian Structure and Productivity in Developing Countries*. Baltimore: The Johns Hopkins University Press.

Béteille, André. 1974. *Studies in Agrarian Social Structure* Delhi: Oxford University Press.

Bhaduri, A. 1973. "Agricultural Backwardness under Semi-Feudalism." *Economic Journal* 83.

Bhattacharya, N. and Saini, G. R. 1972. "Farm Size and Productivity." *EPW* 7:26 (June 24).

Bhattacharyya, Jnanabrata. 1979. "Inequality and Radical Land Reform: Some Notes from West Bengal." *Asian Survey* 19:7 (June).

Bhutto, Zulfikar Ali. 1969. *Let the People Judge* Lahore: Pakistan People's Party.

Bredo, William. 1961. "Land Reform and Development in Pakistan." In Walter Froelich, ed., *Land Tenure, Industrialisation and Social Stability*. Milwaukee, Wis.: Marquette University Press.

Breman, Jan. 1974. *Patronage and Exploitation: Changing Agrarian Relations in South Gujarat, India*. Berkeley: University of California Press.

Brow, James. 1980. "The Ideology and Practice of Share-Cropping Tenancy in Kukulewa and Pul Eliya." *Ethnology* 19:1 (January).

Burki, Shahid Javed. 1976. "The Development of Pakistan's Agriculture." In Stevens et al., eds., *Rural Development in Bangladesh and Pakistan*.

Byres, T. J. 1972. "The Dialectic of India's Green Revolution." *South Asian Review* 5:2 (January).

Casperz, Paul. 1973. "Land Reform in Sri Lanka: Obstacles and Restraints." Institut International des Civilisations Differentes. Mimeographed. Brussels, October.

Central Bank of Ceylon. *Annual Report*. Colombo.

———. 1969. *Survey on Cost of Production of Paddy*. Colombo.

Ceylon Daily News. 1970. *Seventh Parliament of Ceylon: 1970* (Colombo).

Ceylon. *Ceylon Administration Reports* (annual). Various departments.

———. n.d. *Draft Agricultural Development Plan, 1971–1977.* Mimeographed. Colombo.

———. Periodic, *Parliamentary Debates, Official Report.* Hansard.

———. 1951. *Report of the Kandyan Peasantry Commission,* Sessional Paper no. 18 (Colombo).

———. 1952. *Survey of Landlessness,* Sessional Paper no. 13. Colombo.

———. 1954. *Final Report of the Economic Survey of Rural Ceylon,* Sessional Paper no. 11. Colombo.

———. 1955. *Report of the United Kingdom and Australian Mission on Rice Production in Ceylon,* Sessional Paper no. 2. Colombo.

———. 1956. Ministry of Home Affairs, *Plan for the Rehabilitation of the Kandyan Peasantry* Colombo.

———. 1958. *Paddy Lands Act, No. 1 of 1958.* Colombo, February 1.

———. 1962. Department of Census and Statistics, *Census of Agriculture, 1962.* Official publication date varies by volume.

———. 1966. Department of Agrarian Services, J. V. Fonseka, Commissioner, "Report on Cultivation Committees Survey." Colombo.

———. 1969. Commissioner of Agrarian Services, "Country Paper: Ceylon," Joint FAO-ECAFE-ILO *Seminar on the Implementation of Land Reform in Asia and the Far East* Manila.

———. 1971a. Department of Agrarian Services, I. K. Weerawardena, "A Review of the Paddy Lands Act." Mimeographed. Colombo.

———. 1971b. Ministry of Planning and Employment, *The Five Year Plan: 1972–1976.* Colombo, November.

———. 1971c. Land Reform Commission, *Draft Interim Report.* Unpublished.

Chander, N. Jose. 1973. "The Legislative Process in Kerala 1957–1969." Ph.D. dissertation, University of Kerala, Trivandrum.

Chattopadhyay, Suhas. 1973. "On the Class Nature of Land Reforms in India since Independence." *Social Scientist* 2:4 (November).

Chayanov, A. V. 1966. *The Theory of Peasant Economy,* edited by D. Thorner, B. Kerblay, R. E. F. Smith. Homewood, Ill.: Irwin.

Cheema, M. A. 1954. Deputy Secretary, Ministry of Food and Agriculture, Pakistan, "Land Tenure and Land Reforms in Pakistan." Bangkok: UNFAO.

Chenery, Hollis, et al., eds. 1974. *Redistribution with Growth.* Oxford: Oxford University Press.

Chesneaux, Jean. 1973. *Peasant Revolts in China,* trans. C. A. Curwen. London: W. W. Norton.

Cheung, S. N. S. 1968. "Private Property Rights and Sharecropping." *Journal of Political Economy* 76 (December).

———. 1969. *The Theory of Share Tenancy.* Chicago: University of Chicago Press.

Cline, William R. n.d. "Policy Instruments for Rural Income Redistribution." Paper for the Princeton/Brookings Income Distribution Project. Mimeographed.

Cochin. 1949. *Report of the Agrarian Problem Enquiry Committee.* Ernakulam.

Commons, John R. 1968. *Legal Foundations of Capitalism.* Madison: University of Wisconsin Press.

Communist Party of India (Marxist). 1973. *Central Committee Resolution on*

Certain Agrarian Issues and *An Explanatory Note by P. Sundarayya*. Calcutta.

Coulborn, Rushton, ed. 1965. *Feudalism in History*. Hamden: Archon.

Dahrendorf, Ralph. 1959. *Class and Class Conflict in Industrial Societies*. Stanford: Stanford University Press.

Dandekar, V. M., and Khudanpur, G. J. 1957. *Working of the Bombay Tenancy Act, 1948: Report of Investigation*. Poona: Gokhale Institute.

——, and Rath, Nilakantha. 1971. *Poverty in India*. Poona: Gokhale Institute of Politics and Economics.

Dantwala M. L., and Shah, C. H. 1971. *Evaluation of Land Reforms with Special Reference to the Western Region of India*. Bombay: Bombay University.

Darling, Malcolm Lyall. 1932. *The Punjab Peasant in Prosperity and Debt*. 3d ed. London: Oxford University Press.

De Mel, M. L. C. 1980. "Some Observations on the Nationalized Tea Industry of Sri Lanka." Cyclostyled paper for Conference on the Post-War Economic Development of Sri Lanka. Peradeniya, December 16–20.

Desai, M. B. 1958. *Report on an Enquiry into the Working of the Bombay Tenancy and Agricultural Lands Act, 1948 in Gujarat* Bombay: Indian Society of Agricultural Economics.

——. 1971. *Tenancy Abolition and the Emerging Pattern in Gujarat*. New Delhi: Planning Commission.

Dhanagre, D. N. 1975. *Agrarian Movements and Gandhian Politics*. Agra: Agra University.

Dias, Hiran. 1973. "A Land Reform Policy in the Context of High-Yielding Varieties of Seed." Ceylon Studies Seminar, 1973 series, no. 4. Peradeniya, Sri Lanka.

Dias, Hiran D., and Wickremanayake, B. W. E. 1977. "The Gambara System in the Hambantota District." In S.W.R. de A. Samarasinghe, ed., *Agriculture in the Peasant Sector of Sri Lanka*.

Dorner, Peter. 1972. *Land Reform and Economic Development*. Middlesex, Eng.: Penguin.

——, and Kanel, Don. 1971. "The Economic Case for Land Reform: Employment, Income Distribution, and Productivity." In UNFAO, *Land Reform, Land Settlement and Cooperatives*. Rome.

Downs, Anthony. 1972. "The Environment as Problem—Up and Down with Ecology: The Issue-Attention Cycle." *Public Interest* 28 (Summer).

Eckholm, Erik. 1979. "The Dispossessed of the Earth: Land Reform and Sustainable Development." Worldwatch Paper 30. Washington, D.C.

Economic and Political Weekly. "CPI(M): A Profile," 13:16 (April 22, 1978).

——. "Land Reform: False Passion," 13:20 (May 20, 1978).

——. "Land Reform: Concealing the Surplus," 12:26 (July 1, 1978).

——. Special Issue on *Caste and Class in India* 14:7/8 (Annual Number, February 1979).

Edelman, Murray. 1962. *The Symbolic Uses of Politics*. Urbana: University of Illinois Press.

——. 1977. *Political Language: Words that Succeed and Policies that Fail*. New York: Academic Press.

Eglar, Zekiye. 1960. *A Punjabi Village in Pakistan*. New York: Columbia University Press.

Ellman, A. O., and Ratnaweera, D. de Silva. 1974. *New Settlement Schemes in Sri Lanka.* Agrarian Research and Training Institute, Research Studies Series no. 5. Colombo, August.

—— et al. 1976. *Land Settlement in Sri Lanka, 1840–1975.* Colombo: ARTI.

Embree, Ainslee, ed. 1977. *Pakistan's Western Borderlands.* Durham, N.C.: Carolina Academic Press.

Esposito, Bruce J. 1973. "The Politics of Agrarian Reform in Pakistan." *Pakistan Economist* (August 25).

Farmer, B. H. 1957. *Pioneer Peasant Colonization in Ceylon.* London: Oxford University Press.

Feldman, Herbert. 1967. *Revolution in Pakistan: A Study of the Marital Law Administration.* London: Oxford University Press.

Fernando, Nimal. 1977. "A Preliminary Analysis of Recent Agrarian Reforms in Sri Lanka." Unpublished manuscript, Land Tenure Center. Madison, Wisconsin.

Fic, Victor M. 1970. *Kerala: Yenan of India: Rise of Communist Power, 1937–1969.* Bombay: Nachiketa.

Frankel, Francine R. 1972. *India's Green Revolution: Economic Gains and Political Costs.* Princeton: Princeton University Press.

——. 1978. *India's Political Economy, 1947–1977.* Princeton: Princeton University Press.

——, and Von Vorys, Karl. 1972. "The Political Challenge of the Green Revolution: Shifting Patterns of Peasant Participation in India and Pakistan." Mimeographed. Center for International Studies, Princeton University.

Frykenberg, Robert E., ed. 1977. *Land Tenure and Peasant in South Asia.* Delhi: Orient Longman.

Gandhi, M. K. 1966. *Socialism of My Conception,* ed. Anand T. Hingorani. Bombay: Bharatiya Vidya Bhavan.

——. 1970. *My Theory of Trusteeship,* ed. Anand T. Hingorani. Bombay: Bharatiya Vidya Bhavan.

Gangandharan, A. 1970. *Law of Land Reforms in Kerala.* 2d ed. Cochin: K. V. Krishnan, 1974.

Gold, Martin E. 1977. *Law and Social Change: A Study of Land Reform in Sri Lanka.* New York: Nellen.

Gopalan, A. K. 1959. *Kerala: Past and Present.* London: Lawrence and Wishart.

——. 1973. *In the Cause of the People: Reminiscences* Bombay: Orient Longman.

Gotsch, Carl. 1971. "The Distributive Impact of Agricultural Growth: Low Income Farmers and the 'System.'" Presented to the Seminar on Small Farmer Development Strategies. Columbus, Ohio, September 13–15.

Gough, Kathleen. 1965 "Village Politics in Kerala." *The Economic Weekly* 17 (February 27).

——, and Sharma, Hari P., eds. 1973. *Imperialism and Revolution in South Asia.* New York: Monthly Review Press.

Griffin, Keith. 1974. *The Political Economy of Agrarian Change.* London: Macmillan.

——. 1976. *Land Concentration and Rural Poverty* London: Macmillan.

——, with Ajit Kumar Ghose. 1979. "Growth and Impoverishment in the Rural Areas of Asia." *World Development* 7:4/5 (April/May).

Guhan, S. 1980. "Rural Poverty: Policy and Play Acting," *EPW* 15:47 (November 22).

Gujarat. 1976. Directorate of Evaluation, *Evaluation Study of Implementation of Land Reform Measures in Gujarat State.* Gandhinagar.

Gutelman, Michel. 1974. *Structures et réformes agraires: Instruments pour l'analyse.* Paris: Maspero.

Hale, Sylvia. 1978. "The Politics of Entrepreneurship in India Villages." *Development and Change 9.*

Halliday, Fred. 1971. "The Ceylonese Insurrection." *The New Left Review* 69 (September–October).

Hardgrave, Robert L., Jr. 1970. "The Marxist Dilemma in Kerala: Administration and/or Struggle." *Asian Survey* 10:11 (November).

———. 1973. "The Kerala Communists." In Paul R. Brass and Marcus F. Franda, eds., *Radical Politics in South Asia.* Cambridge: MIT Press.

———. 1977. "The Mappilla Rebellion, 1921: Peasant Revolt in Malabar." *Modern Asian Studies* 2:1.

Harriss, John. 1977. "Aspects of Rural Society in the Dry Zone Relating to the Problem of Intensifying Paddy Production." In S.W.R. de A. Samarasinghe, ed., *Agriculture in the Peasant Sector of Sri Lanka.*

———. 1979. "Why Poor People Remain Poor in Rural South Asia." *Social Scientist* 8:1 (August).

Hart, Henry C., and Herring, Ronald J. 1977. "Political Conditions of Land Reform: Kerala and Maharashtra." In Robert E. Frykenberg, ed., *Land Tenure and Peasant in South Asia.* Delhi: Orient Longman.

Heady, E. O. 1947. "Economics of Farm Leasing Systems." *Journal of Farm Economics* 34:3 (August).

Herring, Ronald J. 1972/74. "The Forgotten 1953 Paddy Lands Act in Ceylon: Ideology, Capacity, and Response." *Modern Ceylon Studies* 3:2 (June 1972; published 1974).

———. 1977a. "Land Tenure and Credit/Capital Tenure in Contemporary India." In Robert Eric Frykenberg, ed., *Land Tenure and Peasant in South Asia.*

———. 1977b. "Policy and Ecology in the Origins of Discontinuities in the Land Tenure System of the Hambantota District." in S. W. R. de A. Samarasinghe, ed., *Agriculture in the Peasant Sector of Sri Lanka.*

———. 1978. "Share Tenancy and Economic Efficiency: The South Asian Case." *Peasant Studies* 7:4 (Fall).

———. 1979a. "Zulfikar Ali Bhutto and the 'Eradication of Feudalism' in Pakistan." *Comparative Studies in Society and History* 21:4 (October).

———. 1979b. "The Policy Logic of Land Reforms in Pakistan." In Manzooruddin Ahmed, ed., *Contemporary Pakistan: Politics, Economy, and Society.* Durham, N.C.: Carolina Academic Press.

———. 1980. "Abolition of Landlordism in Kerala: A Redistribution of Privilege." *EPW* 15:26 (June 28).

———. 1981. "Embedded Production Relations and the Rationality of Tenant Quiescence in Tenure Reform." *The Journal of Peasant Studies* 8:2 (January).

———, and Chaudhry, M. Ghaffar. 1974. "The 1972 Land Reforms in Pakistan and Their Economic Implications: A Preliminary Analysis." *Pakistan De-*

velopment Review 13:3 (Fall). Also, Reprint no. 126, Land Tenure Center, University of Wisconsin, Madison.

———, and Kennedy, Charles R., Jr. 1979. "The Political Economy of Farm Mechanisation Policy: Tractors in Pakistan." In Raymond Hopkins, Donald Puchala, and Ross Talbot, eds., *Food, Politics, and Agricultural Development: Case Studies in the Public Policy of Rural Modernization* Boulder, Colo.: Westview.

Hewavitharana, Buddhadasa. 1974. "Non-Monetized Capital Formation in Ceylon—A Marga." Colombo: Marga Institute.

Hilton, Rodney, ed. 1976. *The Transition from Feudalism to Capitalism.* London: New Left Books.

Hinton, William. 1966. *Fanshen: A Documentary of Revolution in a Chinese Village.* New York: Monthly Review Press.

Huntington, Samuel P. 1968. *Political Order in Changing Societies* New Haven: Yale University Press.

India. n.d. *The Turning Point: New Programme for Economic Progress.* New Delhi.

———. 1955. Directorate of Economics and Statistics, Ministry of Food and Agriculture, *Agricultural Legislation in India.* Delhi.

———. 1956. Planning Commission, *The Second Five Year Plan.* New Delhi.

———. 1957. Planning Commission, *Report of the Indian Delegation to China on Agrarian Co-operatives.* New Delhi (May).

———. 1959. Planning Commission, *Reports of the Committees of the Panel on Land Reform.* Delhi.

———. 1961. Planning Commission, *Third Five Year Plan.* New Delhi.

———. 1962. *Agricultural Labour in India: Report of the Second Enquiry*, vol. 7, *Kerala.* Delhi.

———. 1963. Planning Commission, *Progress of Land Reform.* Delhi.

———. 1966a. Directorate of Economics and Statistics, *Farm Management in India* New Delhi, April.

———. 1966b. Planning Commission, National Development Council, *Implementation of Land Reforms.* New Delhi.

———. 1966c. Planning Commission, *Seminar on Land Reform: Proceedings and Papers.* New Delhi.

———. 1968. Department of Community Development, *Report of the Study Team on Involvement of Community Development Agency and Panchayati Raj Institutions in the Implementation of Basic Land Reform Measures.* New Delhi.

———. 1969. Planning Commission, *Draft Fourth Five Year Plan, 1969–74.* New Delhi.

———. 1970. Directorate of Economics and Statistics, *Chief Minister's Conference on Land Reforms: Notes on Agenda.* New Delhi, September 26.

———. 1971. Census of India, *A Portrait of Population, Kerala*, by Census Commissioner K. Narayan. New Delhi.

———. 1971/72. Directorate of Economics and Statistics, *Studies in the Economics of Farm Management in Kerala.* 3 vols. New Delhi.

———. 1972a. Directorate of Economics and Statistics, *Studies in the Economics of Farm Management in Kerala, 1964–65.* New Delhi.

———. 1972b. Ministry of Finance, *Report of the Committee on Taxation of Agricultural Wealth and Income.* New Delhi, October.

————. 1972c. Planning Commission, "Land Reforms: Policy Legislation and Implementation." *Mainstream* 11:10 (November 4).

————. 1973. Planning Commission, *Task Force on Agrarian Relations Report.* New Delhi.

————. 1974. Planning Commission, *Draft Fifth Five Year Plan* (1974–1979), vol. 2. Delhi.

————. 1975a. *Census of India, 1971*, Series 9, *Kerala.* Delhi.

————. 1975b. Ministry of Planning, The National Sample Survey, Twenty-sixth Round (1971–72), *Tables on Land Holdings.* New Delhi.

————. India, 1976. Ministry of Agriculture and Irrigation, *Report of the National Commission on Agriculture.* 15 vols. New Delhi.

————. 1978a. "Country Review, 1978: India," UNFAO World Conference on Agrarian Reform and Rural Development. New Delhi.

————. 1978b. Ministry of Agriculture and Irrigation, *Report of the Committee on Land Reforms.* New Delhi.

Indian Commission of Jurists. 1970. *Report of the Kerala Enquiry Committee.* New Delhi.

Indian Council of Social Science Research. 1980. *Alternatives in Agricultural Development.* New Delhi: Allied.

Indian Journal of Agricultural Economics. 1974. Special Issue, Conference Number. "Wages and Incomes of the Weaker Sections in Rural India" 29:3 (July–September).

Indian School of Social Sciences. n.d. "Survey on Agrarian Structure and Social Change in Selected Villages of Kerala." Draft typescript. Trivandrum.

International Bank for Reconstruction and Development. Annual. *Annual Report* Washington, D.C.

International Labour Office. 1971. *Matching Employment Opportunities and Expectations: A Programme of Action for Ceylon.* vol. 1, *Report*; vol. 2, *Technical Papers.* Geneva.

Isenmen, Paul. 1980. "Basic Needs: The Case of Sri Lanka." *World Development* 8:3 (March).

Jacob, K. T. 1972. *Tiller Gets Land in Kerala.* New Delhi: People's Publishing House.

Jacoby, Erich H. 1971. *Man and Land: The Fundamental Issue in Development.* London: Deutsch.

Jahan, Rounaq. 1972. *Pakistan: Failure in National Integration.* New York: Columbia University Press.

Jannuzi, F. Tomasson. 1974. *Agrarian Crisis in India: The Case of Bihar.* Austin: University of Texas Press.

————, and Peach, James T. 1980. *The Agrarian Structure of Bangladesh.* Boulder, Colo.: Westview.

Jayachandran, T. N. 1976. "Farming Cooperatives in Kerala." *Dharani*, Special Number (November).

Jayaraj, D. 1974. "Coalition Governments in Kerala." Draft Ph.D. thesis, University of Kerala (Kariavattom).

Jha, S. C. 1971. *A Critical Analysis of Indian Land Reforms Studies*, Bombay: Asian Studies Press.

Jones, Philip E. 1978. "Changing Party Structures in Pakistan: From Muslim League to People's Party." Quaid-E-Azam Conference on Contemporary Pakistan, Columbia University, New York, March 9–11.

Jose, A. V. 1973. "Wage Rates of Agricultural Labourers in Kerala." *EPW* 8:4–6 (February).

Joshi, P. C. 1975. *Land Reforms in India: Trends and Perspectives*, Bombay: Allied Publishers.

———. 1978a. "Land Reforms Implementation and Role of Administrator." *EPW* 12:39 (September 30).

———. 1978b. "Perspectives of Agrarian Reconstruction: India in Asian Context." *Mainstream* 16:21–22 (Republic Day).

Jupp, James. 1978. *Sri Lanka: Third World Democracy*. London: Frank Cass.

Kaneda, Hiromitsu. 1969. "Economic Implications of the 'Green Revolution' and the Strategy of Agricultural Development in West Pakistan." Pakistan Institute of Development Economics, Report no. 78. Karachi.

Kanel, Don. 1967. "Size of Farm and Economic Development." *Indian Journal of Agricultural Economics* 22.

Karat, Prakash. 1973. "Agrarian Relations in Malabar: 1925–1948." *Social Scientist* 2:2 (September).

Kearney. R. N. 1971. *Trade Unions and Politics in Ceylon*. Berkeley: University of California Press.

———. 1973. *The Politics of Ceylon (Sri Lanka)*. Ithaca, N.Y.: Cornell University Press.

———, and Jiggins, J., 1975. "The Ceylon Insurrection of 1971." *Journal of Commonwealth Studies* 13 (March).

Kerala. Annual. Administration Report, *Land Board and Land Tribunals*. Trivandrum.

———. Periodic. Land Board, "Notes on the Progress of Implementation of the Land Reforms Act." Mimeographed. Trivandrum.

———. Periodic. Land Board, "Proceedings of the Land Board." mimeographed. Trivandrum.

———. Periodic. Secretariat of the Kerala Legislature, *Gleanings from the Question Hour*. Trivandrum.

———. Periodic. Secretariat of the Kerala Legislature, *Synopsis of the Proceedings of the Kerala Legislative Assembly*. Trivandrum.

———. 1961. *The Kerala Agrarian Relations Act, 1960* (Act 4 of 1961). Trivandrum.

———. 1962. *Kerala Legislative Assembly Who's Who 1962*. Trivandrum.

———. 1964. *The Kerala Land Reforms Act, 1963* (Act 1 of 1964). Trivandrum.

———. 1968. Bureau of Economics and Statistics, *Land Reforms Survey*. Trivandrum.

———. 1968/76. *Land Reforms Survey in Kerala: Report* Trivandrum, 1976. Expanded version of the 1968 *Survey*.

———. 1971. *Report of the Kuttanad Enquiry Committee*. Trivandrum.

———. 1973a. Bureau of Economics and Statistics, *The Third Decennial World Census of Agriculture, 1970–71: Report for Kerala State*. Trivandrum.

———. 1973b. Fifth Five Year Plan, *Report of the Task Force on Land Reforms*. Trivandrum.

———. 1974. Public Relations Department, *New Deal to Farm Labor*. Trivandrum.

————. 1977a. Department of Public Relations, *Kerala Election Reportage, 1977.* Trivandrum.

————. 1977b. Planning Board, *Statistics for Planning.* Trivandrum.

————. 1977c. *The Kerala Land Reforms Manual.* 2 vols. Trivandrum.

————. 1978. State Planning Board, *Report of the Task Force on Land Reforms: VI Five Year Plan 1978.* Trivandrum.

————. 1979. Public Relations Department, *Land Revolution in Kerala.* Trivandrum.

Khan, Akhter Hameed. 1973. "Land Reforms in Pakistan: 1947–1972." In *Three Essays by Akhter Hameed Khan,* Michigan State University, Asian Studies Center, occasional paper no. 20 (East Lansing).

Khan, Mahmood Hasan. 1975. *The Economics of the Green Revolution in Pakistan.* New York: Praeger.

————. 1977. "Land Productivity, Farm Size, and Returns to Scale in Pakistan Agriculture." *World Development* 5:4 (April).

Khan, M. Ayub. 1967. *Friends Not Masters: A Political Autobiography.* Lahore: Oxford University Press.

Khusro, A. M. 1958. *Economic and Social Effects of Jagirdari Abolition and Land Reforms in Hyderabad.* Hyderabad: Osmania University Press.

————. 1973. *The Economics of Farm Size and Land Reform in India.* Delhi: Macmillan.

Koshy, M. J. 1972. *Genesis of Political Consciousness in Kerala.* Trivandrum: Kerala Historical Society.

Koshy, V. C. 1974. "Land Reforms in India under the Plans." *Social Scientist* 2:12 (July).

————. 1976. "The Politics of Land Reforms in Kerala." Ph.D. thesis, Jawaharlal Nehru University, New Delhi.

Kotovsky, Grigory. 1964. *Agrarian Reform in India,* trans. from the Russian by K. J. Lambkin. New Delhi; People's Publishing House.

Krishna, Raj. 1961. "Some Aspects of Land Reform and Economic Development in India." In Walter Froelich, ed., *Land Tenure, Industrialization, and Social Stability.* Milwaukee, Wis.: Marquette University Press.

————. 1979. "The Crucial Phase in Rural Development." *Kurukshetra* 38:3 (November).

Krishnaji, N. 1979. "Agrarian Relations and the Left Movement in Kerala." *EPW* 15:9 (March 3).

Kuhn, Thomas S. 1962. *The Structure of Scientific Revolutions.* Chicago: University of Chicago Press.

Kurien, C. T. 1980. "Dynamics of Rural Transformation: A Case Study of Tamil Nadu." *EPW* 15: 5, 6, 7 (February).

Ladejinsky, Wolf. 1965. *A Study of Tenurial Conditions in Package Districts.* Delhi: Planning Commission.

————. 1972a. "Land Ceilings and Land Reform." *EPW* 7:5–7 (February).

————. 1972b. "New Ceiling Round and Implementation Prospects." *EPW* 7:40 (September 30).

————. 1976. "Food Shortage in West Bengal—Crisis or Chronic." *World Development* 4:2 (February).

————. 1977. *Agrarian Reforms as Unfinished Business,* edited by Louis J. Walinsky. London: Oxford University Press.

Lappé, Frances Moore, and Collins, Joseph. 1977. *Food First: Beyond the Myth of Scarcity*. Boston: Houghton-Mifflin.

Laxminarayan, H., and Tyagi, S. S. 1977, "Tenancy: Extent and Interstate Variations." *EPW* 12:22 (May 28).

Leach, E. R. 1961. *Pul Eliya*. Cambridge: Cambridge University Press.

Lehmann, David, ed. 1974. *Agrarian Reform and Agrarian Reformism*. London: Faber and Faber.

Lenin, V. I. 1938. *Theory of the Agrarian Question*. In his *Selected Works*, vol. 12. New York: International Publishers.

————. 1962. *Collected Works*. Moscow: International Publishers.

Lewis, Oscar. 1965. *Village Life in Northern India*. New York: Vantage.

Lieten, Georges Kristoffel. 1979. "Progressive State Governments: An Assessment of First Communist Ministry in Kerala." *EPW* 14:1 (January 6).

Lipton, Michael. 1977. "The New Economics of Growth: A Review." *World Development* 5:3 (March).

Maddison, Angus. 1971. *Class Structure and Economic Growth: India and Pakistan since the Moghuls* New York: Norton.

Maguire, Jane. 1975. *On Shares (Ed Brown's Story)*. New York: Norton.

Maharashtra. 1974. *Report of the Committee Appointed by the Government of Maharashtra for Evaluation of Land Reforms*. Bombay.

Malaviya, H. D. 1954. Secretary, Economic and Political Research Department, All India Congress Committee, *Land Reforms in India*. Delhi: AICC.

Mannheim, Karl. 1936. *Ideology and Utopian*. New York: Harcourt, Brace, and World.

Mao Tse-tung. 1967. *Selected Works*, 5 vols. Peking: Foreign Languages Press.

Marx, Karl. 1965. *Precapitalist Economic Formations*, trans. Jack Cohen, ed. Eric Hobsbawm. New York: International Publishers.

McCoy, Al. 1971. "Land Reform as Counter-Revolution: U.S. Foreign Policy and the Tenant." *Bulletin of Concerned Asian Scholars* 3:1 (Winter–Spring).

McInerny, John P. and Donaldson, Graham R. 1973. *The Consequences of Farm Tractors in Pakistan*. Washington, D.C.: IBRD.

Melchior, S. X. James. 1979. "Karnataka: Implementation of Land Reforms." *EPW* 14:18 (May 5).

Mellor, John W. 1976. *The New Economics of Growth: A Strategy for India and the Developing World*. Ithaca, N.Y.: Cornell University Press.

Mencher, Joan P. 1975. "Land Ceilings in Tamil Nadu." *EPW* 10: Annual Number (February).

————. 1976. "Land Reform and Socialism." In S. Devadas Pillai, ed., *Aspects of Changing India*. Bombay: Popular Prakashan.

————. 1978. "Agrarian Relations in Two Rice Regions of Kerala." *EPW* 12:6–7 (February).

————. 1980. "The Lessons and Non-Lessons of Kerala: Agricultural Labourers and Poverty." *EPW* 15:41–2–3 (October).

Menon, C. Achutha. 1958. *The Kerala Agrarian Relations Bill: An Interpretation*. New Delhi: People's Publishing House.

————. "Land Reform in Kerala: An Interview with Chief Minister Achutha Menon." *Yojana* 16:13 (1972).

Merillat, H. C. L. 1970. *Land and the Constitution in India*. New York: Columbia University Press.

Minhas, B. S. 1970. "Rural Poverty, Land Redistribution, and Economic Strategy." *Indian Economic Review* 5 (April).

Mirich. 1977. "Announce Tenants' Ledgers." *Mainstream* 12:8 (October 22).

Montgomery, John D. 1972. "Allocation of Authority in Land Reforms: A Comparative Study of Administrative Process and Outputs." *Administrative Science Quarterly* 17 (March).

Moore, Barrington, Jr., 1968. *Social Origins of Dictatorship and Democracy: Lord and Peasant in the Making of the Modern World.* Boston: Beacon.

———. 1978. *Injustice: The Social Bases of Obedience and Revolt.* White Plains, N.Y.: M. E. Sharpe.

Murthy, K. G. Krishna, and Rao, C. Lakshmana. 1968. *Political Preferences in Kerala.* New Delhi: Radhakrishna Prakashan.

Myrdal, Gunnar. 1968. *Asian Drama: An Inquiry into the Poverty of Nations.* New York: Random House.

Nair, Kusum. 1962. *Blossoms in the Dust: The Human Factor in Indian Development.* New York: Praeger.

Namboodiripad, E. M. S. 1952. *On the Agrarian Question in India.* Bombay: People's Publishing House.

———. 1954. *The Peasant in National Economic Construction.* Delhi: People's Publishing House.

———. 1959. *Twenty-Eight Months in Kerala: A Retrospect.* New Delhi: People's Publishing House.

———. 1968. *Kerala: Past, Present and Future.* Calcutta: National Book Agency.

———. 1974. *Conflicts and Crisis: Political India 1974.* Bombay: Orient Longmans.

———. 1976. *How I Became a Communist,* trans. from the Malayalam by P. K. Nair. Trivandrum: Chinta.

Nanjundaiya, B. 1978. "Ceiling on Urban Property." *Yojana* (October 15).

Narayan, R. 1977. "Sharecropper Killing." *Mainstream* 16:12 (November 19).

Narayanaswamy, C. 1973. "Problems, Policies, and Programmes Relating to Paddy Lands in Sri Lanka." Mimeographed. Colombo: ARTI.

Neale, Walter C. 1962. *Economic Change in Rural India: Land Tenure and Reform in Uttar Pradesh, 1800–1955.* New Haven: Yale University Press.

Nehru, Jawaharlal, 1960. *The Discovery of India.* New York: Doubleday.

Newbery, D. M. G. 1975. "Tenurial Obstacles to Innovation." *Journal of Development Studies* 11:4 (July).

Niaz, Shafi. 1959. "Land Reforms in Pakistan." *Economic Digest* 2:3–4 (March–April).

———. 1965. *Study of the Relationship between Land Reforms and Community Development.* Karachi: Government of Pakistan.

Nozick, Robert. 1974. *Anarchy, State and Utopia.* New York: Basic Books.

Obeysekara, Jayasumana. 1973. "Revolutionary Movements in Ceylon." In Kathleen Gough and Hari P. Sharma, eds., *Imperialism and Revolution in South Asia.*

Obeysekere, Gananath. 1967. *Land Tenure in Village Ceylon.* Cambridge: Cambridge University Press.

Oommen, M. A. 1971. *Land Reforms and Socio-Economic Change in Kerala.* Madras: The Christian Institute for the Study of Religion and Society.

———. 1973. "Obstacles and Restraints Impeding the Success of Land Reform in

Developing Countries (Kerala State)." Institut International des Civilisations Differentes. Brussels, October.

———. 1975. *A Study on Land Reforms in Kerala.* New Delhi: Oxford and IBH.

———, ed. 1979. *Kerala Economy since Independence.* New Delhi: Oxford and IBH.

Oommen, T. K. 1971. "Agrarian Tension in a Kerala District: An Analysis." *Indian Journal of Industrial Relations* 7:2 (October).

———. 1975. "Agrarian Legislations and Movements as Sources of Change: The Case of Kerala." *Economic and Political Weekly* 9:40 (Oct. 5).

———. 1976. "Problems of Building Agrarian Organizations in Kerala." *Sociologia Ruralis* 16:3.

Paige, Jeffery. 1975. *Agrarian Revolution: Social Movements and Export Agriculture in the Underdeveloped World.* New York: Free Press.

Pakistan. n.d. Planning Commission, "Working Papers for the Development Perspective (1974–1980)." Typescript. Islamabad.

———. 1952. Ministry of Food and Agriculture, *Report of the Pakistan Agricultural Inquiry Committee, 1951–52.* Karachi.

———. 1954. M. A. Cheema (deputy secretary, Ministry of Food and Agriculture), "Land Tenure and Land Reforms in Pakistan." UNFAO mimeographed. Bangkok.

———. 1956. Planning Board, *First Five Year Plan, 1955–1960.* Karachi.

———. 1959a. Martial Law Regulation no. 64, Notification no. 181/89, *The Gazette of Pakistan Extraordinary* (March 3).

———. 1959b. *Report of the Land Reforms Commission for West Pakistan.* Lahore, January.

———. 1960. Planning Commission, *The Second Five Year Plan, 1960–1965* Karachi.

———. 1962. Ministry of Agriculture, *Census of Agriculture, 1960.* Karachi.

———. 1965. Planning Commission, *The Third Five Year Plan, 1965–1970.* Karachi.

———. 1966. West Pakistan Land Commission, *Implementation of Land Reforms Scheme in West Pakistan.* Lahore.

———. 1970a. Ministry of Food and Agriculture, *Farm Mechanization in West Pakistan* (Report of the Committee on Farm Mechanization). Officially unpublished. Islamabad.

———. 1970b. Planning Commission, *The Fourth Five Year Plan, 1970–75.* Karachi.

———. 1972a. Department of Films and Publications, Zulfikar Ali Bhutto, "Address to the Nation," March 1, 1972. Karachi.

———. 1972b. Department of Films and Publications, *President of Pakistan Zulfikar Bhutto Speeches and Statements* (Karachi).

———. 1972c. Marital Law Regulation 115, Land Reforms Regulation 1972, *Gazette of Pakistan, Extraordinary* (March 11).

———. 1974. "White Paper on Baluchistan." *Dawn* (Karachi, October 20).

———. 1975a. Agricultural Census Organization, *Pakistan Census of Agriculture 1972* (Lahore).

———. 1975b. (draft). *Report of the Agricultural Enquiry Committee.* Typescript. Islamabad, June.

———. 1977. Minister of Agriculture, Shaikh Muhammad Rashid, "Land Reforms—The Dawn of a New Era." Unpublished mimeograph. Rawalpindi.

———. 1979. *White Paper on the Performance of the Bhutto Regime.* Vol. 4, *The Economy.* Islamabad.

Pakistan People's Party. 1970. *Election Manifesto of Pakistan People's Party, 1970.* Lahore.

Panikar, P. G. K. 1979. "Employment, Income, and Food Intake among Agricultural Labour Households." *EPW* 14:34 (August 25).

Pannikar, K. N. 1979. "Peasant Revolts in Malabar in the Nineteenth and Twentieth Centuries." In A. R. Desai, ed., *Peasant Struggles in India* Bombay: Oxford University Press.

Paranjpe, V. M. 1958. "Input-Output Relations in Indian Agriculture." *Indian Journal of Agricultural Economics* 13:1 (January–March).

Pathak, R. P. et al. 1977. "Shifts in Pattern of Asset Holdings of Rural Households, 1961–62 to 1971–72." *EPW* 12 (March).

Patnaik, Utsa. 1972. "Economics of Farm Size and Farm Scale." *EPW* 7:31–33 (August).

Paulini, Thomas. 1978. "Agrarian Movements and Reforms in India: The Case of Kerala." Ph.D. thesis, University of Stuttgart.

Peiris, G. H. 1975. "Current Land Reforms and Peasant Agriculture in Sri Lanka." *South Asia* 5 (December.)

———. 1976. "Share Tenancy and Tenurial Reform in Sri Lanka." *Ceylon Journal of Historical and Social Studies* 6:1.

———. 1978. "Land Reform and Agrarian Change in Sri Lanka." *Modern Asian Studies* 12:4.

Perera, M. S. 1970. "Agrarian Reform in Ceylon." Unpublished MS. Land Tenure Center, University of Wisconsin (Madison).

Pherson, Robert N. 1966. *The Social Organization of the Marri Baluch,* compiled and edited by Frederick Barth. Chicago: Aldine.

Pieris, Denzil. 1958. *1956 and After: Background to Parties and Politics in Ceylon Today.* Colombo: Pieris.

Pillai, Thakazhi Sivasankaran. 1967. *Two Measures of Rice.* Bombay: Jaico.

———. 1976. *The Iron Rod.* Delhi: Sterling.

Pillai, V. R. and Panikar, P. G. K. 1965. *Land Reclamation in Kerala.* Bombay: Asia Publishing House.

Polanyi, Karl. 1944. *The Great Transformation.* New York: Farrar and Rinehart. Originally published as *Origins of Our Time.*

Popkin, Samuel L. 1979. *The Rational Peasant.* Berkeley: University of California Press.

Poulantzas, Nicos. 1968. *Pouvoir politique et classes sociales.* Paris: Maspero.

Pressman, Jeffrey L., and Wildavsky, Aaron B. 1973. *Implementation.* Berkeley: University of California Press.

Proctor, Robert Chelvathurai. 1915. "The Ceylon Peasantry." *Tropical Argiculture.* Issues of August, September, and December of 1914; January 1915.

Punjab. 1938. *Report of the Land Revenue Commission.* Lahore.

Qayyum, Abdul. 1977. "Land Reforms (Pakistan): Review of Implementation." Paper presented to the International Seminar on Agrarian Reform, Institutional Innovation and Rural Development, Madison, Wisconsin, July 14–22.

Radhakrishnan, P. 1980. "Peasant Struggles and Land Reforms in Malabar." *EPW* 15: 50 (December 13).

Raj, K. N. 1975. "Agricultural Development and Distribution of Land Holdings." *Indian Journal of Agricultural Economics* 30:1 (January–March).

Rajaraman, Indira. 1975. "Poverty, Inequality, and Economic Growth: Rural Punjab, 1960/61–1970/71." *The Journal of Development Studies* 11:4 (July).

Ram, Rati, and Schultz, Theodore W. 1979. "Life Span, Health, Savings, and Productivity." *Economic Development and Cultural Change* 27 (April).

Rani, Usha. 1971. "Size of Farm and Productivity." *EPW* 6:26 (June).

Rao, A. P. 1967. "Size of Holding and Productivity." *EPW* 2:44 (November 11).

———. 1968. "Farm Size and Yield Per Acre: A Comment." *EPW* 3:37 (September 14).

Rawls, John. 1971. *A Theory of Justice*. Cambridge, Mass.: Harvard University Press.

Raza, Ameer. 1970. *Evaluation of the Paddy Lands Act*. Rome: UNFAO.

Rehman, Frazlur. 1974. "Islam and the Problem of Economic Justice." *Pakistan Economist* (August 24–30).

Reid, Joseph D., Jr. 1976. "Sharecropping and Agricultural Uncertainty." *Economic Development and Cultural Change* 24:3 (April).

Rizvi, Hasan Askari. 1973. *Pakistan People's Party: The First Phase: 1967–71*. Lahore: Progressive Publishers.

———. 1974. *The Military and Politics in Pakistan*. Lahore: Progressive Publishers.

Robinson, Joan. 1964. *Economic Philosophy*. New York: Doubleday.

Rudra, Ashok. 1968a. "Farm Size and Yield Per Acre." *EPW* 3:26–28 (July).

———. 1968b. "More on Returns to Scale in Indian Agriculture." *EPW* 3:43 (October 26).

———, and Chakravarty, A. 1973. "Economic Effects of Tenancy: Some Negative Results." *EPW* 8:28 (July 14).

———, and Sen, Amartya. 1980. "Farm Size and Labour Use: Analysis and Policy." *EPW* 15: Annual Number (February).

Russett, Bruce. 1964. "Inequality and Instability: The Relation of Land Tenure to Politics." *World Politics* 16:3 (April).

Ruttan, Vernon W. 1966. "Tenure and Productivity of Philippine Rice Producing Farms." *The Philippine Economic Journal* 5:1.

Ryan, Bryce. 1958. *Sinhalese Village*. Miami: University of Miami Press.

Samarasinghe, S. W. R. de A., ed. 1977. *Agriculture in the Peasant Sector of Sri Lanka* Peradeniya: Ceylon Studies Seminar.

Sanderatne, Nimal. 1969. "Ceylon's Crop Insurance Experience." *Indian Journal of Agricultural Economics* 24:2 (April–June).

———. 1972a. "Sri Lanka's New Land Reform." *South Asian Review* 6:1 (October).

———. 1972b. "Tenancy in Ceylon's Paddy Lands: The 1958 Reform." *South Asian Review* 5:2 (January).

———. 1974a. "Landowners and Land Reform in Pakistan." *South Asian Review* 7:2 (January).

———. 1974b. "The Political Economy of Asian Agrarian Reform: A Comparative Analysis with Case Studies of the Philippines and Sri Lanka (Ceylon)." Ph.D. dissertation, University of Wisconsin, (Land Tenure Center).

————. 1977. "Group Farming in Sri Lanka." In Peter Dorner, ed., *Cooperative and Commune: Group Farming in the Economic Development of Agriculture*. Madison: University of Wisconsin Press.

————, and Zaman, M. A. 1973. "The Impact of the Agrarian Structure on the Political Leadership of Undivided Pakistan." Land Tenure Center Research Paper no. 94, Madison, Wis., November.

Saini, G. R. 1969. "Farm Size, Productivity and Returns to Scale." *EPW* 4:26 (June 28).

S. K. Sanyal. 1969. "Size of Holding and Some Factors Related to Production." *EPW* 4:33 (August 16).

————. 1972. "Has There Been A Decline in Agricultural Tenancy?" *EPW* 7:19 (May).

Saradamoni, K. 1980. *Emergence of a Slave Caste: Pulayas of Kerala*. New Delhi: People's Publishing House.

Sarkar, N. K., and Tambiah, S. J. 1957. *The Disintegrating Village*. Colombo: University of Ceylon.

Sayeed, Khalid B. 1967. *The Political System of Pakistan*. Boston: Houghton Mifflin.

Schultz, T. W. 1940. "Capital Rationing, Uncertainty and Farm Tenancy Reform." *Journal of Political Economy* 48:3 (June).

Scott, James C. 1972. "The Erosion of Patron-Client Bonds and Social Change in Rural Southeast Asia." *Journal of Asian Studies* 32 (November).

————. 1974. "Exploitation in Rural Class Relations: A Victim's Perspective." *Comparative Politics* 7:4 (July).

————. 1976. *The Moral Economy of the Peasant: Rebellion and Subsistence in Southeast Asia*. New Haven and London: Yale University Press.

————. 1977. "Protest and Profanation: Agrarian Revolt and the Little Tradition." *Theory and Society* 4:1–2 (Spring/Summer).

Seers, Dudley. 1969. "The Meaning of Development." *International Development Review* 11:4 (December).

Sen, Bhowani. 1955. *Indian Land Systems and Land Reforms*. Delhi: People's Publishing House.

Sen, Sunil. 1972. *Agrarian Struggle in Bengal, 1946–47*. New Delhi: People's Publishing House.

Shea, Thomas W., Jr. 1959. "The Land Tenure Structure of Malabar and its Influence upon Capital Formation in Agriculture." Ph.D. dissertation, University of Pennsylvania.

Sind. n.d. *Report of the Government Hari Enquiry Committee, 1947–48*. Karachi.

Singer, Marshall. 1964. *The Emerging Elite*. Cambridge, Mass.: MIT Press.

Singh, M. L. 1972. "Ceiling on Land Holdings." *Yojana* 16:10 (June 1).

Sinha, Arun. 1977. "Class War Not 'Atrocities against Harijans.'" *EPW* 12:50 (December).

Sivanandan, P. 1979. "Caste, Class and Economic Opportunity in Kerala: An Empirical Analysis." *EPW* 14:7–8 (February).

Sri Lanka. Annual. Central Bank of Ceylon, *Annual Report* (Colombo).

————. Periodic. *National State Assembly Debates, Official Report* (Colombo).

————. 1972a. National State Assembly, *Land Reform Law No. 1 of 1972* (Colombo, August 26).

——. 1972b. National State Assembly, *Agricultural Productivity Law, No. 2 of 1972* (Colombo, September 21).

——. 1979. Central Bank óf Ceylon, *Review of the Economy* (Colombo).

——. 1980. *Third Interim Report of the Special Presidential Commission of Inquiry*, Sessional paper no. 6–1980 (Colombo).

Stevens, Robert; Alavi, Hamza; and Bertocci, Peter, eds. 1976. *Rural Development in Bangladesh and Pakistan*, Honolulu: The University of Hawaii Press.

Stinchcombe, Arthur L. 1961. "Agricultural Enterprise and Rural Class Relations." *American Journal of Sociology* 67 (September).

Stokes, Eric. 1959. *The English Utilitarians and India.* Oxford: Clarendon Press.

Sufian, Abu. 1972. "It's a Fraud." *Pakistan Forum* 3:3 (December).

Tai, Hung-Chao. 1974. *Land Reforms and Politics.* Berkeley: University of California Press.

Tanter, Raymond, and Midlarsky, Manus. 1967. "A Theory of Revolution." *Journal of Conflict Resolution* 11:3 (September).

Tennyson, Hallam. 1955. *India's Walking Saint: The Story of Vinobha Bhave.* New York: Doubleday.

Thorner, Daniel. 1956. *The Agrarian Prospect in India.* Delhi: University Press, Delhi School of Economics.

——. 1973. *The Agrarian Prospect in India*, 2d ed. Columbia University: South Asia Books)

——, and Thorner, Alice. 1962. *Land and Labour in India.* Bombay: Asia Publishing House.

Travancore-Cochin. 1956. *Report of the Minimum Wages Committee for Employment in Agriculture.* Ernakulam.

Tuma, Elias. 1965. *Twenty-Six Centuries of Agrarian Reform.* Berkeley: University of California Press.

United Nations. Annual. *Statistical Yearbook.* New York.

——. 1975. Department of Economic and Social Affairs, *Poverty, Unemployment and Development Policy: A Case Study of Selected Issues with Reference to Kerala.* New York.

United Nations Food and Agricultural Organization. 1979. World Conference on Agrarian Reform and Rural Development, *Review and Analysis of Agrarian Reform and Rural Development in the Developing Countries since the Mid-1960's.* Rome.

——, and ILO, 1970/76. *Progress in Land Reform, Fifth Report* (New York, 1970); *Sixth Report* (New York, 1976).

United Nations Research Institute for Social Development (UNRISD). 1974. *The Social and Economic Implications of Large-Scale Introduction of New Varieties of Food Grains.* Geneva.

Varghese, T. C. 1970. *Agrarian Change and Economic Consequences: Land Tenure in Kerala 1850–1960.* Bombay: Allied Publishers.

Vellupillai, C. V. 1970. *Born to Labour.* Colombo: M. D. Gunasena.

Warriner, Doreen. 1962. *Land Reform in Principle and Practice.* London: Oxford University Press.

Wilson, A. Jeyaratnam. 1974. *Politics in Sri Lanka.* London: Macmillan.

Wimaladharma, Kapila P., and Clifford, John. 1973. "The Operation of the Paddy

Lands Act in a Village in the North Central Province." Ceylon Studies Seminar. Mimeographed. Peradeniya, Sri Lanka.

Wijeweera, Rohan. 1975. "Speech to the Ceylon Criminal Justice Commission." Reprinted in Robin Blackburn, ed., *Explosion in a Subcontinent*. Middlesex: Penguin.

Wolf, Eric R. 1969. *Peasant Wars of the Twentieth Century*. New York: Harper and Row.

Wolff, Robert Paul. 1977. *Understanding Rawls: A Reconstruction and Critique of A Theory of Justice*. Princeton: Princeton University Press.

Wood, Geof. 1973. "From Raiyat to Rich Peasant." *South Asian Review* 7:1 (October).

World Bank. 1952. *Report on the Economic Development of Ceylon*. Washington, D.C.

———. 1974. *Land Reforms*. Washington, D.C.

———. 1975. *The Assault on World Poverty*. Baltimore: The Johns Hopkins University Press.

———. 1979. *Bangladesh: Current Trends and Development Issues*. Washington, D.C.

Wriggins, Howard. 1960. *Ceylon: Dilemmas of a New Nation*. Princeton: Princeton University Press.

Wunderlich, Gene. 1964. "Land Reform in Western India: Analysis of Economic Impacts of Tenancy Legislation, 1948–1963." Washington, D.C.: Department of Agriculture.

Yalman, Nur. 1967. *Under the Bo Tree*. Berkeley: University of California Press.

Yojana "Land Reform in Kerala: An Interview with Chief Minister Achutha Menon," 16:13 (1972).

Zagoria, Donald S. 1971. "The Ecology of Peasant Communism in India." *American Political Science Review* 65.

Index

Administration: decentralization of, 10, 77, 205, 208; difficulties in, 205–10; effect of agitations on, 204; "ordinary," 3, 4, 11, 38–42, 136, 207, 236; popular participation in, 51–55, 173–74, 189, 197, 201–05; reform of, 286. *See also* Bureaucracy; Implementation

Agrarian reform: as distinct from land reform, 13, 265–66, 282

Agrarian structure: changes in, via land reform, 149–52, 210–16, 269–71; as explanatory variable, 4, 54, 76, 158, 235, 237; and local power, 235; political expressions of, 54, 57–59, 170, 218; of South Asia, 27, 270. *See also* Ceylon; India; Kerala; Pakistan

Agricultural laborers: 13, 73, 75n, 79, 83, 84, 96n, 110, 128, 130, 157, 160, 161, 181, 184, 203, 237; claims of, 155, 216; strata of, 162; treatment in land reforms, 83–84, 155, 212–14, 270, 280–81; unions of, 170, 194, 213, 215–16, 270. *See also* Tiller

Baluchistan, 112, 114, 119, 122

Bandaranaike, S. W. R. D., 75, 138

Bandaranaike, Sirimavo, 140, 227–28, 233

Bangladesh, 14, 36n, 97, 106, 122, 125, 237

Bhoodan/gramdan, 134 and n

Bhutto, Zulfikar Ali, 18, 100–03 passim, 117–21 passim, 124–25, 224, 226, 229, 234. *See also* Pakistan People's Party

Bihar, 128n, 129n

Bourgeoisie: position in bourgeois revolution, 10, 86, 121, 155, 219, 220, 224–25, 227n. *See also* "Feudalism"

Bureaucracy: as "embedded" in society, 10, 38–42, 286; role in land reform, 39, 40 and n, 43, 60, 124n, 163, 173–74, 189, 197, 235, 263, 284, 286–87. *See also* Administration; Implementation

Capital, working: 62, 105–06, 157, 252, 258, 282, 284. *See also* Credit, agricultural; Production relations

Capitalist agriculture, 47, 48, 94, 103, 154–55, 161n, 184, 187, 224, 248, 261, 264, 265, 274, 283–84; distinguished from "feudal" by reformers, 87–90, 100, 101–02, 134–35, 165, 166, 212n, 219, 220–21, 225; distinguished from peasant agriculture, 13, 242–43, 260; ideology of, 85–86, 94; interpenetration with traditional forms, 108–10, 123–24; regulation of, 284; rentier component of, 280; strategy of development, 263. *See also* Development strategy; Entrepreneurs, agrarian; Inequality

Caste, 17n, 31–32, 137, 154–55, 157, 171, 214n, 238, 261; and class, 158. *See also* "Untouchables"

Ceiling legislation. *See* Land ceilings

Ceylon: agrarian structure, 56–59, 83–84; colonization schemes, 84, 139, 150–51; cultivation committees, 75–80; land-tenure reform, 10, 19, 22, 24–25, 41, 49, 65, 55–84, 117n, 156, 208, 235, 258. *See also* Sri Lanka

Chayanovian peasantist economics, 243, 247, 257, 260, 265n, 281, 282. *See also* Economic efficiency

China, 43n, 53, 59, 235n, 240n

Class conflict, 13, 224, 287; perceptions of, 60, 67; as result of land reform, 10, 29, 31, 47–49 passim, 137, 172, 193, 210–16 passim, 270; structural vs. overt, 31–38; within leftist agrarian movement, 216. *See also* Landlord–tenant relations; Patron–client relations; Violence

Collective farming, 62, 63, 76, 79, 130, 147, 149, 150, 168–69, 192, 201, 213*n*, 266, 282; economic arguments for, 263–64. *See also* Cooperative farming; Innovation, institutional

Colonial land policy, 21, 44, 85, 92, 97, 129, 145, 159, 233. *See also* Nationalist ideology

Communist Party of India: class composition, 166; conceptualization of land reforms, 10, 135, 163–70, 186–90, 192, 212–15, 280; conflicts between CPI and CPI(M), 10–11, 190–97, 203–05; development of peasant movement, 158–59, 212–16 passim; factions in, 192; governing, 170–74, 185–94, 211; split in, 179; victim of success, 214–16. *See also* Embourgeoisement; Leftist parties

Compensation. *See* Redistributive policy

Congress Agrarian Reforms Committee, 52, 129–31, 163, 232, 240, 280, 281*n*

Congress Party, 128, 137, 159, 196, 214–15, 219; position on land reform, 10, 20*n*, 51, 88, 129, 132, 163, 171, 174–79. *See also* Gandhi, Indira

Constitutional constraints on land reform, 12, 163, 166, 190–92, 198. *See also* Courts; India, Center–State relations

Cooperative farming, 30, 131–33 passim, 140, 146–49, 167, 206, 240, 263–64, 281, 282. *See also* Collective farming; Innovation, institutional

Corruption, 33, 39, 131, 149. *See also* Administration, "ordinary"; Land records, corruption of

Courts: effect on land reform, 43, 66, 69–75, 76, 81, 116, 135, 172–75 passim, 190, 197–202, 204, 206, 208, 235–36, 286. *See also* Legal philosophy and process

Credit, agricultural, 62, 68, 71, 81, 123, 216, 223, 232, 255–56, 258, 260–63 passim, 266, 276, 285 and *n*. *See also* Capital, working; Debt

Crop insurance, 63, 72, 81, 276

Data: as social product, 15; distortions of, by land reform, 13–15, 261, 269. *See also* Land records, corruption of

Debt, 62, 75*n*, 199, 216, 255, 258; bondage, 162–63, 169, 220. *See also* Credit, agricultural

Democracy: parliamentary, compatibility with land reform, 12, 60–64, 65, 163–64, 192, 234–39; participatory, relation to land reforms, 10, 50, 51–55, 77, 79, 85, 87, 91, 172, 174, 190, 281 and *n*; relation to justice, 278

Dependency relations, 64, 66, 92, 106, 167, 217, 232, 235, 278; and democracy, 55,

91, 278, 281. *See also* Patron–client relations

Development strategy: relation to agrarian reform, 3, 121–22, 220, 262–67, 279, 283, 285; "trickle-down" theories in, 267, 277, 278 and *n*. *See also* Entrepreneurs, agrarian; Inequality; Justice

Economic development. *See* Development strategy

Economic efficiency: conceptualizations of, 245–46, 261; economics of scale and size, 91, 143, 230, 240, 242, 245–46, 263; of share tenancy, 254–62; yield-size of holding relationship, 240–52. *See also* Economic theory

Economic theory: critiques of large holdings, 91, 240–47 passim; critiques of share tenancy, 22–24, 104–05 and *n*, 240, 252–54; and effects of land reform, 12, 262, 266; as ideology, 6–8, 12, 24, 239, 274–75; role in policy logic, 6, 12, 233, 267. *See also* Development strategy; Economic efficiency

Electoral politics and land reform, 4, 51, 56–57, 59, 100, 117–18, 124, 132, 139, 146, 148, 163–64, 168, 171, 179, 185–86, 193, 194, 196–97, 210–12, 214–15, 229–31 passim. *See also* Parliamentary systems; Party competition; Political functions of land reform

Embourgeoisement: in electoral politics, 214; as result of land reform, 9, 11, 49, 59, 168, 170, 192, 215, 287

Employment arguments for land reform, 133, 141–43, 243–44, 251–52, 262. *See also* Unemployment

Entrepreneurs, agrarian: favored class in land reform, 85, 87–90 passim, 94, 98, 102, 121, 123, 134, 219; obstacles to, 264; subsidies to, 94, 98. *See also* Development strategy; Landlords

Equality. *See* Inequality; Justice

Exploitation, 2, 17, 20, 40, 59, 133, 248, 286*n*; perceived economic and political consequences of, 17; "self-," 245, 248, 265, 281–82. *See also* Chayanovian peasantist economics; Ideology; Justice

Export crop sector, 121, 142 and *n*, 145–46, 222, 233, 266. *See also* International influences on land reform

Farm management studies, 240–41, 244–45, 247, 248–52 passim

Federalism as political structure. *See* India, Center–State relations

"Feudalism": conceptual problems in, 103, 108–10, 114*n*, 122 and *n*, 164 and *n*, 165, 167; as target of reforms, 10, 85, 90 and *n*, 92, 94–95, 101, 103–07, 121–24, 126, 139 and *n*, 219, 220, 225, 232. *See also* Bourgeoisie; Capitalist agriculture; Dependency relations

Food aid, 233

Food production: relation to land reform, 25, 93, 121, 142, 150, 186, 220, 233, 283

Gandhi, Indira, 7, 86, 127, 135, 191, 196, 238

Gandhi, M. K., position on land reforms, 1, 2 and *n*, 131, 133 and *n*, 134, 154*n*

Garibi hatao. See Gandhi, Indira

Gopalan, A. K., 21*n*, 159*n*, 173, 203*n*, 215. *See also* Communist Party of India; Kerala

"Green revolution," 98, 247, 256. *See also* Development strategy; Technological change

Gujarat, 15, 35*n*, 157*n*

Haq, Zia-ul-, 100, 116

Haryana, 278*n*

Ideology, 2, 4, 6–8, 24, 83–84, 217–18, 237–39, 272; and consciousness, 9, 12, 35, 78*n*, 173, 235, 237, 272–73; and deference, 35; and economics, 239, 274–75; in great traditions, 153; and justice, 271–74; of market economy, 23, 123; of patron–client relations, 37; and policy logic, 4, 24; of rural poor, 272–73. *See also* Development strategy; Justice; Patron–client relations

Implementation, 51–55, 69–70, 111–14, 115–16, 136, 201–05 passim, 205–10, 269, 286; and political conflict, 11, 194–97, 204. *See also* Administration

Incentive structures: economic, 22–23, 93–94, 97–98, 105, 120–21, 255; political, 12, 74, 286. *See also* Rational behavior

Incrementalism, 81–83, 202

India: abolition of intermediaries, 86–88, 126–28, 232; Center–State relations, 12, 126–28, 189–90, 192, 201, 204, 216, 236; concentration of land wealth, 269, 285; Emergency, 3, 41*n*, 54, 136, 209–10; extent of tenancy, 14–16, 269; farm economics, 240–47 passim, 255–61 passim; land ceilings, 86, 126–28, 134–38, 178; "land grab" agitations, 7, 135, 206, 270; land tenure reform, 28–31, 50–51, 178; "regulated capitalism," 284; rural poverty, 277*n*, 278*n*, 285. *See also* Caste; Congress Party; Gandhi, Indira; *Zamindars*

Inequality, 2, 239, 282*n*; "bonus," 277–78; dimensions of, 32–34, 37–38, 91, 218, 265, 278, 282*n*, 287–88; justifications for, 95, 239, 273–74, 276–78; political conse-

quences of, 2, 237 and *n. See also* Development strategy; Ideology; Justice

Innovation, institutional: obstacles to, 38–42 passim, 51–55 passim, 63, 75, 82, 148–52 passim, 189, 197, 263–64

International influences on land reform, 25, 145, 150, 151, 233; foreign exchange and external debt, 121, 138, 145*n*, 150, 251, 266. *See also* World Bank

Investment incentives and land reform, 23, 96–97, 101–02, 221, 234, 235, 253, 259–61, 263, 266, 285

Iran, 236

Jajmani, 31–32, 274*n. See also* Patron–client relations; Production relations

Janata Party, 137

Janatha Vimukhti Peramuna, 140, 145. *See also* Sri Lanka, Insurrection

Japan, 25*n*, 43*n*, 50, 263, 287

Justice: claims of reformers, 1, 2, 3, 12, 19, 20, 96, 144, 153 and *n*, 154–55, 215, 236, 239, 267, 277–78; "entitlement," 280; and ideology, 171–79; methodology of John Rawls, 271–74; noneconomic dimensions of, 278. *See also* Ideology; Inequality; Redistributive policy

Kashmir, 126

Kerala, 10–11, 61, 89*n*, 235–37 passim, 264, 268, 279–81; ceiling legislation, 166–68, 189–90; collectivization of agriculture, 168–69, 192, 201, 213*n*, 264; farm economics, 244, 247, 248–52; first Communist ministry, 163–74; first impact of reforms, 211–16, 270; land-tenure reform, 48, 159, 174–79; land-tenure structure, 157–63, 180–85; treatment of agricultural laborers in reforms, 166–70, 183–85, 211–16 passim; wages of laborers, 162–63, 277*n. See also* Agricultural laborers; Communist Party of India; Malabar

Khan, Ayub, 94–95, 97, 100, 125, 226, 229, 234, 238; impact of land reforms of, 97–100, 101

Labor theory of value, 274

Land: conceptually, 13, 17, 45–46, 156–57, 265–66, 274–75, 282

Land ceilings: conceptually, 8, 85, 287; political arithmetic of, 229–31; political resources from, 227–29; regional comparisons, 86, 125–26, 138, 166, 232, 270; relation to rural democracy, 85, 87, 91, 278; transformational potential of, 85–87, 90–94, 103, 122, 125, 132, 146–50. *See also* India; Kerala; Pakistan; Political functions of land reform; Sri Lanka

Landlordism: abolition of, 13, 93, 211–12,
    268; connotations of, 60–61, 87–88; nor-
    mative defense of, 88–90, 93, 132, 272,
    276. *See also* "Feudalism"
Landlords: and colonial rule, 21, 159; as
    "feudal," 88, 90 and *n*, 92, 165, 212*n*; eco-
    nomic behavior of, 24, 257–61, 264, 275;
    "good" vs. "bad" in policy logic, 24, 87,
    134–35, 147, 166, 264, 266; and political
    instability, 93–94, 97, 122–24 passim,
    226; as sources of power, 32–34, 115,
    218. *See also* Entrepreneurs, agrarian; Pa-
    tron–client relations
Landlord–tenant relations: extraeconomic,
    31–38 passim, 68; landlord services and
    obligations, 35–38, 64, 67, 68 and *n*, 71,
    88–90, 193–95 passim, 258*n*, 275–76;
    overt conflict in, 17, 28, 29, 31, 32, 66,
    68*n*, 88, 137, 159; structural features of,
    31–38, 50, 84. *See also* Class conflict;
    Dependency relations; Patron–client re-
    lations; Rent; Tenancy
Land records: absence of as obstacle to re-
    form, 32, 42, 64, 82, 131, 177, 202, 207–
    08; corruption of, 14–16, 57 and *n*, 58*n*,
    73–75 passim, 82, 84, 107, 111, 116, 135,
    177, 207–08, 269, 286
Land reform. *See* Collective farming; Coop-
    erative farming; Land ceilings; Land-
    tenure reform; Nationalization of land;
    Redistributive policy
Land-tenure reform: conceptually, 8, 17–18,
    42–46, 60–64, 83, 156–57, 287; failure
    of, 9, 17–18, 20, 26, 27, 51, 83–84, 114–
    17, 156, 174–79; reasons for failure of,
    12, 28–46, 50, 52–55, 64–75, 77–79, 81–
    84, 115–16, 131, 176–78; unintended
    consequences of, 37–38, 48, 84, 269, 285–
    86. *See also* Implementation; Landlord–
    tenant relations; Patron–client relations;
    Tenancy
Latin America, 233, 269
Leftist parties: agrarian structural basis of
    left unity, 214; role in land reform, 11,
    43*n*, 56, 83–84, 139, 172, 175, 190–97
    passim, 214, 230, 232, 263–64. *See also*
    Communist Party of India
Legal philosophy and process: importance
    of law per se, 37–38, 41, 47–48, 270; ob-
    stacles to land reform, 44, 61, 70, 116,
    187, 191, 196, 197–99, 235. *See also*
    Courts; Land records
Lenin, V. I., 2, 104, 108, 155, 215, 222, 246,
    288
Liberty: relation to dependency, 91, 278.
    See also Dependency relations

Mahajana Eksath Peramuna, 56, 138
Maharashtra, 28–29, 50*n*, 157*n*
Malabar, 21, 89, 158–59, 167, 171, 223, 237

Mappilla Rebellion, 159
Marshallian position on share tenancy, 24,
    252–54 passim. *See also* Economic
    theory
Marxian theory, xi, 1, 19, 31, 56, 154, 218,
    222, 272; vs. Maoist, in policy logic, 231.
    See also Class conflict; Production rela-
    tions
Mechanization of agriculture, 102 and *n*,
    105*n*, 109 and *n*, 111, 135, 251, 261; and
    eviction of tenants, 116 and *n*, 285–86.
    See also Technological change
Military: as landowners, 229
Minimax strategy of ceiling reform, 229
Modernization of agriculture, 96, 102,
    105*n*, 109; effect on efficiency arguments,
    246–47. *See also* Entrepreneurs, agrarian;
    Technological change
Moral economy, 35, 37, 40. *See also* Ideol-
    ogy; Justice
Moral outrage, 133–34. *See also* Ideology
Muslim League (Kerala), 191, 193, 194, 202

Namboodiripad, E. M. S., 21*n*, 159*n*, 163*n*,
    164, 165, 167–70 passim, 172–74 passim,
    179, 186, 189, 219, 261, 281. *See also*
    Communist Party of India
Nationalist ideology: critique of colonial
    land policy (q.v.), 87, 92, 128, 129, 233
Nationalization of land, 107*n*, 138, 145; re-
    gime imperatives in, 145–46, 233
Naxalite, 197
Nehru, Jawaharlal: on the land problem,
    87, 88, 127; dismissal of Kerala's Com-
    munist ministry, 10, 171
Normative theory: functions in policy anal-
    ysis, 5, 6, 8; legitimation of, 268–69;
    methodology, 271–74. *See also* Ideology;
    Justice
Northwest Frontier Province (Sarhad), 54,
    108*n*, 109, 112, 114 and *n*, 119 and *n*,
    122, 258

Pakistan: agrarian structure, 107–10, 114;
    agricultural laborers, 96*n*, 110; bureau-
    cracy, 115, 124*n*; credit, 258*n*; effect of
    Ayub Khan's reforms, 97–100, 101; effect
    of Bhutto's reforms, 110–17; farm eco-
    nomics, 247, 256–60 passim; farm mech-
    anization, 116 and *n*, 285–86; land
    ceilings, 86, 94–100, 110–14, 232; land-
    tenure reform, 18, 19 and *n*, 45, 114–17;
    National Charter for Peasants, 119; polit-
    ical power of landed elite, 93 and *n*, 94*n*,
    105, 107, 111, 115*n*, 121 and *n*, 124 and
    n, 234; political uses of land reform,
    226–29; tenant evictions, 115–17; yield-
    size of holding relation, 247
Pakistan People's Party, 100, 105, 107;

landed elite in, 121, 124; left faction of, 121, 123. *See also* Bhutto, Zulfikar Ali

Panchayati raj, 51–54, 174. *See also* Democracy, participatory

Parliamentary systems: contributions to failure of reforms, 65, 81; compatibility with land reform, 234–39; role of revolutionary party in, 172–74, 192, 211, 214. *See also* India, Center–State relations

Party competition: effect on land reform, 10, 179, 195, 210, 215, 234–36. *See also* Symbolic uses of land reform

Patron–client relations, 37, 88, 286; conceptually, 34–38; deterioration of, 47 and *n*, 156, 173, 286; effect on efficiency of share tenancy, 260–61; extraeconomic dimensions of, 35, 63, 67–68; "feudal" deference, 78*n*; idealized, 258*n*; moral economy of, 35, 63; patron services, 36, 64, 67, 68 and *n*, 88–89, 260–61, 275–76; and political representation, 217; as social organization of production, 31–38, 68, 260–61. *See also* Class conflict; Ideology; Landlord–tenant relations

Peasant organizations, 9, 34, 53–55, 57, 136, 169, 170, 196; dynamics of mobilization, 158–59, 235, 237; expansion of, 215; role in land reform, 11, 194, 196, 203, 205

Peasantry: class conflict within peasant movement, 214–15; classes within, 27, 166, 181–85, 284; differentiation with modernization of agriculture, 246; differentiation via land reform, 27, 49, 84, 181–85, 211–16; quiescence, 22, 34, 44, 64, 78, 115, 235, 284; revolts, 159. *See also* Chayanovian peasantist economics; Patron–client relations; Landlord–tenant relations; Rational behavior; Tenancy; Tiller

Philippines, 254*n*

Plantation sector, 56–57, 138, 145, 146, 151, 166, 180, 189, 200–01, 222, 233, 266. *See also* Kerala, ceiling legislation; Sri Lanka, ceiling legislation

Police: role in land reform, 33, 43 and *n*, 71, 169, 173, 193, 196, 208, 286; policy of Communist Party, 172–73

Policy models and policy logic: role in policy analysis, 4–9

Political development, 12 and *n*, 82, 267

Political functions of land reform: crisis management, 85, 87, 125, 219, 225; cuing behavior, 124, 233; patronage resources, 79 and *n*, 82, 145, 148, 151, 227–28, 233; political integration, 122, 232–33; preemptive-cooptive, 9, 21, 54, 117–18, 150, 231–32; resource in partisan politics, 3, 79*n*, 148–49, 174, 192–93, 210, 215, 227–29; tactical vs. strategic, 10, 11,

56, 123–24, 225–27. *See also* Symbolic uses of land reform

Political instability: effect on land reform, 64–66, 71, 82, 151, 203; influence of agrarian structure on, 71, 93 and *n*, 94, 97, 122–24, 237

Political structure and land reform: 4, 83, 234–39. *See also* India, Center–State relations

Political will: defined, 285*n*; as explanation, 13, 46, 48, 81, 232, 235, 285

Population pressure: and land reform, 57, 160, 180; and yield-size of holding controversy, 242

Positivist social science, 13–15, 269, 285*n*. *See also* Data

Poverty: effect on farm economics, 245, 253, 260, 277*n*; incidence of, in India, 2, 278*n*, 283, 285. *See also* Development strategy; Inequality; Justice; Redistributive policy

Power: "concentrated," 12, 234–39 passim; of landed elite, 54, 115, 217–18; local, 235, 282. *See also* Democracy; Inequality; Landlords; Political functions of land reform

President's Rule, 179, 203. *See also* India, Center–State relations

Production relations: conflicting models of, 31–38, 109; "embedded," 1, 9, 77; new forms as goal of legislation, 13, 104, 152. *See also* Class conflict; "Feudalism"; Landlord–tenant relations; Patron–client relations

Productivity: as legitimation of land reform, 2, 10, 17, 22, 236, 239, 262. *See also* Economic efficiency

Progressive farmers. *See* Entrepreneurs, agrarian; Development strategy

Punjab (colonial), 23, 33*n*, 39*n*, 259

Punjab (India), 241, 277*n*, 278*n*

Punjab (Pakistan), 55, 92*n*, 108, 109, 114*n*, 117, 119 and *n*, 124, 268

Rational behavior: defined, 9*n*; individual vs. collective, 151; of peasants, 9, 34, 66–69, 73–74, 82, 235, 286; Popkin-Scott controversy on, 68*n*; and productivity, 243, 259; quiescence as, 64, 66–69 passim, 78, 117, 208–09; and risk, 66–69. *See also* Dependency relations

Redistributive policy: compensation in, 92, 98, 117*n*, 129, 136, 144–45, 165–66, 188–90 passim, 201, 220, 236, 280; vs. distributive policy, 79, 82, 150, 191–92; justifications for, 90–91, 267, 279–81, 284–87; objections to, 280–84. *See also* Justice

Regime interests in land reform, 4, 12, 203, 217, 225–29. *See also* Political functions of land reform

Regime type: as explanatory variable, 12, 234–38. *See also* Parliamentary systems

Rent: abolition of, 8, 157, 188, 191, 211; conceptually, 157, 274–76, 280; "fair rent" in legislation, 5, 18–20, 165, 177, 188; labor rents, 220; legitimacy of, 17–18, 153, 274–76, 284, 287; and profits, 13, 280; rack-renting, 17–20 passim, 26, 160–62; relation to security of tenure, 28. *See also* Justice; Landlord–tenant relations

Sind, 88, 117, 119 and *n*, 124, 237, 268

Slaves, agrestic, 157, 162

Socialism: Gandhian, 1, 2 and *n*, 133; Islamic, 153*n*, 227; as symbol, 219, 226–27. *See also* Symbolic uses of land reform

Sri Lanka, 3, 5; ceiling legislation, 79, 126, 147, 222–25, 227, 229–33, 236, 270; cooperative and collective farms, 146–52, 282; farm economics, 241, 254–58 passim, 266; Insurrection, 84, 126, 139–40, 148, 200, 231, 232, 236, 238; international dependency, 145 and *n*, 150–51; rice ration, 141; United Front government, 139. *See also* Ceylon; United National Party

State: and governing class, 218; interests in land reform, 8, 93, 122, 145, 232–33, 238, 270; liberal, 9*n*, 43, 49, 51, 82; relative autonomy of the, 12, 218; and society, 10, 31, 38–42, 286. *See also* Political functions of land reform; Regime interests in land reform

Surplus: appropriation of, 233, 255, 258*n*, 261–62, 267, 275–76, 287; control as source of structural power, 218; marketed, 283. *See also* Rent

Symbolic uses of land reform, 3, 25, 118, 124, 126, 145, 200, 219, 221, 225–27

Taiwan, 43*n*, 50, 263

Tamil laborers (Sri Lanka), 56–57, 151

Tamilnadu, 273*n*

Taxation of agriculture, 76, 120, 122, 281

Technological change, 105, 135, 221, 247, 253, 259, 262, 265, 283; effect on yield-size of holding relationship, 246–47; and tenant evictions, 46–47, 116*n*, 156. *See also* "Green revolution"; Mechanization of agriculture

Tenancy: bargaining position of landless, 20, 34, 43–44, 46, 66, 258, 261; conceptually, 22, 30, 44–45, 61–62, 156–57; economic critiques of, 22–23, 83, 252–54; extent and concealment of, 14–16, 57, 269 (*see also* Land records, corruption of); loss of, through evictions, 17–18, 29, 30, 32, 46–47, 49, 66, 69–75 passim, 77–78, 84, 115, 116 and *n*, 117, 156, 176–78, 197, 277*n*, 285–86; political consequences of, 21, 65, 78*n*, 81, 82, 135, 237; stratification within, 27, 30, 78*n*, 80, 181–83. *See also* Landlord–tenant relations; Land-tenure reform; Rent

Tiller: conceptual ambiguities, 13, 29, 157, 165, 180–85 passim, 187, 212–13, 216, 270

Unemployment: and land reform, 66, 140–44, 148, 162–63, 169–70, 213, 220, 232, 244, 267. *See also* Employment arguments for land reform

United Front governments. *See* Leftist parties

United National Party, 25, 80, 146, 149, 151, 233

"Untouchables," 137, 158, 168*n*, 187. *See also* Caste

Urban wealth: anomalous treatment of, 95, 134, 287–88

Uttar Pradesh, 29*n*, 132, 280*n*

Violence, 2, 4, 7, 17, 21, 26, 29, 54, 66, 135, 137, 159, 160, 193–95 passim, 197, 204, 206, 210, 231, 236, 237 and *n*, 264, 270, 286. *See also* Class conflict; Sri Lanka, Insurrection

West Bengal, 19, 30*n*, 43*n*, 277*n*

World Bank, 3, 22*n*, 150, 259, 266

Zamindars: abolition of, 86, 127–30, 270; critiques of, 87–88, 127, 134, 214; defined, 87 and *n*. *See also* Colonial land policy; Landlords